State, Society, and the Development of Canadian Federalism

This is Volume 71 in the series of studies commissioned as part of the research program of the Royal Commission on the Economic Union and Development Prospects for Canada.

This volume reflects the views of its authors and does not imply endorsement by the Chairman or Commissioners.

State, Society, and the Development of Canadian Federalism

RICHARD SIMEON
AND
IAN ROBINSON

Published by the University of Toronto Press in cooperation with the Royal Commission on the Economic Union and Development Prospects for Canada and the Canadian Government Publishing Centre, Supply and Services Canada

University of Toronto Press
Toronto   Buffalo   London

Printed in Canada
ISBN 0-8020-7319-0
ISSN 0829-2396
Cat. No. Z1-1903/1-41-71E

'

CANADIAN CATALOGUING IN PUBLICATION DATA

Simeon, Richard, 1943–
    State, society, and the development of Canadian federalism

(*The Collected research studies / Royal Commission on the Economic Union and Development Prospects for Canada,*
ISSN 0829-2396; 71)
Includes bibliographical references.
ISBN 0-8020-7319-0

1. Federal government — Canada. 2. Federal-provincial relations — Canada.* 3. Canada — Politics and government — 1867–   . 4. Canada — Economic policy. 5. Canada — Economic conditions — 1867–   .* 6. Canada — Social policy. 7. Canada — Social conditions — 1867–   .* I. Robinson, Ian, 1956–   . II. Royual Commission on the Economic Union and Development Prospects for Canada. III. Title. IV. Series: The Collected research studies (Royal Commission on the Economic Union and Development Prospects for Canada); 71.

JL27.S55 1990   320.971   C85-099613-9
PUBLISHING COORDINATION: Ampersand Communications Services Inc.
COVER DESIGN: Will Rueter
INTERIOR DESIGN: Brant Cowie/Artplus Limited

CONTENTS

When the members of the Rowell-Sirois Commission began their collective task in 1937, very little was known about the evolution of the Canadian economy. What was known, moreover, had not been extensively analyzed by the slender cadre of social scientists of the day.

When we set out upon our task nearly 50 years later, we enjoyed a substantial advantage over our predecessors; we had a wealth of information. We inherited the work of scholars at universities across Canada and we had the benefit of the work of experts from private research institutes and publicly sponsored organizations such as the Ontario Economic Council and the Economic Council of Canada. Although there were still important gaps, our problem was not a shortage of information; it was to interrelate and integrate — to synthesize — the results of much of the information we already had.

The mandate of this Commission is unusually broad. It encompasses many of the fundamental policy issues expected to confront the people of Canada and their governments for the next several decades. The nature of the mandate also identified, in advance, the subject matter for much of the research and suggested the scope of enquiry and the need for vigorous efforts to interrelate and integrate the research disciplines. The resulting research program, therefore, is particularly noteworthy in three respects: along with original research studies, it includes survey papers which synthesize work already done in specialized fields; it avoids duplication of work which, in the judgment of the Canadian research community, has already been well done; and, considered as a whole, it is the most thorough examination of the Canadian economic, political and legal systems ever undertaken by an independent agency.

The Commission's research program was carried out under the joint direction of three prominent and highly respected Canadian scholars: Dr. Ivan Bernier (*Law and Constitutional Issues*), Dr. Alan Cairns (*Politics and Institutions of Government*) and Dr. David C. Smith (*Economics*).

Dr. Ivan Bernier is Dean of the Faculty of Law at Laval University. Dr. Alan Cairns is former Head of the Department of Political Science at the University of British Columbia and, prior to joining the Commission, was William Lyon Mackenzie King Visiting Professor of Canadian Studies at Harvard University. Dr. David C. Smith, former Head of the Department of Economics at Queen's University in Kingston, is now Principal of that University. When Dr. Smith assumed his new responsibilities at Queen's in September 1984, he was succeeded by Dr. Kenneth Norrie of the University of Alberta and John Sargent of the federal Department of Finance, who together acted as Co-directors of Research for the concluding phase of the Economics research program.

I am confident that the efforts of the Research Directors, research coordinators and authors whose work appears in this and other volumes, have provided the community of Canadian scholars and policy makers with a series of publications that will continue to be of value for many years to come. And I hope that the value of the research program to Canadian scholarship will be enhanced by the fact that Commission research is being made available to interested readers in both English and French.

I extend my personal thanks, and that of my fellow Commissioners, to the Research Directors and those immediately associated with them in the Commission's research program. I also want to thank the members of the many research advisory groups whose counsel contributed so substantially to' this undertaking.

DONALD S. MACDONALD

INTRODUCTION

At its most general level, the Royal Commission's research program has examined how the Canadian political economy can better adapt to change. As a basis of enquiry, this question reflects our belief that the future will always take us partly by surprise. Our political, legal and economic institutions should therefore be flexible enough to accommodate surprises and yet solid enough to ensure that they help us meet our future goals. This theme of an adaptive political economy led us to explore the interdependencies between political, legal and economic systems and drew our research efforts in an interdisciplinary direction.

The sheer magnitude of the research output (more than 280 separate studies in 72 volumes) as well as its disciplinary and ideological diversity have, however, made complete integration impossible and, we have concluded, undesirable. The research output as a whole brings varying perspectives and methodologies to the study of common problems and we therefore urge readers to look beyond their particular field of interest and to explore topics across disciplines.

The three research areas – *Law and Constitutional Issues* under Ivan Bernier, *Politics and Institutions of Government* under Alan Cairns, and *Economics* under David C. Smith (co-directed with Kenneth Norrie and John Sargent for the concluding pahse of the research program) – were further divided into 19 sections headed by research coordinators.

The area *Law and Constitutional Issues* has been organized into five major sections headed by the research coordinators identified below.
- Law, Society and the Economy — *Ivan Bernier and Andrée Lajoie*
- The International Legal Environment — *John J. Quinn*
- The Canadian Economic Union — *Mark Krasnick*

- Harmonization of Laws in Canada — *Ronald C. C. Cuming*
- Institutional and Constitutional Arrangements — *Clare F. Beckton and A. Wayne MacKay*

Since law in its numerous manifestations is the most fundamental means of implementing state policy, it was necessary to investigate how and when law could be mobilized most effectively to address the problems raised by the Commission's mandate. Adopting a broad perspective, researchers examined Canada's legal system from the standpoint of how law evolves as a result of social, economic and political changes and how, in turn, law brings about changes in our social, economic and political conduct.

Within *Politics and Institutions of Government*, research has been organized into seven major sections.
- Canada and the International Political Economy — *Denis Stairs and Gilbert Winham*
- State and Society in the Modern Era — *Keith Banting*
- Constitutionalism, Citizenship and Society — *Alan Cairns and Cynthia Williams*
- The Politics of Canadian Federalism — *Richard Simeon*
- Representative Institutions — *Peter Aucoin*
- The Politics of Economic Policy — *G. Bruce Doern*
- Industrial Policy — *André Blais*

This area examines a number of developments which have led Canadians to question their ability to govern themselves wisely and effectively. Many of these developments are not unique to Canada and a number of comparative studies canvass and assess how others have coped with similar problems. Within the context of the Canadian heritage of parliamentary government, federalism, a mixed economy, and a bilingual and multicultural society, the research also explores ways of rearranging the relationships of power and influence among institutions to restore and enhance the fundamental democratic principles of representativeness, responsiveness and accountability.

Economics research was organized into seven major sections.
- Macroeconomics — *John Sargent*
- Federalism and the Economic Union — *Kenneth Norrie*
- Industrial Structure — *Donald G. McFetridge*
- International Trade — *John Whalley*
- Income Distribution and Economic Security — *François Vaillancourt*
- Labour Markets and Labour Relations — *Craig Riddell*
- Economic Ideas and Social Issues — *David Laidler*

Economics research examines the allocation of Canada's human and other resources, how institutions and policies affect this allocation, and the distribution of the gains from their use. It also considers the nature of economic development, the forces that shape our regional and industrial structure, and our economic interdependence with other countries. The thrust of the research in economics is to increase our comprehension of what determines our economic potential and how instruments of economic policy may move us closer to our future goals.

One section from each of the three research areas — The Canadian Economic Union, The Politics of Canadian Federalism, and Federalism and the Economic Union — have been blended into one unified research effort. Consequently, the volumes on Federalism and the Economic Union as well as the volume on The North are the results of an interdisciplinary research effort.

We owe a special debt to the research coordinators. Not only did they organize, assemble and analyze the many research studies and combine their major findings in overviews, but they also made substantial contributions to the Final Report. We wish to thank them for their performance, often under heavy pressure.

Unfortunately, space does not permit us to thank all members of the Commission staff individually. However, we are particularly grateful to the Chairman, The Hon. Donald S. Macdonald; the Commission's Executive Director, Gerald Godsoe; and the Director of Policy, Alan Nymark; all of whom were closely involved with the Research Program and played key roles in the contribution of Research to the Final Report. We wish to express our appreciation to the commission's Administrative Advisor, the late Harry Stewart, for his guidance and advice, and to the Director of Publishing, Ed Matheson, who managed the research publication process. A special thanks to Jamie Benidickson, Policy Coordinator and Special Assistant to the Chairman, who played a valuable liaison role between Research and the Chairman and Commissioners. We are also grateful to our office administrator, Donna Stebbing, and to our secretarial staff, Monique Carpentier, Barbara Cowtan, Tina DeLuca, Françoise Guilbault and Marilyn Sheldon.

Finally, a well deserved thank you to our closest assistants, Jacques J.M. Shore, *Law and Constitutional Issues*; Cynthia Williams and her successor Karen Jackson, *Politics and Institutions of Government*; and I. Lilla Connidis, *Economics*. We appreciate not only their individual contribution to each research area, but also their cooperative contribution to the research program and the Commission.

Ivan Bernier
Alan Cairns
David C. Smith

POSTSCRIPT

Publication of this volume, No. 71 of the Commission's research studies, was delayed because Richard Simeon, the senior author, carried a crushing workload during the Commission's life that rendered impossible the completion of the manuscript within the original timetable. When the Commission's formal life ended, the authors returned to other time-comsuming responsibilities.

As the research for and writing of this volume proceeded, the project became increasingly ambitious by reaching back to Confederation and forward to events that followed the Commission's Report. Thus, happily, its belated appearance has added to the richness and subtlety of the presentation.

This volume owes much to the Privy Council Office for maintaining interest in and support for its publication, and to Ed Matheson, the Commission's Director of Publishing, and Eunice Thorne, both of Ampersand Communications Services, for extending their managerial skills to the publication of this final volume.

As the Research Director most closely involved, I congratulate Richard Simeon and Ian Robinson for their tenacity and for the wisdom and rigour of their analysis. They have greatly enriched our understanding of the federal pilgrimage on which Canadians have been engaged for more than a century.

Alan Cairns
Vancouver
August 14, 1989

PREFACE

This volume is the last of the Research Studies undertaken for the Royal Commission on the Economic Union and Development Prospects for Canada.

Early in their mandate the Commissioners recognized – as did their predecessors on the Rowell-Sirois Commission – that to understand the present and shape the future, we must comprehend the past. Accordingly, they asked that an historical survey of modern Canadian federalism be prepared as one of the Commission's Research Studies. However, when the Commission was wound down in 1986, the task of completing that study remained.

From the outset, we sought a comprehensive theoretical framework which would blend and integrate the roles of economic and social forces, political institutions and political culture. We perceived that the course of Canadian federalism was quite distinct from federations in other advanced industrial countries and we therefore considered it essential to retrace early experience, especially the character of the 1867 Confederation bargain and the experience of the Great Depression in which the tensions between new roles of the state and classical federal forms first appeared. As our work continued, we recognized that we must also come to grips with more recent events, especially the remarkable shift from the pervasive sense of crisis, conflict and disarray which marked the decade from 1974 to 1984 to the more harmonious "collaborative federalism" of the Mulroney era, which, as this book goes to press is being followed by a resurgence of linguistic and regional tensions surrounding debate on the Meech Lake Accord.

We have thus moved well beyond our original assignment. Nonetheless, we believe we have been faithful to the Commission's initial mandate.

We write as political scientists, not as historians. This is not a history of great men and women; nor is it a commentary on memoranda culled from archives. We have relied largely on secondary sources and have concentrated on the role of social and economic forces, institutional constraints, ideas and collective actors which have shaped contemporary federalism. Our analysis and conclusions are very much our own – as are all errors of fact or interpretation.

Richard Simeon
Ian Robinson
Kingston,
1 September, 1989

ACKNOWLEDGEMENTS

We owe many debts.

First, to Alan Cairns for his wisdom, insight and patience throughout a long association and for his faith that this work would eventually be finished.

We also acknowledge the immense contribution of our colleagues at the Commission, staff members, other researchers and consultants from whom we learned much. We are especially indebted to those from the research areas – economics, law and political science – who worked with us on federalism questions.

We also acknowledge our debt to Donald V. Smiley whose contributions to the study of Canadian federalism were a constant source of inspiration.

R.S. AND I.R.

PART I

Introduction

Chapter 1

Overview

In June 1987 the heads of Canada's federal and provincial governments gathered at a lakeside lodge in Quebec to hammer out the "Meech Lake Accord". Two weeks later, after an all-night session in a Victorian office building at the foot of Parliament Hill, they signed the Constitutional Accord, 1987. The images of Canada embodied in the Accord and reflected in the subsequent debates illustrate long-standing political dilemmas which are central to Canadian federalism.

How do we represent relations between the two great language groups in our political institutions? What kind of balance do we strike between regional and national loyalties and interests? How do we reconcile the sometimes competing values embedded in parliamentary government, the Charter of Human Rights and Freedoms, and federalism? What are the appropriate roles of federal and provincial governments, and how should we conduct the relations between them? To what extent should federal principles be reflected not only in intergovernmental relations but also within the central government itself? Does federalism, as it has evolved in Canada, effectively serve democratic values; does it provide the means for effective policy-making in a complex and sometimes threatening environment?

These have all been hotly contested questions throughout the history of the federation. In order to understand these issues and the language in which they are expressed, we must first understand the forces which have shaped Canadian federalism since its beginning. That is our purpose in this study.

First, we explore the dynamic relationship between a federal society, characterized by deeply-rooted territorial and linguistic interests and identities, and a federal state, characterized by the division of political authority between two autonomous yet interdependent orders of government. This relationship is then considered in the context of Canada's position within the larger North American and global political economy and also within the context of the changing role of the state, especially since World War II.

The primary focus of this study is intergovernmental relations in the broadest sense. What are the roles of federal and provincial governments? How does the relative balance of power shift between them? What determines the balance between co-operation and competition, conflict and harmony? What shapes the patterns of intergovernmental relations?

In part, the answers to these questions are found in the actions of federal and provincial political elites deploying the resources supplied to them in the Constitution in order to further their own interests. The central argument of this study, however, is that to understand intergovernmental relations we must explore the economic, social and political settings within which intergovernmental relations are conducted. Without ignoring the role of federal institutions in maintaining and reinforcing the federal and territorial dimension of Canadian society, we give greater weight to the causal relationship between federal society and the federal state. Societal forces, interacting with institutional forms, are chiefly responsible for shifts in the division of powers, fluctuations in the nature and intensity of intergovernmental conflict, and the changing character of the Canadian state. Therefore, this study places special emphasis on the organization, mobilization and activities of collective interests and identities, and on the political parties, interest groups and governments that shape and express them. The relative importance of these contending interests, the language in which they are expressed, and the issues around which they crystalize are central to this analysis.

Such social forces are of two kinds. First are those which are primarily organized along territorial or federal lines – language, region, province. These are the divisions that made federalism necessary in the first place and which remain fundamental to understanding Canadian federalism. Second are divisions which, to varying degrees, cut across or transcend territorial lines, notably class and, more recently, gender. To some extent, such divisions have challenged the preoccupation of Canadian politics with the older divisions and have criticized the political system that entrenches them. As will be seen, the federal system has responded to the emergence of these new social forces and, in turn, has shaped and channeled them.

We do not see the history of Canadian federalism as a natural progression from "traditional" to "modern" cleavages or from decentralized to centralized political authority. Old identities and ideologies have not been displaced by new ones; instead, we contend that old and new identities have been integrated into more or less dynamic syntheses, in which both territorial and non-territorial bargains or accommodations are continually being formed, eroded and reformed. The stimulus for such change comes from both external – largely economic – forces operating on Canada and from underlying social and economic changes within the country. These changes highlight some divisions and overshadow others. They pose new policy challenges to which various groups must respond and they inject new values into Canadian political debates.

In the years following World War II in Canada, as elsewhere, social and economic change has been associated with massive growth in the size of government and the extent of its roles and responsibilities. One of our central tasks, therefore, has been to explain the impact of these developments on federalism. For some, the lesson was clear: federalism was an obsolete form, incapable of responding to new needs and expectations. The prescription was centralization. But the constellation of forces that developed in the early years of confederation ensured that this would not happen. Instead, the "Keynesian welfare state" was established within the largely unchanged framework of the federal constitution of 1867. Both levels of government responded to the new agenda, greatly increasing the interdependence among governments and the opportunities for conflict between them. Again, this distinctively Canadian pattern – the analysis of which takes up the bulk of this work – can be understood only if we understand the foundations laid down previously.

Throughout this study, we treat federalism as both a dependent and an independent variable. As a dependent variable the focus is on the forces which explain the pattern of intergovernmental relationships. As an independent variable, federalism in general and the specific forms which emerged in Canada have had important consequences for the ways in which interests are organized, the strategies they must adopt, the issues which have been debated, and the policy alternatives which have been chosen. Like other countries, Canada adopted the Keynesian welfare state, but its form and timing were greatly influenced by federalism. Much of this study, therefore, explores policy formation within the federal system.

Thus, in the pages that follow, we seek to answer two central questions. First, what drives Canadian federalism; how can we explain change? Second, what differences has federalism made to Canadians as we explore new policy agendas and respond to a changing society and changing values?

Organization

Chapter 2 presents in more detail the theoretical underpinnings which guide our study, linking them to the alternative models which have shaped the analysis of federalism in Canada.

In Chapter 3 we set out the "Confederation bargain" and show that many of the ambiguities and dilemmas which remain with us – in the Meech Lake debate for example – are embedded in the British North America Act itself. The history is set in motion in Chapter 4, as we explain the forces which moved the federation from the centralized, quasi-federal model championed by Sir John A. Macdonald to the more province-centred model endorsed by Wilfrid Laurier.

The Great Depression and World War II provoked the crisis and transformation of the Canadian political economy that we examine in Chapters 5 and 6. The Depression raised two fundamental questions: could democratic capitalism survive its economic and social contradictions, and could Canadian federal institutions effectively implement reform? The war years demonstrated that the federal government could respond rapidly and effectively to extraordinary new demands and that it could command the support of a majority for its national and international purposes; but they also showed that such periods of federal dominance are temporary and conditional.

In Chapter 7 we provide the theoretical basis for our analysis of the modern era. We present and criticize the ideas of those who argue that modernization and centralization go hand-in-hand, displacing territorial divisions with class divisions at the societal level and centralizing authority and initiative at the level of the state. We suggest, instead, that modernization is equally consistent with increased diversity and pluralism in society and with highly dispersed state power. Chapter 8 surveys the post-war reconstruction period from 1947 to 1957, exploring how it was possible to implement the new political economy through intergovernmental cooperation under federal leadership while avoiding major constitutional change. The expansion of the state, however, ruptured the linguistic accommodation and rendered obsolete the classical model of federalism which had prevailed since Laurier's time. In Chapter 9 we explore how these developments combined with the Quiet Revolution in Quebec to pose a fundamental challenge to the federal system. Almost overnight, the dominant coalition in Quebec – previously conservative and anti-statist – became the most activist and interventionist in the federation. It embraced the new political agenda, but sought to implement it through a provincial state, creating intense pressures for decentralization.

Chapter 10, spanning the next decade from 1974 to 1984, describes a "compound crisis" of the federal system. The failure to achieve a new linguistic accommodation resulted in the election of the Parti Québécois, dedicated to Quebec's independence. Further, changes in the global economy, such as the energy crisis and stagflation, exacerbated regional divisions and put great strain on the postwar class accommodations. The response was a serious questioning both of the role of the state, and of the efficacy of federalism.

Two responses were possible: to abandon cooperative federalism in favour of a more centralized, unilateral and competitive model; or to extend cooperative federalism by further decentralization and by institutionalizing federal-provincial collaboration as the dominant mode of Canadian policy-making. After 1980, Prime Minister Trudeau's "New Federalism" sought, with only partial success, to realize the first possibility. Since his election in 1984, Prime Minister Mulroney has sought to realize the second possibility, a process which culminated in the Meech Lake Accord.

In Chapter 11 we trace the Mulroney approach to federalism, exploring its contradictions just as we explored those of the Trudeau model in the previous chapter.

Finally, in Chapter 12, we consider the lessons of our history and relate them to the future of Canadian federalism. We assess the links between federalism and the fundamental political values of democracy, community and political effectiveness as Canada faces challenges arising from changes in both the domestic society and the international political economy.

Chapter 2

Collective Action, Societal Differences and Theories of Canadian Federalism

Canadian federalism has been shaped by two sorts of pressure. First is the pressure exerted by changes in the prevailing conceptions of the appropriate relations between the national and subnational political communities. Such pressure affects changes in the distribution of material resources, legal powers and political responsibilities between the two orders of government – i.e., changes in the degree of centralization. Second is the pressure exerted by changing ideas of social justice. Although the effect of such pressure on federalism is less direct, it nonetheless bears heavily on changing views concerning the economic and social roles the state ought to play. Such changes have fundamentally altered the character of federalism, shifting it from the "watertight compartments" of classical federalism to the "*de facto* concurrency" of modern federalism and a new logic of intergovernmental relations.

Ideas about political community and social justice are ideological aspects of wider political principles. In theory, every individual is able to hold and to press his or her own political views. In practice, however, most participate only at the margins of politics, voting once every four years, or responding to the occasional opinion poll. Their views are relevant to political outcomes only insofar as they are organized into large or powerful "collective actors" such as governments, political parties, religious organizations, private corporations and trade unions (Olson, 1971).

Contemporary Canadian federalism has been shaped by the conflicts between such collectivities which have vied for control over – or influence within – the Canadian state. Each has sought to shape the state and society according to its vision of political community and social justice. But such visions are by no means self-evident; nor are they determined simply by "objective" considerations such as the primary language, region of residence or class position of the members of the competing collective (Levine, Wright & Sober, 1987, pp. 67-84; Przeworski, 1985a). Rather, they are the products of debates, compromises and agreements – conflict and cooperation – within and between the major collective actors (Moe, 1980, pp. 73-113; Sabel, 1984, pp. 127-32, 186-90).

As the relative economic and political power of the collective actors has changed, there have been corresponding changes in the Canadian state, and in the division of powers between the two orders of government. The central role of collective actors in political life suggests that any account of the changing character of Canadian federalism must answer three questions: first, what conditions must be met for a collective actor to occupy an important position in the political space; second, why do the goals and values they pursue change over time; and third, why does one coalition prevail in one period but not in another?

Political conflict presupposes at least two collective actors, each capable of mobilizing large numbers of followers and other political resources. Where this condition is met, there is a discernable "societal cleavage" (Lipset and Rokkan, 1967). Where it is not met, there is a one-sided concentration of power and often severe exploitation, but political mobilization is limited or non-existent (Gaventa, 1980, pp. 1-32). In Canada, for example, class differences were not able to rival the political importance of regional or ethnic cleavages until the settlement of the prairies created a relatively homogenous, well organized class of grain farmers. Industrialization and the growth of trade unions did the same for the urban working class. The emergence of gender-based conflicts is closely correlated with the mass entry of women into the paid workforce, providing more women with more financial independence than they had hitherto possessed. Thus, increases in conflict are often a product of reduced power inequalities between the competing players.

Two factors determine the relative power of a collectivity: the economic and political resources at its disposal; and the solidarity of its membership, including their commitment to protect and promote the interests of the collectivity (McAdam, 1982, pp. 1-65; Moe, 1980, pp. 1-9, 113-44). The material resources available to a collectivity depend, above all, upon its relation to the two most important sites of power in capitalist industrial democracies: the means of economic production and the state. Owners and managers of the principal means of production have more resources at their disposal than non-owners and managers. Governments have varying degrees of economic power, depending upon their capacity to regulate private economic actors, the degree of goverment ownership and their capacity to tax the population (Lindblom, 1977, pp. 170-200).

The ability to control the authority of the state depends on the size of a collective actor's membership, and the capacity of its leaders to mobilize these members to participate in the democratic process. The nature of political institutions is relevant here: if political action entails the "mobilization of bias", political institutions bring a certain bias to bear on the logic of mobilization (Schattschneider, 1960). Federalism, with its provincial governments implies easier access to some measure of political power for groups whose members are clustered together in the same region. It is this characteristic of federal systems that led maritimers and francophones (who recognized that they would become minorities in the new nation) to insist on such institutions in 1867. The enduring impact of the federal structure of the Canadian state has been to make it easier to organize and mobilize collectivities that are territorially concentrated than those which are not. This is one of several reasons why ethnic and other differences that are regionally based have been more dominant in Canada than have class differences.

A nascent popular movement, lacking the material resources required to offer "selective incentives" to its members or potential members must rely more on "non-material" resources such as a sense of moral outrage or a desire for justice to induce them to engage in collective action (Moe, 1980, pp. 113-44). Such "ethical" motives serve as a viable basis for collective action only if individuals have a strong sense of collective identity, self-respect and dignity.

An individual must, for example, think of him/herself as a francophone before he/she will rally to a call from an organization purporting to defend the interests of francophones from some putative threat. A collective identity distinguishes members from non-members, and provides an account of the character and significance of the particular community defined in this way (See, 1986, pp. 1-32). It provides a lens which defines "us" and "them", and which identifies the set of people with whom one shares common goals and interests. Historically, the primary bases of collective identity in Canada have been ethnicity, encompassing language, religion and culture; class, in terms of economic function; and region, as demarcated by political boundaries, first as British North American colonies, and then as Canadian provinces and territories.

While these bases of collective identity have remained relatively constant throughout our history, the substance of each has changed in important ways. Ethnicity, for example, was originally linked to religious affiliation. Today, language is its principal expression.

The relationship between the three primary bases has also changed. In 1867, the community of French Canadians was considered to be Canada-wide. By 1925, it was effectively relegated to the province of Quebec. This produced a new, provincially-based form of collective identity which is today characterized as "Quebec nationalism".

Since most collectivities rely upon their members' sense of moral obligation to their community, it is logical for them to articulate their goals as demands for social justice. Hence, the growing importance of issues of social justice as the extension of democracy encouraged popular movements to mobilize in pursuit of political power. This helps to explain why an ideology which promotes solidarity of its adherents and obliges them to defend the collectivity (as with *nationalism* organized around ethnic and regional considerations, and *populism* organized around class differences) have become the principal challenges to the *status quo* in Canadian politics since 1900. Only an appeal to powerful normative ideals could overcome the lack of access to economic and state power and the material incentives that such power can make available.

This also suggests why governments with plans to implement policies based on such ideologies are more likely to come to power at the provincial level and, once elected, seek to increase the powers of provincial governments. It is easier to develop a sense of solidarity among a relatively homogenous population – in terms of class, ethnicity and region than it is in diverse societies. Having gained provincial power, such collective actors seek to increase the power of provincial governments both to enact their program at that level and, in some cases, to "bootstrap" themselves to power at the national level. This is the logic behind the province-building initiatives that have characterized Canadian federalism at various stages of its development. It also sheds light on why provincial governments have become the principal exponents of communitarian values and solidarity politics in Canada, while the federal government has associated itself more with universalist political ideologies and the Charter of Rights.

Yet, these considerations do not account for other important changes such as the extension of federal power, with little regional conflict, between 1939 and 1957. Nor do they explain the decentralizing trend that began in 1960 or the escalation of regional conflict after 1973.

These examples show that while the structure of Canadian society and of its federal institutions combine to ensure that regional and linguistic divisions are the primary bases of conflict, the forms this conflict takes and its importance relative to class divisions varies. These variations have important consequences for the politics of federalism. For example, a regionalist movement may stress the need to increase its capacity to exercise influence over the central government and extract benefits from it – or it may demand increased autonomy and freedom from the centre. With limited resources of their own, Maritimers have stressed the former; Quebecers have emphasized the latter. Western regionalism has taken both forms. The Progressive movement sought greater influence at the centre; the province-builders of the seventies sought mainly the freedom to control their own resources to pursue provincial autonomy.

In addition, the relative importance of the three chief lines of division we trace throughout this work varies. On the one hand is a long-term trend through which non-territorial class and other interests have grown in importance. On the other hand, economic circumstances and the resulting policy agenda tend to "energize" or tap differing interests and identities at different times. Thus, regional conflict was relatively muted in the immediate post-war era when the broad consensus on constructing the welfare state highlighted class considerations. There was relatively little sense that these concerns would pit British Columbians against Ontarians or Newfoundlanders. But the energy conflicts of the 1970s tapped regional differences of interest directly; they pitted workers and capitalists in Alberta and Saskatchewan against workers and capitalists in consuming provinces. One of our central tasks, therefore, is to trace such shifts in the intensity of conflict across all three divisions, in the articulation of these conflicts by political actors and in the implications of both of these for federalism. Thus, the three lines of social cleavage – language, region and class – and the collective actors which express them – governments, parties, trade unions and others – are the pivotal factors in our analysis. We explore how these divisions change in response to changes in external forces and the domestic society and how these changes then shape the politics of federalism and intergovernmental relations.

It is useful to contrast the approach we employ in this work with those that have hitherto characterized the study of Canadian federalism.

The *public choice* approach explains the driving force of federalism in terms of the competition between rival governments at the federal and provincial levels. Each government is seen to be motivated by the desire to maximize its power (revenues, jurisdiction, etc.) relative to the others, using all the resources available to it, including public support, powerful symbols and constitutional authority. The causal relationship flows from state to society, and from elites to masses.

Some versions of the public choice approach consider the consequences of such elite power-seeking as benign – as competition for wealth in economic markets, for example, is held to maximize consumer satisfaction. Thus, intergovernmental competition for voter support is held to maximize governmental responsiveness to citizen preferences (Breton, 1985). Other versions contend that the process is perverse. They argue that the competition for power is so "imperfect" that it does not constrain state elites; this leads to escalating intergovernmental conflict and a widening gap between government policies and popular preferences (Cairns, 1977, 1979).

We adopt some elements of both variants of the public choice model. Federal and provincial governments have sought to expand their power and political support. To this end, their approach to federalism reflects their institutional interests. But political actors seldom pursue power for their own sake alone. They seek broader goals, defined by their ideologies or vision of the good and the possible, and these considerations both direct and constrain their pursuit of power. Consequently, to explain political action as no more than the drive to increase power is partial and misleading.

Even if all politicians and bureaucrats are "power maximizers", such an assumption provides little help in explaining *change* in the federal system. If the drive for power is a constant, then change must originate elsewhere. And that change must come in the institutional, social and economic environment in which these leaders operate. The environment generates the issues to which they must respond, the bargaining resources available to them and their ability to win popular support. It also generates constraints on their freedom of action. Our approach stresses this environment; it focuses on the social and economic context within which elite activity takes place. Hence, we shift the focus away from elites and institutions to the changing balance of power among the underlying social forces.

The *political economy* approach – or perhaps more properly, approaches – focusses directly on societal actors and structures, making economic classes, rather than political elites, the key collective actors. One version of their approach sees the dynamic of federalism as a struggle between classes or among "fractions" of classes – each concentrated in a particular region and each with privileged access to one or another government. It therefore sees federal-provincial conflict as at root an expression of class conflict. The clearest example of this view is Macpherson's *Democracy in Alberta*, seeing Alberta provincialism as an expression of the class interests of small farmers in opposition to business interests centered in Ontario.

A second version, characteristic of writers such as Underhill (1937) and Porter (1965) saw federalism itself as a device which undercut and blocked the emergence of class-based politics. Their fundamental premise was that the Canadian emphasis on territorial divisions, federalism and "national unity" was a deliberate mystification – or, at best, an atavistic fascination with pre-industrial categories – which limited the role of the state, inhibited the organization of labour, and prevented the emergence of a "creative", class-based politics. A third view suggested that economic developments were creating "new fractions of the bourgeoisie" tied to emergent industries and whatever order of government has jurisdiction over them (Pratt &

Richards, 1979; Stevenson, 1977, 1979, 1981). Hence, federal-provincial conflict was largely a struggle within the business class.

We agree that the political mobilization of the working classes, and the role and strength of the collective actors rooted in a collective identity – such as organized labour and the CCF/NDP – have been relatively neglected forces shaping the evolution of the federal system. They have created pressures to reorient Canadian politics from a linguistic to a class mode and to expand the roles of government, to which federal institutions have had to adapt. Conversely, the federal and regionally diversified characteristics of the Canadian polity have significantly shaped the evolution of class politics in this country (See, 1986, pp. 29-32). We therefore give considerable attention not only to region and language, but also to class throughout this study.

We do not believe, however, that federal-provincial politics can be understood simply in class terms. Class has not been the only important basis of collective identity and mobilization in Canada. Nor do we attribute the persistence of regional and linguistic identities to the manipulations of economic elites and their political servants. We ascribe more autonomy both to these non-class identities and to state institutions. Therefore, we believe that it is inaccurate to reduce the complexities of ethnic and regional conflict to the level of a disguised or confused class conflict. We do recognize, however, that there is frequently a class dimension to these struggles. We agree with Stanley Ryerson when he writes:

> Classes embody relationships of property and work in the context of a mode of production. The nation-community embodies relationships of a different order. Hence, while it is inseparable historically from class structures and modes of production, the national community is more than just an aspect of any one of them. This is so because the nation-community embodies an identity, linguistic and cultural, that is not simply an "effect" of class, however closely its evolution may be interwoven with the shifting patterns of class relations and struggles.
>
> (in Teeple, 1972, p. 224; cited in See, 1986, p. 16)

We also agree with the political economy approach, when it assigns great importance to the changing international circumstances in shaping interregional conflict. Much of our analysis explores the impact of changing global markets on the relative well-being of Canadian regions. Changing global terms of trade also shift the terms of trade – and hence the sources of political conflict – within the Canadian federal system. The energy crisis, for example precipitated by the rise and fall of international oil prices, pitted workers and capitalists in one region against those in others.

The *political culture* approach, like ours, places the fundamental dynamic of federalism in citizens' collective identities, values, and perceptions of their interests, and places alternative concepts of political community and justice at the heart of an understanding of the conflicts that animate Canadian federalism (Bell & Tepperman, 1979; Simeon & Elkins, 1980).

However, this approach has two important flaws. First, if public choice theories write society out of the equation, political culture theorists tend to write out governmental actors, seeing them as simply responding to underlying pressures. We see a dialectical relationship between culture and institutions. Second, like the public choice approach, the political culture approach is essentially static. By definition, "cultures" change relatively slowly; they encompass long-standing ethnic, regional and class identities. But the substance of each of these identities, the issues around which their differences crystallize, the discourse in which they are expressed, the resources each is able to mobilize and its salience relative to the other identities within Canadian society are all *variables* which must be explained. To do this, we must look to the mobilizing activities of collective actors, and changes in objective circumstances of the sort stressed by the political economists.

The *legal-institutional* approach tends not to ask what shapes or changes the character of federal institutions, but rather to ask what effects they have on the society, public policy, and the like. The fact that in Canada federalism builds the territorial dimension of politics directly into our institutional framework is held to entrench and reinforce the strength of provincial identities, and to undermine and weaken other bases of identity. It is also held to explain certain aspects of Canadian public policy, such as the relatively late development of the welfare state and the decentralized form that it took (Simeon, 1972; Banting, 1987).

We agree: federalism does tend to "organize" territorial issues into Canadian politics and to organize other issues out. Constitutional rules certainly provide resources to particular actors in particular circumstances; that is precisely why they have been so hotly contested. But, like the public choice model, the institutional approach does not explain change, the focus of our concern. Changes are not the result of the internal logic of institutions; rather, they derive from the interaction of the institutions and the the underlying society. Indeed, until the advent of the Charter of Rights, what was most striking about the institutions of Canadian federalism was how little formal, constitutional change had occurred, while the politics of federalism underwent dramatic change.

Thus, we seek to avoid the extremes of a society-centered or a state-centered model. We draw on all the approaches discussed above. While the resulting analysis lacks the elegance and drive of a "single factor" model, we believe it captures and makes sense of a complex reality with minimum distortion.

PART II

Classical Federalism: Origins and Dynamics

The forces unleashed by the Depression and World War II changed Canadian society and generated new roles for the state. These changes, in turn, transformed the institutions and practices of Canadian federalism. The state and society so transformed were already fifty years old – linguistic and regional divisions had become entrenched, class cleavages were growing, and federal institutions had taken strong root. This legacy shaped the emergence of modern federalism.

Chapter 3

The Confederation Settlement

The constitution-makers who gathered at Quebec and Charlottetown knew roughly what they wanted to achieve – a new nation, continental in span and capable of building a new basis for economic prosperity now that the era of British mercantilism was at an end. There were two difficult questions; how were they to manage the intense linguistic and religious differences which had wrecked the experiment of 1840, and how could this ethnic accommodation be institutionalized in a workable form? These two analytically distinct questions were bound inextricably together in practice. Any political solution, however principled, which could not be embodied in workable institutions was unconvincing and, hence, was not a real solution. Institutional choices were determined by the values, interests and experiences of the colonial politicians and of the communities and classes they represented. Few were visionaries; familiar institutions were simply bent to new purposes. Britain provided the parliamentary model of government, a device which served the democratic principle of majority rule (however limited that concept was in the mid-nineteenth century), combining it with a powerful executive and the still important residual powers of the crown. Canada's constitution was to be "similar in principle" to that of the United Kingdom.

But the principles of majority rule, responsible government and concentrated authority did not solve the central problem of reconciling deep-seated linguistic and cultural differences. It was this concern which led the Fathers of Confederation to look south of the border, to the model of the United States where some powers were allocated to a central government and others, considered to be crucial to subnational communities, were assigned to states. For the Canadian constitution-makers, this arrangement offered the prospect of reducing conflict and paralysis by disengagement. Federalism was a device which could ensure that the aspirations of one community would no longer be frustrated or overruled by another. With the American civil war fresh in their minds, however, they feared that federalism might easily foster tendencies to fragmentation and dissolution. Canadian federalism, the majority of the framers thought, should be more centralized than its unruly American inspiration.

Federalism in the United States was also part and parcel of a scheme to limit and constrain government authority, intimately linked to the checks and balances in which "ambition" would counter "ambition" (Ostrom, 1987, p. 80 and Ch. 6). No such liberal vision guided the Canadian founders who, steeped in the British and loyalist tradition, were not liberal democrats. Nor, with the task of creating a new country in the face of a forbidding geography, were they inclined to create a weak state.

The third component of the institutional synthesis was the continued colonial relationship to the government of Great Britain. This led to some peculiar omissions in the BNA Act, especially the lack of a domestic amending formula, of a formal power for making and implementing treaties, and of a final domestic Court of Appeal for resolving federal-provincial disputes. Each of these omissions would come to haunt Canadians in their second century.

The vestiges of the colonial model also help to explain some quasi-colonial aspects of the relationship between the new federal government and the provinces. The federal power to disallow provincial laws, and the notion that the Lieutenant-Governor was an agent of the central government with the power to "reserve" provincial legislation for the consideration of the Governor General suggest that, in some respects, the provinces were to Ottawa what Ottawa was to London.

These were the institutional elements from which the new Canadian state was constructed. Each element had its own operating principles and sources of legitimacy and there was considerable tension among them. If they were to be welded together, some means of reconciling conflicts between them which would not impede progress and flexibility in response to changing conditions, had to be found. The criteria were to be found in the larger purposes of the new federation.

The Fathers of Confederation had two basic purposes: to create a new British North American nation, and to establish a new collective political identity capable of inspiring loyalty to its political institutions. They also agreed on the need to create a corresponding economic union – spanning the continent and large enough to achieve prosperity, as in the United States – even if, as seemed likely, all trade preferences with the United Kingdom were to be eliminated.

The Nation-Building Imperative

If there was a core of agreement as to the purposes of the new state, its character and the collective identity which was to underpin it remained unclear and controversial. At one extreme, Sir John A. Macdonald hoped to build a national political community founded on toleration, and commanding strong loyalties from its citizens. He hoped that these loyalties would eventually supersede citizens' identification with provincial political communities. Macdonald expected that if this occurred, the legitimacy possessed by provincial governments in 1867 as articulators and defenders of provincial and community values and interests would "wither away". Provincial governments would ultimately be reduced to administrative arms of the federal government with the status of municipal governments. In a letter to a friend written in 1867, Macdonald predicted that: "If the Confederation goes on, you, if spared the ordinary age of man, will see both local parliaments and governments absorbed in the general power. This is as plain to me as if I saw it accomplished" (Swainson, in Francis & Smith, 1982, p. 53).

At the other extreme were those who did not share Macdonald's view. They saw the provinces as important political communities. They did not wish to see provincial governments stripped of autonomous control over important powers and resources. On this view, Confederation was primarily a device for the preservation and development of its member communities, whether sociologically defined as linguistic and religious, or politically defined as the original colonies. Confederation in this sense was associated with the conception of the BNA Act as a "treaty" made among representatives of the British North American colonies, in which they came together to constitute the new federal government. As E. R. Black observed, the Confederation debates are "replete with reference to the treaty aspect of the resolutions", and in Charlottetown and London all provinces voted as equals (1975, pp. 150-51). Thus, while the Act was formally a law of the British Parliament, there was much support for the view that Confederation was a compact between "races" and provinces. Such a view was particularly strong among French-Canadians, but it was also widely held in the previously separate maritime colonies. (Indeed, it was an Ontario premier who first explicitly articulated the "compact theory"). Prince Edward Island and Newfoundland would not initially join the federation; Nova Scotia was virtually coerced into joining by the British Colonial Office, and moved to regain its separate status soon after 1867.

Despite his long-term aspirations, Macdonald himself recognized the force of these prior identities and loyalties:

> I have always contended that if we could agree to have one government and one parliament, legislating for the whole of these peoples, it would be the best, the cheapest, the most vigorous, and the strongest system of government we could adopt. But, on looking at the subject in the [Quebec] Conference, and discussing the matter as we did, most unreservedly, we found that such a system was impracticable.
>
> In the first place, it would not meet the assent of the people of Lower Canada, because they felt that in their peculiar position – being in a minority, with a different language, nationality and religion from the majority – in case of a junction with the other provinces, their institutions and their laws might be assailed, and their ancestral associations, on which they prided themselves, attacked and prejudiced; it was found that any proposition which involved the absorption of the individuality of Lower Canada – if I may use the expression – would not be received with favour by her people.
>
> We found too, that though their people speak the same language and enjoy the same system of law as the people of Upper Canada, a system founded on the common law of England, there was as great a disinclination on the part of the various Maritime Provinces to lose their individuality, as separate political organizations, as we observed in the case of Lower Canada herself.
>
> (Bliss, 1966, p. 120)

Thus, it was recognized from the beginning by the majority of the founders that linguistic and cultural diversity would be fundamental characteristics of the new country and of any kind of national identity it might develop. George Etienne Cartier, Macdonald's principal francophone Quebec ally, noted in the course of the confederation debates that:

> ...objection has been taken to the scheme now under consideration, because of the words "new nationality". Now, when we were united together, if union were attained, we would form a political nationality with which neither the national origin, nor the religion of any individual, would interfere. It was lamented by some that we had this diversity of races, and hopes were expressed that this distinctive feature would cease. The idea of unity of races was utopian – it was impossible.... In our own Federation we should have Catholic and Protestant, English, French, Irish, and Scotch, and each by his efforts and his success would increase the prosperity and glory of the new Confederacy.... We could not do away with the distinctions of race. We could not legislate for the disappearance of the French Canadians from American soil, but British and French Canadians alike could appreciate and understand their position relative to each other.... It was a benefit rather than otherwise that we had a diversity of races.
>
> (Bliss, 1966, pp. 112-13)

Federalism in Canada, therefore, was primarily justified and debated in terms of the preservation and development of provinces defined as communities, and about the relationship of these communities to the national community. This was an important question during the debates on the American constitution as well. But the Civil War went far to resolve that question, at least outside the South. Federalism in the U.S. was defended largely in terms of the value of dispersed authority. The Canadian model, however, continued to focus primarily, although not entirely, on alternative conceptions of community.

Despite their apparent divergence, the two visions of the new nation shared important common ground that extended beyond the simple recognition that the creation of some sort of new nation was desirable. Ramsay Cook observed:

> ...while it is true that in 1867 the political leaders of Canada were engaged in that characteristic ninteenth-century activity, the building of a nation-state, it is likewise true, and highly significant, that they were rejecting that equally characteristic nineteenth century phenomenon, the nationalist-state. Their concept of Canada was of a community based on political and juridical unity, but also on cultural and religious duality. And the key to that unity in duality was the rejection of the intolerant, conformist, ideological nationalism that was, in these same years, shaking the foundations of Europe and also providing the drive that led to the destruction of the Southern Confederacy by the North in the American Civil War.
>
> (1966, pp. 173-74)

The common ground made a political deal possible, but it was a far cry from a shared vision of the common good and the corresponding purposes of state. Without more extensive agreement on the purposes of the new nation, detailed questions of institutional design could not be fully resolved. The result was a constitutional document which remained deeply ambiguous with respect to the relative priority of national and sub-national political communities in the event that their interests came into conflict with one another. As John Whyte has described it:

> Even if the language of the power allocating sections contains coherent ideas, the arrangement of those sections reveals competition between overlapping themes and ideas. This is not the consequence of poor drafting or faulty articulation of agreed upon arrangements. Rather, the occurrence of conflicting political goals on the face of the Constitution reflects the unresolved tensions that are attendant upon the creation of a federal state... . Each allocation contains an idea of Canada or vision of how the new nation will be politically (and, hence, economically and socially) organized, but these visions are in sharp conflict with each other. The idea of confederation turns out not to be a single idea but, rather, a mere hope that somehow a nation will exist, will grow and will become politically and economically inextricably linked.
>
> (Whyte, 1984, p. 2)

Ambiguities were present at two levels. First, and fundamentally, it was unclear whether the drafters had opted for a centralized but still classical model of federalism, or for a quasi-federal model. The classical model implied that each order of government was sovereign and equal within its respective sphere of jurisdiction; the quasi-federal model implied that provincial governments were subordinate to the federal government, able to legislate, in effect, only where the senior government was silent. Second, even if the classical model were accepted, the precise scope of potentially overlapping federal and provincial powers was unclear. Where, for example, did the federal commerce power stop and provincial powers over property and civil rights begin?

Support for the classical model can be drawn from the preamble to the Act, which began by noting that "the Provinces of Canada, Nova Scotia, and New Brunswick have expressed their desire to be federally united into One Dominion", and from the fact that both sections 91 and 92 refer to powers "assigned exclusively to the Legislatures of the Provinces". Support for the quasi-federal view, on the other hand, can be found in other passages of the Act. Sections 55 and 90 together empowered the Governor-General, which in most instances effectively meant the federal government, to "disallow" or "reserve" provincial legislation, a power which Macdonald would use extensively in his years as Prime Minister (Rowell-Sirois, p. 62). Perhaps more symbolically, the Governor General was also empowered to appoint the provincial Lieutenant Governors, suggesting that they were agents of the Dominion government (Creighton, 1979, p. 83). Finally, section 92.10(c) allowed the federal government to declare "local works and undertakings" to be "for the general advantage of Canada or for the advantage of two or more provinces", thereby gaining jurisdiction over projects which would otherwise fall under exclusive provincial jurisdiction.

The BNA Act was also ambiguous on the question of the scope of the general powers assigned to each order of government under sections 91 and 92. The "residual power" – i.e. the power "to make laws for the Peace, Order, and good Government of Canada in relation to all matters not coming within the Classes of Subjects by this Act assigned exclusively to the Legislatures of the Provinces" – was assigned to the federal government in section 91. But its real scope and meaning depended upon the interpretation of the two general categories of power assigned to the provincial legislatures under section 92: "Property and Civil Rights in the Province" and "Generally all Matters of a merely local or private Nature in the Province".

Some sense of the scope and purpose of these general provincial powers was provided by the more specific powers listed under section 92: the "Solemnization of Marriage"; and the "Administration of Justice in the Province, including the Constitution, Maintenance, and Organization of

Provincial Courts, both of Civil and Criminal Jurisdiction, including Procedure in Civil Matters in those Courts". In addition, section 93 assigned provincial governments the exclusive power to make laws in relation to education, subject to a set of limitations which sought to protect the rights of separate denominational schools which existed at the time of the Union. With these powers, provincial governments – and above all, the province of Quebec – could prevent the national majority from overriding customary forms of community life related to language, religion, education, civil law and public welfare. Finally, responsibility for social policy – public welfare and the municipalities which were responsible for it, insofar as it was not left to private charities and churches – was assigned to the provincial governments (Rowell-Sirois, pp. 51-52).

This is enough to suggest that the preservation and development of existing sub-national communities and identities was considered to be important and was also understood to be primarily the responsibility of the provincial governments. But there was little to provide guidance on how to reconcile conflicts between the perceived requirements of federal nation-building and provincial community preservation. Nor did it provide for cases in which individuals or minorities within provinces might be subject to the tyranny of provincial majorities.

One way of responding to the first type of problem is to supplement the division of powers by devices which incorporate provincial representatives into the federal state. This strategy – "intrastate federalism" as it came to be known a century later (Cairns and Black, 1965) – seeks to represent the federal society in national institutions. It can do so either by ensuring provincial governments a role in these institutions or by representing provincial populations in legislative bodies, tempering simple majority rule with equal provincial representation or something close to it. Canadian constitution-makers had available to them an American model of intrastate federalism with respect to their Senate and Supreme Court. In 1867 the members of the United States Senate were appointed by the state legislatures, each of which had equal representation (two Senators), in a Senate with powers co-equal with the House of Representatives. The same principle applied to the judicial branch, because the justices of the United States Supreme Court were subject to the confirmation of the Senate.

More than six of the 14 days of discussion at the 1864 Quebec conference were devoted to discussion of the Senate, especially the mode of representation and appointment. In the end, the parliamentary model adopted (influenced in part by the desire for a second chamber with some parallels to the British House of Lords) included a Senate whose members were appointed with an eye to regional representation, but with no provincial government or direct citizen participation as to who would be chosen to represent each region.

The selection of judges of the Supreme Court of Canada mattered less than its American counterpart since the final Court of Appeal (until 1949) remained in Britain with the Judicial Committee of the Privy Council. This explains in part why the Supreme Court of Canada was not even created until 1875, although provision for its creation was contained in the BNA Act. Nonetheless, just as with the Senate, the federal government alone made all judicial appointments, without any formal provincial role, although from the start the Supreme Court Act stipulated that two, and later three, Justices should come from Quebec, and there have been informal norms about other elements of regional representation (Hogg, 1985, p. 162).

Considerable attention was also given at Charlottetown to the idea of regional representation in the federal cabinet, and strong informal conventions along these lines soon developed. But again, incorporating regional criteria into an exclusively federal selection process is very different from incorporating provincial representatives into the federal government and its judiciary. The Canadian version of intrastate federalism which emerged from the BNA Act was thus more attenuated and less formal than its American counterpart.

The potential tyranny of federal or provincial majorities could have been addressed by assigning religious and linguistic rights to individuals and leaving it to the courts to enforce them. This was the model the United States chose through the Bill of Rights. But again, the Canadian choices were very different. If the Canadian version of intrastate federalism was more centralized than the American, the Canadian version of religious and linguistic rights was much more decentralized. Provincial governments were assigned primary responsibility for religious and linguistic rights; and the federal goverment, rather than the courts, was assigned responsibility for protecting (some) minorities within provinces. Subsections (1) and (4) of section 93 provided that in any case where a provincial law "shall prejudicially affect any Right or Privilege with respect to Denominational Schools which any Class of Persons have by Law in the Province at the Union", a right of appeal to the federal government would exist, and that (the federal) government would have the power to "make remedial Laws for the due execution of the Provisions of this Section". This section also extended the minority rights existing in Upper Canada at the time of the Union to "the Dissentient Schools of the Queen's Protestant and Roman Catholic Subjects in Quebec". Section 133, in turn, obliged the federal government to recognize the use of both English and French in its courts and legislature, and to publish all legislation, records and journals in both languages. The same obligations were placed upon the government of Quebec.

Thus, the federal government was made responsible for the protection of existing religious minority education rights from the potential tyranny of provincial majorities, and for providing, if not actively promoting, the use of both languages in its institutions and activities. This was a significant role, but it was not nearly as extensive as it might have been. As Donald Creighton has written:

> The British North America Act contained no general declaration of principle that Canada was to be a bilingual and bicultural nation – or, for that matter, that it would remain "a diversity of races". The Fathers of Confederation were as little inclined to lay down the law about the cultural purpose and future of their new nation as they were to issue a general pronouncement on the nature and probable destiny of mankind... . The French language had thus...no official standing in the courts of any of the provinces except Quebec; and perhaps even more important, it was given no protected place in any of the nation's schools.
>
> (1970, p. 12)

Canadians did not simply copy the American model: indeed, it was as much a negative example as a positive one. The Canadian federation was at the outset more collectivist, more centralized, and less focussed on state representation at the centre. In Canada there were few provinces, each of which was characterized by a strong executive and parliament. In the American version there were many more states, each of which (as well as the federal government) was characterized by checks and balances in a Congressional form. All these differences had crucial implications for the future evolution of the two systems. These differences help to explain the extent to which Canadian communities have been defined and expressed by their governments, and why the relations among them are carried out largely, though not entirely, through intergovernmental relations.

The ambiguities of the BNA Act did not cast Canadian institutions and processes in stone. Nor was it inevitable that religious, linguistic and regional differences would remain dominant. Indeed, federalism was declared "obsolete" several times over the next 120 years – in the 1930s, in the 1950s and again in the 1980s. We must turn to the dynamics of state and society to explain why such predications have been, at least so far, always confounded.

The Economic Development Imperative

The objective of creating a viable national market economy – an economic union, continental in scope – provoked much less controversy than the nation-building imperative. It was generally accepted that the state must play a major role in developing the economy. Britain was already in the twilight of its *laissez-faire* state (Mallory, 1954, pp. 30-31); in a frontier society like Canada, sole reliance on private enterprise and markets for economic development was never a serious option. The national economy had to be constructed before there could be any discussion of allowing it to run on its own. As Aitken observed: "On any reading of the historical record, government policies and decisions stand out as key factors." The creation of a national economy in Canada – and even more notably, of a transcontinental economy – was as much a political as an economic achievement (1981).

During the first phase of this development process, the state had two principal goals: the acquisition of the western territories from the Hudson's Bay Company, and the elimination of trade barriers among the British North American colonies. Section 91 granted the federal government exclusive jurisdiction over defence, Indians and lands reserved for them, and naturalization and aliens. Section 146 permitted the federal government to admit Rupert's Land and the North-west Territory into the Union on such terms as it saw fit. Admission of the colonies of Newfoundland, Prince Edward Island and British Columbia was also provided for under the terms agreed to by the federal and the relevant colonial governments. Section 95 provided for concurrent federal and provincial jurisdiction over immigration and agriculture, because the agricultural settlement of the west was expected to be based primarily upon immigrants from outside Canada. With respect to the economic union, section 121 guaranteed that "All articles of the Growth, Produce, or Manufacture of any one of the Provinces shall, from and after the Union, be admitted free into each of the other Provinces".

Beyond these preliminary tasks, the constitution-makers assumed that the state had two important economic development obligations: the provision of a nation-wide transportation and communications network and other types of infrastructure, and the regulation of private resource development activities. These were regarded as part of the essential framework within which private investment and development activity would stimulate economic growth. It seemed clear that only by assigning these tasks to the central government and by enabling it to pool resources and coordinate effort was there any hope of success. The provinces would have a role in the development of infrastructure, but only that which was not interprovincial or international in character. With respect to natural resource development, the (four) provinces were given the principal role within their boundaries, but the federal government was to be responsible for the settlement of the North-west Territory and the development of its resources.

Section 91, which lists 29 specific areas over which the federal government had exclusive jurisdiction, assigned to Ottawa the power to regulate trade and commerce; and responsibility for the postal service, navigation and shipping, currency and coinage, banking and the issuance of paper money, weights and measures, bankruptcy and insolvency, and patents and copyrights. Section 92.10 explicitly excluded from provincial jurisdiction "local works and undertakings" associated with the crucial inter-provincial and international transportation and communications systems – ships, railways, canals, telegraphs – networks that the federal government would need to develop in order to carry out its mandate. This was supplemented by the "declaratory power" which, under subsection (c) of 92.10, assigned the federal government the power to declare any work or undertaking to be in the general interest of Canada, thereby bringing it under federal jurisdiction. Finally, section 145 committed the federal government "to provide for the Commencement within Six Months after the Union, of a Railway Connecting the River St. Lawrence with the City of Halifax in Nova Scotia, and for the Construction thereof without Intermission, and the Completion with all practicable Speed". Such policies with respect to the development of the new nation's infrastructure were by far the most important focus of government expenditure during this period.

Conclusions

The framers of the constitution of 1867 were divided between two competing visions of the new nation and over the appropriate form of its new federal institutions. In drafting the BNA Act, they deliberately avoided these fundamental differences in order to protect the limited agreement they had been able to forge (see Waite, 1962).

By such evasions, many difficult bargains are made, with each party achieving its most pressing and immediate aims and at the same time hoping that when the questions begged arise, the interpretive chips will fall its way. By setting these fundamental questions to one side, the drafters succeeded in securing agreement among themselves, and from their legislatures, on the desirability of a federal union, but this tactic had a price. Unresolved conflicts were incorporated into the text of the BNA Act. The area of greatest agreement and least ambiguity was that pertaining to economic development, for here jurisdictions could be assigned primarily in accordance with the immediate goals of the federation determined by current notions of the appropriate economic and social role of the state. But as the objectives and the roles played by both federal and provincial governments broadened, the division of powers between governments were to become less clear cut. Moreover, the division of taxing powers would become more complicated, so that fiscal arrangements would require frequent adjustment.

As the evolution of the political economy, particularly of the economic role of the state, invalidated many of the empirical and normative assumptions upon which economic powers had been divided, the pressure for a restatement and clarification of those powers increased. The United States, subjected to the same logic, experienced parallel political pressures. Despite the fact that its constitution defined the classical, decentralized model of federalism, Americans responded with major shifts toward a more centralized form after the Civil War and again in the 1930s. Paradoxically, Canadian federalism moved in the opposite direction during the same period, pursuing a decentralizing course after the first Macdonald government. This trend was interrupted only by the First World War. The main reason for the divergence between the two federal systems, as we shall see, was that the constellation of political communities and collective actors that existed in Canada was substantially different from that which developed in the United States.

Chapter 4

The Triumph of Classical Federalism

The BNA Act established the basic framework within which federalism would evolve in Canada's first half century. Its very ambiguities ensured that it would be sufficiently flexible to permit shifts in the balance of powers held by each order of government without formal constitutional amendments. In this chapter we trace the evolution of the social forces which lay beneath the decentralizing path followed by Canadian federalism in these years.

This evolution may be divided into four periods. The early years were dominated by Macdonald and lasted until the election of the Liberal government under Wilfrid Laurier in 1896. The next period, dominated by Laurier, lasted until the First World War. During these years, the economic promise of the National Policy and Confederation seemed to be fulfilled, but religious and linguistic divisions prevented the emergence of a strong sense of national identity. A brief period of centralization during and immediately after World War I foreshadowed the more interventionist roles which the state would play in the modern era under the leadership of the federal government. But the fourth period, the decade of the 1920s, witnessed the rapid retreat of the central government from its war-time dominance. The political initiative shifted to the provinces in response to the emergence of the Maritime Rights movement, conservative Quebec nationalism, and agrarian radicalism. This decade was the apogee of classical federalism.

Federal Society

The first five years of the new federation saw rapid economic growth, fuelled by growth in the rest of North America and Europe and by a spurt in the volume of world trade (Hughes, 1970, p. 144). Then, in 1873, the international economy plunged into what the nineteenth century called "the Great Depression". It would last, with only short and minor respites, until 1896. Its impact on the Canadian economy was immediate and profound. Foreign capital became more difficult and expensive to acquire. Railways, which had been over-extended in the construction boom of the 1850s and 1860s, teetered on the edge of bankruptcy. The Intercolonial Railway, to which the federal government had committed itself in section 145 of the BNA Act, encountered serious financial difficulties. When the Pacific Scandal brought down the Macdonald government in 1873, its Liberal successor sought to economize by putting further extension of the Pacific Railway on a "pay-as-you-go" footing. The result was a virtual halt in new construction. British Columbians threatened secession if the railway were not completed as promised. Other elements of the federal Liberals' economic policies proved equally ineffective and strains within the federation mounted (Lower, 1973, pp. 126-30).

Thus, while the federal government had quickly achieved the territorial goals it had been assigned, it seemed unable to make significant economic progress during the first fifteen years of the federation. Mackenzie's Liberal government bore the brunt of the dissatisfaction attending this failure and Macdonald's Conservatives were restored to power in the 1878 election.

Macdonald had campaigned on the need for a new economic strategy – "the National Policy" – consisting of three interrelated components. First, the railway to British Columbia would be completed with all speed. Second, Canadian tariffs would be raised, thus increasing Ottawa's revenues, a necessity if it were to play the larger role in the promotion of the intercontinental railway that the Policy required. Higher tariffs would also afford protection from import competition to the nascent Canadian manufacturing sector. Third, the government would do everything it could to encourage immigrants to settle as farmers in the western provinces and territories that the new railroad would make accessible. Such settlement would create an expanded and protected market for eastern Canadian manufactures and increase Canadian wheat production and exports. The two-way traffic in these commodities would create plenty of business for the inter-colonial railway (Brown, pp. 22-28, but see also Dales, pp. 29-43, both in Francis & Smith, 1982).

The railroad was completed with remarkable speed. The last spike was driven at Craigellachie in 1885, only four years after the Canadian Pacific Railway received its charter, and four years ahead of its 1891 deadline. The general tariff rose from 17.5 percent to 20 percent, and tariffs on fully manufactured goods ranged from an average of 25 percent to a high of 30 percent (Lower, 1973, pp. 130-31).

Despite these efforts, however, the National Policy did not succeed in restoring economic growth, nor did the surge of immigration and western settlement expected to follow the completion of the CPR materialize. Many of those who did come in this period did not stay long: between 1871 and 1891, an estimated 1,256,000 people came to Canada and an estimated 1,546,000 left the country. The total population grew by only 1,150,000 over these two decades, concentrated in Quebec and Ontario (*Historical Statistics*, A2-14). The Maritime population was virtually stagnant, and the population of Manitoba and the NWT in 1891 still only represented about five percent of a total Canadian population of 4,833,000 (Creighton, 1970, p. 76).

World recovery brought renewed growth of Canada after 1896. As Easterbrook and Aitken put it, "after thirty years of waiting and frustrated hopes, it was at last Canada's turn to be drawn into the world network of trade and investment" (1981, p. 483). Leading the national economy was the growth in wheat production and exports, which had been greatly stimulated by rising wheat prices, falling transportation costs and new technologies (Easterbrook & Aitken, 1981, pp. 477-78). The wheat boom brought to fruition the hopes which had inspired the National Policy of 1879 (Mackintosh, 1964, pp. 40-45).

Rapid economic growth attracted the immigration that Macdonald's National Policy alone could not. Two million immigrants arrived in Canada between 1896 and 1911 (Lower, 1973, p. 142). In 1872, the entire prairie region had a population (including Metis and Indians) of about 73,000 (Conway, 1982, p. 21). Between 1896 and 1913 more than a million people settled in the prairies, increasing the area of occupied lands seven-fold, and wheat production by more than ten times (Conway, 1982, pp. 27-28). The net value of flour and wheat products in the first decade of the new century increased fivefold, almost twice the rate at which the net value of industrial goods such as textiles and steel increased. Wheat exports, which constituted four percent of the value of Canada's total exports in 1901, accounted for 16 percent by 1911 (Easterbrook & Aitken, 1981, pp. 483-85). By 1913, the value of wheat and flour exports alone was greater than the value of all exports in 1896 (Conway, 1982, pp. 27-28).

The settlement of the west by immigrant farmers under a regime of protective tariffs was a major stimulus to the growth of Canadian primary and secondary manufacturing. The first major expansion of hydro-electricity began in this period, as did the manufacture of automobiles. The chemical industry more than trebled in size. Even more important in terms of total value, however, was the expansion of iron and steel production associated with the renewed expansion of railways and the rapid growth of the pulp and paper and mining industries. Only in the maritime provinces was this a period of slow economic growth and depopulation (Mackintosh, 1964, pp. 50-51).

World War I gave further impetus both to western agriculture and central Canadian manufacturing. It quickly pulled Canada out of a recession which had begun in 1912, creating near full employment. Large-scale federal spending on war materials so expanded primary and secondary industry that by the end of the war Canada's industrial output had surpassed its agricultural production (Lower, 1973, p. 154). Between 1910 and 1923, the production of rubber products increased almost ten-fold, of automobiles more than twelve-fold, of electical light and power more than five times, and of chemical products more than four times (Mackintosh, 1964, p. 51).

War boosted wheat prices, as European production dwindled. This resulted in "an unparalleled rate of increase in the area devoted to the production of wheat and other food crops" in Canada. Between 1913 and 1919 the acreage under wheat increased 80 percent, an increase equal to that of the previous twenty years of the wheat boom. The western population expanded rapidly. Between 1911 and 1921, it grew by more than 600,000, reaching almost two million (Easterbrook & Aitken, 1981, pp. 487-88).

The war was also a time of renewed prosperity for the Maritimes. North Atlantic shipping was a great stimulus to ship building in the ports of Halifax and Saint John, and to the ancillary steel and coal industries of the region. For a time, Nova Scotia, "and to a less extent New Brunswick and Prince Edward Island, recovered the advantages for export trade and shipping, which had fallen from her between 1880 and 1900" (Mackintosh, 1964, p. 72).

This rapid expansion brought with it steadily mounting pressure on short supplies of labour and raw materials. By 1916, inflation was eroding the incomes of most workers and shortages of vital materials for war industries were becoming a serious problem. In attempting to control inflation and maintain war supplies, the federal government was drawn into the regulation of ever wider aspects of the Canadian economy (Rowell-Sirois, pp. 120-23).

The armistice of November 1918 was followed by a brief but intense economic boom, lasting until 1920. Then the price and credit structure in Canada collapsed, reaching its lowest point in 1922. Some commodities were particularly hard hit – wheat prices fell nearly 60 percent between 1920 and 1922; dried cod prices fell by more than 50 percent between 1918 and 1923 – and so were the regional economies that specialized in their production. Unemployment had been a serious problem since 1918, due to the rapid demobilization of the armed forces, and to lay-offs while industry converted from war-time to civilian production.

By 1924 economic recovery was under way, but progress was slow and regionally uneven. It was strong in Ontario, Quebec and British Columbia, more attenuated on the prairies, and weakest in the Maritimes. Agriculture's contribution to net national production declined, though with much variation from year to year. Manufacturing increased rapidly from 33 percent in 1920 to 40 percent in 1929. The single most important industry became pulp and paper, at more than twice the value of the second largest – non-ferrous metal smelting – but the latter was the fastest-growing of all the industrial sectors. Other rapidly expanding sectors were automobile manufacturing and hydro-electric power (Mackintosh, 1964, pp. 71-72, 77, 79-82).

Despite the appearances produced by the rapid growth of the 1925-29 period, however, the foundations of the new international economic order, and Canada's renewed prosperity, were terribly fragile. The New York stock market crash of 1929 was the first domino in a sequence of events which, over the next two years, would plunge Canada into the worst depression of its history.

The strength of sub-national Canadian identities was such that even as some sense of membership in the larger Canadian nation began to emerge, Canadians still understood their nation as a collection of smaller communities banded together for various practical reasons. The legitimacy of extensive federal powers, accordingly, depended upon its capacity to make good the claim that it required extensive legal and fiscal powers in order to execute these goals effectively and that it could indeed bring about such results. But the long world recession had seemed to show that there was little which even a highly centralized federal government could do to promote domestic economic development if the international conditions were not propitious. This reduced the plausibility of the federal government's principal claim to those powers, while mounting ethnic conflict created strong pressure for decentralization:

> The provincial governments lacked the financial resources, while the Dominion failed to evoke a spirit of national loyalty. In these circumstances, it was by no means clear, at the end of the period [c.1896], that the equilibrium necessary to a working federalism could be reached. It was not clear whether room could be found for the free play of provincial aspirations without denying to the Dominion the confidence and loyalty it needed for the advancement of common national purposes.
>
> (Rowell-Sirois, pp. 89-90)

The wheat boom might have strengthened federal legitimacy and, with it, Macdonald's quasi-federal ideals; but under Laurier, the federation moved toward the classical model in an effort to douse the flames of ethnic conflict that Macdonald had helped to fan. So the principal moral drawn was that political decentralization and economic growth were compatible, while centralization was no guarantee of anything other than ethnic conflict. We now examine the dynamics of the ethnic and class differences which made the realization of the classical federal possibility in the BNA Act a political necessity.

Ethnic Cleavages

Language, religion, and culture – "race" in the language of the time – combined to form the dominant division in Canadian politics throughout this period. In 1906, André Siegfried, who Frank Underhill was to call "the de Tocqueville of Canada", described Canadian politics as:

> ...a tilting-ground for impassioned rivalries. An immemorial struggle persists between French and English, Catholics and Protestants, while an influence is gathering strength close by them which some day may become predominant – that of the United States. In this complex contest...the whole future of Canada is at stake.... [T]he Canadian problem...is...a very complex one. Hence its difficulty. Hence its profound interest.
>
> (Siegfried, 1966, p. 14)

Because the populations on either side of this cleavage line were regionally concentrated, each could constitute a majority in at least one province while at the federal level each could mount sufficient strength to foil the aims of the other except under the most exceptional circumstances. This made it easier for provincial governments to take uncompromising stands, and more difficult for the federal government to do the same. More importantly the exacerbation of the linguistic divisions meant that the hope of creating a national political community in which both elements would eventually feel at home remained just that – a hope – entertained by a minority, which receded into the future. Canada would not, in the foreseeable future, develop a homogenous national culture in which all would be bilingual and ecumenical.

The primary battlegrounds of the religious-linguistic struggle were not in Quebec, but rather in Ontario and the West. Rapid population growth on the prairies, especially in Manitoba, radically altered the ethnic, religious and linguistic balance in the region. In Manitoba, primarily French-speaking and Catholic Metis had outnumbered the white settlers in Red River by about six to one in 1871. By 1891 the ratio had been reversed, with English Protestants from Ontario constituting the overwhelming majority (Conway, 1983, p. 15, p. 21, p. 36).

These changes underlay the second Riel rebellion – a last protest against the defeat of a traditional way of life. But the geopolitical conditions which gave Riel and his supporters real bargaining power with Ottawa in 1870 were no longer in effect by in 1885. The suppression of the rebellion had broad support in all provinces including Quebec (Wade, 1956, pp. 422-23). It was Riel's conviction for treason by an English-speaking jury, in contrast with the acquittal of his co-conspirator, Henry Jackson, coupled with Macdonald's calculated refusal of clemency which outraged *Canadien* opinion. Even the normally moderate Laurier publicly declared that, had he been in Riel's position, he too would have taken up arms. At the same rally, Honoré Mercier called for the creation of an all-French Canadian political party. Laurier opposed this proposal, but the more extreme wing of the Ontario press made great play of it, calling for the "shattering" of the federation and the "re-conquest" of Quebec. In this atmosphere of polarizing rhetoric, Mercier's Parti national won a majority in the provincial election of 1886.

Laurier's rise in the Liberal Party began with the Riel debacle – he assumed the leadership in 1887 – and so did the party's growing support in Quebec. It also marked the beginning of the decline of the Conservative party in that province, hence Senator Lowell Murray's observation that the Conservative Party "has been waiting for an achievement like this (the Meech Lake Accord) since the day Louis Riel was hanged" (*Maclean's*, June 15, 1987, p.17).

Meanwhile, ethnic conflicts intensified. In 1887 the Mercier government sought to resolve an old Quebec question with the Jesuit Estates Act, but it was bitterly opposed by the Orange protestant factions among the federal Tories. Two years later, having failed in their efforts to have the Quebec legislation disallowed, thirteen members of this faction – variously called "the Noble Thirteen" and "the Devil's Dozen" – agitated for the revocation of the sections of the Manitoba Act (1870) providing for two official languages and protecting the rights of Catholics to public support for confessional schools (Creighton, 1970, p. 19; Wade, 1956, pp. 393-405). They also attacked Mowat's Liberal government in Ontario for allowing the use of French in its schools. Finally, in 1890, they introduced a bill in Parliament proposing the abolition of the French language in the administration and in the schools of the North-west Territory (Wade, 1956, p. 435).

In 1890, the Manitoba Legislature abolished bilingual government services and public funding for separate schools. In Ontario, French separate schools were first required to teach English as a subject in 1885; then in 1890, a regulation was added requiring the (now) bilingual schools to adopt the same curriculum as unilingual English schools, using English textbooks (Symons in Burns, 1971, p. 172). Following Macdonald's death in 1891, the

Orange faction of the Conservative federal government succeeded in passing two ordinances which deprived the North-west Territory of French-language government services and abolished the use of French in most schools (Wade, 1968, pp. 539-45; Joy, 1972, p. 127).

By 1893 the Orange faction had lost the initiative, but the federal Tories could not agree to override the actions of the Manitoba government. Instead, they bought time by referring the question of the constitutionality of the Manitoba legislation – and of any federal "remedial" response under section 93 of the BNA Act – to the Courts. When the Privy Council held that the federal government had the power to act, delay could no longer be justified. The federal Conservatives introduced a remedial bill, but the Liberals blocked it. The issue remained unresolved before the federal election of 1896 (Creighton, 1970, pp. 80-81).

Throughout the Manitoba schools conflict, Laurier's Liberals had taken the position that the federal government should not use its powers to overrule the Manitoba legislation. In part this reflected the Liberal party's commitment to the defence of "provincial rights" and in part it reflected Laurier's own convictions concerning the appropriate relationship between church and state. He opposed the ultramontane doctrines which then prevailed in the Catholic Church of Quebec, and argued that to strike down the Manitoba legislation would be interpreted by many as bending to the Church's persistent demands for federal intervention (Wade, 1956, pp. 364-69). Laurier's position on the issue earned him the denunciation of the Catholic hierarchy: the Vicar-General declared it a mortal sin to vote Liberal in the election (Wade, 1956, p. 437).

Despite the attacks from the extreme wings on both sides of the linguistic divide, Laurier was able to find solid middle ground with his platform of toleration, provincial rights and continuity with the Conservatives' protectionist economic policies. In the 1896 contest the Liberals won 49 of the 65 Quebec seats, against the 37 they had secured in the 1891 election. In the maritimes (except for PEI) and the west, the Liberals significantly improved their standing. The Liberals split Ontario with the Conservatives – despite anti-French backlash and suspicions arising from past Liberal support for free trade – each party gaining 43 seats. Laurier had secured a parliamentary majority with 118 seats to the Conservatives' 88 (Beck, 1968, p. 86). In 1897, Laurier reached an agreement with Premier Greenwood of Manitoba which "allowed bilingual teaching, in French or another language, with English, instruction by a teacher of the same faith as that of the pupils, and religious instruction under prescribed and limited conditions" (Morton, 1963, p. 391).

Laurier's Manitoba policy successfully defused that source of conflict, but the spread of imperialist ardour in English Canada – reflected in the formation of the Imperial Federation League in 1884 and the British

Empire League in 1896 – soon re-opened the ethnic divisions, again raising questions about the character of the Canadian political nationality.

The Canadian imperialists were not uniformly anti-French or anti-Catholic. Some of their leading members, such as Principal Grant of Queen's University, supported Laurier's position on the Manitoba schools issue (Berger, 1970, pp. 136-37). Yet, D'Alton McCarthy, who had spear-headed the Orange crusade in Manitoba, was also closely associated with the British Empire League. Such affiliations gave the League's motto, "One race, one flag, one throne", an ominous ring in *Canadien* ears (Berger, 1970, pp. 4-5).

Laurier sought to contain the spread of imperialist ideas in English Canada by appeals to Canadian patriotism, and the extension of Canada's political autonomy vis-à-vis Great Britain. This nationalist tack found strong sympathy among French Canadians, but it was much less successful in English Canada, where imperialist sentiments prevailed. As a result, imperial policy questions so polarized English and French Canadian public opinion that attempts to locate a middle ground in the politics of national identity on the terrain of Canadian nationalism proved increasingly difficult. The sending of Canadian troops and supplies to South Africa during the Boer war prompted Tardival to call for the foundation "at the hour marked by Divine Providence...[of a] French Canadian nation". In a public reply, Henri Bourassa wrote:

> Our own nationalism is a Canadian nationalism founded upon the duality of races and on the particular traditions which this duality involves. We work for the development of a Canadian patriotism which is in our eyes the best guarantee of the existence of the two races and of the mutual respect they owe each other...the English Canadians are not foreigners, and we regard as allies all those among them who respect us and who desire like us the maintenance of Canadian autonomy.
>
> (Wade, 1956, pp. 534-35)

By 1914, nationalism of this sort was more than ever the exclusive possession of French Canada. Only in the wake of the Great War, which widely discredited the ideology of empire and weakened Canada's economic ties with Great Britain, would national autonomy find stronger support among English Canadians.

Other issues further polarized opinion. When Saskatchewan and Alberta achieved provincial status in 1905, Laurier sought to restore the minority language education rights which had existed in the Territories before 1891, but was forced to back down by English opposition led by Clifford Sifton, the Minister responsible for immigration and western settlement. Dispute over the Naval Bill and Canada's military obligations to Britain was partially responsible for Laurier's defeat in the 1911 election. A popular political cartoon of the period depicted Laurier as a circus rider, astride two horses, one foot on each, as they galloped off in different directions. He himself described his situation in this way: "In Quebec I am branded as a Jingo and in Ontario as a separatist. In Quebec I am attacked as an Imperialist and in Ontario as an anti-Imperialist. I am neither. I am a Canadian" (Beck, 1968, p. 132).

Imperialism and the schools issue would not go away. Borden's attempt to resolve the thorny problem of Canada's contribution to British naval strength was stalled by the Liberal-dominated Senate, and no way out of this impasse could be found before the war broke out (Lower, 1973, pp. 152-53). On the schools issue, the Ontario government approved Regulation 17 in 1912, effectively preventing French-language instruction after Form 1 and limiting the study of French as a subject to one hour per day. Borden refused to challenge the regulation, rejecting the arguments made by Bourassa and Laurier that a federal policy of non-intervention could no longer hope to preserve national unity, and would only serve to discredit the federal govermment in the eyes of French Canadians (Symons, 1971, p. 174).

In 1916, after the Courts upheld Regulation 17 against a constitutional challenge brought by franco-Ontarians, the provincial government enacted even more restrictive legislation. Again, the Borden government refused to act, and party discipline disintegrated when Lapointe introduced a motion to censure the Ontario government: Quebec Conservatives of the Nationalist tendency voted with Laurier's Liberals in support of the motion; western Liberals broke ranks and voted with the Conservatives against it (Rowell-Sirois, pp. 114-15). New fuel was added to the schools issue when, later the same year, the Manitoba government repudiated the Laurier-Greenwood agreement of 1897. In its stead, the provincial legislature made English the sole language of instruction in the public schools and attendence at public schools compulsory. Once again, Borden refused to act (Wade, 1956, p. 440, pp. 546-52).

Despite initial French Canadian support for Canadian participation in the Great War – Bourassa, in *Le Devoir*, called it "Canada's national duty to contribute" – the accumulated hostilities over education and imperialism soon eroded the consensus. Canadians accused *Canadiens* of lower levels of voluntary enlistment and failing to do their share to support the war effort. By 1917, Borden was committed to conscription, but so strong was the opposition to it from French Canadians and farmers that the Prime Minister sought a new electoral mandate and a non-partisan "government of national unity" to carry it through.

In the conscription election of December 1917, English-speaking Liberals deserted Laurier to run with Borden's Conservatives as Union Government candidates. *Canadien* Nationalists deserted their erstwhile

Conservative allies to support Laurier. The election returns reflected this polarization: "the Union Government swept English-speaking Canada while Quebec gave solid support to Sir Wilfrid Laurier's opposition to conscription. Of the 143 candidates elected who were endorsed by the Union Government, all but three were returned in English-speaking Canada; 60 of the total of 77 elected candidates endorsed by Sir Wilfrid Laurier were elected in Quebec" (Rowell-Sirois, p. 117).

The experience of direct federal coercion in the face of determined and united *Canadien* opposition, the realization of the fears which Riel's execution had raised in symbolic form, strengthened *Canadien* convictions that provincial rights constituted the only significant bastion against an English-speaking majority which could be expected to control the federal government in cases where "racial" identities and interests were fundamentally opposed. The hope that the Catholic religion and the French language might flourish in all parts of Canada as part of a dualistic national culture seemed to many of the younger generation of *Canadien* leaders an unrealizable dream, rendered impossible by a combination of immigration, settlement patterns and the actions of provincial governments (see Joy, 1972). This perception promoted the regionalisation of the linguistic divisions: Quebec was increasingly regarded as the only true homeland and protector of the *Canadien* people in Canada. For the first time, a significant Quebec-centred ethnic nationalism emerged.

The definition of the provincial political community entailed by Quebec nationalism was deeply at odds with the vision of Canadian nationality espoused by Cartier, Laurier and Bourassa. It began with a vision of the race or people as primary, endowed by God and history with a particular mission and destiny (Wade, 1956:887-8). The Abbé Groulx, a religious educator, popular historian of Quebec and leader of the Quebec nationalists in the 1920s and 1930s, described the goals of his politics this way:

> To work toward the survival of a great Canada – which, after all, we are not renouncing – is to work for the growth and endurance of a political and economic entity; in short, for a material greatness. "Canada exists solely for political reasons" Siegfried has recently written. But if it is granted that a Catholic people and country represent a value of a higher order; and if, despite our shortcomings and troubles, as a result of historic causes it happens that we embody, here in our land, Catholic spirituality and vitality as no other people does, then to work towards the creation of a French State, towards a climate of liberty for the flowering of human personality and Christian civilization – what is this, in short, but to give our labour and our life to an incomparable end: the survival of one of the highest spiritual realities on this continent?
>
> (in Forbes, 1985, pp. 268-69).

This Quebec nationalism had important implications for the province's economic and social policies. The post-war recession provoked much discussion concerning the degree to which the economy was dependent upon American investment and run by Americans and Anglo-Canadians. In 1920 the Abbé Groulx argued: "Nous avons à choisir ou de redevenir les mâitres chez nous ou de nous résigner à jamais aux destinées d'un peuple de serfs" (Hamelin, 1977, p. 438). With the return of economic prosperity, the economic critique levelled at successive Liberal provincial administrations lost much of its popular support, but it would revive with the economic crisis beginning in 1930 (Hamelin, 1977, pp. 438-39; Wade, 1956, p. 897). So, too, would the phrase "mâitres chez nous" and the concerns it expressed.

The profound political and social conservatism associated with this view also meant a growing gap between Quebec and the rest of Canada about the character and purpose of the state. This gap, more than anything else, accounts for the failure of the federal government to pursue new social and economic initiatives in the 1920s.

Regional and Class Cleavages

The wheat boom and the influx of new settlers radically altered the social makeup of the western prairies. The new agrarian class which it created became a major force in Canadian politics at both the national and the provincial levels. Prairie agriculture was concentrated on the production of a single commodity – wheat – the bulk of which was sold in a volatile international market. The economic interests of western farmers were thus unusually homogenous. This facilitated the development of a collective identity which highlighted conflicts of economic interest between the farmers of the region and the financial, commercial and industrial capital concentrated in central Canada.

New agrarian organizations sought to alter the terms of trade between farmers and the various sectors with which they dealt – manufacturers of implements and other necessities, grain merchants, financiers and transportation firms – and to influence federal tariff, freight rate and grain marketing policies. The Patrons of Industry, a farmer's movement active in the United States and Ontario since the 1870s, established its first western branch in 1891. By 1896, the Patrons had established a number of cooperatively-owned grain elevators and were able to extract from Laurier election promises of reduced tariffs for key agricultural commodities. Not all of these promises were fulfilled, but in 1897 the Crow's Nest Pass Agreement reduced the transportation costs faced by farmers and established the principle of government regulation of freight rates. In 1900 the federal government passed the Manitoba Grain Act, embodying further reforms related to the shipment of grain (Conway, 1983, pp. 46-48).

In the first decade of the new century a series of new agrarian organizations sprouted in the prairies, linking with Ontario organizations in 1909 to form the Canadian Council of Agriculture (CCA). In 1910 a delegation of Prairie farmers descended on the House of Commons, demanding that Laurier's government return to the traditional Liberal policy of reciprocity with the United States. By 1911, the CCA had more than 30,000 members and had developed the first of many "Farmer's Platforms". It focussed on demands for free trade and a halt to rural depopulation. It was partly in response to these demands that the Liberal Party entered the 1911 election advocating reciprocity with the United States (Conway, 1983, pp. 49-55; Lower, 1973, p. 150).

Agrarian mobilization continued after World War I. At the national level the Progressives called for a "New National Policy" and won 65 seats in the 1921 election. But by 1925 – as a result of their declining appeal in Ontario, splits between regional wings of the party, and successful cooptation by Prime Minister Mackenzie King – the party was reduced to 25 seats, virtually all of them from the western provinces.

At the same time farmers were seeking new political forms at the provincial level, with agrarian parties elected in Ontario in 1919, Alberta in 1921 and Manitoba in 1922 (Friesen, 1984, p. 367). While the Ontario farmers were soon defeated, the United Farmers of Alberta remained in power for 14 years. The capacity of the national party system to integrate was now challenged not only along ethnic lines, but also along class lines; moreover, both divisions were becoming more regionally concentrated and, hence, more naturally aligned with provincial governments.

The Maritimes, threatened by population stagnation, economic decline and a diminishing weight in the national political system, gave birth to a very different kind of movement in these years. The Maritime Rights Movement, "which saw all classes united in their demands upon the rest of the country", grew rapidly after 1919. As Forbes goes on to say:

> This did not mean that different classes did not have distinct aspirations of their own; on the contrary, they were probably more conscious of them in 1919 than in any other period before or since. Each held a dream of progressive development in which its own collective interests were directly involved.... But none of these aspirations was capable of realization with the continued decline of the economic and political status of the Maritimes in the Dominion. Just as electricity might channel the usually conflicting molecular energies of an iron bar to produce a magnetic force, so the federal government's adverse policies served to re-align the various "classes" in the Maritimes to produce a powerful social force – regionalism. This force, dressed up in a variety of complex rationalizations, became the Maritime Rights movement of the 1920s.
>
> (Forbes, 1979 pp. 385-86).

Here was a politics rooted primarily in regional identities, as opposed to ethnicity in Quebec and class in the Prairies. The strength of the Maritime Rights movement was revealed in the provincial and federal elections of

1925. At the provincial level, the incumbent Liberals were thrown out of office in each province by the Conservatives who had embraced the Maritime Rights cause. At the federal level, the Conservatives won 11 of 14 seats in Nova Scotia, 10 of 11 seats in New Brunswick and two of four in Prince Edward Island, in each case displacing strong Liberal majorities (Beck, 1968, pp. 160-61, pp. 174-75).

Agriculture remained the focus of class divisions in these years. At Confederation, organized labour barely existed in Canada, but towards the end of the nineteenth century growing industrialization in central Canada, along with labour organizing in primary industries such as logging and mining, set the stage for union growth. Trade unions were exempted from common law anti-combination doctrines in 1872. Between 1880 and 1886 seven bills aimed at regulating working conditions were introduced into the federal parliament but none was passed, partly on the ground that this was an area of provincial jurisdiction. The Trades and Labour Congress of Canada (TLCC) was established in 1886, uniting all existing forms of labour organization. By 1902 there were 960 union locals in Canada, but in that year the TLCC split along craft versus industrial union lines. In spite of this organizational setback, the number of locals rose to 1,741 over the next ten years (Easterbrook & Aitken, 1981, pp. 560-63; Kumar, 1986, p. 108). At the same time, organized labour was developing close connections with the urban reform and social gospel movements which had begun to grow rapidly in the 1890s (Rutherford, 1982, pp. 303-320; Allen, 1982, pp. 271-86).

Governments responded slowly to the organization of labour. None of the pro-labour recommendations of the 1887 Royal Commission on the Relations of Labour and Capital was implemented. In 1900, the Liberal government created a federal Department of Labour and a young man named Mackenzie King was appointed its first Minister. King was instrumental in drafting and passing the federal Industrial Disputes Investigation Act in 1907. In 1908, Ottawa responded to demands for an old age pension scheme from unions and other reform groups by creating a system of federal annuities. Provinces also responded. Ontario passed the first provincial factory act in 1884. Other provinces followed suit over the next 20 years. In 1909, the first provincial Workmen's Compensation Act was passed in Quebec. Ontario's 1914 legislation was hailed as one of the most advanced pieces of compensation legislation in North America (Guest, 1980, pp. 41-44).

World War I stimulated labour organization and militance. Union membership more than doubled between 1914 and 1918. Wartime inflation eroded working class incomes, while the headlines told of business profiteering. The sacrifices in the name of democracy and the general good raised expectations of major postwar social reform. The frustration of these hopes culminated in the Winnipeg general strike of 1919. Its suppression by the federal government undermined the One Big Union movement which had been formed by the more radical unions that had been expelled by the conservative Trades and Labour Congress (TLC).

There was an important regional dimension to the organizational and ideological division between the TLC and the One Big Union movement. The membership of the TLC was concentrated in the older manufacturing sectors of central Canada, while the One Big Union movement was strongest in the rapidly growing primary resource extraction industries of the west, especially in British Columbia. With the disintegration of the One Big Union movement, these western industrial unions had no overarching representative body until the formation of the All-Canadian Congress of Labour in 1927. In the interim, there was no serious attempt by the TLC to organize the rapidly growing automobile and rubber industries in southern Ontario or the burgeoning forestry and mining industries of northern Ontario and Quebec. As a result, the largest and fastest growing sectors of Canada's industrial economy remained largely unorganized in this period (Morton, 1984, pp. 113-38).

Ethnic divisions also plagued the union movement. These achieved institutional form with the creation of the Canadian and Catholic Confederation of Labour (CCCL) in 1921, its membership largely drawn from break-aways from the TLC (Abella, 1973, pp. 2-3). By 1932, the CCCL would encompass about 60 percent of unionized Quebec workers (Hamelin, 1977, p. 445). This fragmentation greatly reduced the cohesiveness and political influence of the trade union movement in this period.

Finally, jurisdiction over labour was also divided after 1925. In 1867 the Fathers of Confederation had not anticipated that organized labour might become a serious political or economic force in Canada, and the BNA Act was silent on the question of jurisdiction. This had not stopped Mackenzie King from drafting the Industrial Relations Disputes Act, which had become law in 1907. There matters stood until the *Snider* case of 1925, in which Lord Haldane of the Judicial Committee of the Privy Council declared that the great bulk of labour-related matters fell under exclusive provincial jurisdiction over "property and civil rights" (Morton, 1984, p. 138). The exceptions were inter-provincial operations (rail, air, shipping and trucking), areas falling under federal jurisdiction owing to the exercise of the declaratory power (such as grain elevators and the uranium industry), banks and the employees of the federal government (including its crown corporations). This amounted to anywhere between 10 percent and 20 percent of the total work force that might be unionized (Kumar, 1986, p. 104). It was an extraordinary decision, and would have profound implications for the future evolution of the Canadian labour movement.

Federal State

The character and intensity of the societal divisions we have just described affected the evolution of Canadian federalism before 1930 in three fundamental ways. First, the weakness of the social forces pressing for an extended role of the state meant its growth was limited. Hence, there was little increase in the levels of jurisdictional overlap and policy interdependence between the two orders of government. The "watertight" bulkheads between federal and provincial functions and powers remained largely intact and there was little need for the development of new intergovernmental mechanisms.

Second, the growing intensity of ethnic and class conflicts – and their increasing regionalization – gave impetus to a decentralizing trend within the parameters of classical federalism, in spite of Macdonald's concerted efforts in the opposite direction and the strong constitutional basis from which he began. This trend was interrupted only by the First World War and federal leadership in reconstruction immediately following it. Otherwise, provincial governments generally took the initiative in whatever new economic and social programs were adopted, the only major peace-time exception being the federal Old Age Pension plan. As a result, there was a continuing need for increased provincial revenues, satisfied partly by new federal transfers and partly by the creation of new provincial taxes. By the end of the period, the provincial governments had achieved a higher level of "fiscal autonomy" (the share of total provincial revenues not deriving from federal transfers) than they have ever had since.

Third, changes in the scope and intensity of federal-provincial conflict were largely a function of whether federal leadership sought to resist these pressures toward classical and decentralized federalism. Macdonald resisted, though less strenuously in his later years; Laurier accepted the process, though not without seeking to set limits on it. The exception of the war period supports this analysis. The one large-scale move away from the limited state role envisioned at Confederation was brought about by the external pressures of the World War. Domestic pressures were not yet strong enough to achieve the same effect. Yet, because these external conflicts temporarily overrode indigenous ones, the extraordinary centralization which took place under the War Measures Act was not attended by significant federal-provincial conflict until the conscription issue inflamed ethnic and class cleavages.

Classical Federalism and the Role of the State

Throughout the early years of the federation the economic and social roles of the state, judged by modern standards, remained highly circumscribed. The primary activity of both orders of government was the stimulation of economic growth through the development of "infrastructure" – railways, canals and, later, roads and electric power. Municipal governments were also required to increase expenditures rapidly for the provision of local services. All three levels engaged in various subsidies and bounties to attract and stimulate industry.

Harbingers of a larger role were evident, however, in the war and immediate postwar years. Attempting to prosecute the war effort and control inflation, the federal government was drawn into regulating wide areas of the national economy. The War Measures Act, unanimously passed in a special session in August 1914, granted sweeping emergency powers to the federal government. Its orchestration of the war economy weakened arguments against more extensive economic intervention. As the Rowell-Sirois Commission report put it:

> People saw how governments could mould their lives and civil servants learned how to do it. Statistical and other information necessary for effective intervention in economic affairs was accumulated. The belief grew that governments could and should use their powers to improve social conditions. The War-time experience with the regulation and direction of enterprise was an important factor in bringing on the wide extension of government control... .
>
> (Rowell-Sirois, p. 123)

There was some indication that, like many other western countries, this activist federal government role would be projected into the postwar era. Inspired by its new leader, Mackenzie King, the Liberal Party's platform of 1919 pledged:

> So far as may be practicable having regard for Canada's financial position, an adequate system of social insurance against unemployment, sickness, dependence in old age and other disability which would include old age pensions, widow's pensions, and maternity benefits, should be instituted by the Federal Government in conjunction with the Governments of the several provinces.
>
> (in Guest, 1980, p. 66)

Yet this program would not be implemented for another quarter century. The delay tells us something important about the factors shaping the evolution of the role of the state in Canada. The Rowell-Sirois Commission argued that under the constitution most of the new policies fell within the sphere of exclusive provincial jurisdiction. This is far from an adequate explanation. Constitutional amendment could have remedied this problem if the national political will had been there. The real question is why that will did not exist in spite of King's apparent reformist sympathies. An answer to this question must focus on the balance of societal forces in Canada. King's inaction was motivated by his fear of antagonizing a Catholic and conservative Quebec, opposed to the extension of the state, and especially the federal government, into new social or economic policy areas. The only thing that could have overridden this concern would have been a united front by organized agriculture, labour and other reform-oriented interests. But no such front would be formed until the Second World War.

The one major exception to this lack of federal initiative – passage of the Old Age Pension Act in 1927 – supports this analysis. Following the 1925 election, King was in a minority position with only 99 seats in the Commons. His political survival therefore depended on support of the third parties, mainly the 24 remaining Progressives. They, in turn, made provisions for the aged and the unemployed a condition of their support. Premier Taschereau of Quebec protested vehemently against the policy, on both constitutional and ideological grounds, but for this brief moment the societal conditions which would be in effect permanently from 1944 were "prematurely" present owing to the distribution of Parliamentary seats. King went ahead with the Old Age Pension Act in spite of Quebec's opposition, but used conditional grants so that the Quebec government was not forced to participate (Guest, 1980, pp. 74-77; Neatby, 1963, p. 109). Much of what the federal government did – and did not do – in this period may be understood as an attempt to minimize ethnic conflict. Indeed, the ability to maintain that accommodation became, under Laurier and then King, the Liberal Party's special talent, the key to its power base in central Canada and the legitimation of its claim to be the natural party of government.

The result, as described by the Rowell-Sirois Commission, was that "in seeking to reduce its old obligations and to avoid new ones, the Dominion yielded the initiative to the provinces" (p. 139). In the wake of federal inaction or retreat, provincial governments led the response to demands for social justice, sometimes conceived primarily in regional terms, sometimes as an inextricable mixture of region and class. The Rowell-Sirois Commission astutely observed the consequences of this division of functions between the two orders of government for the relative strength of citizen identification with provincial and national communities and their governments:

> ...these activities brought the provincial governments into a closer relationship with the people. In their intimate contact with the movements and tendencies of the time, the provincial governments added greatly to their economic and social importance and thus to their political power and prestige. Those which could carry their obligations manifested a new independence of the Federal Govern-

ment and those which could not became more importunate as they focussed on the Federal Government regional protest against the operation of the national policies...the Federal Government, unable to deflect these demands by a vigorous policy of its own, made important concessions to the provinces. The rise of regionalism gave an altered direction to Dominion-provincial relations.
(Rowell-Sirois, pp. 139-40)

With the end of the war there was an explosion of provincial and municipal capital spending on highways, municipal services, public buildings and utilities, housing and agricultural assistance. The distribution of current account spending also changed dramatically, with public welfare expenditures nearly trebling between 1918 and 1921. The principal objects of this increase were newly-introduced mother's allowance and child welfare programs, and enhanced spending on mental hospitals and education. These three years also witnessed the introduction of federal-provincial shared-cost programs to fund the fight against venereal disease and the creation of employment offices, new technical and agricultural education programs, highways and, in 1921, to provide direct relief to the unemployed (Rowell-Sirois, p. 130). This brief interval between the war and the full restoration of a civilian economy foreshadowed the social policy expansion – and the shared-cost methods that would be used to implement it – of the post-World War II years.

The use of conditional grants by the federal government reflected continued leadership with respect to war-related resettlement, health and employment problems. Yet the division of federal and provincial responsibilities which would characterize the decade of the 1920s was already apparent. Provincial and municipal governments were responsible for most of the rather limited extension of the welfare state that took place in these years. Federal participation in these areas was *ad hoc*, unsystematic and increasingly confined to unconditional financial aid. The use of shared cost devices was steadily phased out as the decade progressed; the old age pension program was the exception that proved the rule.

In this context, jurisdictional overlap and policy interdependence was minimal: despite considerable expansion in the roles of the state at the provincial government level, federal government inaction left the classical model of "watertight compartments" intact. This in turn meant that complex intergovernmental machinery was unnecessary. Federal-provincial relations were confined to occasional exchanges between politicians. Before 1930, there were only nine of what we would today call "First Ministers Conferences" (FMCs). All those held before World War I were Interprovincial Conferences, with no significant federal participation. With the exception of the 1887 conference, those held before the War dealt primarily with demands for increases in fiscal transfers from Ottawa to help the provinces meet these new responsibilities. They did not serve as forums for making national decisions and federal governments did not feel much obligation to respond to them. In Armstrong's anaysis the conferences were primarily symbolic, designed to assert and display the Premiers' stature (in Carty & Ward, 1986, pp. 112-52).

Toward the end of the period, however, FMCs began to exhibit more contemporary concerns and characteristics. The Borden government wished for provincial cooperation in such matters as demobilizing returned soldiers. As a result, two federal-provincial conferences were held in 1918. The first was primarily a forum for Ottawa to announce its plans, but at the second the provinces added their demands for better subsidies, an end to the federal income tax enacted in 1917, and the transfer of jurisidiction over lands and resources to the western provinces. Next in 1927, and again in 1931, federal and provincial First Ministers debated procedures for patriation and constitutional amendment, issues which had arisen because of the Balfour Declaration and the subsequent Statute of Westminster. In strong contrast to Macdonald's view, federal leaders did not assert that transfer of authority from Britain to Canada meant a transfer to the federal government. Both federal political parties "were committed to the proposition that there should be 'discussion' or 'consultation' with the provincial governments about constitutional amendments". This implied that "the dominion-provincial conference was likely to become the central forum for such negotiations" (Armstrong, 1986, p. 126). Ontario Premier Howard Ferguson argued that any constitutional change required unanimous consent; Ottawa sought a more flexible formula, but did not press the point. This Canadian inability to reach consensus on an amending procedure meant that ultimate authority over constitutional change would remain in the United Kingdom (Verney, 1986, p. 141; Bothwell, et.al., 1987, pp. 242-43).

Societal Cleavages, Decentralization and Federal-Provincial Conflict

From its inception, the leaders of the new federal government attempted to "develop and nourish a Canadian political community" (Carty, 1986, p. 1). But as we have seen, there was more than one vision of what the substance of this sense of community should be, and what role the federal government should play in promoting it. The competing visions are well represented by Canada's first two great Prime Ministers.

For Macdonald, regional identities should be assigned the same peripheral location in citizen loyalties that they occupied on the national map. Macdonald knew that a unitary state was beyond reach, but believed that the federal government must act as much like one as possible. If successful, this would result in citizens who thought of themselves primarily as Canadians, defined mainly in terms of political institutions: parliamentary democracy, the rights of Englishmen, the rule of law, and a special relationship with the British Empire. These Canadians would just happen to speak French or English, be Protestant or Catholic.

Laurier was as strongly committed to building a Canadian national identity (indeed, he was much more of a nationalist than Macdonald in the sense that he sought to wean English Canadians away from their emotional ties to the British Empire) but the substance of what he understood that nationality to be was very different. He assumed that language and religion were such important constituents of individual identity that they must be central to any compelling version of a national identity. Therefore, national identity must make a virtue of necessity, locating much of its unique character in its dualism. An important part of being a Canadian must therefore be the ability to be at home in both languages and, hence, in all parts of a dualistic nation.

But demographic and political trends were moving in the direction of regional concentration of monolingual cultures increasingly hostile to one another. In such a situation relatively homogenous provincial governments, with no electoral incentives to find a balance or synthesis between the two elements – indeed, with strong incentives to the contrary – would be able to count on much stronger citizen loyalties than the federal government. Therefore, the only alternative to escalating federal-provincial conflict which Ottawa could not win was to acknowledge that provincial governments must play a much more important role in governing a divided nation. For Laurier, this was a tactical retreat – the hope was that eventually the federal government would gain sufficient political strength to protect minority language and religious rights which the constitution gave Ottawa the power and duty to uphold – but he recognized that it might prove a long march.

The evolution of Canadian politics in this era shows how difficult it was to realize either conception of national identity – how many Canadian citizens were inclined to define the nation as either the projection of their own ethnic identities (thus erasing the other from map and mind) or an instrument for the protection of existing ethnic identities and communities from hostile forces both inside and outside the country.

Macdonald sought to use the extensive powers of the new government aggressively, asserting federal power by all the means at his disposal. If the future course of Canadian federalism had been primarily a function of political will, then surely Macdonald possessed the will and the constitutional resources to realize the quasi-federal model. But by the late 1880s Macdonald was running into increasing resistance from many quarters: the national government had neither the political legitimacy nor the economic efficacy to make the centralist model prevail. Laurier understood this: his formula for nation-building was to recognize and accommodate the strength of provincial communities and governments. Laurier's victory in 1896 marked the end of Macdonald's centralizing thrust. But it was as much a result of decentralizing trends already begun as of Laurier's own views. One indicator was the trend of judicial decisions that gradually narrowed the ambiguity surrounding which model of federalism – quasi-federal or classical – would prevail and, closely related, the scope of general powers held by each order of government.

The first step was the recognition that provincial governments were as sovereign as the federal government in their respective areas of exclusive jurisdiction. In *Hodge v. the Queen* (1883), the Privy Council endorsed the view that provincial governments were not subordinate to, but coordinate with, the Dominion: "the local legislature is supreme and has the same authority as the Imperial Parliament or the Parliament of the Dominion, would have under like circumstances" to delegate powers to agencies of its creation (cited in Rowell-Sirois, p. 75).

Once this was established, the definitions of exclusive powers under sections 91 and 92 became much more important. Other cases began to narrow the federal general powers. The earliest cases on this point predated *Hodge*. In *Citizens' Insurance v. Parsons* (1881), the Privy Council held that the federal power to regulate "trade and commerce" did not include "every regulation of trade...down to minute rules for regulating particular trades" (Rowell-Sirois, p. 80). The following year, however, in *Russell v. The Queen* (1882), the Privy Council upheld a federal temperance law on the basis of a broad interpretation of the "Peace, Order and Good Government" clause. Thus, having determined that Canada was, in terms of legal principles, an example of classical federalism, rather than some new constitutional hybrid, the Courts remained uncertain as to how centralized a version of classical federalism Canada would be. A series of cases following these early ones and culminating in the *Local Prohibition* case of 1896, gradually moved in the direction of a less powerful federal government than Macdonald sought to promote. In that case, Lord Watson held for the Court that the concluding words of section 91 did not give the federal government "authority to encroach upon any class of subjects which is exclusively assigned to the provincial legislatures by s. 92". While accepting that the "Peace, Order and Good Government" clause could sometimes justify federal action in areas of "national concern", "great caution" must be used in doing so (Hogg, 1985, p. 375).

In the *Insurance Reference* (1916), *Board of Commerce* (1922) and *Snider* (1925) cases, the scope of the "Peace, Order and Good Government" clause was defined even more narrowly as an emergency clause, justified only in "cases arising out of some extraordinary peril to the national life of Canada, such as the cases arising out of a war" (*Snider*, quoted in Hogg, 1985, p. 304). Under Haldane's leadership, other cases narrowed the scope of federal powers in the criminal law, trade and commerce, and treaty implementation. The Judicial Committee of the Privy Council (JCPC) thus "elevated the provinces to coordinate status with the Dominion" (Hogg, 1985, p. 89).

F.R. Scott (1951) asserted that the JCPC almost single-handedly transformed Canadian federalism, betraying the centralist intentions of the founding fathers. They were, in Eugene Forsey's words, "the wicked stepfathers of Confederation" (quoted in Hogg, 1985, p. 89). There are two problems with this analysis. First, as we have argued, both conceptions of Canadian federalism were embedded in the BNA Act. Second, the decisions which the Privy Council laid down did not so cripple federal powers that the form of decentralized federalism which emerged in this period was constitutionally inevitable. The JCPC left intact the broad federal powers of reservation, disallowance and the declaratory power. So the federal government retained the constitutional right to override the normal division of powers, under a wide range of circumstances, at its discretion. It could – and did in its early years – use these powers extensively to operate within areas of otherwise exclusive provincial jurisdiction, either vetoing provincial laws or transferring jurisdiction to itself. Yet in the latter part of the period these powers were exercised less and less often. Between 1867 and 1876 the federal government disallowed 20 provincial Acts and reserved 37, for a total of 57 direct interventions in provincial jurisdiction; between 1877 and 1886 there were 32 disallowances and eight reservations, for a total of 40 interventions; between 1887 and 1896, only 13 disallowances and 12 reservations, for a total of 25 interventions (Urquhart & Buckley, 1965, pp. 625-26).

We conclude, with Alan Cairns, that "It is impossible to believe that a few elderly men in London deciding two or three constitutional cases a year precipitated, sustained and caused the development of Canada in a federalist direction that the country would not otherwise have taken" (1971, p. 319). The explanation of decentralization in the latter years of the 19th century is, rather, to be found in the fact that organized political support for a centralist vision simply did not exist. As the Rowell-Sirois Commission put it,

> ...there had never been any large transfer of loyalty from the older communities to the new Dominion created for urgent common purposes. The achievement of Confederation and the spectacular activity of the Federal Government in the early years had merely overshadowed or, at most, temporarily subordinated the separate interests of the distinct regions and communities.
>
> (Rowell-Sirois, p. 70-71)

Without an overriding sense of, and commitment to, the national community, most federal politicians came to Ottawa determined to protect or extend the values and interests of their own provincial political communities. Widening linguistic differences increasingly reached up into the federal parties, so dividing them that no federal government could wield decisively even those constitutional powers which it unambiguously possessed. So it was with the Manitoba and Ontario schools and the federal power under section 93. The only coherent alternative was Laurier's: the recognition of a sphere of "provincial autonomy" within which provincial governments would exercise considerable powers free from federal intervention except under exceptional, emergency circumstances.

Because Macdonald sought to run against the provincialism and localism described earlier in this chapter, and against the political logic of decentralization they entailed, federal-provincial conflict intensified under his tenure. Because Laurier recognized and accepted this political logic, although he sought to combat the racism and prejudice that fueled ethnic conflict, federal-provincial conflict subsided thereafter. Borden was less conciliatory, with the result that between 1911 and 1914 the federal government was paralyzed on all questions with important implications for the ethnic division. The outbreak of war afforded a temporary escape from this paralysis, but by 1917 the conscription crisis had torn apart both national parties on ethnic and class lines, paving the way for the emergence of Quebec nationalism and the Progressives, the first of a long series of regionally concentrated, class-based third parties. After 1921 Mackenzie King revived the operating assumptions of his political mentor, Laurier, and federal-provincial conflict, though not the underlying societal conflicts, again decreased.

In 1887, at the height of the struggle between the two visions of the federation and with the active support of Ontario Premier Oliver Mowat, Quebec Premier Honoré Mercier convened the first interprovincial conference in 20 years. Macdonald refused to attend, arguing that demands for greater provincial autonomy were no more than a screen behind which Liberals in power at the provincial level sought to embarrass a Conservative federal government. The Conservative provincial governments of Prince Edward Island and British Columbia followed Macdonald's lead. In the end, five provincial premiers attended. Mercier stated the rationale for the conference at its outset:

The centralizing tendencies, manifested of late years by the federal government and favoured by the obscurity – in some respects – of the British North America Act, 1867, have aroused legitimate fears with regard to the maintainence of our local institutions and render it imperative that there should be an understanding between the provincial Governments with regard to the organization of a system of common defence.

(quoted in Armstrong, 1986, p. 115)

The five Premiers produced a list of demands which included: increased federal subsidies to the provinces, the abolition of the federal power of disallowance, the restriction of the federal declaratory power by a provincial approval requirement, federal acknowledgment that Lieutenant-Governors were representatives of the Sovereign rather than the Dominion, and the right to nominate half of the members of the Senate. It is striking how closely the demands issuing from that conference resemble those of the next major period of federal-provincial confrontation, the 1970s.

Macdonald did not concede to any of these demands. Yet they could not be dismissed, as he sought to do, as the machinations of his Liberal enemies (Creighton, 1970, pp. 66-67; Rowell-Sirois, p. 72). With the advent of Laurier, federal-provincial relations became more harmonious, not because party interests ceased to influence the conduct of governments in their relations with one another, but because the new Prime Minister recognized a sphere of provincial autonomy in which the provinces could exercise considerable powers free from federal intervention. In this context, the initiative flowed to the provinces. Correspondingly, their concerns shifted from constitutional change to the problem of how to acquire sufficient funds to meet their new responsibilities.

Fiscal arrangements were a focal point of concern and negotiation from the earliest days of the federation. Calls for revisions in this area of the BNA Act began almost immediately. Supplementary grants were awarded to New Brunswick and Nova Scotia in 1869. Special financial terms applied to Manitoba, British Columbia and Prince Edward Island as they became provinces. By the Interprovincial Conference of 1887, all provinces were demanding substantial revisions. But the federal government, in difficult economic circumstances too, refused to meet these demands. Unlike questions of centralization, however, these perpetual fiscal problems were amenable to "splitting the difference" compromises and did not lead to escalating intergovernmental rancour. Rather, provincial governments introduced new taxes, including succession duties and corporate and personal income taxes. So, while federal subsidies made up 58 percent of all provincial revenues in 1874, this share had fallen to 43 percent by 1896, and to 28 percent by 1914. After 1896, federal and provincial spending increased at roughly equal paces, but federal revenues grew much faster. In 1906, what was then held to be a "final revision" of federal transfers to the provinces increased them by about a third and provided for automatic increases with population growth (Moore, Perry & Beach, 1966, p. 4).

Federal revenues, spending and debt rose dramatically during World War I, effectively freezing provincial revenues at their prewar level. In addition, the federal government imposed an income tax for the first time, tapping a source hitherto reserved to the provinces. Provincial demands that Ottawa abandon the income tax after the war had ended were to no avail. Nevertheless, as the federal government cut back on its activities, the provinces increased theirs, developing further revenue sources such as gasoline taxes, motor vehicle licensing fees and controlled liquor sales. Thus, on the eve of the Great Depression, the provincial governments had reached their highest historical level of fiscal autonomy: they received, on average, only 13 percent of their revenues from federal transfers (Moore, Perry & Beach, 1966).

Conclusions

By 1929, a decentralized version of the classical model of federalism was firmly in place – sociologically, politically and constitutionally. The strength of sub-national Canadian identities was such that even as some sense of membership in the larger Canadian nation emerged, it tended to interpret that nation as a collection of smaller communities banded together for various instrumental reasons. Accordingly, the legitimacy of extensive federal powers depended upon its capacity to make good the claim that it required extensive legal and fiscal powers in order to achieve instrumental ends. But the long world recession suggested that there was little which even a highly centralized federal government could do to promote domestic economic development if the international conditions were not propitious. This reduced the plausibility of the federal government's claim to wide powers, while mounting ethnic conflict created strong pressures for decentralization:

> The provincial governments lacked the financial resources, while the Dominion failed to evoke a spirit of national loyalty. In these circumstances, it was by no means clear, at the end of the period, that the equilibrium necessary to a working federalism could be reached. It was not clear whether room could be found for the free play of provincial aspirations without denying to the Dominion the confidence and loyalty it needed for the advancement of common national purposes.
>
> (Rowell-Sirois, pp. 89-90)

The economic successes of the wheat boom, corresponding roughly with the Laurier era, might have strengthened federal legitimacy and, with it, Macdonald's centralized quasi-federal ideals. But under Laurier, the federation had already decentralized considerably in response to the flames of ethnic conflict that Macdonald had helped to fan. So the principal moral was that political decentralization and economic growth were compatible. At the same time the cross-cutting issues of imperialism and free trade, exacerbating ethnic and regional/class differences, so fragmented Canadian society that no federal government could develop a position embracing a national majority. Laurier was the victim of this growing fragmentation in the election of 1911. In the next three years, under the Borden government, the federal government was immobilized on all of the four major issues that provoked deep conflict along these lines of dissension: Canada's contributions to the imperial navy, French language instruction in public schools, public funding for separate schools, and free trade with the United States.

The war at last gave the federal government a clear purpose but the consensus behind it had disintegrated by 1917 as francophone, agrarian and labour criticisms of Canadian commitments to an apparently futile European conflict mounted. Nonetheless, the war encouraged urbanization, industrialization and other social changes that many theorists of modernization have argued are likely to lead to the development of national or even cosmopolitan consciousness. Various Canadian commentators have argued that World War I laid the foundations of a broader and deeper sense of national identity. Thus, Prang writes of the War bringing "fresh vigour" to many existing associations and [leading] to the formation of scores of new ones representing a wide spectrum of economic, religious, education, sporting and cultural concerns" (in Carty and Ward, 1986, p. 56).

But the central issue is not whether Canadian nationalism was stimulated by the First World War, but whether that implied the erosion of provincial identities. It did not seem to. Following the war there was a further regionalization of the major social cleavages, and the collective identities that underpinned them. The agrarian reform movement became largely a matter of western mobilization against central Canadian interests; and a powerful Maritime Rights movement erupted in the east. Organized labour remained regionally divided along the lines defined by the Winnipeg general strike. Above all, the conscription crisis transformed French Canadian nationalism into a conservative version of Quebec nationalism. By the 1920s, the federal government had symbolically recognized this when the federal Minister of Justice, Ernest Lapointe, declared that Ottawa accepted the basic assumptions of the compact theory against which Macdonald had fought so hard: that Canada was an agreement among pre-existing parties; that "no substantial change should be made without consulting the contracting parties"; and that "the BNA Act is the charter of the provinces in which power has been fixed and determined between the Dominion and the provinces" (in Armstrong, 1986, p. 123). This new consensus on the meaning of the federal constitution would not survive the Great Depression.

PART III

Crisis and Transformation

Modern Canadian federalism is distinguished from its predecessor by its thorough-going departure from the classical, "watertight compartments" model established in the last years of the nineteenth century. Post-war federalism is characterized by much higher levels of jurisdictional overlap and policy interdependence or, as Albert Breton has called it, *"de facto* concurrence" of jurisdictions. This transformation had two related causes. The first was the dramatic expansion of the economic and social roles played by the Canadian state. The second was the failure of all attempts to implement the new state by means of centralizing constitutional reforms. The first development rendered obsolete many of the old constitutional categories by which powers had been divided between the two orders of government. The second development meant that *de facto* concurrence could not be eliminated by transferring activities to federal jurisdiction, or by moving back toward the quasi-federal system that Macdonald had championed.

The new roles of the Canadian state may be traced to the economic upheavals of the Great Depression. An increasing number of Canadians came to believe that only a fundamentally transformed political economy could resolve the social and political crises, and prevent their recurrence. Many also believed that only the federal government had the powers, resources and expertise to orchestrate the transformation and effectively perform the new roles which would be required of the state. Hence there was a widely shared perception, at least in English Canada, that some form of extensive centralization – perhaps even the end of federalism – must be carried out. While raising these issues, the Depression years brought forth no widely accepted answers upon which a new political accommodation, bridging the major differences that divided Canadian society, could be built.

The experience of the war years provided answers to both questions. It demonstrated that the federal government, stimulating aggregate demand through its war expenditures, could rapidly restore the national economy to full employment, thereby vindicating Keynesian theory and providing Ottawa officials with experience in turning theory into practice. The War shifted the relative bargaining power of labour and capital, generating some of the political pressure that forced Mackenzie King to implement the commitment to the social welfare state which he had endorsed in 1919. Finally, the War led to Canadian endorsement of the American plan to restore market economies, situated within an open international economy, as the foundation of the post-war economic order upon which the high employment welfare state would be superimposed. This ensemble of interlocking policies we call the International Policy.

The War also shaped the means by which Ottawa gathered the powers and resources necessary to meet its new commitments. The conscription crisis weakened Godbout's relatively reformist Liberals, replacing them with Duplessis' conservative Quebec nationalist Union nationale. This eliminated whatever chance there may have been of centralizing the federation through constitutional amendment without a fundamental rupture with Quebec. The political impossibility of such reforms, combined with the imperatives for a more centralized federation, together sealed the fate of classical federalism in Canada.

Chapter 5

The Crisis of Classical Federalism, 1930-38

Both linguistic and class differences in Canada had become more regionalized between 1896 and 1929 as a result of economic, demographic and political developments. The Great Depression destroyed the traditional economic bases of hundreds of thousands of individuals, families, towns and entire regions of Canada. As habitual ways of seeing themselves and their society were shaken, people began to ask new questions about the appropriate economic and social roles of the state, the rights which private capital and organized labour should possess, and the desirability of the regional economic division of labour which the National Policy had created (Mallory, 1976, p. 40).

The proliferation of new political parties in this period demonstrates that Canadians embraced a wide variety of answers to these questions. The traditional parties could stave off the threats posed by these new parties only by adopting programs that they would have rejected out of hand in the previous decade. Thus, in the 1930s, regional and class divisions which had emerged in the previous thirty years were radicalized. Yet, the federal government did not implement reforms on a scale equivalent to those of Roosevelt's New Deal. Nor did Canadian federalism undergo the same process of centralization. The new political economy and the new federalism were not implemented in Canada until after the Second World War. Even then, the form of modern Canadian federalism differed from that in the United States, in spite of the similarities in the new roles which their federal governments would play.

The single most important factor distinguishing Canadian from American politics in this period was, as it continues to be, the existence of a francophone majority in Quebec. The economic crisis provoked some important changes in elite and public opinion in that province concerning the public provision of social welfare programs. But it did not shake the conviction that if new programs were to be undertaken, the provincial government must retain sufficient control over them to ensure their compatibility with the religious and cultural character of the province. What was required, on this view, was not the centralization of constitutional powers, but rather the jurisdictional and fiscal decentralization which would enable the Quebec government to implement such programs.

This position, defended by a solid Quebec bloc, could not have prevented significant movement toward centralization had the other side of the linguistic dividing line – constituting the national majority – been equally united in the conviction that the role of the state must be extended and that this extension must take place at the federal level. But English Canadians, more polarized than ever before on class and regional lines, disagreed on both these points, so only the temporary emergency of war created a national majority, transcending all three lines of division in favour of enhanced central power.

Federal Society

The fragility of the international economic system that was cobbled together in the wake of the Great War was starkly revealed by the New York stock market crash of 1929. The crash precipitated a dramatic fall in commodity prices and credit availability. As competition for shrinking world markets increased, the universal response was recourse to tariff barriers. By the spring of 1933, the volume of world trade had fallen by 28 percent, and its value by 65 percent, from 1929 levels (Mackintosh, 1964, pp. 109-111). In 1929, about one third of Canada's national income was derived from exports, primarily wheat and natural resources. So the precipitous decline in the volume of international trade, combined with the dramatic fall of wheat and natural resource prices, hit Canada very hard (Mackintosh, 1964, p. 111, pp. 113-15). Nearly 25 percent of the Canadian work force was unemployed in 1933, and about two thirds of school leavers and would-be entrants into the workforce were unable to find work (Guest, 1980, p. 83). In 1933, Canadian per capita incomes (adjusted for the falling cost of living), were 74 percent of what they had been in 1926. They had risen to 89 percent by 1936, but at that point a new downturn in the American economy stalled further improvement in both Canada and the

United States (Mackintosh, 1964, p. 137, p. 114). By 1937, Canadian exports were nearly as great as in 1929 (Mackintosh, 1964, p. 119). Yet, as late as 1939 health authorities estimated that one third of Canadians could not afford a diet considered nutritionally adequate (Guest, 1981, p. 83), and unemployment remained at 11 percent (Phillips & Watson, in Cross & Kealey, 1984, p. 22).

Aggregate statistics obscure the uneven sectoral incidence of the depression. Agriculture was by far the hardest hit: in 1928 it had contributed 18 percent of national income; in 1932 it accounted for only five percent of a greatly reduced income. (Mackintosh, 1964, p. 134). The export recovery after 1934 took place primarily in the non-ferrous mining, pulp and paper, and lumber industries. Agriculture experienced no parallel recovery (Mackintosh, 1964, p. 119). Worst off, then, were those dependent upon agriculture, export-dependent primary resource industries, and construction; better off were those working in the service sector and tariff-protected secondary manufacturing industries; best off were those dependent upon investment income (Mackintosh, 1964, p. 123). Thus, it was farmers and workers outside the protected manufacturing sector who "rode the rails" in the generally fruitless search for work, stood in the soup kitchen lines and populated the government work camps.

Major sectoral variations translated into significant regional disparities. The Depression had the least impact where income from protected manufacturing, the service sector and investment was greatest: in central Canada. The recovery after 1934 was strongest where natural resource industries were located: in British Columbia, Ontario and Quebec. The central Canadian provinces, which accounted for more than 60 percent of national income in 1929, increased their share in the decade that followed. The shares of the maritime provinces and British Columbia remained roughly constant, although maritimers continued to have the lowest average incomes in the country (Mackintosh, 1964, p. 134). The Prairies suffered most. Falling wheat prices were exacerbated by low yields due to an unprecedented conjunction of drought and grasshoppers, leaving in its wake the blowing topsoil from which the image of "the dirty thirties" derives. Between 1929 and 1937 *per capita* incomes dropped 72 percent in Saskatchewan, 61 percent in Alberta, and nearly 50 percent in Manitoba. Interest payments alone would have devoured half the value of the 1935 wheat crop. At least two thirds of Saskatchewan's rural population was still on relief in 1937.

The societal effects of the Depression varied accordingly. This accounts in part for the variety of policy responses to the Depression taken by provincial governments, and the order of government with which citizens of a particular region most strongly identified.

Prairie Populism and New Political Parties

The radicalization of the agrarian class was not confined to the prairies – farmers in all regions of the country suffered greatly and responded positively to proposals for change – but the process went further on the prairies than anywhere else. Not only was the economic impact of the Depression greatest there but, in contrast to all other provinces, the farmers constituted the majority of the prairie population. It was therefore imperative for parties to respond to their demands. The radicalization of the farmers was manifested primarily as the rise of prairie political protest.

In 1932, radio evangelist William Aberhart launched the Social Credit movement in Alberta, adapting the economic theories and social criticism of Major Douglas to the farmers' plight. Three years later, Social Credit swept into power in the provincial election (Conway, 1983, pp. 115-18). Premier Aberhart promised that the Alberta government would issue every citizen credit for $25 per month, so that people could afford to purchase more of the goods that the economy was perfectly capable of producing (Neatby, 1972, pp. 152-54). As Keynes observed in his *General Theory* (1936, p. 32, pp. 370-71), the details of social credit theory were often mistaken, but it also contained a crucial grain of truth: government could counter cyclical downturns by increasing the availability of credit. The federal government, claiming that it alone had the power to employ monetary policies, persistently and successfully attacked the Socred programs.

The early 1930s also gave rise to a new federal party defending the interests of the agrarian class and drawing most of its support from western farmers – the Cooperative Commonwealth Federation (CCF). Its Manifesto, made public in 1933 at the founding conference in Regina, stated that:

> We aim to replace the capitalist system, with its inherent injustice and inhumanity, by a social order from which the domination and exploitation of one class by another will be eliminated, in which economic planning will supercede unregulated private enterprise and competition, and in which genuine democratic self-government, based upon economic equality will be possible.
> (in Beck, 1968, pp. 208-9)

The CCF called for the socialization of banking, credit and insurance institutions, as well as major infrastructure industries such as transportation, communications and electrical power. A National Planning Commission was to be created to "coordinate the activities of the socialized industries" and "plan for the production, distribution and exchange of all goods and services necessary to the efficient functioning of the economy". Private ownership was to be preserved in the agricultural sector and provincial governments were to develop regulatory and assistance policies aimed at ensuring "security of tenure". A National Labour Code was to be developed "to secure for the worker maximum income and leisure, insurance covering illness, accident, old age, and unemployment, freedom of association and effective participation in the management of his industry or profession". Finally, "publicly organized health, hospital and medical services" were to be made "at least as freely available as are education services today" (in Bliss, 1966, pp. 291-94).

Article 9 of the Manifesto explicitly addressed the implications of the CCF program for the federal system, calling for:

> The amendment of the Canadian Constitution, without infringing upon racial or religious minority rights or upon legitimate provincial claims to autonomy, so as to give the Dominion government adequate powers to deal effectively with urgent economic problems which are essentially national in scope...
>
> (in Bliss, 1966, pp. 294-95)

The CCF program clearly implied extensive centralization, but it sought to sweeten the pill with references to the maintenance of "provincial autonomy". This, together with the opposition of the Catholic Church to all forms of socialism, deprived the CCF of significant support in Quebec. But it did not stop them from increasing their strength in Ontario and the prairies, the other provinces with a significant agrarian class.

The Organization of Mass Industrial Workers

At the outset, the Depression seemed to spell unmitigated disaster for the Canadian trade union movement. Widespread unemployment decisively shifted economic bargaining power away from the trade unions and toward the owners of capital. Union members in stagnant industries were laid off, and owners refused to recognize unions attempting to organize non-unionized industries. Union membership in 1929 had been 322,000 or 7.9 percent of the civilian labour force; at its lowest point in 1935, it had fallen to 281,000 or 6.4 percent of the labour force (Kumar, 1986, p. 108).

Yet this crisis of the traditional unions created the space for the emergence of new, more radical types of unionism and, with them, innovations in organizing strategy that responded more effectively to the politicization of workers that the Depression encouraged. Wider and better organization was viewed as essential not only for the short-term defence of existing wage levels, but also for the long-term political reformation of the social order (Roberts & Bullen in Cross & Kealey, 1984, pp. 106-23). Between 1935 and 1937, Canadian union membership increased by 100,000 to total 383,000 or 8.5 percent of the civilian labour force, surpassing pre-Depression membership peaks (Kumar, 1986, p. 108).

Even in the early 1930s there were indications of this growing politicization. The leaders of the more radical elements of the trade union movement joined with agrarian and academic reformists to launch the CCF. As in the days of the One Big Union movement, so in the 1930s, it was the natural resource extraction industries such as mining and forestry – ill-paid, dangerous, concentrated in company towns and ignored by the traditional crafts unions – that exhibited the highest levels of politicization. While such industries existed in all parts of the country, they were the principal economic base in British Columbia, which became the stronghold of the communist Workers' Unity League (WUL), formed in 1929. The WUL sponsored eleven industrial unions and claimed responsibility for three quarters of the strikes in Canada in 1933. It alone organized the unemployed and created the Relief Camp Workers' Union that led the "On to Ottawa Trek" of 1935 (Roberts & Bullen, pp. 107-10).

In British Columbia this kind of class conflict, impinging on the daily lives of large segments of the population more powerfully than other dimensions of identity, resulted in the the most class-polarized politics in Canada. Here organized labour enjoyed its most striking electoral gains. In 1933, the CCF formed the official opposition, forcing the provincial Liberal government considerably to the left (Cook, 1963, p. 202). Thereafter, it was excluded from provincial power only by the united front which the capitalist-oriented parties formed against it.

The situation was very different in Ontario, with its secondary manufacturing industries dominated by the old craft unions, represented by the TLC and affiliated with the AFL in the United States. There, paradoxically, the crucial development in the radicalization of organized labour was the Wagner Act of 1935, followed by Roosevelt's triumphant re-election in 1936, in spite of unrelenting business opposition. These developments greatly facilitated the organizing success of the Congress for Industrial Organization (CIO) in the mass production industries, hitherto largely unorganized in both Canada and the United States (Piven & Cloward, 1979, pp. 118-80).

In February 1937 the CIO – in name, at least (Morton, 1984, pp. 158-60) – spilled over into Canada with the Oshawa strike. Premier Hepburn sought to suppress it, but failed, and Canadian CIO-affiliated unions grew rapidly after this victory. Hepburn was able, however, to capitalize on sufficient anti-labour sentiment to increase his majority in the provincial election called shortly after the Oshawa strike. It would take war-time expansion to produce an Ontario labour movement capable of forcing provincial governments to take a more conciliatory stand (Roberts & Bullen, pp. 110-11).

But Canadian union growth was soon stalled by further developments south of the border: the American economy began to slow down and the Canadian economy followed the same course. Moreover, the AFL severed all ties with the CIO, insisting that its Canadian counterpart, the TLC, expel all industrial unions affiliated with it, diffusing the energies available for new organizing in internecine conflicts (Roberts & Bullen, p. 111).

There were domestic political problems as well. Canadian organized labour was never able to extract the equivalent of the Wagner Act from Ottawa, and this meant that organizing activities did not have the extra boost they had in the United States after 1935. It was from that year that American union density shot ahead of Canadian union density, outpacing it by more than 10 percent by 1940 (Kumar, 1986, p. 128).

Yet American union density was no higher than Canada's in the years up to the passage of the Wagner Act, so union density does not explain why organized labour was unable to get the labour legislation that would give it the political muscle to get a Canadian equivalent of the American New Deal. What, then, explained that difference? It is difficult to attribute it to ethnic diversity – and the cross-cutting cleavages to which it gave rise within the union movement – since that was an attribute of industrial workers in both countries. Nor does blaming it on federal institutions, another old standard, help. Both countries shared that attribute as well. Three factors seem to have been relevant: first, the fact that jurisdiction over labour fell mainly to the federal government in the U.S. and to provincial governments in Canada; second, the unique politics of Quebec and its place in the calculus of federal power in Canada; and third, the Congressional versus the Parliamentary systems of democracy.

The first factor – the result of the *Snider* case, as we have seen – meant that Canadian labour had much less to gain even if it could succeed in pressuring the federal government to pass new labour legislation, unless a constitutional amendment re-allocating jurisdiction over labour matters could be secured at the same time. But here the second factor became relevant: such an amendment was virtually impossible given the united opposition of the Quebec political elites, as Bennett discovered in 1935. One can imagine the conservative Southern Democratic elite playing a similar role in the United States, if their consent had been necessary for a more progressive federal government to gain jurisdiction over labour matters, but it was not.

An alternative to constitutional amendment would have been for the Prime Minister to bring pressure on the Canadian Supreme Court to re-think the reasoning in *Snider*, as President Roosevelt pressured the United States Supreme Court to repudiate the reasoning upon which it struck down the principal legislative elements of his New Deal in 1935 (Kelly, et.al., 1983, pp. 487-500). To this end, the Supreme Court of Canada could have been unilaterally declared to be the last court of appeal. The King government introduced a bill to do this in 1939, but immediately referred it to the Joint Committee of the Privy Council. In the *Privy Council*

Appeals Reference, (1947) it held abolition was within federal power and the Bill was enacted in 1949. Ottawa could have increased the number of Supreme Court justices at the same time, ensuring that the new appointments favoured the expansion of federal power. Such a change was within its jurisdiction, in contrast to the President's famous court-packing plan, which needed Senate approval. But Prime Minister King did not make such changes; on the contrary, he signalled the Supreme Court and the Privy Council that he did not much favour the centralization of power, as we show below.

Arguably, he did not exert such pressure on the Courts because he did not need to: the costs of not doing so were expected to be lower than the costs of doing so, but not because the President, who faced an election in 1936, was any less worried about Southern disapproval of the New Deal, and the Wagner Act in particular, than King was worried about facing Quebec in 1940. Rather, organized labour and its allies in support of a Canadian New Deal were less effective at pressuring King on the other side of the equation than their American counterparts. We have already noted that they had roughly the same strength in 1935, as crudely indicated by union density.

It is here that the third factor became relevant. American organized labour was able to use the Congress to keep up the pressure on FDR. The Wagner Act was initially introduced into Congress by Senator Wagner without the President's approval, and the 1934 Congressional elections greatly strengthened his hand by routing the business critics of pro-labour legislation (Piven & Cloward, 1979, pp. 130-33). But the Canadian movement could place much less pressure on a federal cabinet with a majority in Parliament and strict party discipline. Only a federal election could really scare King: in 1935, he didn't need labour's support to defeat Bennett because the latter bore the electoral brunt of five years of economic disaster, while the left was divided. Having won that election, the next one King would have to face was a long way off. As a result, there would be no Canadian New Deal.

The Obstruction of Reformist Quebec Nationalism

In the Quebec of the 1930s, both the industrial working class and the agricultural class were large and politically significant. By 1931, only 42 percent of the French-origin population remained in the rural areas, despite the efforts of successive provincial governments to stabilize the rural population. The Depression froze the drift into the cities, and even reversed it to some extent, but almost six out of ten francophones experienced the economic crisis as urban workers rather than as subsistence small holders (McRoberts & Posgate, 1980, p. 51). As in Ontario and

British Columbia, the internal dynamic of provincial politics was, to a considerable degree, driven by labour-capital conflicts.

But unlike the other two heavily industrialized provinces, class conflict in Quebec was widely experienced by francophones as part of the older and deeper linguistic division. This did not mean that class divisions were unimportant, but that those aspects of class divisions which were reinforced by language differences became the focal point of nationalist class politics. The conflation of class and ethnic politics was rendered easier by the fact that most *Canadiens* were farmers or workers, and the relatively small francophone professional class was largely excluded from positions of power within a business sector dominated by English Canadians and Americans.

Quebec nationalism, then, had conservative and reformist variants. The conservative variant drew a fundamental distinction between the "sphere" of the economy and that of politics and culture. The economy was to be maintained in accordance with the rules of the capitalist order as it was understood in the pre-World War II years: the state would have little role in orchestrating capitalist development, but would intervene on the side of business where major class conflicts threatened it. Culture, the preservation of religion, language and associated institutions, was considered a legitimate sphere for state intervention. Until the Depression, however, this was limited primarily to protecting private sector control of education and social policy from such federal incursions as the 1927 Old Age Pensions scheme.

The reformist variant of Quebec nationalism understood economics and culture as inextricably related; it argued that an extended state economic and social role was essential to the realization of cultural aspirations in Quebec. Class conflict was viewed as one more dimension of French-English power relations. As a result, the reformist variant was more sympathetic to the growing francophone industrial working class and its battles with the predominantly English-speaking business class.

The politics of Quebec in the 1930s centred around the struggle between the forces of conservative and radical Quebec nationalism. It was a complex battle in which the composition of the two sides was constantly changing, with each gaining the initiative at various times. But overall, the conservative variant, led by Maurice Duplessis for most of the period, was to dominate Quebec politics. There was only one hiatus when, with aggressive support from the federal party, the Liberals under Godbout triumphed in the 1939 election.

The short recession following the Great War elicited the first clear statement of reformist Quebec nationalism, captured in the demand of l'Abbé Groulx that French Canadians become "maîtres chez nous". In the conditions of the 1930s these ideas rapidly revived, and greatly extended their influence among both the francophone elite and the general population. Proponents argued that control over the key elements of the Quebec economy must be wrested from the hands of American and English Canadian trusts by the Quebec government. Only popular control of their economic destiny would permit the nation to maintain a balance between the urban and rural life in keeping with its religious and cultural ideals. At the top of the list of English "trusts" were the pulp and paper companies, notorious for their poor wages, and the hydro-electric power corporations, which charged high rates in the cities and showed no interest in rural electrification (Neatby, pp. 115-16).

In these early phases, the resurgence of reformist Quebec nationalism at the popular level was, to a considerable extent, led by elements of the Catholic church. The rudiments of a more urban, labour-oriented, "Christian Democratic" politics had been evolving within the Catholic trade union movement. Many Catholic priests and laymen were confronted with the social and economic problems thrown up by the new industrial Quebec. It politicized them, just as it had the English Canadian proponents of the social gospel since the 1890s. Even before the Depression there had been important signs of these changes. In 1926 the Confederation des Travailleurs Catholiques du Canada (CTCC) had adopted a resolution in favour of Quebec participation in the federal old age pension scheme, much to the chagrin of Taschereau's Liberal government (Bryden, 1974, p. 90). The Depression reinforced social reform tendencies within the leadership of the CTCC.

The social reformers within the Quebec Catholic church were given intellectual support and doctrinal authority by contemporary developments in European Catholicism. Pope Pius X's 1931 encyclical *Quadragesimo Anno*, the most important papal pronouncement on social questions since Leo XIII's *Rerum Novarum* of 1891, rejected *laissez-faire* capitalism, stating that:

> ...the immense number of propertyless wage earners on the one hand, and the superabundant riches of the fortunate few on the other, is an unanswerable argument that the earthly goods so abundantly produced in this age of industrialism are far from rightly distributed and equitably shared among the various classes of men.
>
> (cited in Quinn, in Francis & Smith, 1982, p. 438).

The encyclical also rejected communism and socialism but, in calling for a substantial redistribution of wealth, it required a fundamental re-thinking of the appropriate roles of church and state in Quebec. To the authority of the papal decree was added the apprehension created among the more conservative wing of the Quebec church by the formation of the CCF and the publication of the Regina Manifesto. Its stated commitment to spread its doctrine to all provinces prompted the church to move rapidly from the Pope's statements of principle to a concrete set of proposals for economic and social reform (Quinn, pp. 438-39).

Responsibility for the development of these proposals was entrusted to an organization sponsored by the Jesuit Order, *l'Ecole Sociale Populaire* (ESP). The ESP drew together Catholic laymen playing leading roles in key French Canadian institutions – the CTCC, the farmer's organizations, the credit unions and cooperatives, the patriotic and professional associations, and the universities – and assigned them the task of drawing up proposals for reform in major policy areas. In the fall of 1933 their proposals appeared in the pamplet entitled *Le Programme de restauration sociale*. They called for "steps to strengthen and even extend the agrarian section of the economy"; "an extensive scheme of labour and social legislation which would raise the incomes and provide greater economic security for the working class"; measures to "curb the power of the public utilities and other large business enterprises"; and "legislation which would eliminate patronage politics" by means of electoral and administrative reforms (Quinn, p. 439).

These reforms found articulate advocates among the younger members of the Quebec Liberal party – led by Paul Gouin, the grandson of Honore Mercier – who called themselves *L'Action Libérale Nationale* (ALN). In 1933 the ALN repudiated the informal political leadership of Henri Bourassa, following a series of public lectures in which Bourassa warned young nationalists against racial pride and separatism, in favour of l'Abbé Groulx (Wade, 1956, pp. 904-5). They sought to persuade Premier Taschereau, and the older generation who dominated the Liberal party, to abandon their largely *laissez-faire* stance on economic and social policy in favour of a program based on the ESP recommendations (Quinn, p. 433, p. 439). But Taschereau ignored them, and shortly before the 1935 election they left the Liberal party to ally themselves with the Conservatives, led by Maurice Duplessis. Duplessis agreed to accept the ALN's reformist platform and a new party, the *Union nationale* (UN), was formed (Quinn, p. 440).

The UN captured 42 seats in the 1935 Quebec election, leaving the Liberals in power with 48 seats, but gaining almost four times the representation that the Conservative opposition had held in the previous legislature. With this strength the Union nationale was able to force the creation of legislative committees which proceeded to expose the corrupt practices of the Liberal governments that had dominated the National Assembly since 1896. Premier Taschereau was implicated and forced to resign; he was replaced by Adelard Godbout, who dissolved the Assembly and called an election for August 1936. Godbout sought to undercut support for the UN by incorporating many of their proposals into his election platform. He promised:

> an extension of rural credit facilities, a programme of rural electrification, and the provision of subsidies on certain farm products; an intensified colonization programme; a sweeping reduction of electricity rates throughout the province; a public works programme to solve the problem of unemployment; a minimum wage scale for industrial workers not covered by collective labour agreements, and the introduction of certain amendments to the Workmen's Compensation Act requested by the trade unions; the establishment of a system of needy mother's allowances; and the elimination of the practice of cabinet ministers accepting directorships from companies doing business with the government.
>
> (Quinn, p. 443)

Before dissolution, several pieces of legislation that both parties agreed should not be delayed, including legislation enabling the province to participate in the federal government's old age pension program, were passed (Bryden, 1974, p. 92).

Godbout's last-minute flurry of reform proposals did not save the Liberals – the Union nationale won 76 of the legislature's 90 seats (Quinn, p. 445). This was not, however, the beginning of the era of state activism and social reform in Quebec. Even before the election was over, Paul Gouin had broken with Duplessis over the latter's domination of the party. Premier Duplessis included only a few prominent ALN members in his first cabinet. Thereafter he took steps to wean the ALN rank and file away from their original leadership. None of the important social and economic reforms in the UN platform was carried out, although large deficits were run to fund more traditional conservative programmes aimed at encouraging increased rural settlement (Neatby, pp. 116-17).

Conservative Quebec nationalism became the public philosophy of the UN government. The "Padlock Law" of 1937, granting the cabinet the power to lock up any premises used for "propagating Communism or Bolshevism", revealed the kind of coalition that supported the political stance of the Union nationale: the conservative wing of the Catholic Church, English big business, and party men seeking to weaken the powers of their critics and potential political rivals (Neatby, pp. 116-17).

Thus, while pressures for economic and social reform were mounting in English Canada, Duplessis was able to exclude from his ruling coalition those elements that demanded parallel changes in Quebec. Despite important differences in the social origins and support bases of the Tashereau and Duplessis governments, they shared an adamant opposition to social and economic reforms entailing an extended state role. In particular, both opposed any reforms which were to be carried out by the federal government in areas which they regarded as falling under exclusive provincial jurisdiction. Thus, the Depression shook but did not topple the coalition which had run Quebec since 1896. It did, however, contribute to the disengagement of federal and provincial politics by reducing the new Quebec Liberal party, the bearer of the more reformist strand of Quebec nationalism, to Opposition status for most of the next quarter century.

The 1935 Federal Election

The political implications of the societal changes traced in the last three sections were manifest in the federal election of 1935. Acknowledging the failure of his tariff and Commonwealth preference policies, Prime Minister Bennett had decided by late 1934 that he must face the electorate with impressive new policies, a Canadian version of the New Deal. In a series of radio broadcasts in January 1935 he declared that: "Canada on the dole is like a young and vigorous man in the poor house. The dole is a condemnation, final and complete, of our economic system. If we cannot abolish the dole, we should abolish the system" (Cook, 1963, p. 194).

The Speech from the Throne followed up such declarations with legislation establishing an eight hour day, a forty-eight hour week, the elimination of child labour, a minimum wage, a national employment service and a social insurance scheme. Improved credit for farmers and fishermen was provided for, as was the regulation of trusts, monopolies and financial speculators. Public works, housing and relief programs were created. The package represented a major advance in Canadian social and economic legislation. Its purpose, Bennett declared in the Throne Speech, was "to remedy the social and economic injustices now prevailing and to ensure to all classes and to all parts of the country a greater degree of equality in the distribution of the benefits of the capitalistic system" (Wade, 1956, pp. 830-31).

Many doubtless questioned the sincerity of Bennett's political death-bed conversion to state intervention, but even if this were granted, a deeper problem remained. The avowed purpose of Bennett's new legislation was to reform capitalism, rather than replace it: "When capitalism is freed at last from its harmful imperfections, when government exercises the intended measure of regulation over capitalist groups, capitalism will be in fact your servant and not your master" (in Neatby, 1972, p. 66). This view of capitalism would find wide support in Canada and elsewhere during post-Second World War period. In the Canada of the Great Depression, however, Bennett either went too far or not far enough.

For many westerners, the proposed legislation was too weak. Two radical western-based parties representing this position, the CCF and Social Credit, contested the 1935 federal election. A third, less radical, was formed when H.H. Stevens, a cabinet minister in the Bennett government, resigned in 1935 to found the Reconstruction Party. He argued that Bennett's

Dominion Trade and Industry Commission Act, one of the eight pieces of "New Deal" legislation, was a poor imitation of what the Royal Commission on Price Spreads and Mass Buying (in which he had figured prominently) had recommended for the protection of Canadian consumers and primary producers from the wave of corporate concentration associated with the Depression (Beck, p. 210).

Meanwhile, in Quebec, Liberal Premier Taschereau complained that Bennett had once been "a safe man" anxious to "retain the elements which had made the country great" but had now "torn these leaves from the book of his political life and unfaithful to his past, launched into a Socialistic venture bordering on Communism" (Beck, p. 214). In Ontario and the Maritime provinces each of these polar reactions to the Bennett "New Deal" found significant support. The overall tendency was also to move away from the Conservatives.

King's Liberal party proposed little in the way of major reform in the course of the election campaign. This garnered him 44.8 percent of the vote. More than 20 percent of the voters supported one of the three parties to the left of the two traditional ones, but vote splitting among them ensured many Liberal pluralities. King's Liberals won 173 seats, to the 25 seats secured by the three new parties. The electoral system worked in favour of the Social Credit Party which, concentrated in Alberta, secured 17 seats with only four percent of the national vote. It cut the opposite way, against the the CCF and the Reconstructionists, which secured only eight seats between them, despite having each secured twice the share of popular support received by the Socreds. The Tory share of the national vote fell to 29.6 percent, from 48.8 percent in 1930, and the party secured only 40 seats (Beck, pp. 202-3, pp. 220-21; Brodie & Jenson, 1980, pp. 175-80).

While the King government's policy initiatives in the next five years were much more limited than those which Bennett had proposed, the 1935 election nonetheless marked a turning point in Canadian politics. If King's federal government would not play a more active social and economic role, then those who had supported one of the new parties, or the Bennett New Deal, would look to their provincial governments to achieve these ends. The efforts of several provincial governments after 1935 to expand their activities significantly, and King's efforts to limit such innovations, gave rise to a period of intense federal-provincial conflict which only ended with the war.

Federal State

The Depression produced a fiscal crisis which plagued the federal system until growth was restored by the war. One result was increasing controversy concerning the constitutional division of taxing powers and spending responsibilities. Initially, these debates were conducted within the parameters of traditional assumptions about the appropriate economic and social roles of the state. But as the depression wore on, both orders of government began to depart from the orthodox economic reponses to the crisis which were so obviously inadequate, only to find that the federal constitution significantly limited what they could legally do. As a result, constitutional controversy took on a new depth and urgency after 1935.

Some English Canadian critics argued that only the federal government was capable of carrying out the necessary reforms effectively and, hence, that constitutional change to centralize power was essential. This position was fiercely resisted by a number of provincial governments. The governments of Quebec and Ontario resisted partly because they were opposed to reform *per se*, and partly because, as the wealthiest provinces, they opposed redistribution from them to the poorer provinces. The governments of Alberta and British Columbia resisted because they hoped to undertake such reforms themselves, believing that, given strong central Canadian resistance, Ottawa would never move far enough, fast enough.

To understand the significance of the crisis, we first set out its fiscal dimension, then turn to the broader constitutional conflicts which grew in the latter half of the decade, focussing on the Bennett New Deal, the social credit program introduced by the Aberhart government of Alberta, and the King government's response to both in the years between 1935 and the outbreak of war.

Fiscal Crisis

Canada's transition to a primarily urban and industrial society had rendered obsolete the assumption that social services – above all, public welfare – could and should be provided by private institutions: the extended family, charities and the Church. The growing political power of social gospellers, urban reformers and organized labour ensured that, by the 1920s, the role of the state in these areas had expanded significantly. But the obsolete assumption remained embodied in the BNA Act, which assigned these responsibilities to the provincial governments without giving them the taxing powers necessary to support their extension.

There had been a portent of the economic vulnerability of this arrangement during the 1921-24 recession, when the federal government was forced to rescue over-extended provincial governments with emergency relief grants. But no reforms followed. So, while a constitutional amendment formula was discussed in the 1920s, the impetus was the impending Statute of Westminster and the widening agreement on the desirability of achieving full national independence from Great Britain, rather than a perceived need for a reorganization of fiscal federalism. With the return to economic growth in the latter half of the 1920s, buoyant provincial revenues were sufficient to cover increases in social service spending. Provincial "fiscal autonomy" increased throughout the decade, in spite of their new expenditures. But this autonomy was as unstable as it was in the early 1920s.

The Great Depression triggered a crisis of intergovernmental fiscal arrangements. Total government outlays rapidly increased to provide levels of public assistance that remained inadequate. Government "relief" expenditures, including direct transfers to individuals and expenditures on public works and various agricultural and industrial subsidies, rose from $18.4 million in 1928 to $165.1 million in 1937. Expenditures on old age pensions rose from $1.9 million in 1928 to $38.9 million in 1937 (Rowell-Sirois, p. 174). Excluding relief expenditures, total per capita outlays remained practically the same in 1937 as in 1930, but against the backdrop of a contracting economy the ratio of total government expenditures to National Income increased from 20 percent in 1930 to 26 percent in 1937 (Rowell-Sirois, p. 180-81).

Provincial governments bore most of these new expenses. The municipal governments to which they had traditionally assigned most of the responsibility for the administration and funding of public welfare were utterly incapable of continuing to meet the need. The provinces undertook major cuts in other spending areas, such as education and economic infrastructure, and borrowed heavily. They raised the rates on traditional tax sources and levied new forms of tax: income taxes in Ontario and the west, a wage tax in Manitoba, and retail sales taxes in Alberta and Saskatchewan (Rowell-Sirois, p. 181, p. 183).

Still it was not nearly enough. The federal government had to provide about 46 percent of total government expenditures on relief and public welfare between 1930 and 1937. Most of this federal share took the form of conditional grants, although the four western provinces also received loans totalling $106 million. The ratio of federal to provincial relief spending varied greatly from region to region: the Dominion government provided 85 percent of all relief expenditures in Saskatchewan and 29 percent in Quebec, with the other provinces falling in between (Rowell-Sirois, p. 176, p. 179).

Even this substantial federal aid did not prevent mounting provincial budget deficits, particularly in the west. Despite gradual recovery from the trough of 1932, 20 percent of provincial and municipal revenues were being absorbed just to pay the interest on debts in 1937 (Rowell-Sirois, p. 179, p. 184). Alberta defaulted on payments owed on its provincial bonds in April 1936 and Saskatchewan, in even worse financial straits, seemed destined to follow the same course unless there were significant increases in federal transfers. It was feared that a second provincial default so soon after the first might undermine Canada's international credit rating. The federal government, through the Bank of Canada, stepped in to aid Saskatchewan and default was averted. But these were band-aid measures (Neatby, 1976, pp. 159-61). Large deficits on the current account still existed in Alberta and Saskatchewan and the other provinces were just barely in balance. Others would fall into deficit again if the emergency federal transfers were cut or terminated (Rowell-Sirois, p. 179, p. 184).

The efforts of the federal government to increase its revenues in order to meet its own debt charges and maintain the flow of transfers to the provinces contributed to a burgeoning "tax jungle" which:

> ...added greatly to the confusion and inefficiency of the Canadian taxation system. The joint occupation by the Dominion and the provinces of the progressive tax field (except inheritance taxes) and the corporate tax field led in the one case to inadequate use and in the other to wasteful duplication. As a consequence far too great a proportion of the load of government expenditure was carried by regressive consumption taxes, by real estate taxes, and by economically harmful taxes on corporations and businesses.
>
> (Rowell-Sirois, p. 184)

A constitutional amendment allowing the provincial governments to levy certain types of indirect taxes might have stabilized provincial revenues and reduced federal transfers, making it easier to eliminate double taxation in other areas. By 1936, King and his Minister of Finance were willing to go along with such an amendment. But the Conservatives fiercely opposed the amendment, both in the Commons and in the Senate, where they had a majority. By the time the Senate rejected the Bill, King had reconsidered and no effort was made to revive it. In the next decade, all discussion of amendments relating to fiscal arrangements would start from the presumption that the options were either centralization or the *status quo* (Neatby, 1976, pp. 160-61).

By 1937, new fiscal problems were looming. Relatively speaking, Ontario fared well in the Depression, but rising federal tax levels cut into provincial revenues. After his re-election in 1937, Premier Hepburn attacked the growing federal subsidies to the poorer provinces, arguing that this aid came from taxes collected in Quebec and Ontario. Premier Duplessis of Quebec found this line of argument congenial. Since the 1920s Quebec's position on federal conditional grants had been that they were a violation of provincial autonomy and contrary to the constitution. Changes in the levels of statutory provincial subsidies were likewise argued to be invalid unless approved by all provincial governments (Armstrong, pp. 201-10, pp. 213-17). This was the era of the "Toronto-Quebec axis" against Mackenzie King and the federal government (Creighton, 1970, p. 237).

By mid-1937, then, the financial state of the federation was worse than ever, and there seemed little possibility of achieving consensus on new fiscal arrangements. After much debate within Cabinet as to whether Ottawa should permit Manitoba and Saskatchewan to default, King was persuaded by the provinces of Manitoba and Saskatchewan to appoint a Royal Commission to investigate and make recommendations regarding solutions to the crisis (Bryre, 1986, pp. 192-93). The Royal Commission on Dominion-Provincial Relations – the Rowell-Sirois Commission – was appointed in August 1937 and was instructed to re-examine "the economic and financial basis of Confederation and of the distribution of legislative powers in the light of the economic and social developments of the last seventy years" (Rowell-Sirois, p. 2). To analyze the origins of the crisis was one thing; to arrive at acceptable means of solving it was another. The Royal Commission would be forced to consider the purposes for which federalism existed, and how these purposes could be rendered compatible with the new roles that governments were required to play. Constitutional developments between 1935 and 1940 had great bearing on this larger issue.

New Deals and Constitutional Impasse

Aside from substantial increases in federal transfers, "charity" to which the provinces had no legal claim and which could not be expected to last beyond the economic emergency, the Bennett government did remarkably little in the early depression years. Increased subsidies were made to the railways and the coal industry, and a variety of price support schemes were undertaken for wheat producers (Rowell-Sirois, pp. 171-74), but Bennett launched no dramatic policy initiatives like those in Roosevelt's America (Neatby, 1972, p. 58).

Prime Minister Bennett's reticence cannot plausibly be traced to a keen sense of provincial rights, or of the sociological realities underlying the legal doctrine. When, in 1935, he finally decided that a major departure from conventional economic policies was necessary, he did not bother to consult his own cabinet ministers, much less the provincial governments (Neatby: 1972, p. 65). Nor was Prime Minister Bennett one for worrying about the details of the constitutional division of powers. He seems to have been confident that constitutional grounds for his "New Deal" legislation could be found within the BNA Act.

The principal reason for the relative lack of federal initiative in the early years of the Depression seems to have been that Bennett believed the crisis could be remedied by the policies he campaigned for in 1930: the restoration of access to foreign markets for Canadian goods through Imperial preferences and the use of Canadian tariffs (Neatby, pp. 58-64). Nor did provincial governments press forcefully for the federal government to undertake more radical programs in these early years. They were focussing on the immediate task of meeting their burgeoning relief commitments and their principal interest in the federal government was increased tax room, larger grants, or both. This focus on fiscal arrangements meant that in the first phase of the Depression there was relatively little intergovernmental discussion of fundamental reform to the federal constitution. As in 1927, so in 1931, the Dominion-Provincial Conference discussed the amending formula only because the issue had to be dealt with as part of the Statute of Westminster.

By 1935 the situation had greatly changed. Prime Minister Bennett's radio speeches of that spring had proclaimed the necessity of major changes in national economic and social institutions. These changes, his legislative program implied, had to be brought about primarily by the federal government. This entailed a clear challenge to the existing federal order. Bennett's defeat in the 1935 federal election left King with the dilemma of what to do with the Bennett New Deal. Unlike Bennett, King was highly sensitive to provincial objections (especially from Quebec and Ontario) that the legislation constituted a major encroachment on provincial jurisdiction. One of King's first acts upon being restored to power was to refer all of Bennett's proposed legislation to the Supreme Court of Canada (Neatby, 1976, p. 151).

King then sought to determine whether a consensus on constitutional reform could be found at the Dominion-Provincial Conference of December 1935. He was open to proposals to extend federal authority to regulate wages, working conditions and combines in restraint of trade, but advocated no specific amendments. King preferred to concentrate on the preliminary problem of securing agreement to an amendment formula.

A committee of the conference was assigned the task of exploring the latter issue. Premier Taschereau, who had opposed any discussion of an amendment formula in 1927, now proved receptive to the idea in the twilight hours of his regime. Still, the participants were a long way from agreement on a concrete formula at the end of the conference and it was agreed that federal and provincial officials should immediately begin to meet with a view to developing such a formula (Neatby, 1976, pp. 151-52).

The conference of 1935 was remarkably conciliatory considering the economic stress facing both orders of government, and there was considerable optimism that an amending formula would soon be found. By February 1936 federal Minister of Justice Ernest Lapointe and the provincial Attorneys-General had, with the exception of New Brunswick, reached agreement on a formula: unanimous consent of all legislatures would be required for amendments touching on such crucial areas of the constitution as the educational rights of religious minorities. For other areas, such as social policy, the consent of parliament and two thirds of the legislatures, representing at least 55 percent of the Canadian population, would be sufficient. It was a major advance, but New Brunswick could not be induced to agree to it. King refused to act without unanimous consent, and the recommendations were shelved. Soon federal-provincial conflict began to escalate. The moment for constitutional reform based on unanimous provincial consent had passed (Neatby, 1976, pp. 161-62).

The King government did take some initatives. It negotiated a formal trade agreement with the United States within weeks of taking office. The Bank of Canada, which Bennett had established in 1934 as a "banker's bank", was nationalized, but the federal control thus acquired was not used to go beyond the easy money policy already established under its first Governor, Graham Towers. A National Employment Commission was created with the aim of coordinating the administration of relief expenditures and recommending measures to create employment opportunities. But when the Commission took up the views of Keynes in 1937 and urged the federal government to run a major budget deficit, King balked (Neatby, pp. 82-84).

Early in 1937, the Privy Council rendered its decisions on the Bennett legislation. Its conclusions echoed those of the Supreme Court of Canada on all important matters (Mallory, 1976, p. 53). Two less important statutes, one amending the Criminal Code to strengthen Ottawa's authority to regulate restrictive trade combinations, and the other extending a form of bankruptcy procedure to farmers (Mallory, 1976, p. 51), escaped their scrutiny unscathed. The Dominion Industry and Trade Commission, a watered-down version of the regulatory body recommended by the Royal Commission on Price Spreads, was found to be valid in part (Beck, p. 210; Rowell-Sirois, p. 193). But the five most important statutes were all held to be *ultra vires*.

The three Acts which had together established national standards for minimum wages and maximum hours of weekly work were all found to pertain to "property and civil rights" and, hence, to fall under exclusive provincial jurisdiction. The federal argument that the Acts fell within its treaty power because they enacted obligations assumed by the Dominion under the conventions of the International Labour Organization, was rejected (Rowell-Sirois, p. 194). The Privy Council held that:

> if in the exercise of her new function derived from her new international status Canada incurs obligations they must, so far as legislation is concerned, when they deal with Provincial classes of subjects, be dealt with by the totality of powers, in other words by co-operation between the Dominion and the Provinces. While *the ship of state* now sails on larger ventures and into foreign waters she *still retains the watertight compartments which are an essential part of her original structure*.
> (cited in Tremblay Commission, p, 134, emphasis added)

The Natural Products Marketing Act provided for the creation of a Dominion Marketing Board to regulate "the time and place of and the agency for marketing as well as the quantity, quality and grade of any natural product which was allowed to be marketed at any time" (Rowell-Sirois, p. 196). It was to apply to any natural product if its principal market fell outside the province in which it was produced. Once this condition was met, all marketing transactions in that product, including those taking place within provincial boundaries, would fall under the Act. The Privy Council found this statute *ultra vires* on the ground that the federal "trade and commerce" power did not extend to the regulation of intra-provincial trade (Rowell-Sirois, pp. 196-97). F.R. Scott's reaction to the Privy Council judgment on this point was characteristically caustic:

> We now have two examples of marketing legislation; the first a provincial Act in British Columbia which the Supreme Court threw out because it interfered with interprovincial trade, and this (federal) Act which was thrown out because it interfered with local trade. The courts, in other words, have created a no man's land in the constitution and are able to invalidate any marketing legislation they do not like.
>
> (cited in Mallory, p. 53)

The Employment and Social Insurance Act provided for the creation of an unemployment insurance program to be financed partly by employer and employee contributions and partly by the federal government. It also declared the government's intention to examine public health insurance, and plans for unemployment relief for those ineligible for the benefits provided in the Act (Guest, 1980, p. 88). The Privy Council found that levies on employees and employers was an invasion of provincial jurisdiction over property and civil rights. To the federal government's argument that the Act could nonetheless be justified as an exercise of its general "Peace, Order and Good Government" power, given that unemployment had reached the proportions of a national evil, the Privy Council replied that a long line of decisions had established that this was a power confined to such "temporary and overwhelming emergencies as war, pestilence or famine" (Rowell-Sirois, p. 195).

The effect of the Privy Council's decisions, in Mallory's opinion, was "practically to paralyse the Dominion as an agency for regulating economic activity...the Dominion had practically no jurisdiction over labour, prices, production, and marketing except in wartime" (1958, p. 51). King was now able to blame the constitution for federal inaction. Many accepted this explanation and there was much argument among reformers such as Scott concerning the conservative politics of the old men on the Privy Council.

Yet, as we argued in our discussion of industrial class divisions, King had other options, including constitutional reform and court-packing. Moreover, if he had supported the Bennett legislation, he could have implemented it, awaiting such private challenges to its constitutional status as might arise. If these measures had improved the national economy, or were believed to have done so, the public outcry against their abolition by a foreign court would have backed his demands for constitutional change. This was the strategy being followed at this time by the Social Credit government in Alberta, with growing popular support despite its constitutional defeats. But King did none of these things; instead, he immediately referred the Bennett legislation to the courts. As Mallory observes: "Under such circumstances, it is unlikely that the Court would be led to believe that the government was strongly attached to the legislation" (1976, p. 50).

Why was King against the federal government playing the sort of extended economic and social role implied by Bennett's legislation? It was not because King was an inflexible fiscal conservative. By 1938, albeit with some misgivings, he had been persuaded to undertake a moderately expansionary budget on the Keynesian grounds advocated by the National Employment Commission and his Minister of Labour, Norman Rogers (Neatby, 1976, pp. 247-48, pp. 250-58). Nor can King plausibly be portrayed as a libertarian intent upon maintaining a minimal state. In the same year that King accepted the desirability of running a deficit, he refused to utilize the federal power of disallowance to strike down Duplessis' "Padlock Law" (Neatby, 1976, pp. 233-36, pp. 267-68).

The best explanation for the King government's relative inactivity during the Depression, and his willingness to expand federal social and economic policy thereafter, is not to be found either in the federal constitution or in King's ideas of economics or justice. It is that the first priority of King and his Liberals, for both ideological and party self-interest reasons, was national unity. As long as there was no clear English-speaking majority position on the appropriate role of the state, electoral politics left King with room to manoeuvre. In this context, King preferred to avoid the kind of economic and social policy initiatives that Taschereau denounced in 1935. To his conscience and his diary King justified his refusal to disallow or refer the Padlock Law to the courts, in spite of his personal opposition to it, by arguing that "in the last resort, the unity of Canada was the test by which we would meet all these things" (cited in Whitaker, 1977, p. 286).

King's inclinations were reinforced by the election of a Quebec government, less than a year after his own re-election in 1935, which was a more militant, if still conservative, defender of provincial rights than its Liberal predecessors. But King's strategy of minimal federal activity, informed by his conviction that the principal threat to national unity lay in French-English conflict, was much less effective under conditions of economic crisis than it had been in the 1920s. For while federal inaction minimized the potential for new federal-provincial conflicts related to language, it provoked increasing criticism from those who saw the nation primarily through the lenses of region and class.

These elements argued that only the federal government possessed the fiscal resources and technical expertise to implement progressive social and economic policies. These policies involved redistribution between individuals and regions which could only be achieved in accordance with national conceptions of collective welfare and fairness. Provincial governments, given their accountability to sub-national political communities, could not be expected to take a national perspective on such issues. Poorer provinces, whatever their progressive aims, were hampered by inadequate resources and limited ability to assert claims on the rich, given the mobility of capital. Accordingly, it was deemed essential that the federal government expand its jurisdiction.

Even before the 1937 decisions by the Privy Council, a growing number of English Canadian intellectuals had begun to attack the federal system as a major impediment to the adoption of progressive policies. Foremost among them had been Norman Rogers, who had first argued that federalism had become a "dead hand" in 1931 (*Canadian Forum*, xii, p. 47). Upon entering national politics, Rogers carried his views into King's cabinet. Leading figures within the League for Social Reconstruction and the CCF echoed this conclusion, although there was considerable difference of opinion as to who should be blamed for the constitutional failure. F.R. Scott (1977, p. 47) stressed the culpability of the Privy Council, while Frank Underhill (1937) argued that the deeper source of stalemate was class-based opposition to "the substitution of government power in place of private wealth". Still, all agreed that the solution to both economic and constitutional crisis lay in a centralization of federal powers. Harold Laski (1939), reflecting widely-held views among the Social Democratic left, went further, declaring that federalism was obsolete, a luxury which could no longer be afforded because it denied governments effective control over the forces of "giant capitalism".

Such critics had little influence on King in the latter half of the 1930s. The only party to endorse such views was the CCF and it was able to muster substantial popular support only in the West. The Maritimes remained conservative. So did Ontario, under Hepburn, whose populism became increasingly right-wing following the Oshawa confrontation and his re-election in 1937. So English Canada – above all, Ontario – remained divided on economic justice issues, allowing King to place national unity and his party's image in Quebec above all else. He claimed to be sympathetic to the goals of the reformists, while chiding them for the politically and constitutionally unsound means by which they proposed to implement them. The advocates of a more active state turned to their provincial governments. The most striking example was the Social Credit government in Alberta after 1936.

Inadequate federal responses to the western debt crisis was one of the major reasons for Aberhart's movement from the comparatively orthodox remedies which he introduced in 1936 toward the more radical social credit legislation that his government began passing in 1937 (Mallory, 1976, pp. 57-152). Ottawa's response to Alberta's attempts to increase provincial credit and reduce government and farmer debt was the resurrection, after 13 years of disuse, of the federal power of disallowance, confounding many legal experts who had concluded that this power was now a "dead letter" (Rowell-Sirois, p. 203; Mallory, p. 84). Shortly after the Social Credit legislation was passed in 1937, the federal government referred the question of the validity of its disallowance and reservation powers, along with three provincial Acts, to the courts.

The Supreme Court of Canada ruled on the federal powers question first, holding that they remained intact (Mallory, p. 85). Then, in March 1938, it held that all three of the Alberta bills were *ultra vires*. Moreover, the judges took the extraordinary step of declaring *ultra vires* an Alberta statute that Ottawa had chosen not to refer to the Court – the Alberta Social Credit Act, the cornerstone of the Social Credit program. As Mallory describes it, "the whole legislative edifice of social credit was brought to the ground in a single judgement" (Mallory, p. 87). In spite of these devastating constitutional losses, the Alberta government fought on. Between 1937 and 1941 a total of 11 Alberta statutes were disallowed and a further 10 were declared *ultra vires* by the Supreme Court of Canada (Freisen, 1984, p. 414; Neatby, 1976, pp. 265-67).

Conflict between Ottawa and provincial governments was not confined to Alberta. By August 1937 when King appointed the Rowell-Sirois Commission, federal-provincial acrimony had reached such a level that three provincial governments – Ontario, Quebec and Alberta – declared that they did not recognize the authority of the Commission to conduct such an investigation and would not cooperate with it (Neatby, 1976, p. 245). Their objections to the Commission, and their alternative conceptions of federalism, became clear in the course of the Commission's hearings, to which each provincial government nonetheless made some form of submission in 1938. All provinces considered the existing division of taxing powers and spending responsibilities unsatisfactory, but there was no agreement on how it might be altered. Two polar strategies were available: either the centralization of social and economic responsibilities better to correspond to the existing distribution of taxing powers and capablities, or the decentralization of taxing powers better to correspond with the existing distribution of social and economic responsibilities.

The governments of Quebec, Ontario, Alberta and British Columbia generally opposed any extension of federal jurisdiction. Ontario's Premier Hepburn was most concerned with the redistributive implications of an expanded federal role in social policy, arguing that they amounted to an indirect way of transferring the wealth of Ontarians to the residents of other provinces. Beyond this, the personal emnity between Hepburn and King was such by this time that the Premier delighted in embarrassing the federal Liberals and their Commission (Armstrong, 1981, pp. 209-19). Short-term calculations of provincial self-interest and personal rivalries were undoubtedly factors in the opposition to centralization expressed by Quebec and British Columbia, the other two provinces with economic standards above the national average. But these considerations were probably outweighed in the case of Quebec by Premier Duplessis' conservative nationalist priorities. British Columbia's Premier Pattullo also had distinct reasons for opposing centralization. He was concerned to maintain sufficient fiscal and jurisdictional latitude to undertake the provincial reforms necessary to defuse the CCF threat from his left. Alberta, unlike the other three, was not a member of the club of rich provinces. Premier Aberhart's willingness to line up with them may have reflected continued hope for the prospects of provincial reform, or simply his anger toward the federal government which had recently blocked all of his reform legislation.

The other provinces favoured varying degrees of centralization. Premier Bracken of Manitoba, soon to become the leader of the federal Progressive Conservative Party, was the strongest proponent of this position. As glossed by W.L. Morton, Bracken urged:

> ...that the federal government assume the whole costs of relief and old age pensions and one-half the costs of certain other services. The submission...was an argument for federal assumption of responsibilities which were national and for provincial revenues which would enable all the provinces to maintain the social services public opinion demanded at a level comparable with that of the more favoured sections of the nation. The unuttered alternative was repudiation of debt by the weaker provinces and the migration of their populations into the stronger provinces, with the possible result that their social services also would be overwhelmed. If the new standards were to be provincial, not national, the results would be disastrous for western Canada and serious for the remainder. Only a new concept of the nature and purpose of Confederation could alleviate the distress in the West and restore the unity of the nation.
>
> (Morton, 1967, pp. 431-32)

By 1939, no significant progress on the constitutional question had been made. The debt problem in the western provinces was worse than ever. English Canadians, and provincial governments located in regions where they were the majority, remained divided amongst themselves. It would take the war to break the deadlock.

To sum up, the Depression caused federal-provincial conflict on a scale that had not been experienced since the early battles of the 1880s and 1890s. This time, however, neither order of government was willing or able to develop the new economic and social policies that were required. As a result, the degree of centralization characterizing Canadian federalism remained more or less unchanged in the 1930s, although the fiscal autonomy of most of the provincial governments was greatly reduced. It is tempting to argue that, rather than one government losing powers that the other gained, the courts in this period deprived both orders of government of powers that simply disappeared into a constitutional "black hole". However, to the extent that the decisions of the courts seriously constrained the operations of the federal government, Mallory is surely right when he argues that:

> The paralysing effects of judicial interpretation on the Canadian constitution in the years between the wars was a reflection of the collective indecision of the Canadian people. For much as an increase in the activity of the state was demanded by a large section of the population, this same increase was bitterly contested by other groups who stood to gain more by the old equilibrium than by the new. Thus every halting step in the direction of satisfying collective wants was transformed into a debate on constitutional first principles. The courts were dragged in because of this uncertainty, and, whether composed of Canadian judges or the learned lords of the Privy Council, were torn by the same uncertainties. Their method of reasoning and the whole spirit of the common law itself contributed to the resulting stalemate, but the courts were not more confused than the people for whose constitution they acted as custodians.
>
> (1976, p. 56)

In the final analysis, the principal cause of the stalemate was the fragmentation of Canadian opinion on fundamental questions of economic strategy and social justice. Without even a majority position on these issues, there could be no clear answers concerning the appropriate economic and social roles of the state and the best division of these roles between the two orders of government.

Conclusions

The Depression experience produced major shifts in the terms of debate about Canadian federalism. Some earlier themes, especially the salience of religion in politics, declined greatly. Others, notably language, remained at centre stage. But this cleavage, too, was changed: its territorialization meant that French Canadian identity was increasingly focussed on Quebec-Canada relations, with the Quebec state viewed as the principal institutional guardian of francophone interests. Moreover, the economic and social issues which arose in the 1930s meant that the debate was focussed more on questions of the division of powers and the policy consequences of federalism than on the issue of minority rights. Conflicting visions of Canadian nationality focussed more on economic and social issues and, therefore, on the role of the state.

The relatively homogeneous agricultural base of the Prairies, combined with the ethnic and social distinctiveness which were products of the settlement patterns and political economy of the National Policy, had developed into a strong sense of regional identity. This evolution was partly recognized in 1930 when the three prairie provinces finally achieved equal status with the other six provinces with the transfer of ownership of natural resources from the federal government. The economic crisis, the perceived inadequacy of the federal response to it, and the jurisdictional battles over Social Credit reinforced regional identities and the sense of grievance against the centre. It was in this period that the symbols and rhetoric of "western alienation", a sense of the West as subordinate to a remote federal political authority in thrall to central Canadian business interests, was fully developed.

Industrial working class divisions emerged alongside the linguistic, regional and agrarian class divisions as the most politically salient societal divisions, but rather than displacing them, they intersected in complex ways. Regional variations in class structure meant that the mobilization of class interests also varied: labour made few inroads in the Maritimes; in British Columbia it was concentrated in the resource industries; in Ontario in manufacturing; in Quebec it was incorporated in the primary politics of language and nationalism. On the Prairies, efforts to link labour and agriculture in the CCF met with some success. Federalism, both its societal and its institutional dimensions, thus fragmented and divided class identities and interests. Nevertheless, the agenda raised by organized labour and agriculture called for major changes in the role of the state and, by implication, in the federal system. More than ever before, the legitimacy of federalism itself, not merely one type of federalism, turned on its perceived capacity to respond effectively to economic crisis in a fashion consistent with social justice.

Chapter 6

Interregnum: War Federalism, 1939-46

World War II required massive government intervention to transform moribund consumer economies into high performance war economies. In Canada, the economic challenge was met with striking success. Unemployment had disappeared by 1942, and productivity and output grew by leaps and bounds. By 1945, the share of the economy represented by secondary manufacturing was larger than at any time before or since. Canadians now had an alternative model to the old form of political economy; they also had evidence that it worked.

The war strengthened the elements of the industrial working and agrarian classes allied under the banner of the CCF. It greatly increased the economic and political bargaining power of organized labour, enabling it to extract a new labour law regime from the federal government and compliance from the private sector. As a result, trade unions expanded with unprecedented rapidity, constituting an ever larger and more powerful force in favour of extending state intervention into the post-war period. The agricultural sector did not expand, but war-time grain price supports helped to stabilize the income of those who remained on the land, reducing Prairie antagonism towards Ottawa and convincing farmers of the necessity of forcing Ottawa to continue such policies after the war.

War was also a nation-building force. Here was a national purpose which many believed transcended regional, linguistic and class interests.

Mobilization of the work force for wartime factories and of millions of service men and women, fostered high levels of mobility and intensive contact with Canadians of other regions. The values for which the war was fought – democracy and freedom – were put in universal terms. Regional conflicts and identities were muted and few doubted that conduct of the war was a federal responsibility. Provincial politicans who challenged this assumption paid the electoral price, as Duplessis and Hepburn discovered.

To this general picture, the important exception of Quebec must be noted, for the Second World War exacerbated French-English conflicts, as had the First. King was much more attuned to these dangers than Borden had been, but in the end a second conscription crisis could not be avoided. It did not cost King power in Ottawa, as it had Borden, but it cost him the Liberal government of Quebec and, with it, any hope of dealing with a Quebec government open to centralizing constitutional amendments. In this way, the war and its societal effects brought about the end of classical federalism and set the parameters that would govern the emergence of modern federalism in Canada.

Federal Society

The Second World War had immediate and profound effects upon the Canadian economy. It led to an enormous increase in government expenditures which, in turn, restored economic growth and full employment, above all in the manufacturing sector. Further, it reinforced the tendency toward increasing Canadian economic integration with the United States, ending the old National Policy and the protectionist industrial strategy of import substitution associated with it.

Federal expenditures increased from $680 million in 1939 to $5.1 billion in 1945. The national economy responded: real GNP by 1944 was 80 percent greater than it had been in 1938, and while much of this increased output went to the war effort, personal consumption of goods and services also rose by about 30 percent between 1939 and 1944 (Clement, 1984, p. 89). The rate of growth peaked in 1942 at 18.6 percent, more than twice the highest annual increase that would be achieved in the post-war period. Unemployment had fallen to 4.4 percent by 1941 and 1.4 percent by 1944 (Phillips & Watson, p. 22, p. 28).

Wartime economic growth was concentrated in certain sectors: manufacturing accounted for an average of 22.6 percent of real GDP between 1926 and 1939, but in the war years it rose dramatically, peaking at 32 percent in 1943. Employment in that sector rose by 177.6 percent between 1939 and 1945, compared with employment in agriculture which fell to 83 percent of its 1939 levels (Phillips & Watson: 22,28,31). More than 60 percent of all manufacturing employees were engaged in the production of war materials, so that most of this growth could be attributed directly to government spending associated with the war effort (Clement, 1984, p. 88).

These sectoral developments were associated with major demographic and regional changes. They signalled renewed movement from the farms to the cities in all parts of the country. This had the most profound impact on the Prairies, where it resulted in population decline in Saskatchewan and stagnation in Alberta and Manitoba. In Quebec, the relative decline of agriculture had important cultural implications, given the special place of agriculture in the conservative nationalist ideology dominant in the province.

Canada's regional economies were also changing in their relation to one another and to the world. Specifically, the war increased the rate at which the economies of the regions were becoming oriented to north-south trade with the United States (Granatstein, 1986). Growing continental economic integration was reflected in the ratio of Canada-United States trade to total Canadian trade, and in the ratio of United States investment to total investment in Canada. Imports from the United States nearly tripled in value between 1939 and 1945, while those from the United Kingdom rose very little. By 1944, exports to the UK had risen to about four times their value in 1939 but, in contrast to Canada's earlier trading patterns, these levels were exceeded by the United States for the last four years of the war (Creighton, 1970, p. 252). Between 1939 and 1946, the American share of total foreign investment in Canada rose from 60 percent to 72 percent (Levitt, 1970, p. 66).

This process was not at first a deliberate policy. The war effort required many components and materials that could only be obtained south of the border. The resulting trade imbalance with the United States soon became untenable. The alternatives were either to reduce reliance on United States products or to establish new trade and currency agreements. The federal government initially preferred the first option: foreign exchange controls were tightened; imports of many products from outside the Sterling currency bloc were prohibited; duties on British imports were reduced while excise taxes on American imports were increased. But these measures proved inadequate, even as they upset the Americans. In April 1941, King reversed gears. Under the terms of the Hyde Park agreement, any components imported from the United States, for the production of munitions and other war materiel to be sent to Britain, could be charged to the Lend-lease account that America had created for Britain. Moreover, the Americans would buy between $200 million and $300 million worth of defence material from Canada (Granatstein, 1986).

The Hyde Park agreement helped to crystalize official thinking in Ottawa on questions concerning the character of the post-war international economy and Canada's place in it. By 1943 key Canadian officials were urging the King government to support British and American proposals to seek agreement on a multilateral free trade regime. Over the next year Canadian officials played an important role in the discussions that culminated at Bretton Woods in 1944, where the lineaments of the post-war international economic order were set out (Granatstein, 1986). The United States committed itself to backing the American dollar with gold at a fixed rate, the foundation of a system of fixed exchange rates. The charters for the international credit institutions – the International Monetary Fund (IMF) and the World Bank – were signed. The free trade regime that would later be embodied in the General Agreement on Trade and Tariffs (GATT) was discussed. As a result of these policies, Canada's economy would become more thoroughly integrated with that of the United States than the framers of the original National Policy would have thought desirable. In effect, Canada had quietly embarked upon a new National or, perhaps more accurately, International Policy.

Organized Labour Resurgent

The strength of organized agriculture and labour (and public support for the CCF) grew gradually until about 1942 and then accelerated rapidly. Thus, it had little impact on the fortunes of the CCF in the snap election called by Mackenzie King in 1940. The CCF was only able to field 96 candidates and, in any case, the national agenda in 1940 was dominated by one concern, Canada's role in the war, an issue on which the CCF was divided. By this time the CCF had abandoned its earlier position of strict neutrality, at the cost of J.S. Woodsworth's resignation, but continued to hold that Canada should restrict its efforts to economic aid, sending no soldiers overseas (Neatby, 1972, p. 102).

There was considerable support for this stance in Quebec and the west where opposition to conscription had been strongest in 1917. But the "communist" CCF was still anathema in Quebec, receiving only 0.6 percent of the popular vote there in the 1940 election. In the four western provinces, CCF support ranged between a low of 13 percent in Alberta and a high of 28.6 percent in Saskatchewan; all but one of their eight seats were won in that region. Stronger ties to Britain in Ontario and the Maritimes, combined with negligible support in Quebec, held national support for the CCF to below nine percent of the popular vote (Beck, pp. 232-34). The Liberals, wearing the mantle of the national government in a time of national emergency, secured 51.5 percent of the popular vote (the first time since 1917 that any party had received more than 50 percent of the vote from the Canadian electorate) and 181 seats. The Conservatives received 30.7 percent of the vote and 40 seats; Social Credit, 2.3 percent and 10 seats (Beck, pp. 236-39).

The first significant political victory for the CCF occurred in British Columbia. In the 1941 provincial election, the party won 33 percent of the vote and more seats than either of the other parties. In response, the traditional parties proposed a coalition government to provide wartime stability; its rationale soon became to keep the socialists from power, casting British Columbia politics into the bi-polar mold that would prevail to the present day (Conway, 1983, pp. 146-47, p. 154; Cairns and Wong, in Thorburn, 1985).

Ottawa's paramount concern with promoting the war effort (and the industrial peace essential to it) and the centralization of powers under the War Measures Act, enabled labour to extract important industrial relations concessions from the federal government. To ensure its cooperation with the wage and price controls imposed in 1941, the federal government promised to implement compulsory collective bargaining. Order-in-Council P.C. 2685 of 1940 proclaimed workers' rights to organize and negotiate agreements through their elected representatives. But there were no provisions for enforcement, and the Order was largely ignored by employers, even within the factories owned and controlled by the government (Easterbrook & Aitken, p. 569).

The result was growing labour militance and, perhaps more surprising, mounting public support for labour's demands. In a federal by-election held soon after the breaking of the Kirkland Lake strike in 1942, a CCF candidate closely associated with the defence of the strikers defeated Arthur Meighen – slated to become new leader of the Conservative party – in the "safe" Tory seat of York-South (Roberts & Bullen, pp. 114-15). This upset gave the initiative to the reform-oriented wing of the Conservative party at the Winnipeg Convention in December 1942. The party got a new leader, a new name and a new platform: the "Progressive" Conservative party, now led by John Bracken (the long-time Liberal-Progressive Premier of Manitoba) officially committed itself to "social security, full employment, collective bargaining, and medical insurance" (Granatstein, 1975, pp. 251-52; Brodie & Jenson, 1980, pp. 202-3).

The Kirkland Lake strike pushed the trade union movement into new political ventures. In 1943 the Canadian Confederation of Labour, formed in 1940 by the merger of the All Canadian Confederation of Labour and the Canadian CIO-affiliates, endorsed the CCF as the political arm of organized labour. This contributed to the gains made by the Ontario CCF in the provincial election of August 1943 (Beck, 1968, p. 247 n. 25). The anti-union Liberal government was reduced to a 15 seat rump, and the CCF emerged as the Official Opposition with 34 seats (19 occupied by trade unionists) and 32 percent of the popular vote, only four fewer seats than George Drew's new Conservative government (Granatstein, 1975, pp. 264-65; Brodie & Jenson, 1980, p. 202).

The political gains of 1943 were not confined to the provincial level. Five days after the Ontario election, King's Liberals lost four seats in by-elections: two in the west to the CCF; and one each to the Labour-Progressive party and the newly formed *Bloc populaire* in Quebec. A month later, a survey conducted by the Canadian Institute of Public Opinion revealed that the CCF had the support of 29 percent of the committed vote, surpassing the Liberals and the Progressive Conservatives, at 28 percent each (Brodie & Jenson, 1980, p. 204). To this point, King had insisted that the principal business of his government was the successful prosecution of the war effort, and that the introduction of new social policies must await the end of the war. But these electoral portents persuaded King that he must modify his position if the Liberals were to avoid defeat in the next election (Granatstein, 1975, p. 265, pp. 266-78).

1943 also saw major gains in industrial relations. Industrial strife reached levels surpassing the previous records set in 1919; there were 402 strikes involving more than 218,000 workers (Jamieson, 1968, p. 280). In this context, King agreed to create more effective means of enforcing the promises made to labour in 1940. In January of 1944 the cabinet issued Order-in-Council P.C. 1003 by which:

> Labour was accorded the right to bargaining representatives of its own choosing; negotiations were to be carried on in good faith; employers were forbidden to discriminate against workers for belonging to unions; union organizers were not to coerce workers to join unions nor to canvass business premises on company time; and a War-time Labour Relations Board with equal representation from employers and labour and a neutral chairman was created to administer and enforce the regulations.
>
> (Easterbrook & Aitken, p. 569)

These legal changes, along with heightened political consciousness and full employment, underpinned dramatic membership growth. National membership more than doubled between 1939 and 1946, rising from 359,000 to 832,000, or from 7.7 percent to 17.1 percent of the civilian labour force (Kumar, 1986, pp. 108-9).

Following P.C. 1003, strike levels declined in 1944 and 1945. But as the war drew to a close organized labour, worried that its war-time advances might be lost upon the termination of the War Measures Act, pressed for the incorporation of the principles of P.C. 1003 in a National Labour Code. The federal government increased labour's apprehension by replying that it was constitutionally incapable of doing so. The unions thereupon attempted to entrench their gains in their collective agreements. Most employers resisted, still hoping for a return to the pre-war labour relations *status quo*. The result was a rapid escalation of strikes and lockouts between September 1945 and July 1946. As Easterbrook and Aitken observe:

These strikes were supported by the labour movement as a whole with a degree of co-operation and disregard of jurisdictional boundaries that was quite unusual. They ended with acceptance of the check-off system, large increases in union membership, and a general recognition of the fact that labour's war-time gains had been consolidated.

(p. 570)

The victories of 1945-46 enabled organized labour to build on its much expanded membership base. There would be no reversals of the sort which followed the 1919 strike wave. Nor would King's Liberals fail to live up to their campaign promises on social policy, as they had in 1921.

The Divergence of Agrarian Politics

Organized agriculture did not benefit from the same kind of growth. There was substantial migration out of the Prairies, most going into the armed forces or to the new manufacturing jobs in the central Canadian cities (Morton, 1967, p. 465). At the same time, federal programs and international economic developments stabilized grain prices and farm incomes for those who remained on the land. These new circumstances permitted two very different interpretations of the long-run interests of Canadian agriculture, giving rise to diverging policy prescriptions.

By one analysis, the Depression was over and the smaller, more efficient agricultural sector that remained – if supported, as it was in the war years, by a determined federal government – could weather any future difficulties. Farmers' interests would be best served by ensuring that the federal government retained its war-time price support system in the post-war period. The role of the provincial government was to act as an effective lobby for regional interests in Ottawa. But a second analysis argued that prairie depopulation in the 1940s was further proof of the vulnerability of an economy based on export- oriented production of primary commodities. This view had long underpinned western support for state intervention to promote economic diversification. Unless the new International Policy could be expected to alter significantly the regional division of labour created by the National Policy, this analysis suggested provincial governments would continue to have an important role in economic and social development.

In the war years, the former interpretation prevailed in Alberta and the latter in Saskatchewan. In Manitoba, it appears that the two positions were more evenly balanced. These differences were reflected in provincial election results.

In Saskatchewan, the CCF had been held to 10 seats and 19 percent of the vote in the 1938 provincial election by the "invasion" of Alberta's Social Credit party, which received 16 percent of the vote. But with the death of

Aberhart in 1943, Social Credit's radicalism dissipated. By the 1944 provincial election, the CCF was the only radical farmers' party in the province. The CCF had also broadened its support to encompass urban workers and professionals. The CCF won 47 seats with 53 percent of the vote; its rural support was about 58 percent, and the relatively small urban working class vote was even higher (Conway, p. 142, p. 165).

The 1944 CCF platform closely followed the program of the Regina Manifesto. Its priorities were the "provision of security" for farmers and urban workers, the development of a more diversified economy through crown corporations, and new tax laws aimed at capturing a greater share of natural resource rents for the people of Saskatchewan (Conway, p. 162-64). The CCF promised protection for farmers from foreclosure, crop seizure and eviction, the promotion of the cooperative movement, and pressure for the closure of the Winnipeg Grain Exchange. To the urban workers it offered higher minimum wages, a shortened work week, better systems of workers' compensation and compulsory collective bargaining, and stricter enforcement of all such laws and regulations. It promised extensive reforms to existing social services and the provision of new ones: socialized health services, old age pension increases, new pensions for those unable to support themselves, increased mothers' allowances, new schools, free textbooks and improved teacher salaries.

The new provincial government rapidly brought about those reforms which could be implemented without Ottawa's support (Conway, pp. 165-68). Initially, it focussed on the economy, seeking to stabilize volatile primary commodity markets and to eliminate middlemen by developing cooperative suppliers of goods and machinery and collectively owned marketing agencies. In 1944, the CCF government passed the Farm Security Act, similar in several respects to legislation passed by the Social Credit government of Alberta in the latter half of the 1930s. The Act provided that during years of crop failure mortgage and interest payments on debt would be suspended and the quarter section of land upon which the home was located protected from foreclosure (Morton, 1967, pp. 433-38). When the federal government threatened to disallow this legislation in 1945, Premier Douglas went on the radio to rally his provincial supporters against Ottawa, arguing that:

> We have just finished a war which was fought, we were told, for the preservation of democratic institutions. It would appear that the war is not finished. We have simply moved the battlefields from the banks of the Rhine to the prairies of Saskatchewan.
>
> (cited in Gibbins, p. 181)

The Act was later ruled *ultra vires* by the Supreme Court of Canada, so that exercise of the federal disallowance power proved unnecessary (Conway, 1983, p. 165).

The CCF government was equally innovative in seeking to diversify the province's economy. In a 1946 speech Premier Douglas outlined his government's strategy:

> First, is to process...by means of private industry, public enterprise or co-operative development, our agricultural and other primary products...to turn our wool into clothing, our leather into shoes...to process the by-products of the farm, and...the forest...and so on. In other words, instead of being exporters of base primary products, whenever we can, to carry those primary products one stage further along the course of economic development, with small factories in various communities turning these primary products into more saleable commodities. [This will] provide employment for the people...on these prairies. I do not think that the people are prepared, for ever and a day, to be hewers of wood and drawers of water.... [Then] we should use those industries...to produce revenue to give our people a certain measure of social security.
>
> (cited in Conway, p. 167)

The CCF created many small Crown corporations for the processing of wood, cardboard, wool and leather, and for fur marketing and fish filleting. As Douglas' speech makes clear, the orientation of this strategy was still the security of the family farm, to be achieved within the economy of a predominantly rural society. The era of giant potash and uranium mines was yet to come (Morton, 1967, pp. 433-38).

In spite of their many initiatives, soon to be followed by its pioneering hospital and health insurance programs, the Saskatchewan CCF recognized that the cooperative commonwealth could only be built by the combined efforts of the two orders of government. Thus, in addition to provincial initiatives, it sought to alter federal policies pertaining to transportation price structures, tariffs, and commodity prices.

In Alberta, despite its setbacks, the Social Credit party continued to retain broad support. But it was now the Saskatchewan CCF that fought the constitutional battles with Ottawa. The new Social Credit leader, Ernest Manning, steered the party to the right, decrying the "pinkism" of the CCF as the first step toward "bureaucratic regimentation". In the August 1944 provincial election the Socreds successfully resisted the attempt of the CCF to expand into Alberta from their Saskatchewan stronghold. The Socreds won 51 of 57 seats with 52 percent of the vote to the CCF's two seats and 25 percent of the vote (Conway, p. 158). As Conway notes, Alberta's "agrarian populist crusade for a new Canada, for a new National Policy and a reconstructed political economy, ended with Manning's victory in 1944" (p. 160).

In Manitoba, conflicts over economic strategies were suspended at the outset of the war when all four of the provincial parties – Liberal-Progressive, CCF, Social Credit, and Conservative – agreed to form a joint administration in November 1940. By the 1945 provincial election, the threat of rapidly growing CCF support within the province, reinforced by the recent CCF victory in Saskatchewan, was sufficient to press the three mainstream parties together into a united front (Morton, 1967, p. 442, p. 450). The CCF share of the vote rose to 34 percent, compared with the 12 percent that it had received in 1936, but in a two-way fight this was not sufficient to form the government (Conway, p. 144, p. 154, p. 173).

The Limits of Quebec Nationalism

Two weeks after Canada formally declared war on Germany, Premier Duplessis of Quebec surprised everyone by calling a snap provincial election for October 1939. He believed francophone popular support for the war was weak, and made what he condemned as Ottawa's unwarranted use of the War Measures Act the central issue of the campaign. Duplessis declared that: "Invoquant le pretexte de la guerre, declarée par le gouvernement fédéral, une campagne d'assimilation et de centralisation, manifeste depuis plusieurs années, s'accentue de façon intolérable" (in Quinn, 1979, p. 104). But Duplessis had misjudged the situation. The majority of *Canadiens* in Quebec supported the compromise which had gradually emerged within the Liberal government as it became clear that war could not be avoided: Canada would commit itself to the full support of the Allies, including the sending of expeditionary forces to Europe and the Pacific, but would on no account conscript troops for overseas service.

On September 8, 1939, in the special session of Parliament convened to decide upon the declaration of war, King stated:

> I wish now to repeat the undertaking I gave in Parliament on behalf of the Government on March 30th last. The present Government believes that conscription of men for overseas service will not be a necessary or an effective step. No such measure will be introduced by the present Administration.
> (cited in Quinn, 1979, p. 104)

King left further elaboration and defence of this compromise to Ernest Lapointe, the leader of the Quebec contingent of the federal Liberal party. Lapointe declared that:

> The whole province of Quebec...will never agree to accept compulsory service or conscription outside Canada. I will go further than that: When I say the whole province of Quebec I mean that I personally agree with them. I am authorized by my colleagues in the cabinet from the province of Quebec...to say that we will

never agree to conscription and will never be members or supporters of a government that will try to enforce it.... . Provided these points are understood, we are willing to offer our services without limitation and to devote our best efforts for the success of the cause we all have at heart.... . God give Canadians the light which will indicate to them where their duty lies in this hour of trial so that our children and our children's children may inherit a land where our social, political, and religious institutions may be secure and from which the tyrannical doctrines of nazism and communism are forever banished.

(cited in Wade, 1968, pp. 920-21)

The francophone press responded favourably (Wade, 1968, pp. 922-29). King was delighted, noting in his diary that:

If I had made the speech Lapointe made, the party might have held its own with the Jingos in Ontario, but would have lost the support of Quebec more or less entirely. If he had made the speech I did, he might have held Quebec, but the party would have lost heavily in Ontario and perhaps some other parts on the score that Quebec was neutral in its loyalty. Together our speeches constituted a sort of trestle sustaining the structure which would serve to unite divergent parts of Canada, thereby making for a united country.

(cited in Whitaker, 1977, pp. 286-87)

The Quebec-based cabinet ministers, led by Lapointe, responded aggressively to the challenge from Duplessis, campaigning actively throughout the province. They promised the voters that they would uphold Lapointe's stand on conscription within the King government, and threatened to resign *en masse* if Duplessis were re-elected, leaving no one in Ottawa to prevent conscription. Lapointe put the matter succinctly in a campaign speech: "Nous sommes le rempart entre vous et la conscription" (cited in Quinn, 1979, pp. 105-6). The role of the federal Liberals in the election went beyond this, however:

Not only did the federal party provide the provincial party with the decisive issue but they also threw out the feuding and ineffective provincial organization, and took direct charge of the campaign in its entirety.... . Candidates considered too nationalistic or unreliable were either forced to withdraw or given no financial support. Most importantly of all, the federal party took direct charge of mobilizing the financial resources of English-Canadian capitalism to defeat Duplessis.

(Whitaker, 1977, p. 287)

It is difficult to assess the real impact of the choice – indeed, the threat – which the federal Liberals put to the Quebec electorate. Certainly many of those who had supported the UN in 1936 had ample reason to reject the leader who had dumped the party's reformist platform immediately upon taking office. Whatever the relative weight of these very different considerations in the deliberations of the voters, their verdict was unambiguous.

Duplessis' party was reduced to 14 of the 86 seats in the National Assembly, while Godbout's Liberals captured 69 seats (Quinn, 1979, p. 291).

It was a stunning, but ultimately Pyrrhic victory. Godbout's client status vis-à-vis the federal Liberals, both during and after the 1939 election, left his government vulnerable to the accusation that it was incapable of adequately defending provincial interests and autonomy where these conflicted with federal Liberal imperatives. The evolution of the war, and the politics of social justice in English Canada, ensured that just such conflicts would dominate the national political agenda after 1943. Hence the truth of Whitaker's observation: "The landslide victory of 1939 ironically marked another stage in the prolonged decline of the provincial Liberals" (1977, p. 288).

Godbout incurred the wrath of conservatives and nationalists in 1940 by agreeing to a constitutional amendment transferring jurisdiction over unemployment insurance to the Dominion government (Quinn, 1979, p. 115). A year later, Godbout was again the object of attacks by the nationalists: Premier Hepburn angrily accused him of deserting the fight for provincial autonomy when he failed to join in the attack on the Rowell-Sirois Commission's recommendations at the Dominion- Provincial Conference in January 1941 (Wade, 1968, pp. 943-44). The real crisis for the Liberal government of Quebec, however, was precipitated by the re-emergence of the conscription issue in 1942. The war had been going badly: France had fallen in June, 1940 and the Battle of Britain commenced almost immediately; a year later, Hitler invaded Russia; on December 7, 1941, the Japanese bombed Pearl Harbour and on Christmas day of that year, a large Canadian contingent was lost at the surrender of Hong Kong. The need for more Canadian troops in Europe was urgent and it began to appear that volunteers would not be sufficient to meet it. Early in 1942 King announced that a national plebiscite would be held in April in which "the people of Canada would be asked whether they were willing to release the government from its pledge of 'no conscription'" (Quinn, 1979, p. 107).

King and his Quebec-based ministers campaigned hard for a "Yes" vote in Quebec, but the issue galvanized the disparate nationalist forces into concerted action. *La Ligue pour la Défense du Canada* (LDC) was hastily formed for the purpose of opposing a "Yes" vote:

> The moving force behind the organization of this League was the nationalist intellectuals who belonged to L'Action Nationale, but the anti-conscription campaign was also supported by prominent individuals from many other groups: the farmers' organizations, the Catholic trade unions, the patriotic and youth organizations. It received the blessing of the veteran nationalist leader, Henri Bourassa and was backed by the Montreal daily, *Le Devoir*
>
> (Quinn, 1977, p. 108).

The outcome of the national plebiscite was a division of the country along linguistic lines as profound as that of 1917. Quebec voted 72 percent "No" and the other provinces, taken as a whole, voted 79 percent "Yes", yielding a national average of 64 percent "Yes" and 35 percent "No" with one percent of the ballots spoiled (Quinn, 1979, p. 108).

Reluctantly, King introduced Bill 80, "An Act to Amend the National Resources Mobilization Act" the following month. He described his government's policy as "not necessarily conscription, but conscription if necessary" (cited in Quinn, p. 109). But no hedging could prevent the issue from dividing his party and it forced the provincial Liberals to try to distance themselves from their federal counterparts. One of King's cabinet ministers, P.J.A. Cardin, resigned and the majority of francophone Liberals voted against the Bill in the Commons. In the Quebec National Assembly a Liberal introduced a motion "calling upon the federal government to maintain the voluntary system of recruiting under all circumstances". It passed by a vote of sixty-one to seven (Quinn, 1979, p. 109). Quebecers might reasonably have asked what right anglophone voters had to release the government from a promise it had first made primarily to francophones.

From this point onward, the provincial Liberals were in deep trouble. Duplessis had no difficulty in demonstrating Godbout's dependence in the 1939 election on the federal Liberal party which had just imposed conscription. He claimed that the Union nationale was the sole reliable defender of Quebec autonomy. Godbout's party had already lost the support of the reform-minded nationalists when they formed the LDC to contest the conscription vote in 1942. Following the plebiscite, they transformed the LDC into a full-fledged political party, *le Bloc Populaire Canadien* (BPC), with the intention of contesting the next provincial election. In February 1943, Gallup polls accorded the BPC 26 percent of the Quebec vote, and by April support had grown to 37 percent (Wade, p. 956-57).

Godbout sought to keep the nationalists divided and to attract the support of at least some of their reform wing by introducing new labour legislation, modifying education laws and nationalizing the largest of the English Canadian power trusts – the Montreal Light, Heat, and Power Company (Wade, p. 982; Neatby, 1972, p. 119). These measures, combined with the departure of some of the most prominent reformers in the BPC, reduced its popular support, which had been declining steadily from its high point in mid-1943 (Wade, pp. 980-81, pp. 1011-12). The BPC received only 15 percent of the popular vote in the provincial election of August 8, 1944. Duplessis gained no new votes – indeed, popular support for the Union nationale declined from 39.2 percent in 1939 to 36 percent – but Godbout's Liberals lost most of the 15 percent that went to the BPC, falling from 54.2 percent in 1939 to 37 percent. Vote splitting and rural over-representation distorted these figures into 45 seats for the UN and 37 for the Liberals (Wade, 1968, pp. 1015-16).

Shortly after Duplessis' victory, the conscription issue began to heat up again. In November of 1944, faced with rebellion among some English-speaking members, the federal cabinet felt it could delay no longer in sending conscript reinforcements to Europe. The provisions of Bill 80 were implemented and 16,000 conscripts formerly assigned to home defence were sent overseas. A motion of censure introduced in the National Assembly passed by a vote of 67 to five (Quinn, 1979, pp. 111-12). Duplessis was able to capitalize on this anger to embarrass further the provincial Liberal opposition and entrench his party's role as the strongest defender of Quebec autonomy. At the same time he relentlessly opposed the federal government's new social legislation proposals as unconstitutional and a Communist-inspired threat to Quebec's institutions (Quinn, 1979, pp. 115-16). In this way, the federal Liberals helped to sustain the Duplessis government in power. The pattern of politics issuing from this dialectic would continue for fifteen years into the post-war period.

The war thus demonstrated the limits of Quebec nationalism in three senses. First, it showed that in a national emergency, where Canada's survival might be at stake, provincial obstruction, even for the normally acceptable purpose of preventing federal incursions into provincial jurisdiction, would not be supported. But at the same time, the fate of Godbout's Liberals suggested that no provincial government perceived to be highly dependent upon federal patronage and initiative – to owe the federal government too many favours – would be tolerated, even under the extraordinary conditions of war. Finally, because of the changes that war brought about in English Canada, the degree to which Mackenzie King could steer the federal government's course primarily by reference to Quebec nationalism was limited. By 1944, he was forced to move further than the majority of the francophone political elites, whether conservative or reformist, would approve in order to preserve his party's power in Ottawa.

The 1945 Federal Election

Many expected the CCF to make major gains in the June 1945 federal election, although few expected them actually to form the government because the party remained without significant support in Quebec. National opinion polls showed a decline in CCF support from the September 1943 peak of 29 percent to a range between 24 percent and 20 percent for the remainder of the war. King made his new social and economic programs, announced in the January 1944 Speech from the Throne, the centrepiece of his electoral campaign in English Canada: "Vote Liberal and keep building a New Social Order in Canada". This preemptive policy strike probably stole some CCF thunder. The Liberals also sought to mobilize fear of communism especially among recent European immigrants in the west and francophone Canadians, to undercut CCF support. Advertisements, often viciously anti-semitic, warned the electorate against the perils of the "foreign-born scheme of 'State Socialism' for our democratic way of life" and predicted that under a CCF government "we would become like animals in a zoo. We would lose our individual freedom just as completely as though we had lost the war!" (Beck, 1968, pp. 251-52; Brodie & Jenson, 1980, pp. 205-9).

The strategy proved sufficient to defuse the CCF challenge. It won only 15.6 percent of the popular vote and 28 seats, all but one in the three western provinces. As in the provincial election of that year, the CCF made little headway in Alberta, where Social Credit took 13 of the province's 17 federal seats. Perhaps more surprising, only four of 28 CCF seats – Cape Breton South, Winnipeg North, Winnipeg North Centre and Vancouver East – were in predominantly industrial working class ridings. The rest came from rural constituencies, 18 of them in Saskatchewan. For the first time at the federal level, the CCF received strong support in industrial Ontario. But in contrast to the provincial election fought against more conservative opponents two years before, these gains were not sufficiently concentrated to translate into seats (Beck, p. 253).

Liberal popular support did not regain its 1940 level, but with 40.9 percent of the vote compared to the 27.4 percent received by the Progressive Conservatives, the Liberals received 125 seats to the 67 won by the Tories. Only in Ontario did the Conservatives outpoll the Liberals (Beck, pp. 256-57). Beck has remarked that the federal election of 1945 was characterized by the same fragmentation of the party system apparent in 1921. Just as in that election, Mackenzie King was able to win a narrow overall victory with the aid of a solid bloc in Quebec (1968, p. 241). To this we should add that, as in 1921, the principal threat to Liberal victory came from the left, and that the Liberal response was to defuse the threat by adopting reformist policies. Quebec support might have been necessary to the King victory, but it was not sufficient, and King could not have secured the additional votes in English Canada that he needed, against formidable opposition in both Ontario and western Canada, had he failed to steer his party toward reform.

The question becomes: How was King able to ride out the conscription crisis and adopt the interventionist policies that he needed to defeat the CCF without losing Quebec? The widespread fear of communism which Duplessis had mobilized against Godbout's Liberals in the provincial election counted against the CCF rather than the Liberals at the national level. And insofar as the bitterness which had surrounded the 1944 conscription decision continued to animate Quebec voters, it counted more against the

Progressive Conservatives than the Liberals. The haphazard efforts of disaffected federal Liberals to create a federal equivalent of the Union nationale came to nought. Although it ran a number of candidates, the BPC never fully recovered from the divisions and disappointments of the provincial election (Wade, pp. 1092-94). For francophone Quebec, King's Liberals were once again the least of evils among the parties that stood a reasonable chance of forming the government. They swept the province, with 50.8 percent of the vote and 53 of 65 seats, a number sufficient to carry them through to national victory despite the decline in popular support that they suffered in the rest of the country (Beck, pp. 255-57).

Federal State

As it had in 1914, the external threat represented by war initially increased the identification of all Canadians with the national political community. The sense that all Canadians were fighting a common enemy was widespread, even if citizen allegiances to provincial political communities remained strong (Schwartz, 1967, p. 93 n.5). But in this context, attempts by the most powerful and outspoken decentralists – Duplessis, Hepburn and Duff Pattullo of B.C. – to continue their struggles with the federal government in much the same way as they had before the war, met with strong public disapproval, reflected in the results of the Quebec election of 1939 and the federal election of 1940. In the 1941 B.C. election, Pattullo's Liberals were reduced to a minority, and shortly afterward he was removed in favour of a Liberal-Conservative coalition which governed for the next 10 years. The large-scale economic reorganization which the war effort required legitimated the centralization of federal power for the duration. As in 1914, federal powers approached those of a unitary state under the authority of the War Measures Act, although this did not prevent some newly-elected governments, such as Godbout's and later Douglas', from undertaking new initiatives. Much more needs to be known about the politics of wartime federalism.

As the war continued, increasing attention was devoted to whether at least some of the fiscal and jurisdictional centralization which had taken place should be extended into the post-war period. The societal developments associated with the rise of the CCF ensured that the answer to this question would be affirmative. The question became whether this would be accomplished by constitutional amendment or by new fiscal arrangements within the existing division of powers. Federal-provincial relations went through two phases, and our discussion is organized around these. First we examine the early period during which the character of war-time federalism was determined, focussing on the unemployment insurance amendment to the constitution, the report of the Rowell-Sirois Commission, the January

1941 Dominion-Provincial Conference, and the subsequent Wartime Tax Arrangements. Then we look at the Throne Speech of January 1944, focussing on the White Paper on Incomes and Employment, the Green Book proposals, and the discussions oriented around them at the Reconstruction conferences of 1945 and 1946.

The War-time Fiscal Arrangements

Following Duplessis' 1939 electoral humiliation, the other Premiers who had been strong critics of the federal government in the Depression years, especially Hepburn and Aberhart, toned down their attacks on Ottawa. Premier Hepburn temporarily suspended his sniping at King; Premier Aberhart introduced only one new piece of unconstitutional legislation (Mallory, p. 116-17). Godbout's government, in turn, was not only the most reform-oriented that Quebec had ever elected, but also was indebted to the King Liberals in Ottawa for its election.

These developments made it possible to secure unanimous provincial agreement to a constitutional amendment transferring jurisdiction over unemployment insurance to the federal government. Unanimous provincial agreement was secured in January 1940; the amendment was passed by the British Parliament in July; and the Unemployment Insurance Act received royal assent in August 1940 (Guest, 1980, p. 106). One of the major goals of the Bennett New Deal was thus accomplished, but it would be the only such amendment to the constitution, even under the exceptional conditions of war. Within a week of securing provincial agreement to the amendment, Premier Hepburn was again attacking Mackenzie King. He moved a resolution of the provincial legislature "regretting that the Federal Government has made so little effort to prosecute Canada's duty in the war in the vigorous manner the people of Canada desire to see" (Armstrong, 1981, p. 220). King seized Hepburn's criticism as a pretext for calling a federal election and was returned to office on March 26, 1940 with 57 of 82 Ontario seats and 50.8 percent of the province's vote (Beck, pp. 238-39).

King, distrusting as always the open debate of issues which might undermine national unity, had asked the Rowell-Sirois Commission not to report until after the election. The Commissioners complied, tabling their report in Parliament on May 10, 1940. Their recommendations were based on the desirability of preserving, as much as possible, the classical "water-tight compartments" model of federalism which had evolved over the past seventy years, and the provincial autonomy that it protected. At the same time, they sought to improve the equity and efficiency of federalism by transferring specified economic and social functions, which in the Commission's view required a uniform national policy, to the federal government.

Two essentially national economic functions were identified. The first was the coordinated collection of the progressive taxes that the Commission hoped would become the foundation of the federal government's revenues. Provincial governments were to cease collecting the income tax, corporate tax and succession duties, leaving the federal government as their sole collector. The second function was the introduction of an equitable system of inter-provincial redistribution based on the principle that all Canadian citizens should have access to comparable standards of government services at comparable levels of taxation. National Adjustment Grants, to be calculated on the basis of fiscal need by reference to a standard formula, would replace all statutory subsidies and the numerous conditional and unconditional grants which had proliferated, *ad hoc*, over the years. In addition to these grants, precursors of equalization transfers, it was recommended that the federal government take over all existing provincial debts (Armstrong, p. 221).

The Commissioners also identified two social policy areas that they believed should become the exclusive responsibility of the federal government. The first was a national system of unemployment insurance and ancillary programs for those who did not qualify for benefits under the regular criteria. The second was a contributory old age pension scheme. Ottawa was thus to provide the foundations of a social security system. The Commission took the view that all other forms of social service built on this foundation – provision for the unemployable, widows' pensions, mothers' allowances, child welfare, public health insurance, workmen's compensation, and education – should remain exclusive provincial responsibilities. The National Adjustment Grants should be set at a level sufficient to allow all provinces to maintain these services "in accordance with average Canadian standards", and their unconditional character would preserve provincial control over the scope and character of each type of service (Guest, p. 92).

The Rowell-Sirois Commission's report was the focal point of the Dominion-Provincial Conference held in January 1941 to discuss the long-term reform of intergovernmental fiscal arrangements. Premiers Pattullo of British Columbia and Aberhart of Alberta, unofficially led by Premier Hepburn of Ontario, were adamantly opposed to the recommendations. Premier Godbout of Quebec and Premier McNair of New Brunswick were non-committal. The Premiers of Manitoba, Saskatchewan, Nova Scotia and Prince Edward Island strongly supported the report's major recommendations (Armstrong, pp. 225-26). Lack of provincial consensus precluded any collective decision for or against the Commission's proposals for the long term future of the federation. But King considered the conference a success, believing that it would eliminate any grounds "for protest on the part of the provincial governments once the Dominion government begins, as it will soon be obliged to do, to invade the fields of taxation which up to the present have been monopolized in whole or in part by some of the provinces" (cited in Armstrong, p. 230).

In the April 1941 budget the federal government took over personal and corporate taxes. In return, Ottawa transferred to each province the amount that these taxes had netted it in 1940. This became known as the "tax rental" system. The agreements were to last for the duration of the war, when more permanent solutions to the problems of fiscal federalism would be discussed and decided upon (Tremblay *Report*, pp. 144-45). Failure of provincial governments to vacate these tax fields would result in double taxation. King believed that angry taxpayers would have no difficulty deciding which order of government had the better claim to taxes in the middle of a war. The provincial premiers apparently agreed: eight of the nine provinces rapidly signed the Wartime Tax Agreements. Only a recalcitrant Premier Hepburn held out for a full year before mounting public pressure forced his consent (Armstrong, pp. 230-32).

Designing Modern Federalism

The federal government began concerning itself with post-war reconstruction as early as 1941. One key source of research and ideas was the Economic Advisory Committee (EAC), created to facilitate the reorganization of the war-time economy and led by Clifford Clark and W.A. Mackintosh. Early in 1941, Ottawa set up the Committee on Post-War Reconstruction, led by Cyril James and Leonard Marsh of McGill University. There was considerable overlap between the mandates of the two committees, and not a little rivalry, but both agreed that major reforms were imperative if the anticipated post-war recession was to be averted (Granatstein, 1982, pp. 158-65).

From the outset, macro-economic and social policy were closely intertwined. Great Britain's Beveridge Report, released in November 1942, had a significant impact on planning in both Canada and the United States. It advocated the introduction of a system of universal health services and children's allowances to supplement a welfare state that was already more extensive than those which existed in North America. The Report also argued that it was imperative that postwar British governments commit themselves to the maintenance of full employment, both because it would make the social security system easier to fund and because economic justice was tied directly to employment. As Lord Beveridge put it:

A person who has difficulty in buying labour that he wants suffers inconvenience or reduction in profits. A person who cannot sell his labour is in effect told that he is of no use. The first difficulty causes annoyance and loss. The other is a personal catastrophe. This difference remains even if adequate income is provided, by insurance or otherwise, during employment; idleness even on an income corrupts; the feeling of not being wanted demoralizes.

(cited in Guest, p. 205)

Following the appearance of the Beveridge Report, work on a federal national health insurance scheme and public health proposals accelerated, culminating in the tabling of the Heagarty and the Marsh Reports in March 1943. Prime Minister King and the EAC responded that the programs were too expensive. The EAC created a subcommittee to develop scaled-down social security proposals integrated with more detailed economic reforms. By the summer of 1943, when King's concern with CCF gains made him more receptive to such measures, detailed proposals were ready (Guest, pp. 124-26; Granatstein, 1975, pp. 264-67).

The Speech from the Throne of January 1944, the last before the general election in June 1945, declared the government's support for "a national minimum of social security through adequate standards of nutrition and housing, policies to promote full employment, and insurance against privation from unemployment, accident, ill health, and old age" (Beck, p. 243). To demonstrate the strength of its commitment, the King government implemented family allowances later in 1944. It introduced legislation amending the National Housing Act (1938) to make it more equitable and effective. It also created generous veterans' pensions. New departments – Reconstruction, National Health and Welfare, and Veterans Affairs – were created to oversee these and subsequent policies (Granatstein, 1975, pp. 274-75). All were constitutionally grounded in an expansive interpretation of the federal spending power.

Ottawa was also defining a new role in economic policy. The economic "mandarins" that the war brought to Ottawa convinced their political masters that Keynesian policies would enable the Liberal government to respond to the demands from the left without undermining a capitalist economy. Their task was facilitated by the experience of war-time reflation through government spending and the fear that, in the absence of government action, recession and large-scale unemployment would once again follow the war (Granatstein, 1975, pp. 249-56).

Keynesian economics provided these advocates with a theoretical *media via* between the hard choices with which policy makers had hitherto believed themselves to be confronted. The ideas expressed in Keynes' *General Theory of Employment, Interest and Money* (1936) made conceivable a workable form of political economy lying between the polar opposites of a state-run "command" economy and a *laissez-faire* market economy (Skidelsky in Crouch, 1979, pp. 59-60). In his own words:

It is not the ownership of the instruments of production which it is important for the state to assume. If the state is able to determine the aggregate amount of resources devoted to augmenting the instruments and the basic rate of reward of those who own them, it will have accomplished all that is necessary.

(cited in Przeworski, 1980, p. 52)

Governments could achieve this control by using fiscal and monetary policy to counteract market cycles. There was no reason why economic growth and high employment could not be sustained indefinitely. Within this new policy framework private owners, operating in the context of competitive markets, could remain the principal determinants of the allocation of scarce resources within and between firms. From this standpoint, the social programs demanded by organized labour and a growing segment of the public could be justified to conservatives as "automatic stabilizers".

Early in 1945, Mackintosh and his colleagues in the Department of Reconstruction drafted a policy paper endorsing Keynesian conceptions of the economic role of the state, expressing them in commonsense language. By March, Mackintosh had convinced his Minister, C.D.Howe, that these goals were politically necessary and that Ottawa had the means to implement them. A few weeks later the majority of the cabinet was won over, after a point-by-point exposition by Mackintosh. On April 12, 1945, one month before the federal election, the White Paper was tabled in the House of Commons. Keynes had officially arrived in Canada (Granatstein, 1975, p. 277). The White Paper began from the proposition that:

...a high and stable level of employment and income, and thereby higher standards of living [must be]...a major aim of government policy. The endeavour to achieve [that aim] must pervade all government policy. It must be wholeheartedly accepted by all economic groups and organizations as a great national objective, transcending in importance all sectional and group interests.

(cited in Granatstein, 1975, p. 277)

In order to do this, the federal government would be prepared,

...in periods when unemployment threatens, to incur deficits and increases in the national debt resulting from its employment and income policy, whether that policy in the circumstances is best applied through increased expenditures or reduced taxation. In periods of buoyant employment and income, budget plans will call for surpluses. The Government's policy will be to keep the national debt within manageable proportions and maintain a proper balance in its budget over a period longer than a single year.

(cited in Granatstein, 1975, pp. 227-28)

In addition to setting out the essential features of the new doctrine, the White Paper was also calculated to maintain business support for the

Liberal government. It promised to end wartime controls as soon as possible, to "privatize" most of the Crown corporations created during the war and to promote the expansion of international trade. In short, it sought to reassure the owners of capital that private property would remain the foundation of the post-war economy (Granatstein, 1975, p. 278).

If the political and economic goals of the modern state were reasonably clear, one fundamental question remained: could they be achieved in the Canadian federal state, or would what King's Minister of Labour called the "dead hand" of the constitution combined with the opposition of Quebec and the richer provinces, frustrate it? Some elements of the new plan were clearly within exclusive federal power: Ottawa controlled monetary policy; it now had the Bank of Canada as its instrument; its control over tariffs was unquestioned; unemployment insurance would function as an "automatic stabilizer". Other powers were much more problematic. Wartime fiscal arrangements had centralized taxation, but political agreement would be necessary to extend them into the postwar period. Also necessary would be the capacity to shape the relations between capital and labour. Still other initiatives, especially in social policy and in regulation, remained within provincial jurisdiction. To achieve them would require some combination of transfers of power to the federal government, programs negotiated with the provinces, and independent provincial action. All three devices would be successfully employed in postwar Canada.

By early 1945, the Cabinet Committee on Reconstruction and the Committee on the Dominion-Provincial Conference had been merged to create the Committee on Dominion-Provincial Relations. This Committee identified two fundamental issues on which the federal government must find some sort of agreement at the upcoming Conference: the means of ensuring that the "intrusions" into provincial jurisdiction implied by the federal government's social policy proposals would not be *ultra vires*, and the means of retaining a level of fiscal centralization sufficient to make the tax system an effective instrument of Keynesian fiscal policy.

On August 6, 1945 the leaders of the two orders of government met in Ottawa. Prime Minister King opened the Conference by declaring that:

> The federal government is not seeking to weaken the provinces, to centralize all the functions of government, to subordinate one government to another, or to expand one government at the expense of others. Our aim is to place the Dominion and every province in a position to discharge effectively and independently its appropriate functions.
>
> (cited in Burns, 1980, p. 50)

King's ministers then outlined the federal proposals, known as the Green Book proposals, dealing with old age pensions, unemployment assistance and public health care. The federal government offered to assume full responsibility for a universal old age pensions scheme for those over 70 years of age; it would also meet half the costs of a means-tested scheme for those aged 65 to 69. Ottawa was also willing to accept all the costs entailed by an unemployment assistance scheme, which would extend coverage to three categories of unemployed hitherto ineligible for benefits (Guest, pp. 135-38).

The health care proposals were more complex, involving four distinct elements: federal grants for the planning and organization of provincial programs, financial assistance for hospital construction, a series of grants for specific public health services, and a health insurance program to be introduced in two stages. In the first stage, the federal government would assume 60 percent of the costs associated with the delivery of basic medical services: general practitioner care, hospital care and visiting nurse services. In the second stage, federal aid would be extended, again at the 60 percent rate, to more specialized medical services: consultants, specialists, surgery, dental care, pharmaceutical and laboratory costs (Taylor, 1978, pp. 50-67). This incremental approach to health care programs was a substantial departure from Ottawa's preference as late as the summer of 1944. The earlier strategy had made provincial acceptance of a model health care Act, drafted by the federal government, the precondition of provincial eligibility for federal grants. The more fragmented approach involved a less intrusive use of the federal spending power, considerably increasing provincial flexibility. It was hoped that this would make it easier to get provincial agreement by separating the substantive policy proposals as much as possible from larger questions of provincial autonomy and the division of powers (Taylor, pp. 41-46).

The income security and health care proposals were overshadowed by the controversy surrounding post-war fiscal arrangements (Taylor, p. 66). Ottawa's proposals, to last for a three-year trial period, were comparatively simple: it would provide unconditional subsidies at a rate of $12 per capita, increased or decreased with changes in the Gross National Product. The statutory subsidies granted at Confederation, no longer an important component of federal- provincial transfers, would be discontinued along with all other special payments and grants. The provinces were guaranteed an irreducible minimum of $138 million per year over the three years of the agreement, but it was estimated that their actual receipts in the first year of the new agreements would be $207 million, a figure substantially above the level which they had received in the war years (Burns, 1980, p. 52). In return, the provincial governments were to stay out of the personal and corporate income tax and succession duty fields, which they had vacated under the terms of the wartime "tax rental" agreements of 1941 and 1942.

The Green Book proposals thus followed the Rowell-Sirois Commission's recommendation concerning the tax sources to which the federal government should have exclusive access. But they departed substantially from the redistributive goals of Rowell-Sirois by rejecting its National Adjustment Grants, based on fiscal need rather than a percentage of actual revenues. Ottawa wished to avoid the anticipated objections of the richer provinces – Ontario, Quebec, and British Columbia – which had expressed their fundamental opposition to the National Adjustment Grant approach at the 1941 Dominion-Provincial Conference (Burns, 1980, p. 52, p. 59). However, the equal per capita payments, regardless of individual provincial tax bases, entailed a significant redistributive element. Ottawa also ignored Rowell-Sirois' preference for "watertight" compartments and its warnings against shared cost programs. These were at the heart of its pensions and health proposals; indeed, the shared cost program was to be the characteristic device of postwar federalism.

All premiers complained that the level of compensation proposed for the extension of the tax rental system was inadequate to the responsibilities the provinces would have to bear in the post-war period. Beyond this, their reactions diverged. The poorer provinces tended to support the broad thrust of the federal proposals. Saskatchewan's newly elected CCF government, represented by Premier Douglas, was perhaps the most articulate defender of their interests. Douglas expressed regret that the principles underpinning the National Adjustment Grant system had been abandoned, but he strongly supported the centralization of fiscal and monetary policy, and argued that only Ottawa could mount the new social policies successfully. Ontario, Quebec, and British Columbia, the three provinces with large enough tax bases to do without federal aid, were the most critical of the federal aim of retaining exclusive access to these major tax sources, but they presented no alternative scheme (Burns, pp. 58-59).

It was agreed to create a continuing coordinating committee, made up of federal and provincial finance ministers and officials, to consider the federal proposals in detail and develop provincial responses after the plenary conference ended on August 10, 1945. In January 1946 Ontario introduced an alternative plan that benefitted Ontario and Prince Edward Island, but left the rest of the provinces worse off than under the federal proposal. Only PEI seemed enthusiastic (Burns, pp. 64-66). The federal government countered with a number of concessions to specific provincial worries expressed in the discussions, seeking to sweeten the deal while retaining its essential features. The most important of these were an increase in the levels of per capita transfers, the retention of statutory subsidies, and the promise to limit federal utilization of certain types of tax fields (Burns, pp. 62-63).

Still, when the plenary conference reconvened on April 29, 1946, no agreement had been reached. Nor was one forthcoming in the next six days. British Columbia appeared willing to go along with the modified federal proposal, but Premier Drew of Ontario remained intransigent, holding to his January alternative proposal despite its lack of support from the other provinces. Premier Duplessis, as always, expressed his opposition in principle to any form of centralization but refrained from rejecting outright the federal proposals. Premier Drew of Ontario was thus able to scuttle the modified Green Book proposals single-handedly. R.M. Burns, assessing the reasons for the failure of the Conference, concludes that "while the Ontario government did not set out to sabotage the conference, it had no real concern with its success and was fully prepared to assume its role as a quasi-independent fiscal power within the Confederation" (1980, p. 71).

Unable to secure agreement on fiscal arrangements, progress on the federal government's income security and health care proposals was impossible. Federal leaders expressed their hope that agreement on taxation might yet be achieved and discussion of the social policy proposals revived. Their hopes would be realized, but not in the fashion imagined in the Green Book proposals.

Conclusions

Depression and war laid the foundation for both the post-war role of the state in Canada and for modern federalism. We have examined those elements of society and state – especially organized agriculture and labour, the CCF and the bureaucratic elites – that were the most important forces behind this new order. Organized labour and the CCF, inspired by foreign examples and successful in mobilizing growing public support, pushed the federal Liberal government to adopt new measures. The mandarins in Ottawa and, behind them, the economic theory and political philosophy of Keynes, persuaded King that these demands could be met without undermining the capitalist economy for which his party stood.

Keynesian theory freed the state, politicians and bureaucrats, from the zero-sum logic of the left and right political economic orthodoxies that prevailed in the interwar years. It enabled politicians and bureaucrats to legitimate the state economic intervention necessary to meet some of the basic demands of organized labour without alienating capital, thus providing the new orthodoxy upon which the post-war political economy of most advanced capitalist countries would be constructed:

> The idea that the best thing that government could do to promote recovery was to do nothing, the belief that a balanced budget was in all cases the goal for government fiscal policy, and beyond that the trust in the blind forces of the market inherently conducive to prosperity – all these once firmly held ideas of the past had been abandoned. The debate within capitalism was no longer whether or not government should undertake responsibility for the overall

> functioning of the market system; only the specific means were questioned: how
> best to achieve that end.
>
> (Heilbroner, 1974, p. 160)

In Canada, the legislative foundations of this new political economy were laid between 1944 and 1951. It was a strategy which, like the National Policy before it, was comprised of several interlocking components: counter-cyclical policy would ensure the full utilization of existing capacity; programs such as welfare and unemployment insurance would function as "automatic stabilizers" to this end; the recognition of trade union rights and social policies such as health care, would have some redistributive impacts, as well as contributing to higher domestic levels of effective demand than would otherwise exist; this source of economic growth would then be supplemented by sales to foreign markets.

There would be a large gap between the Keynesian orthodoxy and the policy reality: neither Canada nor the United States would pursue consistent counter-cyclical policies until the 1960s, and they would abandon them again in the early 1970s (Campbell, 1987, pp. 69-99, pp. 190-218). For this reason, we decline to call this the era of the Keynesian state. Keynesian theory and rhetoric is best understood as a necessary part of the new accommodation forged between labour, capital and the state. For, again like the National Policy, the new political economy was as much a political compromise as an economic strategy: full employment, labour rights and redistribution through social policies were the demands from the left that had to be met; the retention of private property and the continued "disciplining" of national organized labour by its situation within an international free market economy was the *quid pro quo* of the right.

The latter point was crucial, as Keohane (1984) and Martin (1986) have argued: the concessions to organized labour dramatically eroded the political and economic power of capital in the context of a closed, national economy. The key, therefore, was to reintroduce the competitive markets, unregulated by an interventionist state, at the global level. The Soviet Union, by seeking to develop trade ties and economic integration with Western Europe on a non-market basis, represented the greatest immediate threat to this strategy, and the Marshall Plan, along with the Cold War, were the principal means by which that threat was averted (Block, 1977; Krasner and Maier in Katzenstein, 1979). It seems appropriate, then, to call the new political economic strategy the International Policy.

Like the National Policy, the International Policy solved old problems, but in ways that created new ones. The long-term political consequences for national economies and their constituent groups of the new continental and global integration were not easy to foresee, but its immediate impact on the three traditional divisions (rupturing the linguistic accommodation of 1896 and permitting the construction of regional and class accommodations for the first time) was evident to all. The effort to rebuild the linguistic accommodation through constitutional reforms to federalism, and to maintain the post-war class and regional accommodations in the face of changes in the international economy which had enormous implications for domestic economic linkages, would dominate the political agenda for the next 50 years.

But all this lay in the future. In 1945, provincial opposition had blocked federal economic and social policy initiatives judged essential to the successful implementation of the International Policy in Canada. It was clear that the classical federalism of watertight compartments would come to an end; it was equally clear that Canada would not become a unitary state. What remained unclear, after the failure of the Reconstruction Conferences, was how federalism would be reconciled with the expanded role of the state that the International Policy required.

PART IV

The Development of Modern Federalism

Chapter 7

Introduction: Federalism and Modernization

The Great Depression starkly underlined the limited capacity of a decentralized federal state to respond to economic crisis. Then the war years provided both the need and the opportunity for the state to play a new set of roles under federal leadership. The central question for the reconstruction era was, therefore, how would the institutions of federalism adapt to the expectations foreshadowed by depression and war? Would federalism become obsolete, remaining nothing more than a vestige of an earlier Canadian society and an earlier conception of the role of government? Or, conversely, would the rigidities of federalism act as an obstacle to the new order, causing an ever-widening rift between political institutions and the character and needs of the post-war society?

Neither extreme prevailed. Federalism shaped the means by which Canada implemented the new order. However, the inability of the federal and provincial governments to agree on the centralizing initiatives outlined in the Green Book proposals did not reduce the social and economic pressures underpinning the commitment to a new National Policy. There was no possibility of a return to the pre-war *status quo*. Nor could the burden of meeting the new commitments be borne by provincial governments. Most contemporary observers agreed that only the federal government was capable of implementing the new policies in a coherent and effective fashion.

So, in contrast to the events following World War I, the initiative for undertaking new programs in Canada did not flow back to the provinces. The foundations of social security in Canada – family allowances, old age security and unemployment insurance – were initiated and financed by the federal government. But other important components of the welfare state – education, social services and health care – remained largely provincial responsibilities. In short, the adoption of new roles for the state was achieved not by the dominance of the central government but by the collaboration of both orders of government, federal and provincial, in the Canadian state. Indeed, federal initiatives were frequently implemented by provincial governments and federal policies were often crucially influenced by provincial governments and officials.

This intermediate response to the problems of post-war federalism was implemented primarily through tax collection agreements negotiated with each province and the extensive use of conditional shared-cost grants from the federal to the provincial governments. This system was, of course, less centralized than that of the quasi-unitary state of the war years. But the federation remained more centralized – in terms of federal control over taxation, share of total government spending and leadership in the development and implementation of new policies – than it had been since Macdonald and the original National Policy. The new National Policy "assigned the provinces a subordinate role in the Canadian federal system" (Smiley, 1970, p. 18). "Cooperative federalism" assumed federal leadership.

This approach had important implications for the evolution of Canadian federalism. The Canadian welfare state evolved more slowly and less systematically than would have been the case under the Green Book proposals, but it grew despite the continued opposition of Duplessis' Quebec. In the process, federalism moved inexorably away from the classical model of "watertight" jurisdictional compartments, towards high levels of jurisdictional overlap and policy interdependence. The fact that federalism responded to new needs through informal accommodations, rather than through constitutional amendment, meant that centralization was never fully institutionalized. It could quickly be reversed when the underlying forces began to push in a more centrifugal direction.

To understand the evolution of federalism in the years following the reconstruction decade, we must look to the forces which determined its form in the beginning. Again, we argue that changes at the societal level were the most important factors. These included the extent to which territorially defined divisions were displaced or transcended by other types of cleavages, the extent to which newly mobilized groups would be organized along provincial rather than national lines, the evolution of Canadian conceptions of social justice and the balance between national and sub-national political identities.

In the first decade following World War II most observers considered renewed decentralization of Canadian federalism, by whatever means, to be no more than a theoretical possibility. "Modernization" and "integration" theorists claimed that the gradual removal of the barriers to the free movement of people, capital, goods and ideas would reduce regional and cultural differences within and between nations. The resulting increased interdependence, they argued, would require an ever expanding scale of government to encompass it. Business, organized increasingly on a national and international scale, would likewise be compelled to think in wider terms and to seek the orderly markets and financial stability that only a national government could provide. The same logic applied to organized labour. The increased importance of scientific, professional and technical knowledge would be at variance with, if not hostile to, the particular cultural considerations associated with territorial politics. As Samuel Beer argued:

> In the United States, as in other modernizing societies, the general historical record has spelled centralization...[T]he main reasons for this change are...to be found in the new forces produced by an advanced modernity.
> (Modernization, p. 52)

Regional and linguistic conflicts, rooted in "outmoded" allegiances to sub-national political communities, were expected to wither away. With modernization, class was expected to become the principal dividing line in society. The intensity of class conflicts would be limited, however, by increasing affluence, the relative growth of the middle class and the increasing heterogeneity of both capital and labour. It was to be the era of the "end of ideology", in which "the great issues of politics are no longer the great issues, if indeed they ever were" (Dahl and Lindblom, 1953). Politics would be about bargaining over how to divide a growing pie in what S. M. Lipset called "the democratic class struggle" (1960, Ch. 7).

If cultural and regional differences initially made federalism necessary, and subsequently determined the acceptable degree of centralization, then the erosion of these differences, the theorists argued, might be expected to result in the steady centralization of Canadian federalism. Federalism, which emphasizes and reinforces territorial politics, would be increasingly at odds with a society organized around alternative concepts of identity and interest, in which different cleavages would predominate. In 1957, Alex Corry suggested with some regret that federalism, which depends on a balance between provincial and national loyalties, might now be obsolete (1958, p, 99). A decade earlier, F. R. Scott had made a similar observation, and applauded the prospect of a federalism more in keeping with Macdonald's aspiration, to create a federalism "freed from the doctrine of state's rights, which had so largely contributed to the American civil war" (1947, p. 25).

Such sociological trends were reinforced by the logic of the new economic functions which the state would assume. They would require the concentration of financial resources in the hands of central governments. This fiscal power was expected to be "an effective device for control and initiative from the centre" which would "seriously limit provincial autonomy" and "starve areas of provincial jurisdiction in which the federal government is not interested". Provincial governments would be unable to do much planning because they could not know "when the lightning of federal generosity is likely to strike next" (Mallory, in Crépeau and Macpherson, p. 9, p. 11). In a similar vein, A.R.M. Lower concluded that

> Cooperative federalism, with its virtually total interweaving of federal and provincial finances, might well be a way-station on the road to a unitary state. But does not every tendency of the time...drive us closer to this unitary state?
>
> (Lower, 1958, p. 48)

Whether or not federalism would entirely disappear, it was clear to Alex Corry that in the future:

> A province cannot hope to run successfully against the tide of national development... . The most it can hope to hold is freedom for minor adventure, for embroidering its own particular patterns in harmony with the national design. It can hope to be free to decide to have rather more public ownership and rather less public enterprise, more or less social security and provincial regulation of economic life. It can hope to adjust policy on education and conservation of natural resources to distinctive provincial needs and aims, and so on. But it is everywhere limited in the distance it can go by being part of a larger, though not necessarily a better, scheme of things. Its own role now is to lighten the curse of bigness.
>
> (1958, p. 108)

The modernization theorists – Beer, Scott, Corry, Lower, Mallory and others – were wrong, at least in the short run. Canadian political developments after 1958 were characterized by increasing levels of federal-provincial conflict and decreasing levels of centralization. One of our tasks in the following chapters is to show why this was so.

Our position, simply stated, is that the modernization theorists were correct in identifying the economic and sociological trends which they lumped under the heading of "modernity" – industrialization, urbanization, secularization, class formation and so on – as the most important determinants of the evolution of the role of the state. They were also correct in anticipating the changing role of the state and that this would require major changes in the character of federalism. Modernization theorists were mistaken, however, in assuming that current trends could be extrapolated indefinitely in a linear fashion. As neo-marxist theorists and others have since argued, the very progress of those tendencies which the modernization theorists identified gave rise to tensions or "contradictions" which had the effect of limiting or even counteracting and reversing those trends. They have generally assumed that the only level at which such contradictions will arise in industrial capitalist democracies is at the level of class identities and interests. In this respect, they share a second assumption of modernization theory: that the new identities, interests and ideologies, outgrowths of modern capitalist social relations, would simply displace those which had preceded them.

It is our contention that the displacement assumption is as inaccurate as the assumption of linear or teleological social evolution. Rather than being displaced, older bases of collective identity have been interwoven into the new ones in complex ways. Personal identity is a more-or-less coherent amalgam of the past, the present and the projected future; it is not a thin slice of immediate concerns and objectives. It is more accurate, therefore, to speak of the interweaving of older and newer identities than of the systematic, mechanical displacement of old identities by new ones. This interweaving is even more true for groups, policies and political institutions. Moreover, it is clear that modernizing forces may intensify rather than erode regional differences, especially when such forces press on an already highly regionalized society, with strong regional identities.

In the context of the Canadian state and society, the evolving synthesis has exhibited different dynamics in different regions and at different times. The dominant form of Quebec nationalism throughout the 1950s, for example, remained locked in its anti-statist form, with the provincial government fighting a rear-guard action against the new agenda championed by Ottawa. By the 1960s, however, its dominant strand had become secular and reformist, embracing the new economic and social agenda, but seeking to attain it through the provincial state. In this form it challenged anglophone dominance of both the economy and the distribution of power in the federal state. By the 1980s, declining faith in the efficacy of the state as the principal instrument of national development had partially undermined this state-based nationalism, and another phase in the evolution of Quebec nationalism had begun.

A somewhat different pattern of evolution characterized regional and provincial identities in the western and Atlantic provinces. In these regions, as in Quebec, "traditional" bases of collective identity remained strong throughout the post-war period. But in contrast to Quebec the substance of these collective identities remained comparatively unchanged, oriented as always around a sense of their economic and political role within the federation and of what constitutes a fair division of labour and rewards between the regions.

During the reconstruction decade, when the new National Policy was perceived by most in both Atlantic and western Canada to be a major step toward a more just economic order, the persistence of strong regional identities was compatible with a decline in both regional protest parties and in levels of federal-provincial conflict. At the margin, it appears to have been consistent even with the idea of abolishing federalism. (One opinion poll conducted by Gallup in 1945 suggested that, regardless of region, most English Canadians would accept the abolition of federalism.) At that time, the federal government was viewed as being favourably disposed to the interests of regional development, and was thought to be the only government capable of effectively achieving it. Provincial governments, therefore, became less relevant as defenders of regional interests against the exploitative power of a federal government dominated by central Canadian interests.

By the early 1970s, however, a federal politics oriented primarily toward Quebec combined with major changes in oil and gas prices to revive the sense of alienation from the federal government and disatisfaction with the political economy. The turn to provincial governments as defenders of regional interests was quick, and federal-provincial conflict escalated to its highest level since the Great Depression. By 1982 further changes in economic circumstances resulted in declining intergovernmental conflict and renewed concern with regional representation at the centre. Thus, the logic of how best to defend and advance the interests of provincial communities and to reconcile them with other dimensions of individual identity and commitment changed in response to changes in material circumstances.

The persistence of older bases of identity also helps to account for the ways in which the new agenda took root in Canada. It meant a stronger labour movement would remain divided by regional and linguistic identities. It meant that social democratic parties, the CCF and later the NDP, would have great difficulty building support in Quebec and the Maritimes and would therefore be unable to challenge the two traditional parties at the national level. It also meant that in provinces less divided by regional and linguistic differences, organized labour and social democratic parties could enjoy greater success. Still, as long as these conditions of success varied significantly across regions, there could be no unequivocal national move toward the "creative" class politics predicted by John Porter and Gad Horowitz. If the increased strength of organized labour and social democracy increased the political importance of redistributive issues, many Canadians would remain more comfortable discussing them in regional and linguistic terms than in the language of class.

Much of the tension within Canadian politics in the postwar period can be understood as a debate between contending principles for the organization of political life. Each set of principles is rooted in differing conceptions of which interests or identities are most important. Is politics mainly about class and class interests? Region and Provincial interests? Language and linguistic interests? Or something else, such as religion or gender? The answers have vital implications for institutional structure and practice, for policy prescriptions, for party ideologies and much more. Each entails its own internal logic, each is an alternative "axis" around which politics can be organized. In the fifties and sixties, left-oriented observers such as Porter lamented the "obsession" of Canadian politics with federalism and national unity, viewing them as barriers to the full emergence of class politics. More recently, a variety of movements – feminists, advocates of native rights and multicultural groups, for example – have condemned federalism for its preoccupation with language and region and for its reliance on processes such as intergovernmental decision making, which leave little or no room for their input and participation.

Despite these clashing conceptions of the central dynamics of politics, predictions of the disappearance of regional interests or of dramatic centralization were confounded. Nevertheless, the intensity of regional conflict, the forms in which it was expressed, and the issues around which it crystallized all fluctuated considerably. The reasons for such fluctuations are subtle and complex; they are a result of the efforts of the major social actors to mobilize populations around their definitions of the crucial interests, and of the economic and institutional resources they can deploy in this effort. In these struggles older groups changed, and new ones struggled to emerge. The results had crucial implications for federalism. For example, the struggles in Quebec between traditional conservative catholicism and an emerging more secular force, including a more powerful labour movement, led to the triumph of a modernizing state-based nationalism which radically altered and intensified conflicts between Quebec and Ottawa.

To take another example, the experience of war and depression led to a broad concensus on the need to construct in Canada, as elsewhere, the Keynesian welfare state. The interests this project reflected and promoted were linked much more to people's economic or class interests than to their regional position. The issues of the welfare state did not, in themselves, divide Ontarions and British Columbians; they did not engage regional identities. While federalism was a critical factor in the building of the welfare state, as we shall see, federal-provincial conflict was muted in the years after World War II. By contrast, many of the economic developments of the 1970s exacerbated and promoted regional differences. Accordingly, the dominant issues of the period energized regional identities and then contributed directly to intense federal-provincial conflict.

Thus exogenous events arising from Canada's position in the North American and global political economies had a direct effect on the interests, goals, strategies and bargaining power of domestic groups, and therefore on federal-provincial relationships. By far the most important of these external forces was the growing economic integration with the United States which strengthened north-south linkages while eroding east-west ones.

The final set of factors central to the post-war developments in federalism was the rapid growth of the state.

Postwar population and urban growth precipitated a massive expansion of education at all levels – health services and urban infrastructures such as roads, parks and the like – all of which were primarily the responsibility of provincial and local authorities. The growth of government in postwar Canada, therefore, occurred at both levels. Indeed, throughout the period the rate of growth of provincial-municipal spending exceeded that of the federal government. In some cases, provincial governments also sought to develop thorough-going industrial policies which, relative to their size, were more ambitious than those of the federal government. While provincial and local civil servants represented half the Canadian total in 1946, they constituted approximately two thirds by 1966.

This rapid growth of both orders of government in Canada had several important implications. First, the proliferation of new policies dramatically increased the level of policy interdependence which characterizes Canadian federalism. The interweaving of a growing number of policy areas meant that there was an increasing tendency for policies developed by one order of government to spill over into other jurisdictions. This reduced Ottawa's ability to act unilaterally without impinging on the plans and policies of provincial governments. Similarly, provincial actions often had national ramifications. Increasingly, the federal government found itself in the position of having to consult, coordinate and, inevitably, compromise or face mounting federal-provincial conflict; the declining efficacy of a federal system that increasingly required intergovernmental good will to function coherently.

Thus, postwar federalism can be viewed through the same analytic prism used in the earlier discussion of the prewar period. The central focus of the postwar period is the interaction between politically mobilized collective identities organized around the major cleavages. The intensity of conflict and the forms and outcomes of this conflict are shaped by international forces and driven by economic and social structural changes. They are also influenced by the power and strategies of competing domestic collective actors each trying to protect or advance its interests under changed circumstances, and by the federal and parliamentary institutions within which this competition takes place. The follwing chapters chronicle the development, and subsequent unravelling, of two sets of policies, each of which was designed to reconcile conflicts along the major fault lines of Canadian society. First is the "historic compromise" among capital, labour and business according to the outlines of the Keynesian welfare state. The second, closely linked, is the accommodation between regional and national interests, and between the federal and provincial governments, embodied in "cooperative" federalism.

There are parallels between these two sets of accommodations or bargains. Both emerged from depression and war. Both enjoyed remarkable success for a generation. Both were constructed under highly favourable domestic and international circumstances. Both provided a formula for reconciling fundamental differences.

The Keynesian welfare state sought to promote both economic efficiency and economic justice on the assumption that workers' and capitalists' interests were fundamentally compatible. Similarly, cooperative federalism sought to promote aggregate national growth and regional sharing on the assumption that growth in accordance with market allocation processes was ultimately compatible with regional economic development. Both, in Canada, were the product of a complex mixture of popular mobilization and elite bargaining. Each supported, but also constrained, the other. Cooperative federalism was the essential vehicle for attaining the Keynesian welfare state, but also affected its timing and scope. In turn, the economic and social success of the new state policies helped sustain the conditions for cooperative federalism.

By the 1970s, both were unravelling. Critics of both left and right argued that social and economic changes had generated tensions and contradictions in the Keynesian welfare state which could no longer be papered over. At the economic level, writers talked of the "fiscal crisis of the state", at the political level they talked of "overloaded governments" and the "crisis of governability"; at the ideological level they talked of a "crisis of legitimation" (O'Connor; Huntington et al; Habermas; Offe). Whatever their differences, critics agreed that the Keynesian *middle way* was obsolete and that the only options were to move toward increased state regulation of the economy and society, or toward reduced state intervention in a more *laissez-faire* system (Goldthorpe in Goldthorpe, 1984). As a result, the apparently irreconcilable differences which had dominated the political economic orthodoxies of the left and right during the 1930s began to reappear.

The developing crisis of the role of the state in the early '70s translated into a crisis of federalism. The growth of government had already multiplied the potential for intergovernmental contradiction, duplication and mutual frustration. Intensified linguistic and regional conflicts were also being addressed in the context of growing disagreement as to the fundamental priorities of the state and the best means of carrying them out within a federal system. So long as there was consensus on building the Keynesian welfare state, managing intergovernmental interdependence was an essentially technical problem, allowing always for the exception of Quebec. In this new context, however, it became an intensely political, and ultimately a constitutional, problem.

Again, common factors were at work to unravel the two accomodations. On the one hand there was a less favourable international environment. On the other hand, domestic social changes were widening the gap that the accommodations had to bridge. Moreover, new grounds of identity (gender, environmentalism, etc), were emerging with corresponding new definitions of the political agenda and challenges to older institutions. As the old accommodations disintegrated, increasingly polarized programs for the future were articulated, whether "neo-conservative" versus "interventionist" or "centralist" versus "provincialist" This polarization, in turn, led to the search for new bases of accommodation.

By the early 1970s the preconditions for cooperative federalism no longer existed. By then federalism was characterized by a growing tension and preoccupation with the politics of region and language and increasing federal-provincial conflict and decentralization.

In Chapters 9 and 10, devoted to the years 1958 to 1973, and 1974 to 1982, we describe these shifts. Finally, our analysis of the period 1984 to 1988 in Chapter 11 shows both the culmination of the constitutional evolution of the period and the dilemmas posed by this evolution. Both these aspects are evident in the debates on "National Reconciliation" and on the Meech Lake Accord. But first we must examine the decade of unprecedented peacetime centralization and harmony during which modern federalism was constructed.

Chapter 8

Construction of Modern Federalism, 1947-57

The rejection of the Green Book proposals did not reduce the pressure on the federal government to implement the International Policy. Alternative means had to be found, and in the reconstruction decade the two orders of government succeeded in finding them. In retrospect this task looks easier than it actually was. Creative solutions were reached that made it possible for class and regional accommodations to be maintained. But finding such solutions is an uncertain and often harrowing business. Many a union leader and government official was purged amidst Cold War fears and allegations. Duplessis fought a determined and bitter holding action against the expansion of the central government, although ultimately his defensive posture limited its effectiveness. It was hardly an epoch of peace and harmony.

Still, it was a time when the federal government could generally count on the support of nine of the ten provincial governments, and at least two thirds of the population, for its most important goals. The image of bold new federal initiatives combined with high levels of federal-provinical cooperation has given the Reconstruction decade the same golden age status in the hearts of advocates of strong central government as the Tremblay Commission, the great defender of classical federalism, reserved for the 1920s.

Federal Society

The rapid decline in government spending, combined with the increase in the civilian workforce associated with demobilization, had resulted in deflation and high unemployment after the Great War. Many expected a repeat performance following World War II. But while GNP fell briefly, it grew constantly thereafter, except for the short recession following the end of the Korean war in 1954. The real average GNP growth rate between 1947 and 1957 was 5.1 percent, and official unemployment averaged 3.2 percent. This was achieved with relatively low, though more widely fluctuating, inflation rates, ranging from a high of 14.4 percent in 1948 to a low of -0.9 percent in 1953 (Wolfe, 1984, p. 51).

This growth was associated with the same large-scale shift out of agriculture that the American and West European economies were experiencing. In the 1930s about one-third of the Canadian labour force was still employed in agriculture. By 1951, the ratio had fallen to 18.4 percent, and by 1961, to 11.2 percent. Agriculture's contribution to the total net value of production in Canada, while growing in absolute terms, fell from an average of 19.9 percent between 1935 and 1939 to an average of 8.5 percent between 1969 and 1973 (Gibbins, 1980, p. 78). There was a roughly equal increase in the size of the service sector, which out-grew the manufacturing sector both relatively and absolutely. Within the industrial sector the growth areas were natural resources, particularly the oil and gas industry after the discovery of the Leduc reserves in 1949, and automobile manufacturing (Brodie & Jenson, 1981, pp. 216-25).

These economic and demographic changes had important regional implications. The growth of the service sector took place in all regions, with the result that all provincial economies became more diversified. The decline of agriculture also changed the distribution of populations between country and city in all parts of Canada, so the agrarian population declined in size and political muscle throughout the country.

The impact of diversification and urbanization was probably greatest in the Prairie provinces. The region's share of all Canadian farms actually rose from 40 percent in 1941 to 48 percent in 1971. But within these provinces, the number of occupied farms fell 41 percent in the same period. By 1971, only 16 percent of the Prairie labour force was employed in agriculture, an average skewed toward the high side by Saskatchewan's 27 percent (Gibbins, 1980, p. 78). Between 1941 and 1951, many of those who left Prairie farms also left their provinces, resulting in a net out-migration of 268,000 people. The Prairies have never since equalled the 1931 peak when they held 23 percent of the Canadian population. Between 1951 and 1961, this outflow was reversed in Alberta by the impetus of the oil and gas boom, but continued in Saskatchewan (Gibbins, 1980, pp. 16-17, 66-67).

There was a dramatic movement out of agriculture in Quebec as well. In 1941, 41 percent of the population were rural farm residents; this was reduced to 13 percent by 1961 (Behiels, 1984, pp. 11-12). In the 1940s, most left the farms for the growing primary, natural resource industries. In the 1950s, however, the rural outflow shifted increasingly toward the secondary manufacturing and service sector jobs. This trend was associated with the rapid growth of cities, especially Montreal (Behiels, 1984, Ch.1).

The Atlantic provinces, which included Newfoundland after 1949, experienced some growth in their traditional staples, but nothing on the scale of western mineral resource expansion or central Canadian manufacturing growth. Consequently, disparities in average income before government transfers did not diminish in this period and outmigration of population was on an even larger scale than in the West.

British Columbia, Ontario and Quebec were the fastest growing provinces. For the first time since the 1920s, most of the new immigrants who now began arriving in large numbers settled in these provinces (Gibbins, 1980, pp. 71-72). Thus, despite the impressive aggregate figures, the regional incidence of economic growth in the period from 1947 to 1957 was very uneven. High growth rates in central Canada and the two most westerly provinces did not "trickle across" to poorer provinces and regions in such a way as to alter significantly their relative standards of living.

Class Conflict Restrained

Few within the labour movement believed that King's shift to the left went far enough. Morton and Copp estimate that, at war's end, at least a third of the CCL's members were organized in Communist-run unions. The proportion was lower in the TLC, but the Canadian Seaman's Union, also Communist led, was one of the most dynamic unions in that federation (Morton, 1984, p. 203; Palmer, 1983, pp. 245-52). Most rank and file members were not Communists, but they were more oriented to fundamental political change than ever before. The political demands of the CCL in 1945, in addition to the kinds of measures that King proposed, included social ownership of banking, insurance companies, war plants, coal mines and transportation (Williams, 1975, p. 184). Strike levels and union solidarity in 1946 and 1947 were unprecedented as organized labour sought, against determined employer resistance, to incorporate the major gains of the war years into their contracts (Easterbrook & Aitken, 1980, p. 570).

By 1948, however, the Canadian union movement was locked in an internecine struggle of unparalleled proportions. Class conflict had not come to an end in Canada; it was turned in upon itself. The federal government did not live up to its promise of deploying counter-cyclical fiscal and monetary policies to maintain high employment (Campbell, 1987, pp. 69-116, 190-97). Still, expanding international trade, particularly with the United States, and rising levels of American investment in Canada were sufficient to maintain rising standards of living and job security for most Canadian workers. Good economic times reduced the persuasiveness of radicals who argued that the system itself was unsound. This helped to shift the balance of power within the union movement in the direction of the CCF and, in some cases, more conservative elements.

The CCF-Communist struggles were bitter. In most unions, the United Auto Workers, for example, the CCF managed to push Communists out of leadership positions. Where such internal strategies proved ineffective, they turned to expulsion: the Mine-Mill Workers in 1947; the Seamen's Union and United Electrical Workers in 1949; the United Fishermen in 1954. In addition, thousands of workers were black-balled, not only by employers but by their former unions (Abella, 1973; Palmer, 1983, pp. 245-52; Morton, 1984, pp. 201-212).

While these struggles were going on, the labour movement continued to push hard for the extension of war-time gains in collective bargaining rights. Centrist federal and provincial governments, seeking to demonstrate that they were anti-Communist but not anti-union, generally responded with new labour laws. In 1948, federal legislation extended the P.C 1003 regime into the post-war period for the approximately 10 percent of the non-agricultural workforce deemed to remain under federal jurisdiction following the termination of the War Measures Act. By 1950, all provinces except PEI had implemented legislation incorporating the main lines of the federal law (Morton, 1984, pp. 196-97; Jamieson, 1968, pp. 293-94). In this more favourable legal environment, trade union membership rose from 29.1 percent in 1947 to its pre-1972 peak of 34.2 percent of paid non-agricultural workers in 1958 (Kumar, 1986, p. 109).

In the wake of the Communist expulsions, the movement's centre of political gravity shifted to the right. One casualty was probably the movement's level of commitment to organizing the rapidly expanding new sectors of the economy. Union growth in this period was concentrated in the industrial sectors – forestry, mining, construction, transporation and public utilities – pioneered by the CIO and Communist unions in the more militant 1930s and 1940s. These industries were largely organized by the mid-1950s. A concerted effort by the CCL to organize Eaton's department store employees between 1948 and 1951 ended in failure. No further efforts to expand into the private, white collar sector were made in this period (Morton, pp. 215-16). As a result, union density flattened out in the mid-1950s and did not rise again until the mid-1960s, when public sector workers (outside of Saskatchewan) were organized for the first time (Kumar, 1986, pp. 107-110).

In failing to coordinate a sustained push on white collar public and private sector workers, the most rapidly growing segments of the workforce, the union movement effectively conceded that it would represent only a minority of Canadian workers for the foreseeable future. This created an unnecessary (as Western European unions demonstrated in these years) ceiling on the economic and political power of the Canadian labour movement (Brodie & Jenson, 1980, pp. 226-27).

A further consequence of the shift to the right was the failure to develop and promote an alternative conception of the political system among even the minority of Canadian workers who were union members. In its absence, as Brodie and Jenson observe, workers tended to view themselves and their unions as just another economic interest group, and the CCF as "Liberals-in-a-hurry" (Brodie & Jenson, 1980, pp. 1-17, 226-52). Thus, while organized workers were much more likely to support the CCF than other voters in this period, the majority of them still voted for one of the traditional parties (Brodie & Jenson, p. 250-51). At the same time, the CCF was losing its traditional pillar of support – the farmers – especially in the West. By the 1957 federal election, the CCF had been reduced to 10 seats in Saskatchewan and five in Manitoba. A year later, in the Diefenbaker sweep, their support fell to a single Saskatchewan seat (Gibbins, 1980, p. 112).

The disinclination to organize new sectors meant that if unions wanted to grow, the growth would have to be at each other's expense. This had been acceptable to the mainstream leadership as long as there were Communist unions to raid, but when this pool had been exhausted the costs of raiding became intolerable. The TLC unions had already abandoned their craft principles in the scramble to capture the benefits of war-time industrial expansion, thus eliminating one of the old reasons for maintaining separate federations. Pressures to eliminate raiding therefore mounted in a context while the barriers to merger fell. The result was the creation of the Canadian Labour Congress (CLC) in 1955 (Morton, 1984, pp. 216-17, 222-24).

The merger was also facilitated by a compromise on another old source of dissension, political partisanship: the CLC would create a political education department, one of its tasks being "the creation of a new party linked to trade unions, cooperatives, farmer organizations and other progressive blocks" (Palmer, 1983, p. 254). The 1958 CLC Convention voted to bring about a "fundamental re-alignment of political forces in Canada", and three years later the New Democratic Party was born (Morton, 1984, pp. 237-38). But the re-alignment did not take place in this period, or in the next.

Regional Conflict Muted

The Maritime and western provinces had always viewed the original National Policy as a form of state intervention which structured the national economy against their regions' interests. Ottawa's commitment to a freer international trade regime signalled the beginning of the end of one cornerstone of the old National Policy – the system of tariffs protecting central Canadian manufacturers. Moreover, Ottawa's new social programs would not only benefit individuals, but also would help protect the regional communities to which they belonged from the worst effects of international commodity price fluctuations. This would reduce the advantages of the two central Canadian provinces in the competition to provide their citizens with a minimum of social and economic security. Thus, the International Policy was widely perceived to be economically advantageous and fair in these regions. Moreover, as with organized labour, any elements that did not accept this diagnosis were marginalized and unable to mobilize effectively. As a result, there was no equivalent of the Maritime Rights movement that had followed the First World War. Perhaps more strikingly, after a few battles between Ottawa and the new Saskatchewan CCF government, federal-provincial conflict in the prairies also subsided.

The end of the war brought economic and demographic decline to the Atlantic provinces, just as it had in 1918. But there was still no class base from which a powerful third party movement paralleling the farmers in the West could arise. In the absence of third parties, the political reaction to this decline focussed on demands for a more equitable distribution of the national benefits of the economic union through increased transfers from the federal government. The commitment of the King government to the expansion of the welfare state – and the implicit equalization contained in the formulae by which it calculated Maritime entitlements under the tax rental agreements – went further than any federal government had hitherto gone toward meeting these demands. So the Atlantic provinces were strong supporters of federal power and initiative.

Newfoundland was the most striking example of the coincidence of a powerful regional identity and federal-provincial harmony. A colony of Britain prior to 1949, its inhabitants had a deep sense of their uniqueness as a political community. So deep, indeed, that the 1949 referendum on the question of union with Canada was very close. Joey Smallwood, leader of the pro-union forces, was primarily interested in modernizing the economy and extending to Newfoundlanders the social benefits associated with the Canadian welfare state. The colony did not possess the tax base to support such programs, which left him committed to a central government strong enough to capture and redistribute to his province a significant share of the benefits of the economic union. Smallwood became the Premier of

Canada's tenth province, with close ties to the federal Liberal party. Both Smallwood and the federal Liberals remained in office for the remainder of the Reconstruction decade. So, despite their strong sense of community, most Newfoundlanders' sense of what was in the best interests of their community and what constituted a fair deal with the rest of Canada, was such that regional interests and values were not seen to be in conflict with Ottawa's imperatives.

On the Prairies, the old stronghold of third parties and their agitations against the National Policy, several factors were shunting politics onto a less conflictual track. The agrarian class declined in size and political clout, relative to the total Prairie population. At the same time, those farmers who remained enjoyed improved economic fortunes: good crop prices, falling tariff barriers and new social programs made life considerably easier for them. The shift into the service sector along with the oil and gas boom produced more diversified provincial economies. This took some of the fire out of claims that Ottawa would never permit Prairie economic development and, hence, that provincial governments must acquire the economic resources and constitutional powers necessary to stimulate diversification. The new industrial and white collar classes, in turn, favoured the new federal policies which had helped to bring them into existence and appeared to guarantee their continued prosperity. The degree to which this picture held true varied considerably from one province to the next. These differences are reflected in provincial electoral politics and in government policies.

In Manitoba, the Conservatives deserted the union government coalition in 1950 but the Liberal-Progressive alliance remained in power until 1958, when the provincial Conservatives were able to capitalize on the momentum of the Diefenbaker sweep to displace the Liberals at the provincial level. There was, however, no major change in policy orientation in 1950 or in 1958. Successive Manitoba governments supported the International Policy (Gibbins, 1980, p. 126).

In Alberta, the Social Credit party rode the oil and gas boom from one electoral success to the next. The provincial government was content to allow foreign private investors to develop and sell the resource. By no means all Albertans agreed, but with an average of 51 percent of the popular vote, the Socreds were able to secure an average of 84 percent of the seats in the legislature between 1935 and 1967 (Gibbins, 1980, pp. 136-37). Ottawa, having transferred control over the development of natural resources to Alberta and Saskatchewan in 1930, encouraged the Alberta government to pursue a development strategy that fit well into its own market-led approach. There was little Ottawa-Alberta rancour.

The same cannot be said of Saskatchewan, where the CCF remained in power throughout this period, retaining more of the old agrarian protest agenda. The ratio of farmers to other occupations was more than twice that of the other two Prairie provinces, and the rate of population decline higher (Gibbins, p. 66, p. 78). The two statistics were closely related: without a more diversified economy, moving off the farms meant moving out of the province. The costs of relocation for those remaining behind in the rural communities, with diminished human resources and tax bases, were high. In this less happy economic context, the pressures on government to play a more interventionist role were greater. The CCF responded to them and, as a result, there were more policy areas in which its activities came into conflict with those of Ottawa.

Saskatchewan was the polar case, however, and even there provincial government activism and associated conflicts with Ottawa died down after 1948. Poor economic performance by many of its public corporations, as well as constitutional battles lost to Ottawa, fed doubts concerning the capacity of the provincial government to manage large-scale economic development. Cold War anti-socialist propaganda also eroded support for more interventionist CCF policies. The urban working class continued to support the CCF in the 1948 provincial election, but there were losses in rural areas. While the CCF retained its legislative majority, its share of the vote fell from 53 percent in 1944 to 48 percent in 1948. It pursued a more conservative strategy for the remainder of this period, consolidating existing programs and focussing on social policy initiatives that led it to look for fiscal support, rather than policy autonomy, from Ottawa (Conway, 1983, pp. 168-71).

These changes in the orientation and assumptions of Western provincial politics were also reflected in federal electoral results. The national CCF became more and more a party of the urban blue collar workers and less a party of the farmers, in the West as much as in the East (Brodie & Jenson, 1980, p. 250). The federal elections of 1957 and 1958 might, at first glance, appear to indicate growing regional disenchantment with Ottawa. But, as Gibbins (1980) points out, the 1957 election was won not in the West, but in Ontario, where the Tories captured 39 percent of the popular vote and 61 of 85 seats. The Tories captured only 29 percent of the prairie vote, and 14 of 40 seats, a result of the continued strength of third party support, which averaged 43 percent across the three prairie provinces. So, while the Tories significantly improved their standing as compared with their fortunes since 1935, it was mainly at the expense of the Liberals.

This shift did not reflect a growing disenchantment with the federal government, but with Liberal arrogance, coupled with fondness for a native son articulating an appealing vision of national politics (Gibbins, 1980, pp. 99-100, 103). David Smith agrees:

He gave to the Prairies for the first time in their history the same sense of dynamic and central participation in nation-building that his predecessor, John A. Macdonald, had given to central Canada after 1867.... John Diefenbaker's policies, when he came into power in 1957, were policies of national integration that typified the Prairie conception of Canada. His emphasis upon 'unhyphenated Canadianism' reflected 50 years of watching the new community in its efforts to find its own character by assimilating its disparate national elements into a single, dominant, English-speaking personality.

(cited in Gibbins, p. 104)

The 1958 federal election represented a decisive realignment of party support on the prairies but, again, it was not inspired by a decentralizing or provincialist thrust. On the contrary, it was a movement away from regional protest parties toward full fledged support for one of the national parties, particularly by the farmers. Ever since 1958 the Conservative Party has reaped most of the benefits of this shift.

Conservative Quebec Nationalism Entrenched

If class and regional cleavages were less salient in these years, the same cannot be said of language. The Union nationale remained in power throughout the period in spite of the rapid social changes brought about by war and post-war economic expansion. The ideological knitting together of the various elements of francophone Quebec that supported the UN did not change. Duplessis continued to portray the expanded role of the federal government as morally deplorable and constitutionally invalid, and his party as the most effective defender of provincial autonomy against federal incursions. Consistent with this position on the appropriate role of the state, Duplessis refused to use the provincial government to channel societal change within Quebec in directions more compatible with the values which he claimed to defend. As Duplessis put the matter in response to demands by a trade union delegation for increases in government old age pensions in 1951, "Le meilleur système est encore celui qui dépend le moins de l'Etat" (in Quinn, 1979, p. 84).

Duplessis came under increasing cricicism from two perspectives that sought to modernize and democratize Quebec. The reformist wing of Quebec nationalism, led by figures such as André Laurendeau, with the support of the editors of Le Devoir and L'Action nationale, sought to redefine nationalism, to render it compatible with an expanded, secular Quebecois nation-state. The anti-nationalists, led by figures such as Pierre Trudeau and Gerard Pelletier, and centered on the small but influential journal Cité libre, argued that only by discarding nationalism itself could Quebec break free of a stultifying past. The two factions were allies against Duplessis on many of the major social and political issues of the day, although they would part company almost as soon as they had defeated Duplessis' political vision (Behiels, 1984).

If the Quiet Revolution of the 1960s is understood as a sudden movement by the Quebec state to adopt the more active role endorsed by both reformist elements, why, given the same economic forces that affected Ontario, did it fail to change in 1945 or earlier? Two further questions follow: why was Duplessis so adamantly opposed to an extended government role in Quebec and how was he able to maintain sufficient electoral support to retain political power for so long?

Duplessis' position on the role of the state was the product of two important factors. Conservative Catholic social thought in the province held that the state's role in education and social welfare should be confined to supplementing the efforts of private institutions, led by the Church (Coleman, 1984, pp. 46-64). Duplessis' willingness to support this view won him the political backing of this section of the Church. By refusing to extend the economic activities of the state, except intervening to limit the effectiveness of organized labour, Duplessis also secured the financial and political support of many elements of English-dominated business and industry. The support of these two powerful forces explains in part how he was able to maintain power, even though his position on economic matters was rejected by the growing progressive wing of the Church. Similarly, his educational policies and his attitude toward civil liberties were antithetical to the liberal sentiments of the English-speaking business elite and such influential intellectuals as F.R. Scott and P.E. Trudeau.

Given Duplessis' strenuous and consistent opposition to the trade unions and the growing militance of their leadership in this period (Quinn, pp. 91-97), alternative coalitions, with organized labour at their core, seem plausible. The progressive wing of the Catholic church had been supporting the unions against Duplessis since the Asbestos strike of 1949. To this, an anti-Duplessis party might have added a large segment of the agrarian class, so as to form the francophone equivalent of the CCF. Or it might have drawn support from the English and French liberal professions by stressing Duplessis' lack of respect for civil rights and the rule of law.

Duplessis recognized the possibility of a francophone version of the CCF and cultivated the support of farmers with an extensive programme of rural assistance and praise for their role as the privileged bearers of the values of ancient Quebec. This strategy succeeded in making rural Quebec the most reliable basis of Union nationale support. Of the 51 predominantly rural constituencies in a National Assembly of 92 or 93 seats, Duplessis never lost more than six to the Liberals in the elections of 1948, 1952 and 1956 (Quinn, p. 98). This rural bloc alone would have been sufficient to keep Duplessis in power as long as its effect was exaggerated by the electoral system. As urbanization increased and constituency boundaries remained unchanged, rural over-representation steadily increased. By 1951, the 33 percent of the population that lived in rural Quebec controlled 55 percent of the seats in the National Assembly (Quinn, p. 85).

Moveover, Duplessis was able to obtain 45 percent or more of the vote in working class districts in every election he fought (Quinn:101). Why did so many working class voters support a party that became increasingly anti-labour in the 1950s? Quinn argues that nationalist allegiances out-weighed class interests for this segment of Quebec workers (Quinn, p. 102). McRoberts and Posgate, on the other hand, argue that the Liberals' position on labour issues was little better, so that Duplessis did not need nationalism to compensate for a relatively poor labour position. They locate the success of the Union nationale in Duplessis' populism – his ability to speak effectively in the vernacular, and his cultivation of anti-bourgeois sentiments among workers and farmers. To this are added the advantages of a governing party with no compunctions about the extensive use of patronage, and the rapid economic growth of this period, which made it easier to ignore those who criticized its economic policies (McRoberts & Posgate, 1980, pp. 81-85).

Both analyses are plausible as accounts of why some workers supported the UN, but they take for granted the existence of a two party system when this is part of what has to be explained. A left nationalist party was not unthinkable – the position articulated by Laurendeau, for example, could have become the platform for such a party. But it did not receive the financial and political support that it would have needed to counter the Duplessis political machine effectively. For the reasons noted above, the only source of such support would have been the trade unions, which represented about 32 percent of industrial wage earners by 1951, compared with 20 percent in 1941 (Quinn, p. 292). But despite their impressive aggregate growth, Quebec's trade unions remained divided and incapable of concerted action. The Catholic CTCC and the industrial unions affiliated with the CCL staunchly opposed Duplessis from the Asbestos strike of 1949. But the craft unions affiliated with the TLC remained favourable to the UN in the 1952 and the 1956 elections (McRoberts & Posgate, 1980, p. 85). Threatened by the rapid expansion of the CCL unions after 1935 – and by the CTCC as well after the sweeping changes in leadership and the more radical intepretation of Catholic social philosophy which it adopted in 1946 – the TLC affiliates remained the largest of the three elements of organized labour in this period and looked to the Duplessis government as an ally in fending off the gains being made by other unions (Quinn, pp. 86-90, pp. 121-22, p. 157).

In the absence of an effective political opposition elements of the labour movement, along with their potential coalition allies, tried to make the best of Duplessis. This tendency was reinforced by the fact that, with the exception of anglophone Quebec liberals, all of the potential allies against

Duplessis – the leaders of the Catholic social reform movements, the professional elites and large sections of the working classes – were strongly committed to the preservation of what each group understood as the Quebec nation. At the same time, English Canada and the federal government were perceived as moving in directions threatening to the provincial autonomy (Quinn, pp. 119-29).

That the different elements of Quebec nationalism could not agree among themselves as to the true "essence" of the Quebec nation did not matter in this context. All believed that provincial autonomy must be retained if their vision of the Quebec people and their political community – Catholic, liberal, socialist, or narrowly linguistic and cultural – was to remain (or become) a reality. Duplessis, as a more tenacious defender of provincial rights than the Liberal party of the day could credibly claim to be, was therefore the best available choice. Recognizing this to be the foundation of his power, Duplessis focussed on the federal-provincial conflicts that highlighted nationalist issues, successfully making provincial rights "the dominant issue in every election [from 1944] until 1960" (Quinn, p. 117). A self-reinforcing dynamic of federal-provincial conflict which helped to sustain UN support was thus maintained.

Federal State

The federalism of the Reconstruction period was primarily concerned with how to implement the International Policy. The federal government retained the political initiative throughout these years, and its first priority was to develop and implement its new economic, social and cultural policies. But at the same time, the federal government was concerned to minimize the degree to which these initiatives antagonized a Quebec which continued to resist the broad thrust of the new political economic order. In the absence of large-scale political mobilization along class or regional lines, this concern with political damage control in Quebec became the principal determinant of the means by which Ottawa's new policies were implemented. Hence, Ottawa's decision to rely on fiscal arrangements, especially shared cost programs, rather than constitutional change.

The Political Limits of Constitutional Reform

There were several important changes in the federal constitution in this period. With one exception, however, they aimed at fulfilling the territorial objectives of Macdonald and the national sovereignty hopes of Laurier and Borden, rather than the new economic imperatives. In 1949, Newfoundland joined the federation. In the same year, the federal government introduced a new section 91(1), giving the federal Parliament alone the right to amend the constitution as it affected federal jurisdiction. The new section was worded as a general amending power, subject to "exceptions" – the powers, rights and privileges of the provinces, the rights of citizens with respect to schools and language use, and the term of Parliament. At the same time, the Supreme Court of Canada, to which Ottawa alone appointed the judges, was made the final court of appeal for all Canadian cases. This cut off all appeals to the Privy Council, which Quebec had come to regard as the defender of a decentralized and classical model of Canadian federalism, and raised the constitutional question of the legal status of the precedents which the Privy Council had laid down.

These amendments to the BNA Act, as well as the abolition of appeals, were requested by Ottawa and granted by the British Parliament without seeking or receiving provincial consent. The federal government argued that this was justified because these amendments had no effect on the provinces. But several of them, led by Quebec, disagreed. Many institutions of the central government had an important federal dimension, so that changes to them would alter the character of Canadian federalism. By this reasoning, they should not be subject to unilateral federal government amendment any more than the division of powers. Abolishing appeals to the Privy Council was a case in point, because a federally appointed Supreme Court might be expected to interpret federal powers broadly, including those subject to future unilateral amendment under section 91(1). The scope of section 91(1) would be tested in the Senate Reference case of 1978.

From the vantage point of Quebec, the federal initiatives of 1949, taken together, suggested a confident St. Laurent government poised to usurp large areas of provincial jurisdiction. At the federal-provincial conference of January 1950 Premier Duplessis declared: "Nous considerons que ceci est absolument opposé au 'fair play' britannique et au fondement même du régime fédératif" (Proceedings, Constitutional Conference, January, 1950, p. 16). Federal efforts at the conference to gain provincial agreement to a more general amending procedure made little progress, largely as a result of provincial reaction to these federal initiatives. Provincial fears proved groundless. The federal government did not use its new powers to centralize the constitution by amendment, nor did the Supreme Court of Canada overturn the major precedents upon which twentieth century Canadian federalism had been built.

The only other constitutional amendment of this period occurred two years later, in 1951, when the federal government sought and secured unanimous provincial approval to bring old age pensions under federal jurisdiction. section 94a, as amended, permitted the federal government to establish old age pensions, while recognizing provincial paramountcy in the field. The latter qualification, which had not accompanied the unemployment insurance amendment of 1940, would become important in the Canada Pension Plan debate of the 1960s, since it would provide the basis for Quebec's claim that Ottawa's proposed Canada Pension Plan could not be enacted over Quebec's own scheme (Simeon, 1972, p. 202). Ottawa's Old Age Security Act provided a federal pension of $40 per month to all Canadians over the age of 70 who had resided in the country for at least 20 years. The companion Old Age Assistance Act provided a means-tested pension to those aged 65 to 69, on a shared cost basis (Guest, 1980, p. 145).

Defending National Cultures

If constitutional changes ended in 1951, the issue of Ottawa's role in culture and education continued to worry Quebec. The International Policy implied unprecedented levels of economic integration with the United States. While federal Liberals in this period were generally sanguine about the economic implications of this trend, they were concerned about the cultural implications of their policies. The Massey Commission was assigned to consider strategies for dealing with the danger of cultural assimilation with the United States. The Quebec government and many conservative francophone intellectuals were equally worried by the cultural and political implications of increased integration into the Canadian community and the new social and cultural policies being pursued by Ottawa. These concerns were eloquently articulated, and their implications for modern federalism systematically explored, in the report of the Tremblay Commission.

The Royal Commission on National Development in the Arts, Letters and Sciences (the Massey Commission) was appointed in April of 1949. The Order-in-Council creating the Commission stated that "It is in the national interest to give encouragement to institutions which express national feeling, promote common understanding and add to the variety and richness of Canadian life, rural as well as urban". The Commission soon extended this mandate to include investigation of the advisability of federal grants to support university education.

For Quebec nationalists, any move by Ottawa to involve itself in cultural matters was cause for apprehension. Singling out the educational system, one of the bastions of *Canadien* culture and values, for special federal attention was particularly suspect. The conditions attached to eligibility for federal grants could be expected to create new pressures to alter the structures and curricula of the Quebec system so as to render them compatible with anglophone educational values. Duplessis declared the Commission to be an unwarranted intrusion into provincial jurisdiction and called for a boycott of its proceedings (Coleman, 1984, p. 66, pp. 68-69).

The Commission's report was tabled in May 1951. Many Quebec nationalists were impressed by its sympathetic approach toward francophone Canadians (including calls for a second French broadcasting network in Canada, a French radio station to serve Acadians in the Maritimes, and the use of existing French-language stations in the West to broadcast national programmes) but the Commission also stressed the need for an extended federal role in culture and communications. National cultural institutions like the CBC, the National Film Board, the national museums and galleries, must be strengthened and new ones, such as the Canada Council, created. The extension of federal financial support to Canadian universities, hitherto confined to grants of $150 per registered war veteran, was also endorsed on the ground that when these grants terminated in 1951 many universities which had expanded rapidly to absorb the post-war influx of veterans would be forced to raise tuition to prohibitive levels to avoid financial crisis (Coleman, 1984, pp. 69-70).

The Commission argued that the federal government had the political responsibility and the constitutional right to promote the general education of all Canadians:

If the Federal government is to renounce its right to associate itself with other social groups, public and private, in the general education of Canadian citizens, it denies its intellectual and moral purpose, the complete conception of the common good is lost, and Canada, as such, becomes a materialistic society.

(cited in Coleman, p. 71)

The report recommended that Ottawa provide annual grants in support of Canadian universities. The federal government acted on this recommendation, beginning per capita grants to the universities in 1951-52 (Coleman, pp. 69-71).

Premier Duplessis responded by appointing the Royal Commission of Inquiry on Constitutional Problems (the Tremblay Commission) in February 1953. Its Chairman, Judge Thomas Tremblay, was a friend and confidant of Duplessis. He was prepared, however, to defer to the two most important intellectual contributors to the report. Esras Minville, Director of the HEC and Dean of Social, Economic and Political Sciences at the Université de Montréal, wrote the sections concerned with culture; Père Richard Arès wrote most of the historical and federalism sections (Coleman, pp. 73-75).

Duplessis hoped that the Commission would report quickly, providing him with arguments and recommendations that could be used in his battles with Ottawa over educational grants. But Minville and Arès viewed the new federal policies as a fundamental challenge to the constitutional order and conceived the Commission as the intellectual defender of classical federalism against the modern federalism advocated by Ottawa and the other provinces. The Commission held 97 public hearings and received 217 briefs, becoming a forum for the universities and other groups suffering as a result of Ottawa-Quebec fiscal conflicts. By the time the Tremblay Commission finally submitted its four-volume report to Premier Duplessis in February 1956, he had lost interest in it. Ottawa's concessions of 1954 had eased the immediate fiscal crisis in Quebec and the 1957 fiscal arrangements (both discussed below) promised to be more favourable to the province. At this level, then, the report was obsolete before it was published. More profoundly, the report attempted to explain and defend a Catholic conception of the Quebec political community which was rapidly disappearing.

Nonetheless, as Coleman observes, the secular conceptions of the Quebec nation which displaced the religious view defended in Tremblay remained indebted to the report's vision of Canadian federalism. Fundamental to this vision were three premises: first, that Confederation was a compact between two founding races or peoples (see Black, 1975); second, that the province of Quebec was the home of one of these peoples; and third, that its government was the principal defender of the rights and interests of francophones. This made the Quebec government unique among the provincial governments, none of which could claim to be a "national" government in this sense. Quebec was thus accorded a special status and its government viewed as the equal of Ottawa, each representing one of the two founding peoples. From these premises the Commissioners developed their positions on the major issues of post-war federalism.

On the question of powers to levy and collect taxes, the Tremblay Report argued that if Quebec was a sovereign government within its spheres of jurisdiction, dealing with the federal government as an equal, it could not be dependent upon federal transfers for the revenues needed to meet its responsibilities. Provincial governments – or, at least, Quebec – needed primacy over the federal government in some tax fields. It proposed that direct taxes be treated in this way, both because the BNA Act singled them out as the provincial base and because it could be argued that they have the most direct impact on the culture and way of life of the citizens. These direct taxes were to include not only personal income taxes and succession duties but, less convincingly, corporate income taxes. This approach to fiscal arrangements would inform the demands of all subsequent Quebec governments until the late 1970s (Coleman, pp. 73-80).

Social policy must remain under provincial jurisdiction because it has more direct consequences for individuals and communities than the tax system. Exclusive jurisdiction over unemployment insurance and old age pensions, brought under federal jurisdiction by constitutional amendments in 1940 and 1951 respectively, should be restored to the provincial governments. The regional character of much unemployment in Canada was argued to be sufficient reason for granting provincial governments a role in manpower policy. Finally, the provinces should also have control over educational and cultural matters.

The Tremblay Commissioners did not believe that securing these provincial rights and powers would be sufficient to ensure that its conception of Quebec as a nation would survive. As Coleman glosses their analysis, they recognized that:

> ...a serious gap had developed between the character of the traditional institutions of French-Canadian society and the way of life of many members of that society. The way of life of the industrial working class was a matter of special concern. Quebec had become industrialized. With industrial capitalism had come economic and political practices and institutions of British or American origin which had created among French Canadian workers a movement towards individualism, liberalism, and materialism.... People began to think and act according to the orientation of the places where they worked rather than the places where they prayed, played, and were educated. The commission saw tensions between the increasingly dominant values of the workplace and those of the nation and its institutions. The pressures on the educational system and the health care system...were gradually and surreptitiously changing them to conform to the values of the industrial capitalist world.
>
> (Coleman, p. 83)

For this reason, the Commission rejected Duplessis' minimal state as incapable of achieving the conservative ends which (insofar as Duplessis was genuinely committed to them) they shared with the UN government of the day. In articulating a constitutional position predicated upon an activist Quebec state, the report anticipated the constitutional position of a long succession of Quebec governments in the years following Duplessis' death. Paul Gerin-Lajoie, soon to be a cabinet minister, understood the shape of the new politics when he argued that "a more equal relationship between Ottawa and Quebec would require three things absent in the Duplessis period: comprehensive planning, legislation and administrative reform to put it into effect, and greater interprovincial cooperation" (1957, pp. 62-68).

Fiscal Arrangements: In Place of Constitutional Reform

Most of the burden of adapting Canadian federalism to the requirements of the International Policy that could not (as with trade policy) be undertaken unilaterally were met by restructuring federal-provincial fiscal arrangements. The requirements of Keynesian macro-economic policy legitimated federal demands for sufficient control over taxation and spending to influence overall levels of demand. The tax rental agreements provided such control on the revenue raising side of fiscal policy. Social policies, some of which fluctuated counter-cyclically with unemployment, provided control over the expenditure side. The federal government did not need to control all aspects of social policy design and implementation in order to achieve this control as long as every province met certain minimum standards. Conditional grants permitted this limited federal control.

Tax Collection Agreements: The Origins of "Tax Abatement" and "Equalization"

After the breakdown of the discussions based on Ottawa's Green Book proposals, the federal government negotiated extensions of the tax rental agreements on a province-by-province basis. Under the 1947 arrangements, Ottawa set the base and the rates for personal and corporate income taxes. The provinces then received unconditional transfers from Ottawa, calculated to increase in relation to population and GNP growth.

Ontario and Quebec did not agree to this arrangement, retaining the right to levy their own personal and corporate income taxes. Non-participation had heavy costs. In the absence of a federal-provincial accord, Ottawa continued to occupy these fields. In this context, any attempt by Ontario or Quebec to levy their own taxes amounted to double taxation. Duplessis was reluctant to incur the wrath which he believed would be visited on his government should it be perceived as the cause of such actions. Consequently, Quebec received neither provincial tax revenues from these sources nor federal transfers on a tax rental basis (Quinn, pp. 116-17).

The result was a fiscal crisis in Quebec which intensified with each year of federal-provincial stalemate. One of the casualties was the Quebec educational system which was starved of adequate funding. A powerful lobby, centred around the Chambre de Commerce de Montréal (CCM), formed with the purpose of forcing the two orders of government to come to a compromise agreement. The CCM convinced the Chambre de commerce de la province de Québec (CCPQ) that Ottawa ought to allow residents to deduct provincial taxes from their federal tax payments beyond the five percent level specified in the existing federal tax law. A letter making this case was sent to Prime Minister St. Laurent in June 1951. He was not receptive, but this proposal would eventually be adopted by Ottawa as the means of breaking the impasse.

In 1952 new tax collection agreements were negotiated under which the federal government considerably increased the size of its "rental" payments. At this point, Ontario signed on with respect to personal income taxes, leaving only Quebec outside the system. The formula for calculating the transfers to each province continued to be based on criteria – population and the pace of national economic growth – unrelated to the size of the tax base in a particular province. This formula implicitly entailed an important redistributive element: poorer provinces received exactly the same number of federal dollars for each of their citizens as did much richer provinces.

By 1954, the cost of remaining outside the system had become intolerable for Quebec. Responding to powerful pressures from Quebec educators and businessmen, reinforced by the arguments of several Tremblay Commissioners, Duplessis finally acted. Quebec levied a personal and corporate income tax equal to 15 percent of the federal tax. "Double taxation" had arrived in Quebec. Ottawa was surprised by the move, and Prime Minister St. Laurent, wishing to avoid any appearance of recognizing special status for Quebec, offered to reduce federal taxes in these fields by 10 percent for any province not signing a tax rental agreement. All other provinces had signed the agreement in 1952 so, in the short run, the offer applied to Quebec alone (Coleman, pp. 73-74; Quinn, p. 117). This approach became known as "tax abatement" because the federal transfer had become the equivalent of an abatement of federal income tax. It had the virtue of permitting an increase in provincial tax revenues while maintaining the same overall level of taxation.

All provinces found tax abatement attractive and when the next tax collection agreement was signed in 1957, it was formalized and applied to all of them. In this way, Ottawa eliminated the *de facto* special status which had existed since 1954 without completely abandoning the tax sharing system. Under the new system, federal transfers were to be calculated as a percentage of the revenues which would have been raised in each province if they had levied their own taxes at a uniform rate. The federal transfer between 1957 and 1962 was to be 10 percent of the personal income tax, nine percent of the corporate tax and 50 percent of succession duties.

The tax abatement system spelled the end of the implicit inter-provincial redistribution which had existed under the tax rental system. As a result transfers calculated on this new basis were, for the first time, supplemented by "equalization" payments to the poorer provinces, calculated to bring their average yield from these tax sources up to the average of the two wealthiest provinces. In 1957-58, federal equalization payments amounted to $139 million and all provinces except Ontario were recipients (Moore & Perry, 1966, p. 58). In addition, special "adjustment grants" for the Atlantic provinces were made. The National Adjustment Grants proposed by Rowell-Sirois had become a reality.

Under the new arrangements the federal government continued to control both the definition of the tax base and the rates which applied to it. Ottawa continued to act as the collection agent for the provinces, relieving them of the administrative and political burden of collecting their own taxes and ensuring that citizens would have a single tax form to complete. This approach successfully reconciled harmony in the tax system with provincial autonomy.

Shared Cost Programs

Shared-cost programs had been used following the First World War to fund public works projects aimed at infrastructural development and relief measures in response to the post-war depression. These programs had been phased out in the 1920s, with the notable exception of the old age pensions established in 1927, primarily in response to Quebec's strenuous constitutional objections. After the Second World War, however, this method was extensively employed both to encourage national infrastructural development projects such as the Trans-Canada Pipeline and to extend the welfare state. Considered in terms of the amount of money involved, the infrastructure projects were the most important component of shared-cost programs in this period.

But the most innovative shared-cost programs were in cultural and social policy. Perhaps the most controversial federal initiative was increased financial support for post-secondary education, a Massey Commission recommendation. The proposal angered Quebec nationalists, who regarded it as unconstitutional, but Duplessis was persuaded to accept the federal aid for one year while seeking to persuade the federal government to change its policy. When the year expired Duplessis forbade Quebec's universities to accept further federal grants. The Quebec government now had to find the funds to make up the difference itself. Added to the losses already sustained by Quebec's refusal to participate in the tax rental agreements, these conflicts with Ottawa were rapidly leading to a crisis of provincial finances until Ottawa's 1954 tax abatement concessions.

After Ottawa's 1944 family allowance program, the first important extension of social policy was the expansion of old age pension benefits made possible by the 1951 constitutional amendment. All subsequent extensions of the welfare state in Canada were made by means of shared-cost programs. The first of these was the Blind Persons Act of 1951, followed by the Disabled Persons Act of 1954. The new legislation enabled the federal government to enter into agreements with provinces to help fund programs aimed at individuals between 18 and 65 years of age, below a specified income, and falling within one of these categories (Guest, 1980, pp. 145-46). Next came the Unemployment Assistance Act of 1956. It enabled the federal government to provide 50 percent of the costs of general assistance to "those in financial need not covered by the existing categorical programmes of old age assistance, blind and disabled allowances, mother's allowances, and war veterans' allowances" (Guest, p. 146). In all these programs, provincial governments retained broad discretion in setting rates of support and other conditions, with the result that there were wide differences among them.

The most important development in welfare related shared-cost programs in this period came in 1957 – health care. Up until now, the provinces had been the major innovators in this area. As early as 1936, British Columbia and Alberta had passed legislation providing for public insurance against the costs of physician and hospital care, but fiscal constraints had prevented implementation of the plans. In 1946, following the failure to achieve a national accord at the Reconstruction Conferences, Saskatchewan's CCF government introduced legislation to establish a universal, compulsory hospital care insurance system, covering virtually all types of hospital service, with eligibility for benefits conditional upon prior payment of premiums of $5 per adult to a maximum of $30 per family (Taylor, 1978, pp. 101-2).

The Saskatchewan program became a model for other governments. British Columbia introduced a similar program two years later, and Alberta followed with a more limited program in 1952. By 1955, the Ontario Tories had decided to develop a similar system, but only if they could get financial help from Ottawa. Within two years, Ontario and the three Western provinces – along with Newfoundland, which brought its own "cottage hospital" system with it into Confederation in 1949 – had persuaded a reluctant federal government to revive its 1945 Green Book proposal to help fund such a project. At this point, federal involvement in this field was confined to the 10 small separate conditional programs, including those for hospital construction, provided for under the 1948 National Health Program.

In 1957, the federal government passed the Hospital Insurance and Diagnostic Services Act, agreeing to meet approximately 50 percent of the costs involved in the provision of provincial health insurance plans covering most forms of hospital care. In order to qualify for this aid, provincial governments had to make the benefits of the programme available to all citizens within their province, on uniform terms and conditions, regardless of age, sex, or physical condition. By March 1963, when Quebec joined the plan, 98.8 percent of the Canadian population was covered by hospital insurance (Guest, 1980, pp. 147-48). The "windfall" transfers which the Saskatchewan government received from the federal government after 1957 would enable its government to launch its medical care insurance, thus beginning the next cycle of innovation in public health policy (Taylor, 1978, pp. 104-8, 158-67, 234-38).

Conditional grant programs helped achieve, piecemeal, the goals of the International Policy. They reflected the wide consensus on equalizing standards, a consensus shared by professionals within governments as well as the wider population, at least in English Canada. Shared cost programs rose from $58 million in 1946 to $144.8 million in 1957. In the next period, such programs would increase even more rapidly: by 1965, conditional transfers had surpassed $1 billion (Bird, 1970, p. 282; Carter, 1971, pp. 24-26). All these programs were examples of federal initiatives in areas of provincial jurisdiction, with no constitutional mandate except an implicit and undefined "spending power". It was based on the assumed power of the Crown to distribute funds it had legitimately collected to any person or institution, and to attach appropriate conditions. In an era of government expansion, this was clearly a powerful tool for influencing national policy through providing inducements to provinces. Yet, apart from Quebec, there were few cries that these were unwarranted or coercive "intrusions" into provincial jurisdiction. Indeed, there seemed to be an implicit agreement not to test their constitutionality in the courts.

There were several reasons for the widespread acceptance by the provinces of federal ventures into provincial territory in this period. First, the instrument was far less coercive than the declaratory or disallowance powers. Second, power was not taken away from the provinces: they were free not to participate and still retain formal jurisdiction. Third, and related, the federal conditions tended to be loose, never entailing the kind of detailed supervision and control characteristic of "grant-in-aid" programs in the United States. Moreover, the conditions attached to federal transfers in Canada were often developed in cooperation with provincial officials sharing common goals and professional standards with their federal counterparts. Fourth, far from weakening the provincial governments, shared cost programs strengthened them, allowing them to increase their revenues, expand their bureaucracies and deliver programs that their citizens wanted. Most important, even if there were disagreement on detail, there was fundamental agreement on the goals underlying these programs and in the legitimacy of federal leadership in promoting them. In some cases, such as hospital and medical insurance, provincial governments had actually pioneered programs and were only too glad to receive federal assistance in expanding them.

Intergovernmental Mechanisms

The scope of new economic and social policies remained relatively limited in this period. The federal government's focus on macro-economic policy, given the control secured by the tax collection agreements, meant that there was only limited policy interdependence in that sphere. Moreover, as we have noted, federal efforts actually to pursue Keynesian counter-cyclical policies were, in any case, limited. Federally initiated infrastructural development projects obviously needed coordination with provincial programs, but these were relatively few. The limited expansion of the welfare state – relative to the original Green Book proposals – meant that the pressures for extensive policy rationalization within governments, and for increased coordination between them, was correspondingly limited. Ottawa's active role in the construction of the GATT and other international institutions did not require any provincial role, and none was sought.

These limits were reflected in the developing intergovernmental coordination mechanisms. Line department officials concerned with the administration of social policies met with increasing regularity to coordinate their activities. The creation in 1955 of a Continuing Committee of Officials on Fiscal and Economic Matters indicated a growing conviction that such meetings should become less *ad hoc*. But such formal consultation and coordination efforts remained primarily at the official level, seldom moving up to the political level at which policy goals, as distinct from means of implementation, were determined. In 1957 there were still only five federal-provincial meetings at the Ministerial level, while in each year of the next period there would be an average of about twenty. Similarly, there were only three First Ministers' Conferences in the 1950s, as opposed to nine in the 1960s, and 10 in the first half of the 1970s (Veilleux, 1979).

Federal-provincial relations thus followed what Stefan Dupré (in Simeon, 1985, pp. 1-32) calls a functional pattern, meaning that they were conducted primarily between line ministers and officials at both levels. Such a pattern facilitated the building of "trust networks" as officials shared common program objectives, common professional standards and criteria, and common interest group clienteles. Lubricated by the 50-cent dollars associated with shared cost programs, officials at each level could form alliances to promote their interests, exerting leverage on their respective treasury boards and finance ministers. This pattern was also facilitated by the continuation of "ministerialism" in which individual ministers, with relatively independent bases of power played a primary role in party organization and the operation of Cabinet (Smith, 1981, p. 52). Strong central agencies concerned with "system-wide" policy coordination had not yet emerged. In their respective fields ministers had considerable autonomy.

Nor was there much interest in Ontario's repeated calls for more elaborate and systematic consultative machinery. But changes were afoot. By 1957, R. B. Bryce, Clerk of the Privy Council, argued that the need for coordination was greater and the channels for doing so less adequate than ever before. Foreshadowing the next period, he wondered whether we would not soon see "intergovernmental ministers plenipotentiary" or "envoys extraordinary" (IPAC, Proceedings, 1957, p. 164). Concerns about the implications of extensive federal-provincial cooperation for responsible Parliamentary government were also beginning to emerge. In a 1955 speech in the Commons, Conservative MP Gordon Churchill worried about the effect of federal-provincial conferences on the future "authority and prestige of Parliament", especially if they were to become vehicles for developing policy (Hansard, 1955, p. 3647).

Conclusions

The extensive use of shared-cost agreements meant that the distinction between the jurisdictions formally assigned by the constitution was blurred. By incorporating fairly detailed conditions to federal grants, the federal government exerted considerable control over the size, scope and substance of policies which, in a strictly legal sense, still fell within exclusive provincial jurisdiction. The classical federalism of "water-tight compartments" was thus effectively brought to an end. A policy of "offering to subsidize what it cannot directly compel...[opened] to the federal government a wide road into positive social planning based on induced provincial consent" (in Lower, 1958, p. 78).

The fiscally based approach to realizing the new political commitments increased the share of total government revenues passing through the hands of the central government and reduced provincial fiscal autonomy. If transfers are considered to be federal spending, the federal share of total expenditure was about 64 percent in both 1949 and 1957. If they are considered to be provincial spending, the federal share was 53 percent in 1949 and 56 percent in 1957 (Bird, 1970, p. 280). In this sense, the system was much more centralized than it had been in 1929. But, on the other hand, the provinces were responsible for the administration of the new social policies funded on a shared-cost basis. This meant that they grew most rapidly, both in terms of their share of total government expenditures and their share of all government employees. The share of the federal budget devoted to transfers to the provinces rose from 3.6 percent of total spending in 1945, to 9.4 percent in 1955, to 18.4 percent in 1965 (Macdonald Commission, *Report*, 1985, Vol.3, p. 228).

Simple talk of centralization or decentralization is therefore fraught with difficulty. The most that can be said uncontroversially is that in 1947 the federal system was less centralized than it had been under the War Measures Act – in terms of the stringency of the conditions attached to Ottawa's shared cost grants, the level of provincial fiscal autonomy, and the relative size of government bureaucracies and expenditures – and considerably more centralized than it would become between 1958 and 1980.

This was an era of constrained federal-provincial conflict. Negotiations surrounding the fiscal arrangements of 1947, 1952 and 1957 were tough, but agreement was always reached in the end because – with the exception of Quebec – both federal and provincial governments were committed to the construction of the new political economy. By later standards, federal-provincial conferences were "decorous affairs". The Duplessis government resisted the whole trend of these developments, refusing to accede to the post-war extension of the tax rental agreements, and to participate in a number of the shared-cost programs. Yet precisely because Duplessis had no wish to create provincial versions of the federal programs, there was no attempt by Quebec to make full use of available provincial jurisdiction, much less to extend it. As D. V. Smiley observed, Duplessis' attempt to resist the new political economy was of limited success because it was defensive; he "failed to use the effective range of provincial autonomy for positive purposes" (1970, pp. 63-64).

The serious battles over jurisdiction – hence the renewed concern with constitutional amendment – would not arise until the conservative nationalist vision of Quebec had been reduced to minority status in the 1960s. In the meantime, fiscal arrangements proved a flexible instrument for accommodating Quebec's uniqueness. Thus, conflict between Ottawa and Quebec City – while the product of deep differences – did not prevent the effective extension of the role of the state in the rest of the country.

Many of the participants in the much more contentious federalism of the 1960s and 1970s would look back upon the Reconstruction decade as a "golden age" of Canadian federalism, characterized by low levels of conflict and a high degree of policy coordination under federal leadership. As they saw it, the flexibility which the BNA Act provided – particularly the availability of the federal "spending power" – permitted federalism to adapt successfully to the new roles required of the Canadian state. Sustained by the postwar "nationalization of sentiment" and by the broad consensus on the directions of policy, there were few impediments to acceptance of federal leadership outside Quebec. The major issues of the day did not divide the country primarily along regional lines, and the federal government itself maintained the historic pattern of conflict avoidance associated with Laurier and King. As a result, regional conflict was muted, and there was little debate about the fundamental character of the federal system.

This image of reconstruction era federalism is correct as far as it goes, but it is incomplete – it is undeniably an Ottawa-centred and, to a lesser extent, an English Canadian interpretation of the major developments of these years. In the character of the new role of the state and the cooperative federalism associated with it, and in their very successes, lay the seeds of the much more difficult period to come.

Chapter 9

The Era of Executive Federalism, 1958-73

By 1958 some of the contradictions of the International Policy and its politics of economic growth were becoming apparent. Growth and associated changes in the structure of the economy gave rise to new classes and collective actors and changed the goals and strategies of the older ones. Political values – democracy, community and equality – were emphasized, in contrast to the economic focus of the Reconstruction decade. Demands that these values be more fully realized threatened the post-war regional and class accommodations, and also fueled the Quiet Revolution in Quebec.

Federal and provincial governments struggled to meet these demands by extending Reconstruction era commitments and expanding into new policy fields. Social policies expanded more rapidly than at any time before or since. Aggregate demand management was supplemented by the first explicitly regional and sectoral policies. The scope of state economic regulation also expanded dramatically as new standards for occupational health and safety, and environmental and consumer protection were promulgated. Finally, governments sought to reform their own decision-making processes to achieve not always compatible increases in government openness and accountability, citizen participation, policy coherence and efficiency of execution.

The expanded role of the state was evident in all industrial democracies. In Canada, for the reasons examined in the last chapter, this trend involved the rapid expansion of both federal and provincial governments and, with it, new problems of jurisdiction and coordination. Growing constitutional uncertainty and institutional complexity would have given rise to difficult technical problems of internal organization and inter-governmental coordination, even if the representatives of both orders of government had continued to agree on their political priorities and the best means of achieving them. But such agreement began to fragment. The movement from a focus on the supposedly technical problems of economic management to the fundamentally political problems of what ends the new prosperity should serve resurrected the old and difficult normative issues that had been set aside in the first phase of the politics of growth. The revitalization of popular concern with political values, what some have called the politicization of society, thus brought with it a renewal of deep political conflict.

These conflicts carried over into federal-provincial relations, most spectacularly but by no means exclusively, in relations between Ottawa and Quebec City, manifested in the growth of reformist Quebec nationalism. For Quebec's political elites, the fate of the francophone Quebec community had always been a fundamental concern. It had always been recognized that the preservation of this community might require some economic sacrifice, such as was sustained in the Duplessis years. But now an increasing number of Québécois, while retaining the sense of the priority of political community that underpinned all Quebec nationalism, defined that community in more secular, materialist and individualist terms, as the Tremblay Commission had foreseen. The new nationalists did not want to make economic sacrifices and they did not believe that they had to. They believed that the Quebec state, if run by politicians committed to modernizing the economy and backed by technically competant bureaucrats instead of patronage appointees, could effectively promote both economic growth and political and cultural autonomy.

The triumph of reformist over conservative Quebec nationalism was gradual, but as it advanced successive Quebec governments demanded increasing fiscal and jurisdictional autonomy as well as constitutional recognition of the province's special status. Ottawa responded by making significant fiscal and jurisdictional concessions, but offered them to all provinces in an effort to deny any recognition of special status to Quebec.

By the late 1960s, several western provinces were also demanding decentralization. Again, this was primarily in response to changes in economic conditions and political coalitions. J. E. Hodgetts, expressing the surprise of those who assumed that western regionalism was a thing of the past, exclaimed: "Almost overnight, regionalism in Canada has become the current fashion and a subject for much intellectual speculation as well as administrative concern" (1966, p. 3).

Taken together, these trends led to a more decentralized federalism in conjunction with rapidly-expanding state activities. Edwin R. Black and Alan Cairns sought to capture this new dynamic with the term "province-building" (1965, p. 35). In some respects, their analysis exaggerated the shift in political initiative and political power that characterized the period. But changes in the rhetoric and practice of intergovernmental relations certainly were occurring. Provincial governments now claimed equal status for themselves in negotiations with Ottawa: Dominion-Provincial meetings became Federal-Provincial Conferences (FPCs); Prime Minister and Premiers alike were called "First Ministers". The number of regular intergovernmental meetings and interactions increased dramatically and efforts to formalize them were made. At the same time, the government actors who engaged in these discussions were changing. As federal and provincial politicians became more concerned with the way large political questions bore on federalism, control over particular programs shifted from the bureaucrats in the line departments to the offices of First Ministers and newly-created ministries of intergovernmental relations.

The re-politicization of Canadian society and federal-provincial relations spelled the end of administrative federalism. It was replaced by the executive federalism which prevails to this day. Political analysts of the period identified the changes and speculated on their implications for social harmony and economic efficiency. Black and Cairns argued that if the question of the 1940s had been whether the provinces could withstand the centripetal pressures of the International Policy, it was now "whether the federal system can successfully contain the powerful decentralizing pressures welling up from below without losing its essential character" (1965, p. 30). Don Smiley argued that,

...the federal and provincial governments are now locked into a system of mutual interdependence in such a way that each level, in pursuing its objectives, will be frustrated to an intolerable degree unless some degree of intergovernmental collaboration is affected.

(1970, p. 217)

For all the foreboding that surrounded the emergence of executive federalism, the tenor of federal-provinical relations remained cooperative. Only in the next period would Smiley's fears be borne out.

Federal Society

As the international economy became more competitive and national economies became more dependent upon trade for their future prosperity, the pace and scale of social and economic change in all capitalist industrial democracies accelerated. These changes had important implications for the three traditional divisions characterizing Canadian society. Class conflict, reflected in the unprecedented strike levels of the late 1960s, re-surfaced. Issues of the appropriate role of the state in directing and facilitating the process of economic transformation also re-emerged as debates about the need for a national industrial strategy and, closely related, for the achievement of greater independence from the United Stated, began and ended the period.

The resource boom continued to fuel western economic growth based on the export of natural resources. But in the late 1960s actual and threatened declines in international commodity prices, owing to rising levels of production in the Third World, led to a renewed desire for the regional economic diversification that market forces alone did not generate. Provincial governments rose and fell on the issue. As economies in the Atlantic provinces stagnated, demands for increased federal transfers and improved regional development policies intensified.

International and domestic economic change also had implications for the politics of identity. Mobility often brought increased economic opportunities, but it also eroded individual ties to traditional communities of various kinds. This process was often experienced as simultaneously liberating and a threat to the foundations of identity and what Simone Weil (1978) termed "the need for roots". One result, manifested in many western countries, was the emergence of subnationalist political movements embracing "modernity" but seeking to control its impact on traditional communities and their values.

In Canada, the largest and most politically powerful instance of this phenomenon was the triumph of reformist nationalism in Quebec. However, the emergence of organizations aimed at protecting and promoting the interests of Canada's native people can also be understood in this way. A second trend was the emergence of new social movements seeking to redefine the foundations of individual identity – environmentalism, consumerism, feminism and other movements for personal liberation.

The growth of the state created a large new class of state employees with an interest in and corresponding ideological predisposition toward the maintenance or expansion of government. Although white collar, they were not part of the private sector managerial stratum and did not share its suspicion of expanded social policy. The growth of the state was also associated with the decline of legislatures vis-à-vis the executive branch of government, and reduced scope for citizen participation in the political process. Concern for the possibility of participatory democracy grew in this context.

Economic expansion now made it plausible to claim that the resources existed to address these political issues (Skidelsky, in Crouch, 1979). The new bureaucratic class tended to support them, particularly from the late 1960s when it was incorporated into organized labour in Canada. Demographic trends – the "baby boom" generation entered political life in the 1960s – also supported this reassessment of political priorities: the young, the affluent and the well-educated were more apt to place a high value on political participation and accountability, and their numbers were increasing relative to the total population (Inglehart, 1977; Arseneault, 1988).

This shift in priorities was reflected in growing demands to push the welfare state beyond its counter-cyclic and "safety net" functions to serve egalitarian ends; for increased regional redistribution; for increased regulation to control technological and environmental changes; for increased bureaucratic accountability to legislatures; and for increased worker participation. James Draper captured the spirit of the time well: "It is concerned with the development of communities and the self-growth of individuals within them...its worth especially lies in enhancing citizen dignity" (1971, Introduction). The result was the extension of the state into areas of social life hitherto left to private actors.

Class and the Roles of the Canadian State

The evolution of the Canadian state has always been shaped by the changing balance of class power. Only when the organized interests challenging the status quo have been able either to gain political power or pressure conservative forces into reforms, has the role of the Canadian state been fundamentally changed. This balance of power, in turn, has been shaped by the changing character of the international economy, by Canada's changing situation within it, and by the domestic economic and social trends to which these changes give rise.

In this period, organized agriculture continued its decline as a share of the working population. At the same time, it became more politically conservative and re-aligned with the two established parties. In the 1958 federal election many farmers deserted the CCF for John Diefenbaker's Progressive Conservatives. The number of CCF seats fell from 25 to eight, all of them in the West. When, in the wake of that debacle, CLC and CCF leaders asked farm organizations in Alberta, Manitoba and Saskatchewan to support the formation of a new party with a stronger labour base, all three refused to participate (Williams, 1975, pp. 218-20). By 1964, when

Ross Thatcher's Liberals formed the new government of Saskatchewan, the CCF had been wiped out in its last Western stronghold (Conway, 1983, pp. 182-83).

Organized labour also languished for most of this time, with union density fluctuating between 34.2 percent and 29.4 percent of non-agricultural paid workers until 1973 (Kumar, 1986, p. 109). The forces within the CLC favouring an explicit political role for organized labour grew steadily stronger and the collapse of CCF support convinced most that it was better to create a new party than to try to prop up the CCF. Accordingly, the New Democratic Party (NDP) held its founding convention in Ottawa in August 1961. However, this advantage had been gained with important concessions. Bowing to TLC elements that continued to dislike any permanent party affiliation, and to public sector unions that worried about endorsing any party, the CLC leadership decided that affiliation by unions would be voluntary and would take place at the local union level, with dissenters free to opt out of any contribution to the NDP. Morton and Copp sum up the immediate consequences of this ambiguous birth:

> ...the "hands off" strategy did not save the party from charges of labour domination – fatal for potential farm and middle-class backers – while it did deny it effective organizational and financial backing. The former CCFers, exhausted and a little disillusioned with their "New Party", were left to take up the struggle. The new party, in consequence, looked steadily more like the old one. In its first two elections, it could attract only about one union member in five and a total vote of between 12 percent and 13 percent (1984, pp. 243-44).
>
> (1984, pp. 243-44)

The one bright spot for organized labour, though it did the NDP no good, was the 1960 electoral triumph of reformist nationalism in Quebec.

Until the late 1960s, then, organized labour and the NDP were too weak to alter much of the political landscape, beyond pulling the two traditional parties slightly to the left. Probably the most important event was the recession of 1957-61, the worst since the Depression. Unemployment reached 7.1 percent in 1961, and the rate of growth of Gross National Expenditure plummetted from 8.4 percent in 1956 to 2.4 percent in 1957. It would be almost 20 years before these unemployment figures were exceeded (Wolfe, 1984b, p. 51). The recession weakened confidence in the capacity of the government to maintain economic growth by means of the macro-economic instruments alone. Closely related, dramatic differences in the regional impact of the recession heightened the growing recognition that even in times of rapid national economic growth, major disparities in regional income and employment would remain and could only be reduced by more focussed regional policies.

Moreover, the application of the same reasoning to Canada's location in an increasingly continental economy fed concerns about the consequences of the drift to closer integration of the Canadian with the American economy. The recession, after all, was largely the product of the termination of the Korean war and its impact on the American war economy. The Massey Commission forcefully expressed such concerns with respect to culture. But successive federal Liberal governments, like Duplessis in Quebec, assumed that cultural and political independence were compatible with, or even required, extensive foreign investment and economic control. Now this assumption was challenged by the report of the Gordon Commission – the Royal Commission on Canada's Economic Prospects (1958) – created by the Liberal government before Diefenbaker's electoral victory. The Commission argued that lagging Canadian productivity gains in the key secondary manufacturing sector required more extensive government/industry coordination, more focussed use of government purchasing policies and the regulation of foreign investment (Final Report, pp. 13-14, p. 250; cited in Pal, 1981, pp. 299-303).

Other voices joined in. The Senate Committee on Manpower called for encouragement of technological innovation, increased specialization, the promotion of new investment and new machinery for intergovernmental cooperation (CAR, 1961, p. 185). The Chairman of the Canadian Tax Foundation called for "a national plan and national objectives" and the creation of a Ministry of Economic Affairs (CAR, 1961, p. 183). Industrialist E. P. Taylor argued in 1961 that "The time for longer-range planning or rationalization of our economic affairs is now upon us" (CAR, 1961, p. 183). These developments stimulated considerable discussion and conflict within the Ottawa bureaucracy as well. Many of the policy ideas which became so familiar in the 1970s – controls on foreign portfolio and direct investment, the creation of the Canada Development Corporation, the institutionalization of business-government consultations on economic policy in key sectors, and the restructuring of domestic financial institutions – were first mooted in the Departments of Finance, Trade and Commerce, and Labour during these recession years (Pal, 1981, pp. 334-38).

Some of the popular appeal of Diefenbaker's "Vision of the North" derived from its claim to address industrial and regional problems with decisive state action and to reduce economic, political and military integration with the United States (Beck, 1968). Diefenbaker's anti-American rhetoric proved more powerful than his policies. Trade dependence on the United States was not substantially reduced as he had promised, but he did develop a rudimentary regional policy in the National Stabilization Act of 1958. The Conservatives also developed a National Oil Policy, announced in 1961, that sought to stimulate the Canadian energy industry, hard hit by the slump. It encouraged more exports to the United States and reserved the Canadian market west of the Ottawa River for Western Canadian producers.

The recession ended in 1962, again largely due to economic developments south of the border. From that year to the end of the period, Canada experienced a boom based on a rising tide of exports and a wave of new investment from both domestic and foreign sources. New projects and industries were begun: subways in Toronto and Montreal, hydro-electric power developments from Churchill Falls to the Columbia River, and potash mining in Saskatchewan. Old industries grew rapidly: grain exports in the prairies, oil and gas in Alberta, and a revitalized auto industry under the Auto Pact. Real output rose by an average of 4.6 percent per year between 1957 and 1966, and 5.3 percent in the following five years. Real per capita income rose at an average of 2.4 percent per year in the first five years and 3.9 percent in the second. Productivity growth was healthy, and both unemployment and inflation moderate. It was the longest sustained boom in Canadian history.

Economic pressures to develop an alternative economic strategy to the Liberals' market-led continentalism dissipated. The Ministry of Finance, hostile to increased state economic intervention and briefly deprived of its traditional ascendency in economic policy matters by Diefenbaker and the recession, re-established its hegemony (Pal, 1981, pp. 334-38). The Liberal Party, returning to power under Lester Pearson in 1963, was not keen to modify its traditional trade and industrial policies, and the economy obligingly continued to grow without any apparent need for increased intervention.

Instead, the Liberal Party of the 1960s distinguished itself from Diefenbaker's Conservatives by becoming the more aggressive champion of social policy expansion. With restored economic growth and rapidly growing tax revenues, the Liberals were able to launch the largest-scale expansion of the welfare state in Canadian history. In 1964 Pearson's government passed a Youth Allowances Act, broadening and and extending family allowances. The Canada and Quebec Pension Plans, dramatically expanding the previous old age pension scheme, were passed in 1965 and the Canada Assistance Plan, consolidating and increasing federal contributions to provincial welfare and social services, followed in 1966. Under Pearson's successor, Pierre Elliot Trudeau, these policies were extended: the Medical Care Act of 1968 created a comprehensive, publicly funded health care system; the revised Unemployment Insurance Act of 1971 made the unemployment insurance system an important instrument of regional redistribution – something close to a guaranteed annual income scheme. As the period ended, the federal and provincial governments embarked on a joint review of the whole field of social security and proposals for a guaranteed annual income were being discussed (Guest, 1980).

Meanwhile, organized labour was breaking new ground in Quebec. By the early 1960s Quebec unions were the most politicized in the country, due to the powerful synthesis of class and linguistic identities. The CCCL unions severed ties with the Catholic Church in 1960, renaming themselves the *Confederations syndicale nationale* (CSN). The leader of the CSN, Jean Marchand, was a close ally of Jean Lesage and the Liberal Party. He kept the CSN out of the CLC, thereby depriving the NDP of the financial and political support of almost half of the Quebec labour movement. The CLC-affiliated *Federation des Travailleurs du Quebec* (FTQ), with the same nominal ties to the NDP as all CLC unions, joined Marchand and the CSN in backing the Lesage Liberals to defeat Duplessis prior to the formation of the NDP, and ties remained strong until 1970 (Palmer, 1983, pp. 257-84; Morton, 1984, pp. 258-59).

Together, the two federations helped to give Lesage's government a social democratic cast. In the Lesage years, the left wing of the *Parti liberale* prevailed over the right in most of the major cabinet battles (Fraser, 1984, p. 30). All remaining private hydro-electric companies in the province were nationalized and consolidated into the provincial Crown corporation, Hydro Quebec. René Levesque, the Minister of Natural Resources, declared that the takeover represented a giant step towards the "emancipation" and "democratization" of the Quebec economy (Thompson, 1984, p. 248). "It is we alone through our state, who can become masters in our own house" said Levesque, invoking the slogan of the Abbé Groulx (in Cook, 1966, p. 15).

Over the next two years, Quebec created three more important Crown corporations. SIDBEC was formed to set up a fully integregrated steel complex near Montreal so that Quebec's major iron ore deposits could be processed in the province instead of being shipped to Hamilton or the United States. SOQUEM was to engage in the exploration and development of mineral resources. The SGF was "to provide financial assistance, as well as managerial and technical expertise where needed, to those Quebec firms with modest capitalization, often family-owned, which were struggling for survival" (Quinn, pp. 192-94). In 1965, following creation of the Quebec Pension Plan (QPP), the government created the Caisse de dépôts et de placements du Québec, which would use the pool of capital deriving from the QPP to increase levels of new capital investment in Quebec (Thompson, 1984, p. 193).

Lesage repaid his union allies in 1964 with legislation that granted every Quebec employee – including all government employees, with the exception of policemen, firemen and a few narrowly defined categories of "essential" workers – the right to bargain collectively and strike. Morton suggests that the legislation bore the imprint of Jean Marchand on one important point: "Civil servants could not affiliate with any organization that openly backed a political party. By backing the NDP, the CLC's affiliates were shut out; Marchand's.... [CSN thus] had an inside track on a large array of public employees" (1984, p. 259).

These developments had important implications for the national labour movement. Before the victories in Quebec, Saskatchewan had been the only provincial government to grant its workers the right to strike. After the Quebec victory of 1964, Canadian organized labour demanded the same collective bargaining rights for public sector workers in Ottawa and the other provinces. The NDP backed union demands and its share of the vote rose from 13.1 percent of the popular vote in 1963 to 18 percent in the 1965 federal election (Beck, 1968, p. 371, p. 397).

The Trudeau Liberals also responded to labour's demands for public sector worker rights. In 1967, the federal government passed the Public Service Staff Relations Act, granting federal public sector workers the right to organize collectively and the option to strike, as well as extending the bargaining rights to several other groups not covered under the its 1948 legislation. This was followed by major revisions to the Labour Standards Code in 1971 which addressed growing union concerns about technological change. It required, among other things, notice of layoffs and severance pay for employees of more than five years' service. It also established, in response to the 1967 Royal Commission on the Status of Women, a more stringent definition of the requirement of equal pay, and made provision for enforcement by government supervision as opposed to individual complaint (Morton, pp. 279-80).

More favourable labour laws were also passed at the provincial level by the NDP governments that came to power in Manitoba (1969), Saskatchewan (1971), and British Columbia (1972). But the demonstration effect extended beyond these provinces. By the end of the period, only Alberta, Ontario, PEI and Nova Scotia still denied provincial employees the right to strike, and even these provinces had made important concessions. In Ontario, where the NDP formed the Official Opposition after 1972, the Tory government passed laws recognizing workers' right to refuse unsafe work, and provisions for imposing "first agreements" on recalcitrant employers (Panitch & Swartz, pp. 27-31; Morton, 1984, pp. 286-94).

The unionization of the public sector gave an immense surge to the growth of the Canadian labour movement: the organized share of the civilian labour force rose from its 1962 low point of 22.2 percent to 24.5 percent by 1966 and 29.2 percent by 1973 (Kumar, 1985, p. 109). It also altered the balance of forces within the Canadian labour movment in four important ways. First, it increased the white collar component of the movement to a point of near equality with the blue collar component: by 1975, the Canadian Union of Public Employees was the largest union in Canada. Moreover, it brought large numbers of women into the union movement and, with them, a new set of concerns like pay equity and daycare, already being articulated by feminists.

Public sector unionization also changed the balance between national and international unions. As late as 1965, international unions claimed 75 percent of all Canadian unionists and dominated the CLC. By the 1974 CLC Convention, the two elements were in rough balance (Morton: 1984, p. 261, p. 275, p. 312). The shift was important because the internationals tended to be more oriented to the "business unionism" of their American majorities, while the nationals were more receptive to "social unionism" and, consequently, were stronger supporters of the NDP and economic nationalist economic strategies (1973, pp. 188-212; Laxer, 1976, pp. 43-176, pp. 255-78).

Finally, public sector unionization changed the regional concentration of organized labour in Canada:

> ...in 1962, three provinces – Ontario, Quebec, and British Columbia – accounted for more than three quarters of total union membership in Canada, and union density by province ranged from 15 per cent in Prince Edward Island to 45 per cent in British Columbia. By 1981, the gap in union density had narrowed from 30 to 18 percentage points, largely because of the spread of unionization among public service employees and workers in education and health.
>
> (Kumar, 1985, p. 116)

In short, in the mid-1960s a process was begun which would change the regional strength of organized labour in Canada. Especially notable was the relative growth in Quebec and the Maritimes. Between 1961 and 1981 Ontario moved from being the second most organized province (after B.C.) to being the second least organized (Kumar, 1985, p. 116).

The result of these changes was a Canadian labour movement which, after 1965, grew much more rapidly than its American counterpart. This growth took place in all parts of the country rather than in just a few provinces, and was more social democratic in orientation than it had been since the 1930s. The increased power and politicization of organized labour contributed to the greatly improved showing of the NDP in the 1972 federal election, when the NDP won its largest caucus to date (32 members, enough to bring down the Liberal minority government) enabling the NDP to extract several important concessions from the Liberals on social policy and economic nationalist issues.

The revival of economic nationalist concerns in the late 1960s was also a product of American economic and military policies. As the American trade balance deteriorated, successive administrations developed policies potentially damaging to the Canadian economy. Canada was able to secure exemption, at a price, from the 1964-65 and the 1968 capital controls, but not from the provisions of the 1971 Domestic International Sales Corporation (DISC) program, one of the components of President Nixon's New Economic Policy of that year. Speaking in Ottawa shortly after it had been announced, President Nixon declared that it was time "for us to recognize that we have very separate identities; that we have significant differences; and that nobody's interests are served when these realities are obscured" (Martin, 1983, p. 21). Aside from economic frictions, the American political system, from 1968, began to look increasingly violent and repressive – the assassinations of Robert Kennedy and Martin Luther King, race riots in major cities, the Chicago Democratic Convention debacle, the escalation of the Vietnam war, Watergate – among other events on a list that seemed to go on and on.

The combination of these economic and political developments was a potent one. Surveys in the 1950s had revealed that a majority of Canadians in all regions of the country believed that free trade with the United States would be beneficial. As late as 1965, 59 percent of English Canadians and 47 percent of French Canadians favoured an economic union with the United States. By 1967, however, 60 percent of Canadians felt that enough American capital had been invested in Canada and, by 1971, less than 20 percent of English and French Canadians continued to favour economic union (Manzer, 1974, pp. 170-71).

Two major economic nationalist movements emerged in these years. The Committee for an Independent Canada argued, as had the Liberal government of Quebec since 1960, that governments must encourage the development of a national business class capable of displacing foreign owned companies in key sectors. The NDP, particularly its "Waffle" wing, argued that the motives and goals of Canadian capitalists were not significantly different from their American counterparts. Hence, more extensive state intervention was essential if Canadians were collectively to gain more control over their economic evolution and a more just distribution of wealth and opportunity (Kresl, 1974, pp. 4-6). But for various reasons, including the antipathy of the international unions that they criticized, the Waffle were expelled from the NDP in a bitter battle in 1972, weakening the pressure from the left (Morton, pp. 289-90).

The Liberals responded to the rising tide of public opinion by initiating more official inquiries. The Watkins Task Force, appointed in 1968 to investigate the structure of foreign investment in Canada, recommended the creation of a state trading agency, a national venture capital development corporation, and the reform of restrictive trade practices legislation aimed at promoting sectoral concentration. The 1970 report of the Standing Committee for External Affairs and National Defence – the Wahn Report – proposed various methods to achieve its target of 51 percent Canadian ownership of the economy. Finally, the Gray Report of 1972 called for the creation of an agency to monitor and regulate foreign investment in Canada with the aim of ensuring that such investment was, on the whole, beneficial to the Canadian economy (Clarkson, 1982, pp. 12-13).

For all the research and recommendations, the party of the International Policy remained internally divided on economic nationalism (Wolfe, 1985) and preoccupied with the questions of culture, language and the constitution. Most federal Liberal initiatives, therefore, focussed on strengthening Canadian cultural industries through protection and subsidies for publishing, broadcasting and film. Only two policies of this period can be described as serious ventures into economic nationalism: the creation in 1971 of the Canada Development Corporation (CDC), a venture capital holding company, along the lines proposed by the Watkins Task Force; and the creation, in 1973, of the Foreign Investment Review Agency (FIRA), with a mandate to ensure that foreign investment and take-overs of Canadian firms resulted in "significant benefits" for Canada. In addition, the government did briefly explore the possibility of reducing dependence on the American market by expanding Pacific Rim and EEC markets – the so-called "Third Option".

The mandates of the CDC and FIRA, reluctant responses to changing public opinion and NDP pressure in parliament, were vague. The Third Option, according to Denis Stairs (in Stairs & Winham, 1985) was never pursued with the vigour and commitment necessary to assess its real possibilities before it was abandoned. These half-hearted and *ad hoc* responses did not amount to a coherent strategy, and the federal Liberals were never committed – as they were, say, to official bilingualism – to developing such a strategy. Thus, there was no federal Liberal counterpart to the breakdown of the conservative distinction between culture and economy which heralded the Quebec Liberals' Quiet Revolution in 1960, and no federal parallel to the integrated economic nationalism pursued by provincial governments in Quebec from Lesage onward.

Region

As we argued in Chapters 7 and 8, regional identities were not destroyed by the processes of modernization. But between 1958 and 1968, regional conflict remained low. Provincial electorates and their governments demanded that federal policies be made more regionally sensitive and that the benefits of the economic union be more fairly distributed. But after 1968 the character of the demands issuing from the four Western provinces changed, as their citizens increasingly looked to their provincial governments to promote economic diversification. Western provincial governments responded by developing their own industrial strategies with varying degrees of sophistication and ambition.

In the following section we explain the increasingly regional focus of economic fairness and development demands that occurred during this period, setting out the federal policy response. We then ask why the form this regionalism took – in Western Canada as opposed to Atlantic Canada – was so different, particularly after 1968.

The Growth of Regionalism and Regional Policy

The recession that began in 1957 hit the "peripheral" regions harder than central Canada, suggesting that special relief measures were warranted, in addition to the overall effort to reflate the economy. It also pushed many politicians and officials to take a hard look at the ten years of experience that had accumulated since the new policies were put into effect. They saw that unemployment rates in the peripheral regions – above all, in Atlantic Canada – were consistently much higher than in the central region. Thus, success in achieving low average national unemployment might still leave unemployment unacceptably high in some regions. Western and Atlantic provincial governments brought pressure to bear on Ottawa to supplement its macro- economic stabilization policies with regionally-and sectorally-specific development policies.

Furthermore, good data on regional per capita income differentials began to become available in the early 1960s. Williamson's 1965 study showed that Canada had the highest level of regional inequality among the six most industrialized nations and that it was the only nation to show no significant reduction in these disparities in the postwar period (discussed in Mansell & Copithorne, in Norrie, 1986, pp. 2-3). A host of subsequent studies supported these findings, culminating in the Economic Council of Canada's comprehensive study, *Living Together* (1977). It concluded that the economic advantages of the richest provinces – Ontario, Alberta and B.C. – had been "increasing relative to other regions for the last several decades... . Regional disparities in incomes and job opportunities are indeed substantial and remarkably persistent in spite of the amount of labour migration that has taken place over the years" (1977, pp. 59-60).

In another period such inequalities might have been tolerated provided that all were made at least somewhat better off, but by the 1960s, as Donald Smiley observes, "there was developing a consensus favouring a more equalized range and more equalized standards of basic public services throughout Canada". Large disparities were now seen as "indefensible" and the federal government had a responsibility to mitigate them (Smiley, 1970, pp. 58-59). In this political context, regional unemployment and income data supported demands that Ottawa develop policies to promote the economic growth in the worst-off provinces, with the long-term aim of reducing their need to rely on federal tranfers.

This shift did not initially entail a reorientation to provincial governments or increased federal-provincial conflict. On the contrary,

Diefenbaker's 1958 electoral victory represented the high point of postwar support for a strong federal government in the Atlantic and Western provinces. Diefenbaker swept both regions, overwhelming Depression era third parties in the West and traditional Liberal strongholds in the Atlantic provinces. The Conservatives won all but one of 48 seats in the Prairies, receiving an unprecedented 56 percent of the region's vote. In British Columbia, they received 18 of 22 seats, the remaining four going to the CCF. In the Atlantic provinces the Conservatives captured 25 of 33 seats with 47 percent of the vote (Beck, 1968, pp. 326-27).

Many of Diefenbaker's new industrial policies – agricultural initiatives, the shared-cost Roads to Resources Program, federal support for railways to Lynn Lake in Manitoba and Pine Point in the North West Territories – had a regional, as well as a sectoral, focus. So did later Liberal initiatives, such as the Auto Pact (1965), and a wide variety of programs to assist manufacturing industries, the benefits of which were concentrated in Ontario and, to a lesser extent, Quebec.

But the first step toward an explicitly *regional* component of federal economic policy making was the creation of the advisory Atlantic Development Board in 1962. Diefenbaker subsequently argued the need to extend such policies, on the ground that it was Ottawa's responsibility to ensure "an equality of development throughout the Dominion" (cited in Lithwick, 1986, p. 118). The goal of regional policy, in the Diefenbaker years, was generally assumed to be the reduction of provincial per capita income differentials, as opposed to economic "development" measured in terms of degrees of economic diversification or the size of the secondary manufacturing sectors. Given the recent prosperity of the the west, this placed the primary emphasis on the Atlantic provinces.

In Opposition, the federal Liberals had asserted their commitment to a "comprehensive" and "planned" attack on regional disparities (CAR, 1960, p. 4). Upon forming the government in 1963, Prime Minister Pearson extended the agricultural and regional policies that Diefenbaker had initiated. The Atlantic Development Board (later the Atlantic Development Council) was expanded. The Agricultural and Rural Development Act (ARDA) was enlarged and reoriented, with special emphasis on designated development areas. A fund for rural economic development (FRED) was created in 1966. Incentives for investment were provided by the Regional Development Incentive Act, administered by the Area Development Agency within the Department of Industry. The Federal Business Development Bank also provided loans to investors in depressed regions at reduced interest rates.

The Pearson government also developed a more expansive definition of the goals of regional policy. Henceforth it would apply to slow growth areas in all provinces, even those with high average levels of income and employment, and it would seek to address the structural causes of slow growth, as opposed to its income effects. This evolution was driven by at least two forces: intellectual logic and international markets. The burgeoning literature on the causes of Third World "underdevelopment" had a significant impact on the thinking of academics, bureaucrats and politicians concerned with regional economic development in Canada.

After 1967 a series of adverse international commodity market developments reinforced intellectual trends, demonstrating how vulnerable western economic prosperity – with its continued reliance on a few primary resource exporting sectors – remained. In 1967 the International Grain Agreement fell apart in the face of over-supply and wheat and other grain prices plummetted. Realized net farm income in Saskatchewan fell from its 1967 peak of $489 million to $202 million in 1969. The experience of the agricultural sector in the other two Prairie provinces was similar. As the potash market was largely determined by the demand for fertilizer, the potash boom also went bust. Prices in 1969 were half of their peak value in 1965. Saskatchewan's per capita income fell from 93 percent of the national average in 1966 to 72 percent in 1970 (Richards & Pratt, 1979, pp. 202-05). Then, in 1968, a major oil field was discovered at Prudhoe Bay, Alaska, raising doubts about the long-run security of American markets for Alberta oil and gas. There was a steep decline in exploration activities in Alberta, as drill rigs moved north in search of other northern deposits: "Alberta's share of total Canadian net cash exploratory expenditures declined from a 1966 peak of 74 percent to 54 percent in 1970" (Richards & Pratt, p. 169).

Mounting evidence that regional disparities were intractable and the collapse of key primary commodity prices constituted a powerful one-two punch. Supplementing grain with potash or oil was now perceived as an inadequate base for stable economic development. Federal regional policies aimed at strengthening existing resource industries were likewise seen as insufficient. What was really required, on this analysis, was substantial economic diversification, particularly into the secondary manufacturing industries for which domestic demand fluctuated less than did international market demands for primary commodities. Pressure grew for more extensive government intervention aimed at the kind of diversification that market forces had not brought about.

All three prairie provinces soon elected governments which promised to pursue such policies more aggressively. The Conservative government in Manitoba was the first to fall, in 1969, when the NDP, led by Ed Schreyer, secured a one-seat majority. The NDP consolidated this slim margin in the election of 1973. In 1971 the Liberal government in Saskatchewan was defeated by the NDP, now led by Alan Blakeney (Gibbins, 1980, p. 126, p. 131). In the same year, Lougheed's Conservatives formed the a new government in Alberta, securing 49 of 75 seats. Finally, in 1972, the NDP, led by

Dave Barrett, defeated the Social Credit government in British Columbia (Richards & Pratt, 1979, pp. 164-66; Conway, p. 189).

Of the new provincial governments that took office between 1969 and 1972, then, three were NDP. That the fourth was Conservative may seem anomalous, and indeed it did reflect the much stronger indigenous business class associated with private oil and gas development in Alberta, but Lougheed's party shared many of the NDP's economic assumptions and some of its methods. From the time that Peter Lougheed took over the moribund Conservative party in 1965, he criticised the Social Credit government for its failure to channel the revenues from the petroleum industry into new industrial development which would sustain the provincial economy after the oil resources ran out. The Conservative victory of 1971 was based on capturing Liberal and NDP votes: Social Credit's share of the popular vote fell slightly from 45 percent in 1967 to 41 percent in 1971, but the Conservative rise from 27 percent to 46.5 percent was primarily at the expense of the Liberal party (its share fell from 11 percent to one percent) and the NDP (its share fell from 16 percent to 11 percent) (Richards & Pratt, p. 166). The economic policies of all four governments exhibited broad similarities:

> Without exception, although there were clear differences between the Alberta Tories and the three NDP governments, the new regimes promised a bigger role for provincial governments in planning and pacing resource development, as well as aggressive new tax and royalty schedules to increase returns to public treasuries. Although the NDP regimes, especially those of Blakeney and Barrett, promised a signficant public role in resource development through crown corporations, the Lougheed Tory government proved also to be surprisingly interventionist.

> (Conway, 1983, p. 190)

When Trudeau succeeded Pearson as Prime Minister in 1968 he seemed to be in touch with the new perspective, arguing that there was an important link between regional development and national unity: "If the underdevelopment of the Atlantic provinces is not corrected – not by charity or subsidies, but by helping them become areas of economic growth – then the unity of the country is as surely destroyed as it would be by the French-English confrontation." An essential element of the "Just Society", Trudeau had argued in his 1968 campaign, "was to put each region of Canada in a position where it can best help itself and the country as a whole" (cited in Lithwick, 1986, p. 126). Trudeau launched a major policy review, aimed at rationalizing and coordinating the various programs which had grown so rapidly over the previous decade. It led to the creation of the Department of Regional Economic Expansion (DREE) in 1968 and the strategy of creating "growth poles" across the country (Lithwick, p. 127).

These initiatives were not enough to forestall a disastrous Liberal showing in the West in the 1972 election. In an effort to demonstrate greater sensitivity to Western interests, the Liberal minority government proposed a Federal-Provincial Conference on Western Economic Opportunities. Prime Minister Trudeau seemed to accept the basic premise of the provincial industrial strategies when he argued that Canada must move to reduce regional economic specialization: it must promote "balanced and diversified regional economies across our land" (Tupper, in Pratt and Stevenson, 1981, p. 91). The economic division of labour implied by the doctrine of comparative advantage in a market economy – the foundation of the International Policy – was, apparently, being rejected by the federal government. But this proved to be largely rhetoric.

A 1973 internal review identified the need for greater coordination of DREE activities with other government departments, the private sector and the provinces. It recommended that DREE be decentralized, with a group of regionally based assistant deputy ministers given considerable freedom to work out agreements with their provincial counterparts in the form of a "General Development Agreement" (Aucoin & Bakvis, 1984; Lithwick, 1986, pp. 128-31). But no new consensus emerged within the federal government on the appropriate model of regional economic development and, without it, institutional reforms remained cosmetic.

The absence of consensus should not be surprising for fundamental issues of political economy and justice were at stake. Was the regional distribution of economic activity a function of "natural" forces – distance from markets, population size, resource bases and the like – or was it "unnatural" – the product of past and present exercises of political power such as the National Policy? If the former, should government simply allow the market to work itself out or should it intervene to induce alternative outcomes? In either case, should the central Canadian bias at the federal level, resulting from the concentration of voters in that region, be regarded as natural and inevitable? Surely not if that population concentration reflected a distribution of economic activity which was itself the product of the original National Policy. But then how should that bias be counteracted in the interest of a more just distribution of national economic activity? Should political power be redistributed by transferring more of it to provincial governments or by reforming the institutions of the central government?

Given Ottawa's inability to take a clear line on these issues, the initiative for such policies fell to provincial governments which had much less difficulty in deciding where they wanted to go. The next natural resource boom, led by four-fold increases in the price of oil in 1973 and parallel potash price increases between 1972 and 1974 (Richards & Pratt, p. 259), did not alter their commitment to the political and economic imperatives established during the earlier bust phase of the cycle. If anything, the boom's extraordinary character reinforced perceptions that it could not last long, and that every possible step must be taken to capture its windfall gains while they lasted and channel them into more permanent development prospects. As we shall see in the next chapter, provincial attempts to do so would soon lead to major federal-provincial confrontations.

Two Faces of Regionalism

The governments of the Atlantic provinces, in contrast to their Western Canadian counterparts, did not develop ambitious provincial industrial policies and assert claims against Ottawa for the jurisdictional room to implement them. They continued to support the primacy of the federal government in regional development policy. Their demands were confined to increased federal expenditures and increased provincial input into the uses to which these funds were put.

Three factors account for this difference in the logic of regionalism. First, the western resource endowment gave the provincial governments the wherewithal to undertake ambitious industrial policies. The Atlantic provinces had no equivalent, at least until the prospect of off-shore wealth became apparent. Second, and closely related, the rapid development of Western resource industries created large new industrial and tertiary sector management and working classes, and these became pivotal actors in the new political coalitions that underpinned activist provincial governments. The same phenomenon was occurring in central Canada, most dramatically in Quebec, but slow and sporadic growth in the Atlantic provinces made this a much less important factor. Finally, Westerners were disaffected from the Liberal governments which ruled in Ottawa from 1963 to 1979 and, hence, were more inclined to turn to their provincial governments than other less politically alienated Canadians. The geographic distribution of natural resources requires no comment here, but we need to explore the other two factors in more detail.

New Provincial Class Structures   Western economic growth had led to the emergence of important new classes in the 1950s. These included a business class oriented to resource extraction and a corresponding working class as well as civil servants associated with the rapid growth of the state. There was an equally rapid growth of the private service sector associated with the expansion of the cities. Together with the still important agrarian class, these new elements constituted a much more complex society with the potential for new political coalitions, new governing parties and new collective goals at the provincial level. These configurations could give rise to more than one type of political coalition, as Pratt and Richards have shown in their comparison of the changing bases of party support in Saskatchewan and Alberta in the post-war period.

Lougheed's Conservatives drew the core of their support from the "upwardly mobile urban middle class...leading indigenous entrepeneurs, managers and upper-income professionals...linking private and public sectors in a quasi-corporatist alliance" created by the oil boom. The resource boom was smaller in Saskatchewan, and accordingly these classes were weaker and less politically important there. Agriculture remained a much larger component of the Saskatchewan economy and organized agriculture was still a more important political force. With the support of organized agriculture and the organized labour that had become an important force in the cities and the mining towns, the NDP were able to do without the support of the Saskatchewan equivalents of Lougheed's core supporters, basing the party on a populist coalition and platform (Pratt & Richards, 1979, pp. 164-67, pp. 200-02, pp. 252-55).

The two new governments thus shared the goal of diversification. But the instruments that they chose to realize it were shaped by the different class bases upon which their electoral support rested. The Alberta Conservatives sought to nurture the development of an indigenous, entrepreneurial business class and, hence, favoured state-supported private enterprise. The NDP government of Saskatchewan sought instead to create an economically skilled bureaucratic class dedicated to the public interest and capable of effectively managing large-scale public corporations and joint ventures.

Western Alienation   In the first part of this period, Westerners sought and received increased participation in the national decision-making process in Ottawa. Between 1957 and 1963, the Diefenbaker governments marked the high water mark of this orientation. If Diefenbaker appealed to national rather than provincial identities in his election campaigns, he was nonetheless sympathetic to western concerns and made an effort to incorporate them more effectively into national policies. What most Westerners wanted was not special treatment, but rather more effective participation on the national stage (Gibbins, 1980, pp. 186-92). The defeat of the Diefenbaker government in 1963, despite sustained support on the Prairies, was therefore a setback, depriving the majority of its inhabitants of what they could regard as a strong voice in Ottawa.

The memory of Diefenbaker's policies, and expectations that another Conservative government would extend them, probably account for some of the continuity in prairie support for the Conservatives in this period. But it these were not the main reasons. The Liberal government in Ottawa was perceived by many Westerners as more and more preoccupied – indeed, driven – by its response to the new nationalism emerging in Quebec after 1960, as manifested in the Bilingualism and Biculturalism Commission, official bilingualism and the constitutional discussions. But the majority of Westerners did not recognize this as their agenda. They were more concerned with transforming the basic structure of the Canadian economy than with questions of linguistic and cultural identity which had long ago been resolved, on a "melting pot" model, on the Prairies (Gibbins, pp. 176-80).

Westerners felt that the Liberal party was ignoring a region with an insufficient population to remove them from power in Ottawa. The circle was a vicious one, from a Western standpoint, because many francophones suspected that the federal Conservatives harboured anti-French, anti-Quebec views which led them consistently to reject the Conservative option in Quebec. The Tories were unable to improve their representation in that province despite sustained efforts by Robert Stanfield after 1967. They received 19.5 percent of the Quebec vote in 1963, 21.3 percent in 1965, the same in 1968, and 17 percent in 1972 (Beck, 1968).

Liberal power depended on central Canada – winning Quebec and then convincing a majority of Ontario voters that the issues raised by Quebec were fundamental to the maintenance of national unity. The success of this strategy kept the Liberals in power, thereby excluding western concerns from substantial representation within the governing party between 1963 and 1979. In the context of mounting conflicts of regional economic interests, a federal government drawing the great bulk of its support from central Canada was widely assumed to generate policies hostile to Western aspirations for economic diversification.

Even if these assumptions were false, as David Smith (1981, p. 93) and Ken Norrie (1976), among others, have argued, their prevalence ensured that federal economic policy, to say nothing of official bilingualism, would be perceived by Westerners as the product of a process which gave insufficient weight to their beliefs and interests. So the Western sense of alienation from Ottawa and its policies revived following the defeat of Diefenbaker. This process culminated in the federal election of 1972. The Liberal party won a quarter of the votes in Saskatchewan and Alberta, but only one seat. It won 30 percent of the Manitoba votes, but only two seats. In 1953, by way of contrast, the Liberals had won 17 seats and received between 35 percent and 40 percent of the vote in these three provinces.

Thus as regional conflict intensified, the sympathies of Prairie citizens were generally aligned with their provincial governments and a national party which appeared permanently relegated to Opposition. Their provincial governments possessed political resources and political authority; the federal Conservatives did not. This dynamic strengthened the sense of regional identification with the group and with the governments that claimed to defend them. Such a reinforcement of sub-national identities could take place, with decentralizing pressures as one of its results, even in the absence of dramatic conflicts of regional economic interest. But they would be greatly reinforced by the battle over resource revenues after 1973.

Language: The Dialectics of Nationalism

The triumph of reformist Quebec nationalism occurred just as Canadian nationalism reached new heights in response to the changing character of politics in the United States and Quebec. Out of this dialectic of identities arose a new politics of community. We have already sketched the growth of Canadian economic nationalism. Here, we look first at the evolution of reform nationalism, including indépendentisme, among the francophones of Quebec. We then turn to the anglophone response to the new politics of Quebec, reflected in the federal government's Official Bilingualism and Multiculturalism policies.

Reformist Quebec Nationalism Ascendent

There were many variants of reformist Quebec nationalism. On the political economy axis there were left and right variants. On the political community axis there were federalist and indépendentiste variants, reflected in constitutional demands and attitudes toward federal-provincial relations. These axes intersected, creating four distinct political possibilities. Each of these positions was expressed by some political party in this period, and the changing strength of those parties, along with changes in their location along these two axes, allows us to track the rapid evolution of reformist Quebec nationalism in this period. There was a steady movement toward the left on the political economy axis and toward indépendentisme on the political community axis.

The Quiet Revolution The "Quiet Revolution" has come to mean many different things. For our purposes, it signifies the end of the phase of Quebec politics which began in the 1920s and which was dominated by battles between reformist and conservative Quebec nationalists. No fundamental political re-alignment of this kind takes place over night. Conservative Quebec nationalism persisted, in Caouette's Créditistes and in the Union nationale, for the remainder of this period, and beyond, but it was reduced to a minority current of provincial politics.

That the most dramatic political indication of this re-alignment occurred in 1960, rather than 1964 or 1966, was almost an accident. In the last years before the 1960 Quebec election, the major political groups opposed to Duplessis – notably the reformist wing of the Catholic church, the trade union movement, many francophone intellectuals and professionals and some elements of francophone business – had been consolidating their strength and moving toward a united front to defeat Duplessis. But they would not have had sufficient political might to defeat the UN in 1960 had it not been for a number of important external, and fortuitous internal, developments. Even so, it was a very close call (Latouche, 1986, pp. 14-20). However, this in no way undercuts the point that the broad movement of economic, social and political forces in Quebec made it highly likely, if not inevitable, that something along the lines of the Quiet Revolution would develop at some point in these years.

In the 1950s, the reform nationalists rallied around *Le Devoir*, taking effective aim at the corrupt electoral practices and patronage of the Duplessis regime. They developed a more comprehensive program of economic reform than their predecessors in the ALN or the Bloc Populaire, while maintaining a strong defence of provincial autonomy. The demographic and economic developments associated with industrialization or urbanization made it possible to link economic reforms and nationalism in a more powerful synthesis than ever before. Growing economic inequalities between French and English, and cultural assimilation of French-speakers in Montreal, demonstrated to many francophones that Duplessis' stand was as serious a threat to the future of the francophone community as federal centralization. This missile found its target. Despite their small numbers and lack of party organization, Duplessis reserved his most bitter invective for them (Quinn, 1979, pp. 153-57).

Francophone businesses, concentrated in small and medium-sized firms, most organized on a family basis, were suffering increasingly from the influx of large anglo-dominated corporations and the fact that insufficient credit was available from the anglophone financial establishment. Many became convinced that they could only survive if state intervention created a more favourable economic and cultural environment (Coleman, 1984).

The trade union movement was overcoming some of its deepest internal divisions. The national merger of the TLC and the CCL in 1956 extended to their branches in Quebec, which became the *Federation des Travailleurs de Quebec* (FTQ). The Catholic trade union movement had become more secular and more militant since the Asbestos Strike of 1949. These developments made it easier for them to form a united front against Duplessis, which happened in response to the Murdochville strike of 1957. The new solidarity carried over into the field of politics for the first time in 1959 (Quinn, pp. 157-60).

The reform wing of the Catholic Church, with the support of lay Catholics such as Gérard Pelletier, had long been a vocal critic of the Duplessis regime. But by 1950, it had become influential in the Quebec Church. In that year, the province's bishops issued a pastoral letter declaring that henceforth it was not merely a right but a duty for workers to organize collectively. The bishops also supported recent demands by the CTCC for worker participation in management, profits and ownership of industry. Finally, they acknowledged that industrialization was a permanent feature of Quebec society, abandoning previous efforts to maintain a predominantly agrarian form of society and economy. A powerful support for Duplessis' anti-modernizing, anti-union nationalism had been removed (Quinn, pp. 160-67).

As the strength and unity of the groups opposed to Duplessis' policies grew, the Liberal party was recovering from the disaster of the 1948 election. In 1952 it won 46 percent of the vote (though only about one quarter of the seats). As its platform developed in a more reformist and autonomist direction, it succeeded in garnering more of the opposition support. The 1956 provincial election was a slight setback – Liberal support fell to 44 percent of the vote and less than a fifth of the seats – but the party was making progress in the rural ridings, essential to success, given the skewed distribution of seats (Quinn, pp. 171-74).

In 1958, federal party politics intruded in an extraordinary way. For the first time since 1887, the federal Conservatives defeated the Liberals in Quebec, winning 49.6 percent of the vote and 50 seats to the Liberals' 45.7 percent and 25 seats (See, 1986, p. 88). This enabled Diefenbaker to form a majority government in Ottawa. The Duplessis machine had worked hard to bring about that victory, though neither leader embraced the other (Beck, 1968, pp. 321-55). Its connections with the federal Tories deprived Duplessis of the arguments that he had used to good effect in 1944 (that the provincial Liberal Party was subservient to federal Liberal government interests) but no-one made much of this at the time. Federal-provincial relations had greatly improved with the signing of the 1957 fiscal agreements (Latouche, 1986, pp. 14-18). More important, the Liberal defeat in Ottawa brought many able politicians into the provincial Liberal Party. One of them, Jean Lesage, the Minister of Northern Affairs and National Resources under St. Laurent, became the new leader in 1958 (Quinn, pp. 174-80).

Lesage extended the directions in which Lapalme had moved the party since 1950. During the 1960 election, the Liberals campaigned on the Programme of the Quebec Liberal Party, a document of 54 articles and more than 200 specific proposals, calling for a sweeping modernization of Quebec society and its relations with English Canada (Thompson, 1984, p. 84). There were proposals to develop a hospital insurance plan that would provide Quebecers with the same coverage as the 1957 federal plan, an extensive program of educational reform, increased benefits for the blind, the disabled and the aged, and reform of industrial relations. The apparatus of government was also to be modernized by the creation of new Departments of Cultural Affairs, Natural Resources and Federal-Provincial Relations, creation of an Economic Planning and Development Council, and civil service reform (Quinn, pp. 180-81; Coleman, pp. 94-99).

Duplessis died in September 1959. His successor, Paul Sauvé, sought to undercut reformist support for the Liberals by moving the UN in the same direction, promising "un revolution des cent jours". But he died only three months later, leaving no clear leader less than six months before the provincial election. Having lost two leaders in less than a year, and with no clear successor to Sauvé, the UN went into the June 1960 election in a shambles. The outcome of the closest Quebec election in post-war history was victory for Lesage. The Liberals took 51 seats with 51 percent of the popular vote, to the UN's 43 seats and 47 percent of the vote (Latouche, 1986, p. 19; Quinn, p. 182).

Lesage's victory brought to power a government that fundamentally rejected Duplessis' attitude toward the state. As Lesage himself put it, "the only power at our disposal is the state of Quebec.... If we refuse to use our state, we would deprive ourselves of what is perhaps our only means of survival and development in North America." (in See, 1986, p. 139). The Liberals introduced legislation expanding Hydro Quebec and creating other Crown corporations in key sectors of the provincial economy. New social policies, including comprehensive hospital insurance and a universal pension plan, were created. New laws sought to secularize higher education, improve its quality and increase its accessibility to students from low income families. The civil service was reformed – making merit a more important criterion for promotion by revitalizing the Civil Service Commission – to render it capable of effectively peforming all of these new tasks. Finally, electoral campaign financing laws were introduced, the electoral map was redrawn to reduce (but not eliminate) over-representation of the rural population, and the voting age was reduced from 21 to 18 (Quinn, pp. 190-95; Thompson, 1984, p. 193, p. 248; See, 1986, pp. 139-41).

In the course of the 1960s, Quebec politics polarized around the issue of Quebec's status within the federation – between 1962 and 1973 popular support for Quebec independence rose from eight percent to 17 percent (Hamilton & Pinard, 1982, p. 209) – and the best strategy for Quebec's economic development. Among the federalists, the conservative forces defeated in the 1960 election re-grouped around Daniel Johnson, the new leader of the Union nationale at the provincial level, and Réal Caouette's Créditistes at the federal level (see Stein, 1973). The federalist left found its home in Lesage's Liberals.

The first organized expression of indépendentiste ideas was the left-wing Rassemblement pour l'indépendence nationale (RIN), formed in 1960 by a small group of intellectuals. In 1964 the Ralliement national (RN) broke away from the RIN, retaining its commitment to independence but decrying its left-wing political orientation. In the provincial election of 1966, the first real measure of their electoral strength, the RIN captured 5.6 percent of the popular vote while the RN gained 3.2 percent, although neither party won any seats (Quinn, pp. 243-44).

These defections helped to undermine the Liberal government (See, 1986, p. 144). An astute UN strategy of focussing on the rural vote, still electorally over-represented, did the rest. Johnson's party won 56 seats with only 40.9 percent of the vote; the *Parti liberale*, with 47.2 percent, retained only 50 seats (Quinn, pp. 222-23). Despite his appeal to traditional values, Johnson made no effort to rein in the growth of the Quebec state. On the contrary, the UN extended SIDBEC, authorized Hydro Quebec to embark on the enormous Churchill Falls project, and created two new Crown corporations to undertake exploration for oil and gas (SOQUIP) and to conserve and develop forest resources (REXFOR) (Quinn, 1979, pp. 231-32).

Instead, Johnson sought to distinguish the UN from the Liberals on the political community axis. The year before the election Johnson had published *Egalité ou Indépendence*, in which he posed the alternatives for Quebec's future as the complete re-writing of the Canadian constitution – based on the assumption that the Quebec and federal governments had equal status as the representatives of the two founding peoples of Canada – or political independence for Quebec: "Si la sécession devenait pour les Canadiens français le seul moyen de rester eux-mêmes, de rester français, alors ce ne serait pas seulement leur droit, ce serait même leur devoir d'être séparatistes" (cited in Quinn, p. 212).

The rise of these indépendentiste parties, combined with electoral defeat, precipitated a crisis within the provincial Liberal party. The former Minister of Natural Resources, René Levesque, sought to convince the Liberals that the party should adopt the goal of political independence for Quebec, coupled with the negotiation of a new form of economic association. When the 1967 Party convention rejected this proposal, Levesque withdrew and formed the Mouvement souveraineté-association (MSA). By 1968 he had persuaded the RIN and the RN to join with the MSA to form the Parti québécois (PQ) (Quinn, pp. 243-49). The PQ, like the MSA before it, was primarily a party of young, of students and intellectuals, of professionals and white collar workers. The support of organized labour would only come later (See, 1986, pp. 144-45).

These developments spurred Premier Johnson's drive for what he termed "vastly increased powers for Quebec under a completely new constitution", and "the establishment of some form of international status for Quebec, particularly among the French-speaking community of nations" (Quinn, p. 233). But an aggressive stand on federalism was not sufficient to prevent the UN from being outflanked, and ultimately destroyed, on the issue of language. Premier Johnson died in September 1968. His successor, Jean-

Jacques Bertrand, was immediately faced with a crisis. The St. Leonard Catholic School Commission decreed, against strong parental protest and the English-language press, that Italian immigrants must send their children to French schools. Both sides in the dispute demanded that the government take action, either to apply the policies to all immigrants or to strike it down, but the UN was deeply divided. After much hesitation, Bertrand decided that he must support the freedom of choice of the immigrants and seek compromise between the two camps. The result was Bill 63 which, owing to abstentions and defections from his own party, was only passed with the support of the Liberals. It was a courageous decision, but it weakened the claim of the UN claim to be the pre-eminent nationalist party (Quinn, pp. 254-56).

The Parti libérale, now under the leadership of Robert Bourassa, sought to defuse nationalist criticism of its support for the Bill by focussing attention on economic problems. The only way of expanding growth and employment, Bourassa argued, was to rely more on foreign investment and private sector initiative. To nationalist arguments that increased integration was the major source of the current economic woes and, hence, that increased political autonomy was essential to their solution, Bourassa responded by reasserting the traditional distinction between culture and economy. The appropriate strategy was "souveraineté culturelle" combined with economic integration. Bourassa even followed Johnson and Bertrand in declaring that his party's support for federalism depended on its economic benefits, "le fédéralisme rentable" (Quinn, pp. 258-59).

That the chief "federalist" party in Quebec—the nominal ally of a federal Liberal government headed by a French Canadian — should take such a position suggested how tenuous Quebec's commitment to federalism had become: contingent federalism was judged to be the minimum concession that might retain sufficient popular support, given the growth of indépendentiste sentiments. Thus, by 1970 the Liberals were roughly on a par with the UN on internal linguistic questions (Bill 63) and on federalism, but added to this a strong pro-business strain in contrast to the UN's continued populism. The Parti québécois now embraced the left and right wings of the indépendentiste movement. The UN was thus located in the centre on both the nationalist and the class axes of the political field.

In the 1970 provincial election, support for the UN plummetted to 19.6 percent of the popular vote and 17 seats. The PQ outstripped the UN in popular support with 23 percent of the vote, although it received only seven seats, all but one in the working class east end of Montreal. Support for the Parti libérale actually declined marginally to 45.4 percent, but vote-splitting by the other two parties helped to translate that plurality into 72 seats (Quinn, p. 265). The Liberal victory over the PQ was closer than these figures suggest in one important respect: they had won 20 of their 72 seats only on the strength of anglophone votes (See, 1986, p. 146).

The electoral collapse of the UN encouraged an exodus of economic conservatives to the Liberal Party, further strengthening the re- orientation on this axis that Bourassa had initiated. It was completed when the FLQ crisis of October 1970 brought about a dramatic decline in PQ support – party membership fell from 80,000 to 30,000 between 1970 and 1971 – and sent the PQ leadership scrambling for support from organized labour. The PQ got that support in the spring of 1971, when the FTQ joined with the CSN and the Corporation des Enseignants de Québec (CEQ) to establish a common front for an independent, socialist Quebec (See, 1986, pp. 146-47). In 1972, the common front, on behalf of 200,000 Quebec state employees, sought without success to negotiate new contracts. The result was the biggest strike in Canada's history, beginning on April 11. Ten days later, Bourassa pushed back-to-work legislation through the National Assembly. When the unions refused to terminate the strike, their leaders were jailed. The divorce of the unions from the Liberals (with the exception of 40,000 members who broke away from the CSN in the aftermath of the general strike) and their attachment to the PQ, was thus cemented (Morton, 1984, pp. 282-86).

Reformist Quebec nationalism, having vanquished its conservative opponent, was now thoroughly polarized on both the economic and the community axes, between two parties. This process was completed in the provincial election of October 1973, when the Liberals were returned to office and the UN was wiped out, failing to win a single seat. The PQ, with 30 percent of the vote, became the Official Opposition in the National Assembly, despite the fact that the vagaries of the electoral system reduced its contingent to a mere six seats. The politics of Quebec, and Canada, had entered a new era.

The Roots of Indépendentisme   Just as the religion-based, normative differences that traditionally separated English and French Canadians sank into relative insignificance, federal-provincial tensions intensified and a large-scale, popularly-based Quebec separatist movement arose for the first time in Canadian history. How can this paradox be explained? What explains the growth and timing of indépendentiste ideas and sentiments? Both of the parties that emerged from the political struggles of this period had answers to these questions, and it is useful to begin with them.

Indépendentistes, exemplified by Claude Morin (1972), argued that increased public support for them sprang from growing frustration with the limits that federalism placed on the capacity of the Quebec state to realize the economic and cultural aspirations of its people. Federalists, such as Albert Breton (1964), understood indépendentisme as the logical extension of reformist Quebec nationalism and characterized the latter as the ideology of a "new middle class". Independence was expected to give the Quebec state maximum latitude to create new, highly-paid positions for this class within the state apparatus and, through language laws that would give French speakers a competitive advantage, in the private sector as well.

Both explanations suffer from obvious problems. If, as Morin suggested, indépendentisme arose out of frustrations with the federal constitution, why did it grow most rapidly in the 1960s when the Quebec state was rapidly expanding without constitutional impediments and Ottawa was making major concessions to provincial management and modification of existing and new federal programs? Conversely, why did support for independence level out from about the end of this period and fail to rise further as federal-provincial conflict escalated in the 1970s? Moreover, if it was a response to frustrations felt by all Quebec francophones, why did it fail to rise above 20 percent at any time (Hamilton & Pinard, 1982), even with the encouragement of the Quebec state after 1976? If, on the other hand, indépendentisme was a phenomenon confined to a section of the new middle class (as Breton and others suggested), then how could it exist before that very class was created by the Lesage state? Moreover, even after 1960, indépendentisme was endorsed by significant elements of other classes. This became impossible to ignore after the labour movement endorsed the PQ and sovereignty-association in 1971. But the federalist account provides no explanation of the nature of the attraction for those who were not members of the new middle class.

To fill in the explanatory gaps left by each account, we must recognize that there were at least three elements to what we have so far been content to call "reformist Quebec nationalism". Each implied different state policies and, at different points, these policies received more-or-less broadly-based support within Quebec society. Changes in the level and support bases for each element help to explain changes in the overall level of support for various versions of Quebec nationalism, including indépendentisme.

The first element was the demand for equality of economic opportunity for francophones. This, aside from the preservation of the language, was the function of the language laws, beginning with the Liberals' Bill 22 in 1974. These laws benefitted all francophones who competed with anglophones for jobs, and these jobs were concentrated in the cities, particularly among the better educated. Precisely because of its widely diffused benefits, no political party could attack such legislation with impunity, and none did after Bill 63 and the destruction of the UN. The new state enterprises also benefitted at least some members of all classes in their initial phase. Later, the new francophone business class that they helped to create demanded a halt to state expansion through Bourassa's reconstructed Liberal Party.

The second element was the demand for equal respect to be shown by English toward French Canadians. This demand resonated for all francophones, regardless of class, as long as they were discriminated against by virtue of their status as francophones. One result was the demand for constitutional recognition of the equal status of the two founding peoples – what in English Canada was known as "special status" for Quebec.

The third element was the demand that the Quebec state be allowed to function unimpeded by any federal entanglements as the instrument for the construction of a Quebec society that would be as different from contemporary English Canadian society as Duplessis' Quebec had been. This was a smaller group in 1970 than it had been in 1960, and it would be smaller still by 1983 as various elements, beginning with the new business class, reached what they considered the desirable limits of Quebec government activity before they reached the limits of its constitutional power. By the end of our period, only one element of the new middle classes – the state elites – and one element of the working classes – that committed to moving beyond capitalism – could plausibly argue that an escape from federalism was essential to the realization of their vision of the good society.

It became increasingly clear that the first and second demands could be realized within the federation. The first, especially provincial language and education legislation, would have to be protected from constitutional reforms that might undermine them; and the second would require a constitutional reform by its very nature. But the prospects of attaining both of these goals within the federation came to seem increasingly realistic. The third goal could not be achieved within the federation, by definition – this was the continuing heart of the indépendentiste drive – but given how much had been achieved within the federal context, the numbers adhering to that vision did not grow much after 1973. In short, as long as independence seemed to be required in order to realize all these goals, they could be united to create a movement with a very broad base and great moral power. But as the first two goals began to be realized within confederation, they separated and the movement weakened.

If an analysis of the character of modern Quebec nationalism in terms of these three basic demands clears up some problems, it does not explain why those demands arose when they did. After all, inequalities of economic opportunity, the lack of respect for francophones by anglophones, and the desire for a more just, non-capitalist social order all predated the 1960s. We have already traced the gradual reorientation of the key groups that forged the original anti-Duplessis coalition – the growing strength of the reform wing of the church, the radicalization of the trade unions, and so on. But that only pushes the question of timing one step back. Why were these groups changing as they did? The answer must lie in the basic societal trends that changed the experiences and ideas of the individuals that constituted them – urbanization, secularization and assimilation.

Urbanization facilitated the formation of an organized francophone working class capable of mobilizing to challenge its economic subordination. Industrial workers could act collectively much more easily than small scale farmers, as the relative political insignificance of the Quebec farm movement in these years attests. The proximity of urban life, combined with improved communications, increased awareness of difference and of inequality. It was much easier for larger numbers of francophones actually to "see how the other half lives" in Montreal. Research on the regional distribution of support for unilingualist and separatist policies found both to be highest in cities where much of the population is bilingual (See, 1986, p. 150).

Urbanization also encouraged secularization, for the Catholic Church had always been much stronger in the rural areas than in urban areas. Secularization meant that the basis of self-esteem for a growing number of francophones was no longer their status as an island of Catholic faith in a sea of Anglo-Saxon protestantism and materialism, the vision articulated by l'Abbé Groulx. Now their capacity to control their own lives, individually and collectively, and to realize their this-worldly aims (secular power) increasingly became the principal basis of self-esteem. The normative transformation of Quebec society meant that English and French Canadians were now competing on the same terrain for the same rewards.

As long as these rewards were denied to francophones, not on the basis of claims about individual merit but by virtue of their status *qua* francophones, the pursuit of secular goods and power could only be effectively pursued by organizing and acting collectively, by overcoming their own doubts about their worth and then forcing "the other" (English Canada) to acknowledge their equality. This was the essence of reformist Quebec nationalism – a celebration of the virtues of being a French speaker and a demand for equal status – and this was why it resonated so powerfully for the great majority of the population, not merely a few elites.

Secularization had another powerful and somewhat paradoxical effect on francophones. On the one hand, the erosion of the power of the Catholic Church was often seen as a liberation. But on the other hand, a French Canadian identity rooted in language alone was less substantial and clearly defined than it had hitherto been. One could be a French speaker and almost anything else as well – language *per se* provided no sign posts to the good life or the good society. Moreover, a language-based identity was more vulnerable to the demographic forces that threatened to push the francophone population below the "critical mass" essential to the maintenance of a living language than a religion-based identity (Coleman, pp. 130-35, pp. 180-89).

Studies began to appear predicting that if existing trends continued unabated, French would cease to be a living language in Quebec. Henripin's famous 1962 study of trends in Montreal found that a growing portion of the total francophone population was living in that city. The fate of the French language, then, increasingly hinged on what happened in Montreal. But the growing numbers of non-French-speaking immigrants entering Quebec, most of whom settled in Montreal, usually chose to have their children educated in English. Hence the importance of Bill 63 and subsequent education legislation. Moreover, the traditionally high birth rate of the French Canadians had fallen precipitously, becoming the lowest in Canada by the late 1960s (See, 1986, pp. 142-43). Extrapolating these trends, francophones would cease to be the majority in Montreal within two decades, and this would hasten the process of assimilation in the province as a whole (Hamilton & Pinard, 1982, p. 206). It was necessary to act at once, before these trends became irreversible.

Thus, urbanization and secularization made it impossible to continue to think of culture and economy as essentially distinct spheres of life. The economy had to be made primarily French-speaking if francophones were going to move out of the occupational ghettos to which they had hitherto been confined without stepping into the "melting pot" in the process. And francophones had to move out of those ghettos and into an expanding, modernizing Quebec economy if they were to fulfill their new ambitions. The result was the new kind of Quebec nationalism, espoused by key collective actors and successive Quebec governments.

English Canadians Face Quebec

Developments in Quebec challenged the English Canadian conception of national identity which had evolved since the Second World War. Most English Canadian commentators greeted the end of the Duplessis era and the election of the Lesage government with enthusiasm. As they viewed it, Quebec was about to throw off the shackles of tradition and join "modern Canada". Past conflicts were assumed to be the result of divergent traditions, so it was expected that that the country would enter a new era of French-English harmony (Behiels, 1984, p. 4). Only gradually did English Canadians recognize the very different significance of the Quiet Revolution. A modernized Quebec would, indeed, be more like English Canada in important respects. But this meant that now French and English Canadians would increasingly want, and compete for, the same things: cultural and linguistic pre-eminence (or, at least, equality), political authority, and economic status and wealth.

Change in Quebec threatened some of the fundamental assumptions upon which postwar Canada had been built, both at the level of the majority conception of the national purpose and identity, and at the level of the new economic and federal orders which in part embodied it. In constructing the post-war order, Pierre Trudeau observed, English Canada had "calmly assumed away the existence of one-third of the nation" and the initial success of that order was possible only because of "Quebec's inability to do anything about it" (in Crepeau & Macpherson, 1965, p. 32). D. V. Smiley agreed, arguing that nationalism could no longer serve as the cement of national unity; any new national policy now must involve the "dominant men and movements in Quebec in the most positive and fundamental way" (in Russell, 1965, p. 108).

Changes in the ways that anglophones and francophones viewed themselves, hence one another, hence the Canadian nation they shared, were not new. The old options articulated by Cartier and Bourassa against Tardivel and l'Abbé Groulx, remained the central ones: integration or disengagement. Either Canadians could strive to create a nation in which everyone would be bicultural and bilingual, or they could recognize that for the forseeable future two distinct peoples would remain harnessed together within the same nation, and strive to adapt the federal system to permit maximum room for each to live without getting in the other's way.

We have seen the growing popular support among Quebec francophones for the disengagement option, manifested in the growing provincialism of successive Quebec governments and the growth of grass roots support for indépendentiste parties. But francophones in Quebec remained divided. The end of the period under consideration saw them sending strong integrationists such as Pierre Trudeau to Ottawa, and electing a Liberal provincial government that attempted to reduce the political salience of Quebec nationalism by claiming that it had little place in economic, as opposed to cultural, matters.

English Canada was similarly divided, particularly between those who were of British and non-British origins, a factor that varied with regional settlement patterns. Electoral results in Quebec helped us to read developments among the francophone majority. The same approach reveals the oscillations of the anglophone majority between the two models, and the regional differences that partially determined those oscillations.

Diefenbaker, despite the strong Quebec support which he received in the 1958 election, had little understanding of, and less sympathy for, the disengagement option. There was no strong Quebec leadership in his Conservative Party and many of the new Tory MPs from Quebec had little in common with Diefenbaker's views (Cook, 1966, pp. 8-9). His opponents alleged that the Conservative electoral strategy was to "write-off" Quebec, concentrating on building a majority in the rest of Canada. Diefenbaker made a number of financial concessions to the provinces. But his commitment to an "unhyphenated Canadianism" and his love of the British connection left him unsympathetic to the developing ideas in Quebec. When André Laurendeau, editor of *Le Devoir*, proposed a full-scale national enquiry into the relations between French and English, Diefenbaker was not interested.

Lester Pearson, who succeeded him in 1963, was open to limited disengagement. The 1963 Liberal election platform emphasized respect for provincial jurisdiction and the strengthening of equalization and fiscal decentralization in the form of increased fiscal tranfers and the introduction of provisions to allow provinces to "opt out" of certain federal programs. In adopting this line, Pearson partially accepted some of the premises of Quebec nationalism – that Quebec is a distinct society, a "nation" at least in the sociological sense of the term; that the essence of Canada was that it was a partnership between "two founding peoples", and that Quebec, as one geographic and political "home" of one of these peoples, has a special status within the federation which ought to be recognized. In the course of the 1963 election campaign, Pearson declared:

> It is now clear to all of us, I think, that French speaking Canadians are determined to become directors of their economic and cultural destiny in their own changed and changing society...they also ask for equal and full opportunity to participate in all federal government services, in which their own language will be fully recognized... . [The federal government must recognize] the greatest possible constitutional decentralization and...special recognition of the French fact and the rights of French-speaking Canadians in Confederation.
>
> (in Bothwell, et.al, 1981, p. 289)

In office, Pearson's Liberals responded to the challenge from Quebec by expanding francophone participation in the public service, enhancing the federal capacity to provide French-language services, and promoting bilingualism in public services across the country. Also, in the tradition of Henri Bourassa, they sought to create and sustain national symbols and a national identity which was unifying rather than divisive. This was the motive behind the decision to adopt a new Canadian flag. Ironically, a change aimed at reducing symbols of historic divisions proved, in the short run, a new focal point for that old controversy.

By the mid-1960s, however, the federal government was becoming unhappy with the results of efforts to accomodate Quebec nationalism (Simeon, 1972, pp. 66-68). In 1965, Pierre Trudeau, Jean Marchand and Gérard Pelletier (former publisher of Quebec's largest newspaper, *La Presse*), came to Ottawa to steer the federal government onto an unambiguously integrationist course. Explaining their decision to enter federal politics, the three wrote:

...the objective situation has changed: Quebec has become strong and the central power has become weak. The Quebecers more and more turned towards the provincial sphere, and it is this sphere which attracts the most dynamic politicians and the competant bureaucrats. The Quebecers continue to be governed by Ottawa, they still pay it half their taxes, but they are less and less present there, intellectually, psychologically, and even physically.

(Simeon, 1972, pp. 171-72, n. 22)

They found the Pearson government receptive to their diagnosis and prescriptions. Trudeau quickly became Parliamentary Secretary to the Prime Minister, and then Minister of Justice. From this time forward, the federal Liberals took the view that disengagement would reduce the links between Quebec citizens and their national government, while strengthening those between citizens and the Quebec government. The legitimacy of the federal government in Quebec, and ultimately the legitimacy of the Canadian nation itself, would be called into question. The role of Quebec MPs in Ottawa would become increasingly anomalous as they voted on federal programs which would not affect their own electorates. On this logic, further concessions would lead inevitably to special status and, from there, to associate statehood and independence.

Henceforth, the federal government would resist concessions to Quebec's search for greater authority and, particularly, any formal recognition of special status. It was time to draw the line against "creeping separatism" (Burns, 1967). Quebec nationalism could be defused only by making sure that, as Trudeau put it, Quebec is "not a ghetto for French-Canadians, that all of Canada is theirs". The federal government must say to the Québécois: "No, not only the Quebec government can speak for you; on the contrary only the Ottawa government can give the French-Canadians their due across the country" (CAR, 1968, p. 71). It was clear that, to accomplish this, Canada's bilingualism must be given more recognition in the symbols of the country; minority language services must be provided across Canada; the public service must become a truly bilingual institution, able to serve francophones in their own language and to represent them fully, especially at the higher levels. Further, the federal government must become a more active presence in Quebec, through regional development and other programs. All of this implied major changes in anglophone attitudes to francophones, and in the national institutions affecting both.

If the integrationists had won out within the Liberal Party by 1968, this was not true of the other two major federal parties. Robert Stanfield, Progressive Conservative leader since 1967, succeeded against considerable opposition in opening his party to the new Quebec. At a party conference in Montmorency, Quebec, the Conservatives adopted the concept of "two founding peoples/deux nations", an ambiguous formula which allowed Pierre Trudeau to hang the label "two nations" on Stanfield, despite his dislike of "special status" (Beck, 1968, pp. 408-09; CAR, 1968, pp. 37-38). The New Democratic Party did advocate special status, arguing that, as the "centre of the French-speaking community in Quebec" the province required powers to deal with matters which "affect the community". This departure from the NDP's historic centralism sprang from several sources. Its leadership was concerned about the "poisonous antagonisms" being created by official bilingualism, particularly in the West, from which the NDP drew much of its strength. Tommy Douglas, the NDP leader and former Saskatchewan Premier, accused Trudeau of having "divided this country as it has never been divided before" in the pursuit of a strategy with little long run hope of success (CAR, 1968, p. 61). The NDP also argued that the kind of federal government activism it sought would not be possible unless Quebec were permitted to exempt itself, at least to some degree, from such initiatives. By recognizing special status, they argued, "Canadians elsewhere can seek action in these fields without creating misunderstandings, frustrations and intolerable strains to our federation" (CAR, 1968, p. 35).

In the 1968 election, Trudeau attacked these alternative visions of the appropriate response to Quebec head on, arguing that they represented a sell-out to the nationalists. His success in that election, particularly in Quebec where he gained 53.6 percent of the vote (Beck, pp. 418-19), virtually ruled out further political exploration of the special status concept. Increasingly the alternatives were posed in the terms that Levesque and Trudeau saw them: full sovereignty for Quebec versus full integration on the bilingual model.

English Canadians were as divided in their reaction to "official bilingualism" as the major national parties. The distinction between those who were and were not of British origin was particularly important on this issue. If the Red Ensign had symbolically excluded the francophone third of the Canadian population from membership in the national political community, the language of dualism, with its emphasis on equal partnership between the "two founding peoples" excluded the one-third of the Canadian population who were neither British nor French in origin. Were there not, they asked, many founding peoples? Did not singling out two for special status relegate the rest to an inferior status?

The federal government responded to these challenges by distinguishing language from culture. As one federal cabinet minister, John Roberts, put the matter in the late 1960s, "What we stand for is one country, two languages, and a plurality of cultures". Thus, the struggle to formulate a conception of the national community capable of undermining the appeal of the Quebec autonomists led to the federal embrace of "multiculturalism". A Ministry of State for Multiculturalism was created in 1972.

In this way, Quebec's struggle to redefine its notion of political and cultural community created strong pressures to do the same, not only at the level of the nation called Canada, but also at the level of the many ethnic groups which collectively comprised the nation. This encouraged the rise of native people and other ethnic minorities to hitherto unprecedented levels of political activism.

Federal State

The structural and normative changes discussed above combined to generate powerful pressures for a renewed round of state expansion. Many now argued that economic growth required micro-economic in addition to macro-economic intervention by the state. Demands for greater equity and social justice between classes and regions entailed a greater state role in regulation and redistribution, whether or not this was perceived to be compatible with economic efficiency. Regional, sectoral and social policies were advocated on the grounds of both efficiency and equity.

This state growth had two major implications for Canadian federalism. First, and most directly, new government roles meant new problems of coordination and coherence. Second, and equally important if less direct, state growth shaped the evolution of societal forces which, in turn, constrained the responses that Canadian federalism could make to the new problems. We have seen, for example, how the growth of provincial governments in Alberta and Quebec stimulated the formation of classes many of whose members espoused a kind of regionalism or nationalism which led them to favour the further extension of provincial government economic activities.

The whole process was reflexive because state and society were so thoroughly integrated. The growth of the state *per se* created a profound need for intragovernmental and intergovernmental coordination. The more integrated programs had to be, the greater the need for an integrative philosophy of government and the authority to execute it. Thus, state growth underpinned the shift from "administrative" to "executive" federalism.

Executive federalism could respond to coordination problems in two ways: by improving the quality of intergovernmental communication and coordination, or by reducing the need for it. The former strategy led to efforts to develop new intergovernmental mechanisms. The latter strategy implied constitutional reforms to redraw the jurisdictional boundaries in ways that would reduce overlap. Which of these options received most emphasis, and how successful it proved, was not determined by state growth rates but rather by societal developments. In this period, the limited re-emergence of regionalism combined with the triumph of reform nationalism in Quebec to give the initiative to provincial governments favouring decentralization and higher levels of intergovernmental coordination. This was, consequently, the period in which the intergovernmental machinery expanded most rapidly. But as these tensions grew, interest in constitutional amendments grew.

State Growth and Canadian Federalism

The role of the state grew at an unprecedented rate in this period, even more rapidly at the provincial level than the federal. One dimension of this growth was the degree to which government regulates private enterprises. An Economic Council of Canada study (1979) estimated that there were 12 new federal regulatory statutes in the 1950s, seven in the 1960s and 25 in the 1970s. At the provincial level, there were 177 in the 1950s, 218 in 1960s and 262 in the 1970s. Another dimension was the degree to which governments expanded their economic role through public enterprise (Laux & Molot, 1988, pp. 11-36). The total assets of federal Crown corporations, as surveyed by the Comptroller General, increased from $6.5 billion to $35.1 billion between 1960 and 1980. Provincial Crowns grew from a combined $5.1 billion in assets in 1958 to $55.6 billion by 1980. According to one estimate, 58 percent of federal Crown corporations were created between 1960 and 1980. Of 233 provincial corporations, 75 percent were created in the same two decades, and 48 percent during the 1970s (Vining & Botterell, in Pritchard, 1983, pp. 303-67). Thus, on both dimensions, both orders of government were growing at an accelerating pace, but provincial governments were expanding most rapidly.

Figures based on government expenditures and employment, as a share of the entire economy, show the same patterns. Total government expenditures rose from 30 percent to 37 percent of GNP between 1960 and 1970, despite the rapid rate at which GNP grew (Macdonald Commission, *Report*, 1985, pp. 34-35). Between 1946 and 1971, employment in the federal public service almost doubled, from 120,577 to 216,488. In the same period, provincial employees increased five-fold, from 38,370 to 209,760. By 1975, 24 percent of the workforce was employed directly by the state: 24 percent by the federal government, 44 percent by provincial governments, and 31 percent by municipal governments (Howard & Stanbury, 1984, p. 13).

This pattern of state growth was not unique to Canada, or to federal states. Cameron found that all OECD countries grew rapidly in the years between 1960 and 1975. Of five explanatory variables he explored, the strongest correlation was with the "openess" of the economy – the share of GNE deriving from trade. The greater that share, the greater the rate of state growth measured as a percentage of GNE. The second highest correlation was with the organizational and political strength of the trade union movement: the more powerful the trade unions, the higher the rate of state growth. OECD nations with comparable levels of openness to Canada (such as the Netherlands, Belgium, the Scandinavian countries) manifested higher rates of state growth than Canada but they also had stronger trade union movements. It is consistent with Cameron's findings that Canada, with a higher than average level of openness, should be in the upper echelon of the rapidly growing states, but with a relatively weak trade union movement, should be near the bottom of that group (Cameron, 1978, pp. 1243-61).

Cameron also found one institutional variable linked to state growth between 1960 and 1975 – federalism: the correlation was negative. This finding is consistent with Wilensky's comparative work on social policy, which concluded that federalism was associated with a relatively smaller welfare state (1975, pp. 52-54). Our discussion of the inter-war years, and of the Reconstruction decade, supports these impressions. In the first period, we saw how federalism helped the political elites of Quebec to delay the expansion of the federal welfare state. In the second, we saw how Ontario's opposition to the fiscal arrangements that Ottawa deemed necessary to fund its Green Book proposals slowed the implementation of the new policy commitments that followed from the historic compromise.

Yet from 1963 to 1973, the Canadian state grew rapidly at the same time that federal institutions were decentralizing. On the Cameron/Wilensky account, we should expect to find accelerating state growth associated with centralizing tendencies. What is missing from the simple model of federalism that Cameron tested is a sense of the societal dynamics that underpin both the evolution of state policy and the character of federalism. In this period, the dynamic of Canadian federalism was the product of a federal government seeking to realize an ambitious social and economic policy program, faced with provincial governments equally if not more ambitious, and no longer willing to concede federal leadership. This unusual conjunction of expansive, ambitious federal *and* provincial governments lies behind the unusual combination of accelerating state growth and decentralization. Both were responding to heightened citizen expectations.

The Emergence of Executive Federalism

The growth of the state had important implications for the internal structure and operation of governments. The proliferation of ministries and specialized agencies responding to a more diversified set of clienteles placed a higher premium on coordination within governments, and on more "rational" policy-making techniques, such as PPBS. Efforts to combat confusion and duplication led to the creation of new central agencies such as the Prime Minister's Office. This new organizational structure was less compatible with the pattern of cross-government functional relationships linking parallel ministries characteristic of cooperative federalism. The tendency was to move intergovernmental relation "up the ladder" to Ministers of Finance and First Ministers, where broad issues of power, status and ideology were more salient. This tendency was reinforced as federal-provincial relations became more preoccupied with Quebec. Increasingly, individual issues were considered within a global framework, developed at the peak of the bureaucratic hierarchy and imposed on those below.

These trends placed new demands on Canadian federalism and new limits on how those demands might be met. In the heyday of administrative federalism, the chief requirement had been to permit the implementation of the new national policy without dramatic centralization, and without the support of the Quebec government. Fiscal arrangements permitted this objective to be realized with tolerable departures from the principles of equity and efficiency. Now that Quebec demanded greater autonomy and resources, fiscal decentralization proceeded more rapidly than it had in the 1950s (or would in the 1970s). Between 1950 and 1960 federal spending, before transfers, as a proportion of all government expenditures changed only marginally – from 58.1 percent to 59.3 percent. After transfers, it declined slightly, from 51.9 percent to 50.5 percent. But between 1960 and 1970, the federal share before transfers dropped more than 10 points, to 49 percent and, after transfers, dropped even further to 38 percent. In the next decade, again, there was virtually no change (Macdonald Commission, *Report*, 1985, p. 37).

But fiscal decentralization did not solve the new coordination problems and it may well have exacerbated them by providing provincial governments with the resources to expand rapidly. The first response was to develop more and better intergovernmental mechanisms in the hope of improving consultation and facilitating cooperation and compromise. But the number of policy areas in which the interests of the two orders of government seemed in conflict, and the degree to which these conflicts were linked together into comprehensive visions of Canadian nationality and federalism, was making interdependence less and less manageable. Interest in constitutional reform therefore revived.

Fiscal Arrangements: Managing Decentralization

"Tax Sharing"   Quebec opened a major breach in the tax rental system when Ottawa agreed to "abate" or transfer tax room, which Quebec could then occupy without subjecting its citizens to "double taxation". Under the Federal-Provincial Tax Sharing Arrangements Act, passed in 1956, provinces had two options: they would either receive federal payments equal to 10 percent of the federal personal income tax raised in the province, nine percent of the corporate income tax and 50 percent of succession duties; or they could impose their own taxes and the federal taxes would be reduced accordingly. Equalization would bring the yield from these sources up to the average per capita yield of the top two provinces.

In opposition, Diefenbaker had been critical of the 1957-62 fiscal arrangements and, in 1957, with the formation of a Conservative minority government, a Federal-provincial conference led to changes. In 1958, the provincial share of the personal income tax was raised from 10 percent to 13 percent, and equalization was supplemented with a special Atlantic Provinces Adjustment Grant, with special provisions for Newfoundland.

In 1960, negotiations began for the next set of arrangements to cover the period from 1962 to 1967. At a conference in July 1960, the first attended by new Quebec Premier Jean Lesage, the wealthier provinces, citing the rapid increases in provincial responsibilities, argued for a larger share of the major revenue sources. The poorer provinces argued, as before, for a greater commitment to equalization. Lesage argued that in the Reconstruction years the federal goverment had possessed good grounds for claiming priority of access to tax revenues, given its mandate to forestall recession and implement social security. But now, he claimed, the major problem was inflation, not recession, and it was provincial priorities – resource development, local economic development, education and social services – which were growing most rapidly (Thompson, 1984, p. 369). In the same vein, Ontario called for "a new deal", demanding 50 percent of all three major tax sources. But the Atlantic provinces and Saskatchewan opposed the end of tax rentals: "the clock was to be turned back", said Saskatchewan Premier Douglas, "to the 'dog-eat-dog' competition of the prewar period" (CAR, 1960, p. 45). Further meetings were held in October 1960 and February 1961.

The result was the termination of the tax rental system which had been created during the war, and of Ottawa's right, which would be identical in all provinces, to set major tax rates unilaterally. Now all provinces would pass their own tax legislation, although Ottawa would continue to act as their tax collection agent, except in Quebec. As long as provinces did not alter the base used for calculating taxes, they could now set their own rates; only citizen expectations and provincial government competition for new investment, would keep them from diverging.

Double taxation would still be avoided through federal "abatements". Ottawa would reduce the level of its taxes on a given base so as to make room for provincial tax increases which, under the new proposals, would rise from 13 percent to 16 percent of the federal tax in 1962, and to 20 percent in 1966. The corporation income tax and succession duty abatements would remain the same. By January 1, 1962, all provinces had passed their own personal and corporate income tax legislation and all but Ontario and Quebec joined the collection arrangements. Only Manitoba and Saskatchewan took the opportunity to raise their own taxes above the level of the federal abatements.

The election of a Liberal government in 1963 signalled a new round of pressures to increase the provincial share of these major tax revenues. The negotiations were now caught up in the vortex of issues surrounding Quebec's pressures for special status at the same time as the federal government had an ambitious agenda of new shared cost programs. Quebec led the provincial demands, calling for a provincial share of 25:25:100, one quarter of both personal and corporate income tax revenues and 100 percent of succession duties. As part of a complex deal made in March 1964, it was agreed that the provincial share of the personal income tax would rise to 24 percent by 1966, and that the provincial share of income taxes from power utilities would rise from 50 percent to 95 percent. In addition, the governments agreed that the allocation of tax sources should be put on a more carefully planned basis. A federal-provincial Tax Structure Committee was established to examine projected revenues and expenditures for the 1967-72 period for each level of government. Its purpose was a "complete and fundamental re-examination of federal-provincial fiscal arrangements," the first since Rowell-Sirois. The work was carried out by the Continuing Committee of Officials on Fiscal and Economic Matters, and coordinated by A. W. Johnson, Assistant Deputy Minister of Finance and a former Saskatchewan Deputy Treasurer. The Committee was a remarkable exercise in collaborative analysis, but it did little to provide a "rational" basis for allocating revenues. The fiscal needs of both orders of government were growing so rapidly that no agreement on likely future revenues and expenditures was possible.

By the mid-1960s federal officials had become convinced that the piecemeal transfer of revenues to the provinces was undermining the capacity of the federal government capacity to manage the economy and pursue its own priorities. It was time to draw the line. No longer would Ottawa "make room" for the provinces by reducing its own taxes. Each level of government must be responsible to its taxpayers. At a meeting of the Tax Structure Committee in October 1966, Finance Minister Mitchell Sharp declared:

> We must get away from what is tending to become a conventional wisdom that the federal government can and should be expected to give greater tax room to the provinces when they find their expenditures rising more rapidly than their revenues. This has been possible, and has been done in the past decade, but it cannot be regarded as a general duty.
>
> (in Simeon, 1972, p. 76)

Henceforth, while the tax collection agreements were renewed, the only further abatement of tax room would be associated with the new federal funding of post-secondary education. Nonetheless, in the space of a decade the provincial share of total income tax revenues had more than doubled.

Equalization   The shift to the tax sharing system made an equalization program essential, for the yield of the major taxes varied dramatically from province to province. From 1957 to 1962, the federal government transferred to each eligible province, without conditions, a grant sufficient to bring the per capita yield of the three major taxes up to the average of the richest two provinces. It provided an additional adjustment grant for the Atlantic provinces.

In the 1962-67 arrangements, the equalization standard was reduced to the national average, but the formula was broadened to incorporate natural resource revenues. Provinces were also guaranteed payments no smaller than they would have received under the previous formula. This process of broadening the range of taxes to be incorporated into the equalization formula culminated in 1967, when it was decided to incorporate all provincial revenues and to bring their yields up to the national average. The approach sought to be comprehensive; even revenue sources not themselves tapped by the federal government or not used by every province would be equalized. Overall federal payments were to be determined by the sum of provincial revenue-raising decisions. This approach is known as the "representative tax" system and remains, with modifications, the model employed today.

Deciding what taxes to include did not determine the appropriate levels of equalization. To address this issue, it was necessary to articulate more clearly its purposes and assess the level of transfers required to achieve them. The conception of intergovernmental equity that lay behind equalization was formulated for the first time, in the fashion which continues to be accepted today, in 1966. The object of equalization transfers, Mitchell Sharp stated, was to ensure that each province was able to provide an "adequate level of public services without having to resort to rates of taxation substantially higher than those of other provinces" (Courchene, 1984, p. 47). The result was a large increase in total equalization payments.

Not all provincial governments supported the new formula. Some wished a more global measure of provincial fiscal capacity, such as per capita income. Others wished the formula to take greater account of variations in expenditure needs and the cost of providing services from province to province. Wealthier provinces continued to balk at the extent of redistribution involved. British Columbia's Premier Bennett argued against the approach on the ground that Ottawa should subsidize individuals equally, wherever they lived, rather than regions and provinces. As with all other fiscal discussions, each government's approval or disapproval of a specific formula depended upon the perceived benefit of the formula for it.

Despite such grumbling, there appears to have been a remarkable level of agreement on the principle of equalization. It represented a striking blend of what are often seen as opposites: on the one hand, the commitment to national equity that was part of the postwar philosophy of the welfare state and, on the other hand, an acceptance of a relatively high degree of decentralization. The equalization program said, in effect, that lack of fiscal capacity should not prevent the provinces from pursuing the priorities which the federal constitution otherwise granted their citizens the right to determine. To achieve this, the federal taxing power would be used to generate revenues which would be transferred without conditions to provincial governments. This open-ended commitment would be determined not by federal calculations of provincial requirements, but "automatically" by the sum of provincial taxing decisions. By 1970 per capita provincial revenues, which had once diverged widely, were very close together (Simeon and Miller, 1980, pp. 246-47). Provincial spending converged. In 1972, three of the Atlantic provinces and Quebec had the greatest per capita levels of spending. A measure of equalization was also introduced into other shared cost programs. Thus, the medicare program, while based on total provincial spending, made equal per capita payments to provinces. Similarly, the 1971 reforms to Unemployment Insurance, with special "fisherman's benefits", and contribution and payment periods linked to local unemployment rates, made the program much more regionally redistributive.

Taken together, tax sharing and equalization underlined a central premise of cooperative federalism: there would be no assumption that the expanded role of the state would automatically accrue to the central government, or to the one with the greatest tax revenues. Rather than shifting responsibilities to Ottawa, resources would be shifted to the provinces. And it would be national policy to ensure, through equalization, that all provinces had a comparable financial ability to undertake their responsibilities. Equalization went a long way to reconciling the idea of provincial autonomy with horizontal equity.

Shared Cost Programs   Shared cost programs were perhaps the characteristic device of modern federalism. By 1960, they were providing more than a quarter of provincial revenues, but objections, both practical and in principle, were growing. It was argued that such programs skewed provincial priorities, that they fostered more uniformity than was desired in the federal state, that conditions were often onerous and blocked provincial innovation, that they were begun, modified and terminated by the federal government without sufficient consultation, and that they failed to take into account variations in provincial capacity to raise matching funds, thus leading to greater federal contributions in some richer provinces than in other poorer ones. Provinces complained they were being "bribed with their own money" (for a summary, see Carter, 1971, pp. 88-89).

Several provinces argued that conditional grant programs had served their purpose and become "so entrenched that their continued existence is no longer in question". Hence, conditions should be removed, and they should be converted into block grants (Douglas, quoted in Carter, 1971, p. 89). Quebec went further when, in 1960, Premier Lesage argued that many programs were now "sufficiently well-established on the provincial scale to enable the Federal government to...vacate these fields. Obviously, in such a case, it would be necessary to compensate the provinces fully for the additional financial responsibilities assumed by them" (in Carter, 1971, p. 89). The compensation, Lesage argued, should take the form of increased tax point abatements, appropriately equalized. The federal Liberals made this proposal a plank of their 1961 election platform. But at the same time, the federal government was rapidly expanding its social policies. International economic change required that education and manpower policies be re-cast to facilitate more rapid and effective economic adjustment. Both tendencies seemed to require further federal action in areas falling primarily, if not exclusively, under provincial jurisdication. Ottawa and Quebec City, if not yet the two orders of government as such, were on a collision course on the issue of the direction in which shared cost programs should move.

The result was an extraordinary set of negotiations between Ottawa and the provinces in 1963 and 1964. Federal activism and provincial assertiveness led to sharp clashes on a wide variety of issues, from tax sharing to pensions. In the end, a new agreement was reached: the Established Programs (Interim Arrangements) Financing Act of 1965. As part of a broader agreement between Quebec and Ottawa, provinces could "opt out" of a number of shared-cost schemes, including hospital insurance, old age assistance and related welfare programs, health grants, vocational training and others. "Compensation" would take the form of an additional transfer of 20 tax points, together with cash payments for a number of smaller programs. An additional tax transfer was to compensate Quebec for opting out of the new federal youth allowance program. Opting-out was available to all provinces, but only Quebec exercised the option.

One of the other provisions of the agreement concerned the new Canada Pension Plan (CPP). Faced with Ottawa's proposal, the Quebec government had formulated an alternative with two attractions: it was more generous and it created a large fund which, if assigned to the equivalent of the Quebec *Caisse de depôts*, could be used by provincial governments as an instrument of economic development (Laux & Molot, 1988, pp. 125-50;

Huffman et.al., in Simeon, 1985b, pp. 140-44). Not only was Quebec able to implement its alternative, but it became the model for the CPP as well, with the fund it generated made available to provinces for their purposes. Provinces were also assured a high degree of control over any future amendments to the Pension Plan.

In a sense Ottawa's opting-out concession was mainly symbolic: it was for an "interim" period, during which provinces would maintain existing program standards. The agreement specified that an "opting out" province would maintain its "present obligations" under the programs and continue to account for expenditures to Ottawa. It said nothing about future programs (Pearson letter, in Moore, Perry and Beach, App. G, p. 143). Meanwhile, Ottawa was able to get on with the new education policies that it regarded as essential to the country's future economic well-being. In 1967, the federal government assumed responsibility for paying half the operating costs of post- secondary institutions, although in deference to Quebec and the new climate in federal-provincial relations, there was no federal policy role and the payment took the form of a combination of "tax room" and cash, an important precedent for the future. Yet, combined with the agreement on a separate Quebec contributory pension plan, the 1965 agreement was understood as a major step towards a distinctive fiscal position for Quebec. Jean Lesage declared: "I have made use of all the means which Providence granted me...so that Quebec, finally, could be recognized as a province which has a *statut special* in Confederation, and I have succeeded" (in Simeon, 1972, p. 59).

The very fact that it was open to this interpretation soon led the federal government to reconsider the desirability of these provisions. Now the federal government sought to implement desired policies within its own jurisdiction, before having recourse to new shared cost programs. One strategy was employed in the area of manpower training policy. The original shared cost programs in this area had been oriented to provincial priorities, concentrating on the creation of technical and vocational schools aimed at youth. In 1966, Ottawa's new Ministry of Manpower and Immigration employed a new method to reorient its spending to programs focussing on the re-training of older persons in the workforce in order to facilitate economic adjustment. It arranged with the provinces to pay allowances directly to trainees and purchased services for them from provincial governments (see Dupre et.al., 1973; Simeon, 1972, pp. 80-81).

The more common strategy for avoiding further recognition of special status was to require that all provinces meet broad and general conditions, rather than the more detailed ones of earlier schemes. Thus, the Youth Allowances Act made provision for provincial modifications to bring the federal program into line with their existing policies. Eligibility for federal medicare transfers required only that provincial programs meet four criteria – comprehensiveness, universality, public administration of the program and portability of benefits – and even these were loosely defined. Similarly, the Canada Assistance Plan, introduced in 1966, was characterized by "conspicuously few" conditions. Provinces were free to set their own rates of assistance and to define "need" themselves. The only federal condition was that there be no residence requirements. The major new commitment to federal financing of post-secondary education, launched in 1977, would entail no conditions at all. In this way, the federal government hoped to defend its application of the same standards to all provinces – that is, its refusal to recognize the right of any province, including Quebec, to opt out in these new programs with any compensation – against the charge that it did not allow for Quebec's particularity.

This strategy did not succeed. Pressure from Quebec to extend the right to opt out to these new programs intensified. The federal government responded by proposing that, under the 1967-72 arrangements, the right to opt out with compensation be extended to all provinces for the three major social programs: hospital insurance, the Canada Assistance Plan and health grants. Thus, when more generalized conditions proved inadequate to meet Quebec's demands without conceding *de facto* special status, opting out was extended to all provinces for all major programs, without their ever having asked for it (Burns, 1967, p. 65). The 1967-72 arrangements also produced a new tax abatement (of 17 points), and a cash payment, together with an adjustment grant, to ensure that no province received less than it would have under a continuation of the previous system. After 1970, federal transfers would no longer be linked to actual program costs, but rather to general increases in per capita income. The only mechanisms left to ensure program uniformity would be intergovernmental consultations, continued federal technical assistance if a province desired it, and provincial agreement to maintain uniform residence requirements (Carter, 1971, p. 94).

In spite of these major concessions, Quebec maintained its position that the shared cost instrument ought to be abandoned and that it would enter no new shared cost programs. Other provinces rejected Quebec's position. Other fiscal issues mattered much more to them. Manitoba and Saskatchewan objected to the idea in principle, arguing that federal withdrawal would lead to increasing disparities in program standards and tax rates. No agreement was reached; but the idea would be revived in the next decade. Thus, the imperatives of responding to Quebec and avoiding special status, led to greater decentralization than the federal government and most of the provinces wanted.

To conclude, the federal-provincial context in which Canadian social policy was extended in this period was very different from what it had been during the first wave of policy expansion in the 1940s and early 1950s. An activist federal government was dealing with far more active and expansive provincial governments, especially in Quebec. The Quebec government was no longer opposed to the welfare state as such, but it was determined that it must control the impact of these changes by developing its own welfare state. These demands did not prevent the realization of the federal initiatives, but they ensured that their form would be significantly different from those of the Reconstruction decade. The growing strength of the provincial governments made policy-making more complex and difficult. Nevertheless, federalism did not stand in the way of a decade of major expansion in Canadian social policy. In this decade and the next, a period of restraint and retrenchment in social policy, it was not the institutions of federalism, but larger social and economic forces which drove and constrained policy change.

Intergovernmental Mechanisms

In the 1960s the search for better mechanisms for coordination became a cottage industry, for as W. R. Lederman (1971) pointed out, if a clarification of roles and responsibilities was impossible, only better machinery for collaboration would succeed. Indicators of the need for such machinery could be found in the rapidly increasing number of more-or-less *ad hoc* interactions between governments at various levels. The number of ministerial and officials' meetings increased strikingly. For example, 64 formal federal-provincial meetings took place in 1957, and 125 in 1964 (Gallant, 1965, p. 8). In the beginning, the primary subjects were fiscal and social policy matters; in later meetings, attention turned increasingly to the constitution and economic policy coordination. From 1964, the Finance Ministers met annually in December to discuss the economic outlook and coordinate budget policy (McLarty, 1967, pp. 412-20).

In 1960, Jean Lesage proposed that there be an annual First Ministers Conference, together with a permanent intergovernmental secretariat. Such meetings would canvass the whole range of general policy and give the provinces a direct voice in federal policy formation. While others echoed Lesage's proposal, no agreement to hold annual conferences was reached. Nonetheless, nine such meetings took place in the course of the 1960s, and ten occurred in the first half of the 1970s. In 1960 Lesage also initiated the practice of annual Premiers' Conferences, arguing that such meetings were "necessary and urgent" in order to allow provinces to seek agreement on "the large number of questions that divide them among themselves and from the federal government" (Thompson, 1984, pp. 334-35). Provincial cooperation, Lesage argued, could forestall unilateral federal action and lay the groundwork for a confederal pattern in which provinces could design national programs in areas of provincial jurisdiction, without the necessity of federal intervention. This vision of interprovincial cooperation received little support from the other Premiers in the 1960s. Ontario Premier Leslie Frost, for one, insisted that the meetings avoid any "ganging up" on Ottawa. But conferences focussing primarily on interprovincial issues did take place.

Provinces also began to cooperate on a regional basis. The Maritime premiers had been meeting annually since 1956, but in 1971 – following the report of a commission appointed by the Maritime premiers and chaired by J. J. Deutsch, which had studied the possibility of "Maritime Union" and the pooling of resources in areas of shared concern (1970) – a Council of Maritime Premiers, backed by a secretariat, was created. The three Prairie provinces founded the Prairie Economic Council in 1965. Originally concentrating on regional economic problems, it later expanded to include British Columbia, changing its name to the Western Premiers Conference. By this time, it focussed mainly on contentious federal-provincial issues. An Ontario-Quebec Permanent Commission was created in 1969.

The growing number of high level meetings prompted governments to create new ministries to ensure that the discussions and negotiations between governments in one policy area were consistent with those simultaneously taking place in others. In the 1950s, the only such agency was the Federal-Provincial Relations Division of the federal Department of Finance. In 1961, Quebec established a separate ministry of Federal-Provincial Relations. This was later renamed the Ministry of Intergovernmental Affairs and assigned major international responsibilities as well. In 1964, the Federal-Provincial Relations Office was created within the Privy Council Office. There was a strong federal-provincial relations section in Ontario's new department of Treasury, Economics and Intergovernmental Affairs, which later evolved into a separate Ministry of Intergovernmental Affairs. Not until 1972 did the first Western province create a separate ministry: Alberta's powerful Ministry of Federal and Intergovernmental Affairs, modelled closely on Quebec's. It was an important signal that the focus of attention was about to shift to the West.

Constitutional Deadlock

From the Depression to 1960, the focus of constitutional reform discussions had been on what powers the provinces would give up to allow Ottawa to assume its new roles. But from 1960 to 1980 the focus was reversed to determine what powers Ottawa would give up in response to provincial, especially Quebec, ambitions. With Sections 91 and 92 of the BNA Act obsolete as a guide to action and conflict resolution, a second potential constitutional thrust was to reallocate powers and responsibilities between the two orders of government. However, this would require consensus not only on the functions of government, but also on the order of government best able to carry them out, and there was none on either point.

The 1960 Quebec Liberal platform called for early patriation of the constitution. Soon after the election, Davie Fulton, the federal Minister of Justice, proposed to the provinces a two-step procedure by which patriation should come first, and then Parliament would enact an amending formula agreed on by all governments. Ontario and other provinces disagreed, holding that the two had to go together. If not, they feared, once patriation had been achieved, there would be no incentive for the federal government to agree on an amending formula which gave the provinces a clear legal role.

In subsequent discussions, provincial positions ranged widely. At one pole, Saskatchewan's CCF government still looked to strong federal leadership and a highly flexible amendment formula, making it easy to delegate powers among governments. At the other pole, Quebec wanted a formula that would entrench as many powers as possible and sought changes to the amending procedures set out in the 1949 amendment. Quebec was also reluctant to permit delegation, which it feared might be used by English Canadian governments to centralize the federation. As negotiations following Fulton's initiative dragged on, discussion of an amending formula was caught up in the growing nationalist ferment in Quebec. Quebec negotiators were torn between their desire to resolve the issue and their fear of nationalist criticism. As the debate continued, a wider range of constitutional options for Quebec were canvassed.

Following the return of the Liberals in 1963, new attempts were made, spurred by the desire to complete the process before Canada' approaching centennial. Patriation, in Pearson's view, would complete Canadian nationhood and, along with the new flag, be a unifying symbol. The Quebec government, considering the possibility of substantive constitutional changes, and now more explicitly favouring special status, sought a flexible amendment procedure and proposed to accept delegation, but with the new element of "fiscal compensation" for provinces which wished to retain responsibility.

In October 1964 agreement to the "Fulton-Favreau formula" was reached. It included "patriation", meaning that no future British laws would apply to Canada, and a strongly provincialist set of amending procedures. Provisions respecting provincial powers, use of the English and French languages, denominational rights in education, and representation in the House of Commons could only be amended with the unanimous consent of the 11 governments. Other provisions respecting the monarchy, Senate representation and the like could be amended by Ottawa with the concurrence of two-thirds of the provinces comprising more than half the population. There was some flexibility in a delegation procedure.

At last success seemed at hand. Lesage agreed to the formula. Presenting it to the National Assembly, he said that it opened the door to special status in a federal system which would permit varying autonomy for the provinces. But nationalist opposition, led by the Union nationale, and including significant elements within the Parti libérale, was intense. The formula, they said, failed to recognize Quebec's fundamental aspirations; it was a strait-jacket for the future. In January, 1966, Lesage informed the Prime Minister that he had decided to "delay indefinitely" proceeding with the proposal. The Fulton-Favreau formula was dead.

It was not to be the end of constitutional discussions; rather, the stakes had been raised prior to another round. When the Union nationale, under the leadership of Daniel Johnson, formed the new provincial government in 1966, it declared in its first Speech from the Throne that:

> In accordance with the mandate granted to it by the people, the government intends to strive to the utmost to achieve a new constitutional order which will be the instrument not of an artificial unity, but of a true alliance between two co-equal peoples.

The precise constitutional implications of Premier Johnson's call for "l'égalité ou l'indépendence" were never spelled out in detail, and larger constitutional goals were often subordinated to the exigencies of negotiations on specific issues. Nevertheless, a new era in Canada's constitutional history was beginning.

In 1967, the Ontario government decided that it had a role to play in mediating what it regarded as a dangerous escalation of constitutional conflict. It opened a new round of constitutional discussions by convening the Confederation of Tomorrow Conference to "examine Confederation as it is today, to take stock after 100 years, to examine the areas of agreement and disagreement and to explore what can be done to ensure a strong and unified Canada" (Robarts, in Simeon, 1972, p. 91). Three broad positions emerged. For Quebec, constitutional change was essential. Ontario, New Brunswick, Nova Scotia and Prince Edward Island had no constitutional grievances but, as Nova Scotia Premier Gerald Smith put it, "If developing a new constitution will help [to preserve and improve Canada] then surely it is worth trying" (in Simeon, 1972, p. 93). A third group of provinces was hostile. Premier Smallwood pronounced himself "absolutely opposed not only to a new constitution, but to any change whatsoever in the existing constitution". Saskatchewan's Liberal Premier, Ross Thatcher, said that on a one hundred item list of the country's problems, the constitution would be the hundred and first. Alberta's Social Credit Premier Manning stated: "It is my sincere belief that in the present context, it is not realistic ...to think that sufficient measure of agreement could be attained among the

Canadian people to make possible at this time the writing of a new constitution for Canada" (in Simeon, 1972, p. 93).

Since the failure of Fulton-Favreau, Ottawa had been reluctant to enter into new constitutional discussions on the ground that the process would inevitably take place on provincialist premises and the lack of consensus could only mean further strains in the fabric of Confederation. But now, fearful that the provinces were gaining the initiative, the federal government committed itself to a constitutional review which would be "both broad and deep". Prime Minister Trudeau acknowledged that new rules were necessary "because the federal and provincial governments were stumbling over each other, completely out of kilter, like characters in one of those Chinese plays" (in Simeon, 1972, p. 95).

The first formal federal-provincial constitutional conference was held in February 1968. Opening the conference, on the eve of his retirement, Prime Minister Pearson stressed the stakes: "Here the road forks. If we choose wrongly, we will leave our children and our children's children a country in fragments... . What is at stake in my opinion is no less than Canada's survival" (CAR, 1968, p. 73). The federal government set out its conception of how the discussions ought to proceed. Under Trudeau's influence, it sought to redefine the terms of the debate. A total review must begin with the rights of individuals and implementation of the recommendations of the Royal Commission on Bilingualism and Biculturalism regarding the status of the French and English languages across Canada. It proposed to entrench political, legal, equality and linguistic rights in a constitutional Charter of Human Rights. The reform of central institutions should then be examined. Only after both of these matters had been resolved should the focus shift to the division of powers between the two orders of government. Quebec countered that discussion must begin with the division of powers.

The disagreement over process reflected conflicting conceptions of Canada and the forms of federalism required to embody them. The Quebec government sought greater resources and jurisdiction, limits on federal powers and special status. The federal government, convinced that further decentralization and, above all, special status, was a slippery slope leading to the disintegration of the federation, desired reforms which would increase its responsiveness to the interests of French Canadians and Quebecers as well as constitutional guarantees of the rights of English and French speakers to protect minorities from provincial majorities.

The struggle between these conceptions remained unresolved and continued to hinder progress on constitutional reform. Nevertheless, some headway was made. There was a tenuous agreement on language rights and a general agreement to proceed with a full-scale constitutional review, which would include linguistic and human rights, the division of powers, central institutions, regional disparities, amendment procedures and mechanisms of intergovernmental relations. The first ministers established themselves as a continuing Constitutional Conference, with a committeee of officials, chaired by Gordon Robertson, and a permanent secretariat to assist them. Determined to take the constitutional initative, Ottawa now began to develop and advance its own views in a series of discussion papers. Most other governments remained by-standers; their worries had not yet taken constitutional form.

Following the February 1968 conference, the officials' committee set to work to compile "propositions" submitted by the various governments. Meanwhile, the political climate was changing. Pierre Trudeau had become leader of the Liberal party and swept to power with a majority in the 1968 election. At the same time, there was a power vacuum in Quebec: Daniel Johnson, ill through much of 1968, died on the eve of the second Constitutional Conference, in February 1969. None of the major issues was resolved, but it was agreed to continue discussions and committees of ministers were established to examine specific topics.

At a third meeting, in June 1969, attention focussed on two federal papers: *Taxing Powers and the Constitution*, and *Federal-Provincial Grants and the Spending Power of Parliament*. In the latter, the federal government proposed strong limitations on its spending power. New programs could proceed only with the support of Parliament and the majority of legislatures in each region. Moreover, governments not agreeing could formally "opt-out" and would receive compensation, in the form of direct payments to citizens rather than to provincial governments. A further conference took place in December 1969, followed by a private working session in September 1970. Despite the lengthy discussions, progress was slow.

Then, political events intervened once again. In April 1970 the strongly federalist Bourassa government was elected in Quebec, with the Parti québécois as the Official Opposition. Six months later, the country was wracked by the FLQ Crisis. Federal leaders felt it was essential, in order to control events in Quebec, that there be some progress on the constitutional front. At another working session, in February 1971, there seemed to be a breakthrough on patriation and an amending formula. A final meeting to ratify the details was scheduled for June 1971, in Victoria. Roadblocks remained, however; notably Quebec's desire for movement on the division of powers. Quebec now sought paramountcy in social policy, by adding family and youth allowances, occupational training, and unemployment insurance to Section 94A as concurrent powers with provincial paramountcy. This was much more than the federal government was prepared to concede.

Yet, in June 1971 the First Ministers seemed to reach agreement. In three days in Victoria, they tentatively adopted a "Canadian Constitutional Charter, 1971". The Charter contained an entrenched bill of rights, including provisions making English and French the official languages of Canada, and a complex set of more limited language rights (excluding education) applying to several individual provinces. Provincial governments were assured a role in the selection of Supreme Court judges and Quebec was guaranteed that at least three of the nine judges on the Supreme Court would be drawn from that province. On the division of powers and intergovernmental relations there were a number of important provisions, including a commitment to equalization. Ottawa's power to enact family, youth and occupational allowances was to be confirmed in the constitution, but there would be provincial paramountcy in these fields and a commitment by Ottawa to consult in advance of legislative action. Annual First Ministers' meetings were made a constitutional requirement. For most changes, the amending formula required the assent of the federal government, together with all provinces which had ever had 25 percent or more of the population (assuring a veto for Quebec and Ontario), plus any two Atlantic provinces and any two western provinces, together comprising at least half the region's population. The package thus combined elements of both the Quebec and federal proposals.

But upon his return to Quebec, Premier Bourassa, like Lesage before him, was faced with a barrage of opposition to the deal that he had negotiated. The CSN, the FTQ, the Federation of St. Jean Baptiste Societies, the PQ, the UN, and even the Quebec wing of the NDP, formed a "common front" against the new Charter. Faced with such broadly-based and intense opposition, Bourassa backed down.

Thus, the internal dynamic of Quebec politics led governments to articulate ever-wider demands and to take highly symbolic positions which then proved very difficult to compromise. The other provinces remained bystanders for the most part; they felt little pressure to come to agreement and were incapable of mediating what was essentially a battle among Quebecers, in Quebec City and Ottawa, about their future. A victim of this logic, constitutional reform initiatives had failed again. Ottawa did not claim, as it would in 1982, that the amendments could go forward without the consent of Quebec. For the moment the negotiations were ended. They would be revived in even more difficult circumstances following the election of the PQ in 1976.

Conclusions

In the years between 1958 and 1973 intergovernmental relations became a central preoccupation of Canadian governments and a crucial arena for policy-making. Cooperative federalism seemed in danger of disintegrating, undermined by the challenge from Quebec. There was a "deepening awareness that the federal system was in crisis" (Smiley, 1970, Intro.). The greater state activism that was the proximate cause of the crisis was rooted in the changing balance of societal forces supporting competing conceptions of the appropriate economic and social roles of the state. The shifting balance, in turn, was traced to fundamental structural changes – above all, secularization, urbanization, and the dramatic growth of the private and public service sector.

The new politics of Quebec rendered obsolete the political logic upon which the original model of post-war Canadian federalism had been based. At that time, the federal government had been the principal threat to the limited role of the state which Duplessis championed. Hence, his principal goal had been to prevent the intrusion of the federal government into new areas of social and economic life. The federalism of the Reconstruction years was, to a considerable extent, tailored to respond to Duplessis' kind of Quebec. It sought few major centralizing constitutional amendments, permitting the Quebec government to decide not to participate in the federal tax collection agreements and shared cost programs, though not without financial penalty.

These arrangements were inappropriate to the role which the Quebec state sought to play after 1960. The new Quebec agenda extended across the full range of intergovernmental issues. The Quebec government needed access to the funds which the federal shared-cost programs made available in order to carry out its own social policies, but it would not accept the conditional strings which the federal government attached. Moreover, Premier Lesage and his successors sought to develop provincial economic policies in areas where only the federal government had previously operated, and which might be regarded as falling under federal jurisdiction. This required more than the acknowledgement of the right of the provincial government to refuse to participate in new federal programs; it required new constitutional rights that fiscal arrangements could not easily accommodate. It also required changes in intergovernmental relations: there would need to be greater collaboration among the provinces and a greater provincial voice in the making of national policy. This, in turn, required new institutional mechanisms. The perceived need for constitutional change meant that federal-provincial relations became an intensely political, as opposed to a largely technical and bureaucratic, process. Federalism had to adapt to these new demands and, in so doing, the era of "executive federalism" was born.

In short, in the era of executive federalism, the coordination of the two orders of government, hitherto achieved primarily through fiscal arrangements, had become both more necessary and more difficult. These changes implied an important shift in the meaning of the term "cooperative federalism". The talents required of federal leaders, said former Minister of Justice Guy Favreau, "are no longer those of chieftaincy, but those of diplomacy" (Simeon, 1972, pp. 172-73). Cooperation meant Ottawa must now work with and through provinces. "In this ménage à onze, there is no room either for gung-ho centralizers or table-pounding provincialists.... Keeping Canada together may...mean that federal politicians will sometimes need the courage to appear weak themselves" (Favreau, 1965, pp. 50-51). Another cabinet minister, Maurice Sauvé, said "Cooperative federalism is halfway between the fédéralisme de tutelle, which existed until 1963, but which is no longer acceptable to French-Canadians, and confederative federalism which is no longer satisfactory for present day problems and which English Canadians would not accept" (in Cook, 1966, p. 22).

Donald Smiley saw the new pattern of federalism as a serious "attenuation of federal power". R. M. Burns suggested that the "conciliatory" attitude of the centre in the face of provincial expansionism "may be incompatible with the effective conduct of our national affairs". If there had been grounds to question whether the provinces were effective units after the war, there were now grounds to question whether Ottawa was "a continuing economic and fiscal force in the nation" (1965, p. 515). A federal offical, A. W. Johnson, worried that further decentralization would result in a "halting and uncertain" monetary and fiscal policy "muddied by compromise, the misallocation of resources as provinces competed for economic development, and diminished authority for Canada in international councils". He concluded that it foreshadowed a "diminished sense of Canadianism" and an erosion of the commitment to equality (1967, pp. 17-18).

If federal leaders saw erosion, others saw in these developments what Jean-Marc Leger called "the new face of centralization". In his view, no diminution of federal intervention in areas of provincial jurisdiction had occurred: "Very certainly Ottawa will have to revise its initial project, consent to modifications, optional formulae, particular schemes for this or that province: little of importance, the essential will be achieved." Thus, he concluded, "we are witnessing the beginning of the most vigourous centralizing offensive yet launched by Ottawa, an offensive all the more dangerous, since it wears the mask of cooperation" (1963, pp. 155-56).

The truth lay somewhere in between, although the extreme quality of these perceptions reveals an important truth about the atmosphere within which federal-provincial relations were conducted in latter part of this period. Fears that the provinces would pursue independent fiscal policies, for example, proved groundless. Guy Favreau sought to "bury the misconception" that the federal government had been stripped of its power and would henceforth be condemned to "preside over the gradual, though inexorable, disintegration of our country" (1965b, p. 48). Nevertheless, the strong, and largely unexpected, provincial reaction to the initiatives of the

Liberals' "sixty days of decision" in 1963 led federal officials to believe that prior consultation and more effective intergovernmental coordination were essential. As Don Smiley summed it up: "It had become apparent at the highest political levels in Ottawa and in most if not all of the provincial capitals that this was essential to governance and even to the existence of the Canadian federation itself" (Smiley, 1970, p. 93).

Chapter 10

The Compound Crisis of the Postwar Order, 1974-84

The years between 1974 and 1984 were the most difficult for Canada since the 1930s. International forces and domestic developments threw into question the country's capacity for sustained economic growth and the very survival of Canada as a federal community. The economic theories and political compromises upon which the postwar order had been built were discredited in the eyes of many and there was renewed debate on fundamental questions concerning the role of the state.

The word "crisis" permeated political discourse. The optimistic assumptions characteristic of the postwar period – that only the political will was required to make the world a better place, that business cycles could be tamed, that growth and equity were compatible, and that governments could be effective and benign instruments of social change – were shaken. The McCracken report, *Toward Full Employment and Price Stability* concluded that "public confidence in the ability of governments to manage the economy had waned, and belief in the likelihood or even desirability of continued economic growth in the industrialized world had weakened" (OECD, 1977, p. 11). Conservative academics wrote of "government overload" (Crozier, *et al*, 1975) and neo-marxists warned of the "fiscal crisis of the state" (O'Connor, 1973). Jurgen Habermas (1975) wrote of the "legitimation crisis" faced by governments that staked their legitimacy on their capacity to deliver the economic goods.

There were as many explanations of the crisis as there were locations for it. Conservatives complained that there were too many well organized interests able to make effective demands on the state. Interest group liberalism, in short, was becoming too democratic (Brittain, 1977; Olson, 1982). Some political economists explained it as a structural contradiction between the Keynesian welfare state and an increasingly competitive international market economy (Keohane, 1984; Martin, 1986). As Zysman put it, "the political capacity of the advanced countries for managing change has diminished, at the same time as the adjustments they must make have become more difficult" (1983, p. 16). Still others saw the problem as a "revolution of rising [and unrealistic] expectations", rooted in something akin to human nature. "Once upon a time," wrote Anthony King, "man looked to God to order the world. Then he looked to the market. Now he looks to government.... And when things go wrong, people blame not 'Him' or 'it', but 'them'" (1975).

In Canada the crisis was above all a crisis of the federal system. Social and economic developments made the harmonization of government goals and policies at once more necessary and more difficult to achieve (see Hueglin, 1984). Moreover, as each grappled with deficits and the need for expenditure restraint, there was increased conflict over fiscal transfers and a tendency for each to pass on its fiscal problems to the other. If much intergovernmental conflict in the 1960s had been shaped by the competitive expansion of governments into new areas, now conflict was also engendered by fears of withdrawal. At the same time, the Parti québécois won power in Quebec in 1976. The politics and economics of energy divided the country along regional lines perhaps as never before. Finally, many of the new social movements were demanding that federalism be constrained by a greater concern for individual rights, and that the processes of intergovernmental decision making be rendered more democratic. Faced with a bewildering array of intractable problems, many citizens experienced a profound sense of institutional failure.

Intergovernmental relations were poisoned by the emergence of mutually exclusive "nation-building" and "province-building" ideologies by which each order of government rationalized its claims. Federalism became more and more competitive. Prime Minister Trudeau became increasingly convinced that the provinces had grown too strong, that cooperative federalism did not work, that the economic union was eroding, and that Ottawa must reestablish the preeminence of the country-wide community which it alone represented (Milne, 1982, pp. 2-3). In 1980, following the defeat of the PQ in the referendum and the collapse of the September 1980 constitutional negotiations, the federal government announced that it was abandoning the assumptions of cooperative federalism in favour of a new, "competitive" federalism. In the future, Ottawa would seek unilaterally to undertake constitutional reform, develop a National Energy Program, tighten the conditions governing transfers to the provinces, and establish more direct links between the federal government and Canadian citizens.

The New Federalism represented, in Bruce Doern's estimation, "the most coherent assertion of political belief and principle since the early years of the Pearson government" (1982, p. 1). As such, it intensified the battle among the rival visions of federalism. But the BNA Act was not rooted in such mutually exclusive visions of the federation, so each ideology implied major constitutional reforms. It was no accident, then, that these ideological struggles culminated in the battle over Ottawa's effort to patriate the constitution. The unilateral process reflected the New Federalism, and so did the substantive reforms that Ottawa proposed. The ensuing fight bitterly divided the country, but at the eleventh hour an agreement on the constitution – to which the government of Quebec, alone, was not a party – was signed. It provided Canada with an amending formula, a Charter of Rights, and a number of other significant constitutional changes. On April 17, 1982 that constitution became the new law of the land.

Federal Society

In the decade between 1974 and 1984 international competition for the sale of primary commodities and secondary manufacturing goods intensified. Third World countries were producing larger quantities of more raw materials for sale to the First World. Japan and, behind it, western Europe and the low-wage "Newly Industrializing Nations" (NICs) such as South Korea and Taiwan, were beginning to attain North American productivity levels in many manufacturing sectors while maintaining lower wage costs.

The economic shock of these changes was greatest in countries which had hitherto been relatively free from such international competition – the United States, Canada and Great Britain. Many sectors of these economies operated with outdated capital equipment. But even more important, they did not meet this crisis with political- economic institutions and strategies designed for rapid adaptation, as did the countries forced to "catch up" at the end of the Second World War (Zysman, 1983, pp. 285-320; Katzenstein, 1985). "De-industrialization" was the most immediately obvious result, as many traditional industries went out of business (Bluestone & Harrison, 1982).

The internationalization of industrial production also intensified competition for the investment essential to modernizing production (Laux & Molot, 1988, pp. 11-36). The result was a decline in the bargaining power of organized labour and the state vis-à-vis capital (Nye, 1983; Martin, 1986).

The declining power of organized labour was reflected in static real incomes for workers. Reduced state bargaining power was manifested in rising budget deficits, as the capacity to tax capital while maintaining adequate levels of new private capital investment – reflected in the share of all revenues represented by corporate income taxes – declined. At the same time, the costs of economic adjustment – welfare, unemployment and re-training expenditures – increased (Wolfe, 1985).

Such structural changes would have been disruptive enough, but two OPEC oil price hikes were superimposed. In the short run, these increases resulted in a massive transfer of purchasing power from oil consumers to oil producers, and dramatic shifts in the character of international demand. This increased unemployment in the less competitive countries and stimulated domestic inflation, which had been rising in the OECD countries since the late 1960s due to intensifying distributive conflicts between labour and capital (Goldthorpe, 1978, pp. 186-214).

These developments probably account for much of the "stagflation" that gripped the OECD countries in this period. They also helped to shift the balance of social forces to favour business-oriented responses to the crisis by weakening organized labour. This was reflected in the tendency to give priority to fighting inflation over unemployment. (Barry, 1985). The shift also influenced the ways these priorities would be pursued. In the countries where organized labour was economically and politically weak – Great Britain, because of its severe structural problems, and the United States, because of its low union density – monetarist techniques were favoured over tripartite corporatist approaches which required significant concessions to organized labour in return for wage restraint (Goldthorpe, 1984). In Canada, inflation was also the top government priority in the 1970s, but the heavy-handed monetarism of Britain and the United States did not prevail (Campbell, 1987, pp. 166-189).

As an oil-producing country like Norway, Holland or Great Britain but, unlike them, with a national government willing to hold domestic oil prices below world prices, Canada was at first cushioned from the economic impact of the OPEC shocks. Between 1973 and 1976 the Canadian growth rate was relatively high, partly as a result of the favourable impact of increased energy and commodity prices on Canada's competitive position, and partly as a result of expansive fiscal and monetary policies aimed at stimulating the economy and moderating the impact of higher energy prices. Canada's inflation performance was also somewhat better than the OECD average (though worse than the U.S., Germany and Japan) until 1980. Canadian unemployment, while remaining high relative to Europe and Japan, did not increase as much as in other countries. Overall, Canada fared considerably better than other OECD countries between 1975 and 1980 (Macdonald Commission, *Report*, Vol.2, 1985, pp. 46-52).

Still, this was a serious deterioration by post-war Canadian standards. GDP growth had averaged 5.6 percent annually between 1960 and 1973; it fell to 3.4 percent between 1973 and 1979. The Economic Council of Canada declared that "economic growth at the high rates prevailing in the sixties can no longer be taken for granted.... Steady growth of the economy is far from assured, and appears to be subject to many influences which on the whole were far less favourable in the past decade than before" (Annual Review, 1979, p. 16). Then, between 1980 and 1984, growth rates deteriorated to an annual average of 2.0 percent. Consumer price inflation had averaged 2.4 percent between 1960 and 1968 and 4.6 percent between 1969 and 1973; now it rose to 9.2 percent between 1974 and 1979, and to 11.2 percent between 1980 and 1982, before the recession brought it down. While prices rose steadily, so did unemployment. The change was dramatic: from 4.8 percent of the workforce between 1960 and 1968, unemployment rose to 5.4 percent between 1969 and 1973, to 7.2 percent between 1974 and 1979, and to 9.9 percent between 1980 and 1984. Finally, productivity growth rates (measured as real GNP/GDP per member of the civilian work force) fell from an average annual rate of 2.7 percent between 1960 and 1973, to 0.5 percent between 1974 and 1979, to 0.4 percent between 1980 and 1984 (Macdonald Commission, Final Report, Vol.2, 1985, pp. 48-49).

The recession that began in 1981 hit Canada harder than many of the other OECD countries. Canada's one percent average growth rate between 1982 and 1984 compared with an OECD average of 2.4 percent, and a United States average of 2.8 percent. Canada's 11.5 percent average unemployment level for the same years compared with the OECD average of 8.4 percent, and an American average of 8.9 percent. Slower growth and higher unemployment did not prevent Canada from exhibiting a higher inflation rate as well: 6.8 percent, compared to the OECD average of 5.6 percent, and the average in the U.S. of 4.5 percent. Finally, productivity growth in Canada showed a 1.1 percent increase between 1982 and 1984, close to the Americans' 1.2 percent, but well below the OECD average of 1.9 percent (Macdonald Commission, Final Report, Vol.2, 1985, pp. 48-49). It appeared that the post-war economic order was in the midst of a fundamental crisis in these years and that Canada, in spite of its oil resource windfall, was in a worse position than most.

This extraordinary deterioration of economic performance, and the fears that it engendered, placed unprecedented strains on the political accomodations upon which the post-war order had been constructed. We now examine how these developments were played out along each of the major cleavage lines.

Class

A decade of stagflation, followed by a world recession, threw into question the compatibility of the interests of capital and organized labour – especially the values of equity and efficiency, growth and social justice – as never before in the postwar period. Organized labour and capital defined their differences in terms of the economic role of the state. Goldthorpe (1984) divides these responses into two diverging paths of political economic evolution which he calls "dualist" and "corporatist". Great Britain and the United States represent the clearest cases of countries which moved in a dualist direction, cutting back the allocative and redistributive dimensions of the state's role, and encouraging the formation of a growing pool of unorganized and low paid workers. Sweden, Norway, and Austria, on the other hand, became more corporatist, re-forging incomes policies initially undermined by the economic upheavals of the 1970s. In return for the cooperation of organized labour, those governments moved to increase worker control over investment and production decisions by various means, the most striking of which was the Meidner Plan (Martin, 1984; Cameron, 1984).

But Canada did not move toward either of these poles in this decade. Between 1972 and 1974, with Liberal power in Ottawa dependent upon NDP support, national policy remained consistent with a commitment to high employment and free collective bargaining. Finance Minister John Turner declared in his 1972 and 1973 budgets that the reduction of unemployment was his priority. He introduced "supply side budgets" which aimed to increase jobs by using corporate tax reductions to induce new investment. At the same time, Old Age Security and Veterans' Pensions were indexed to inflation in 1972, as were personal income tax brackets and exemptions in 1974. The result was a federal deficit of almost $1.5 billion over two years during which economic growth averaged over 6.5 percent. Such spending was likely to increase inflation, which rose from 4.6 percent in 1972 to 7.6 percent in 1973, but the government was prepared to tolerate some inflation in return for significant decreases in unemployment. So monetary policy remained liberal (money supply growth averaged 14.5 percent) and the policy-makers did not resort to wage and price controls. (Campbell, 1987, pp. 177-81).

Turner's corporate tax cuts had two immediate effects. They raised the underlying level of inflation, upon which dramatic OPEC oil price hikes were soon superimposed, with the result that inflation was almost 11 percent by 1974. This convinced many Liberals that the fight against inflation must now take precedence over unemployment, and that new inflation-fighting techniques – tight monetary policy and wage and price controls – must be developed.

The corporate tax cuts provoked the NDP into voting against the budget, bringing about the 1974 election. The Liberals promised they would deliver to workers what the NDP only talked about. Progressive Conservative advocates of wage and price controls were ridiculed. The NDP share of the popular vote fell two points (from 17.7 percent to 15.4 percent), but the territorial distribution of this marginal decline translated into an almost 50 percent decline in seats (from 31 to 16). Support for Robert Stanfield's Conservatives actually increased marginally, but the number of Tory seats fell from 107 in 1972 to 95. Thus, limited Liberal gains against the NDP and the Créditistes raised the Liberal share of the popular vote from 38.5 percent to 43.2 percent. These small shifts were sufficient to push Liberal Parliamentary representation to 141 from 109 seats – the largest electoral majority since Diefenbaker's 1958 sweep. The Liberals were freed from the need to maintain NDP support for their policies (Penniman, 1975, Preface, pp. 292-301).

The reduced political power of organized labour in Ottawa was soon reflected in Liberal policy changes. In 1975, Finance Minister Turner urged the CLC to accept a voluntary guideline of eight percent on wage increases in 1976. The CLC responded that it would help if the government "guaranteed higher old age pensions, monitoring of professional fees, rent controls, full employment, regulation of oil and gas prices, and a promise that real wages would rise" (Morton, 1984, p. 302). In September 1975 Turner resigned. A month later the new Minister of Finance, Donald Macdonald, announced the Liberals' new plan: three years mandatory wage and price controls and a commitment to holding increases in federal spending at or below the rate of GNP growth. Meanwhile the Bank of Canada, under Gerald Bouey, embraced monetarist theories and curtailed the rate of growth of the money supply (Campbell, 1987, p. 184, pp. 187-88).

The Finance Minister declared that these new initiatives were part of a wider move "into an era of government intervention in the economy". A few months later, business leaders called Prime Minister Trudeau a socialist when he echoed this theme in a New Year's television interview. Business fears proved exaggerated. The only serious reduction of private corporate power was in the energy sector where, in 1974, the control of foreign multinationals was reduced by the creation of PetroCanada, under NDP pressure and, again in 1980, when the National Energy Program increased the power of PetroCanada and Canadian-owned private capital.

Thus, from 1975 until its defeat in 1984, punctuated by the Clark government hiatus of 1979, the federal Liberals defied Goldthorpe's generalization by pursuing a path which involved a high level of state intervention, contrary to the dualist model, but without the support of organized labour, contrary to the corporatist model. The closest parallel was probably the Gaullist state in France. There, a powerful Left was excluded from all post-war national governments until Mitterand's 1980 victory. Yet the Left was strong enough to ensure that the ruling party must take responsibility for economic development and employment (see Zysman, 1977, pp. 159-214; Hall, 1986).

The Canadian state was much less centralized than the French, so the Canadian Left could not be excluded from government in the same way. NDP governments continued in British Columbia until 1975, in Manitoba until 1977 and in Saskatchewan until 1982. And, in 1981, the NDP regained power in Manitoba. Moreover, the PQ after 1971 had strong support from organized labour in Quebec, and when it came to power in 1976, proceeded to repay that support with favourable policies (Morton, 1984, pp. 304-06). Nonetheless, after 1975 most provincial governments tended to move in the same direction as the federal government: more intervention and fewer connections with organized labour. This was most obviously true in the western provinces in which NDP governments were defeated, and in Quebec after the PQ's 1983 break with organized labour, but the process had begun within those NDP governments before they were defeated.

The capacity of the NDP to retain its provincial toe-holds was enhanced by its ties with a dynamic, expanding labour movement. Canadian union density rose further, principally as a result of continued organizing success among public sector workers, from 29.4 percent of the civilian labour force in 1974 to 31.3 percent in 1979, before the recession drove it down to 27.4 percent in 1981. By 1984, it had reached pre-recession levels. In the United States, by contrast, union density levels never passed the war-time peak, and had fallen to half the Canadian level by the early 1980s (Kumar, 1986, p. 109, p. 128).

Nor did the NDP repudiate its ties to organized labour. Nonetheless, ties between organized labour and the NDP, and between national and provincial elements of the NDP, were severely strained as a result of two developments: Ottawa's wage and price controls, and energy policy.

The mandatory wage and price control program covered the public sector and 1,500 large private firms with a total of about four million employees. Wage increases were to be limited to 10 percent in the first year, eight percent in the second, and six percent in the third. Price increases were to be limited to increases in actual costs. An Anti-Inflation Board (AIB) was created to administer the program, with the power to roll-back offending price and wage increases. All ten provincial governments agreed to participate. Eight agreed to include their public employees within the program; the other two, Saskatchewan and Quebec, established parallel programs.

The national NDP, led by Ed Broadbent and supported by the leader of the Ontario NDP, Stephen Lewis, condemned the program. Organized labour was bitterly opposed. The CLC and CSN announced that they would pull out of the Economic Council of Canada. A "day of protest" was staged across the country in the fall of 1976. But all three of the western provincial NDP governments cooperated with the federal initiative. This caused deep splits within the NDP along federal/provincial and east/west lines, and between the Western provincial NDP governments and organized labour.

Organized labour was able to make offending governments – NDP and otherwise – pay a price. In British Columbia, it gave NDP Premier Barrett only lukewarm support in his 1975 re-election effort, in part because of his participation in the controls, thus contributing to his defeat (Morton, 1984, pp. 302-05). Union support for the PQ in 1976 was instrumental in bringing down Bourassa's Liberals (See, 1987, p. 149). The new PQ government immediately cancelled the enforcement provisions of the Quebec version of the Anti-Inflation Board. Other governments paid attention. In 1977 NDP Premier Ed Schreyer of Manitoba pulled his province out of the program, although not in time to save his government from decisive defeat that autumn. In Alberta, Lougheed's Conservative government followed suit, albeit for different reasons. The other provinces remained in the program until its termination in 1978.

Unable to defeat the program politically, organized labour turned to the courts, claiming that the program exceeded the federal government's jurisdiction. Ottawa argued that the program was justified under the general powers of "Peace, Order and Good Government" because inflation was a problem of "national dimensions". The majority of the Supreme Court of Canada held that the program was within the federal jurisdiction, but on the narrower ground – advanced by some provinces – that a temporary state of national emergency existed. The distinction was important: if a problem as broad and multidimensional as inflation had been determined to be a national concern, Ottawa would have had a broad mandate to intervene in many aspects of labour relations, not to mention other provincial jurisdictions.

The narrow basis of the Supreme Court's decision was some consolation for the provincial governments that had supported labour's constitutional challenge. But the Court nonetheless upheld a government policy that deprived organized labour of what its leadership had come to view as its principal raison d'être: the right to negotiate wages and working conditions with employers. Faced with economic and legal crisis, some CLC leaders re-considered their positions on the relative merits of free collective bargaining and corporatism. Meanwhile, elements of capital were moving in a parallel direction. The Business Council on National Issues (BCNI) was created to give the major corporations operating in Canada a single voice in dealings with government. The Council was much less hostile to the tripartite idea than the newspaper editors who inveighed against Trudeau's New Year's musings concerning the corporatist future that lay in store for Canada (Morton, p. 308).

At its 1976 convention, the CLC's President, Joe Morris, presented delegates with what Morton describes as "the most radical document ever to come before a major Canadian labour body", *Labour's Manifesto for Canada*. It argued that free collective bargaining might soon become a thing of the past and that wage and price controls should be seen as harbingers of a new, and potentially more equitable, process of tripartite cooperation. Labour must respond constructively so that this potential would be realized. The Manifesto also called for the increased CLC control over affiliates deemed necessary to bargain with government and business with one voice. The Manifesto was unanimously adopted by the CLC after only a brief debate (Morton, pp. 305-06).

In this atmosphere, Ottawa produced *The Way Ahead* (1976), a position paper that sought to define a new relationship between business, government and labour in the management of the economy. Proposals for a formal tripartite mechanism followed in *Agenda for Cooperation* (1977). A year later, the federal government launched two major tripartite initiatives: the Tier I and Tier II consultative forums on industrial policy (see Brown & Eastman, 1981). This was followed by the Blair-Carr Task Force on major industrial projects, which sought ways to ensure full participation of the Canadian manufacturing industry in large-scale resource developments (see Blais, 1985).

Despite the flurry of interest and activity, however, corporatism had not arrived in Canada. The consultative exercises were only preliminary, and the proposals of the Blair-Carr Task Force soon fell victim to the extreme drop in oil and other primary commodity prices. Moreover, the immediate crisis provoked by controls was over and other problems soon displaced Ottawa's limited interest in tripartism. The moment had passed within the CLC as well. The Manifesto was given a "discreet burial" at the 1978 convention (Morton, pp. 307-08). If corporatism was to emerge in Canada, it would have to be under the auspices of a social democratic, rather than a Liberal, government.

The other major source of tension within the NDP and between elements of organized labour was energy policy. The federal NDP helped the Liberals bring down the Clark government in late 1979, alienating the western provincial members of the party. The Liberals sweetened the deal with a National Energy Policy (NEP) that increased the role of PetroCan and promised to be the first step toward "Canadianizing" other key sectors of the national economy. Economic nationalism, with a prod from the NDP, as in the years of minority government, seemed to be back on the Liberal agenda. But when the Liberals were returned to power with a majority, the appropriate parallel proved to be 1974 rather than 1972. The NDP was no longer necessary to Liberal power, and the wider Canadianization element of the plan was abandoned in the face of American hostility (Clarkson,

1982). The Liberals gave less ground on the revenue and management elements of the NEP, which were the focus of their tough bargaining with the Western provinces.

If the 1980 federal election and party divisions over energy were serious setbacks for the NDP, the recession that began in 1981 was a serious blow to some elements of organized labour. Between 1980 and 1983, the United Steelworkers of Canada lost 25 percent of its membership, and the United Autoworkers, 29 percent (Morton, 1984, p. 317). Union density fell from 31.3 percent in 1978 to 30.6 percent in 1981 (Kumar, 1986, p. 109). The CLC was also weakened in May 1981 by the withdrawal of twelve building trades unions, closely tied to conservative, American-based internationals, representing about 230,000 Canadian workers (Palmer, 1983, p. 295). The growing power of the public sector and other national unions was making the CLC a more activist and social democratic movement than it had ever been.

In June 1982 the federal government again imposed wage and price controls, which became known as the "Six and Five" program. This time they were mandatory for federal public sector workers, restricting their wage increases to six percent in the first year and five percent in the second, but voluntary for the rest of the economy. A private sector "Six and Five Committee", chaired by CPR president Ian Sinclair, was set up to encourage voluntary cooperation by businesses. In July the government announced that it would use the lever of government contracts and grants to extend the range of participation: firms receiving such contracts and grants had to convince the government that they were abiding by the guidelines in their own operations. The program also specified that prices administered by the government, including those of Crown corporations, would exceed the Six and Five limits only under exceptional circumstances.

This time there was no call for formal agreements with the provinces, most of which had already embarked on their own restraint programs. A private meeting between the Prime Minister and the Premiers to enlist provincial support was held, but the Premiers were sceptical, arguing that the program dealt with only part of the economic problem and that provinces should be free to develop their own responses. Nevertheless, in the following months all provinces introduced public sector wage restraint programs of some kind. Because most of these programs followed the federal lead in targetting public sector workers' wages as the principal budget villain, they frequently involved the imposition of new limits on public sector collective bargaining rights (Panitch & Swartz, 1985, pp. 43-57).

In Quebec, the PQ government actually took back some of the increases granted at the time of the 1980 referendum and, in the process, ruptured its links with organized labour. Bill 70 suspended the existing collective agreement and reduced the wages of 300,000 public sector workers by an average of 19.5 percent in the first three months of 1983. Bill 105 decreed that public sector wage increases, from March 1983 until December 1985, would be held to levels equal to the Consumer Price Index inflation rate minus 1.5 percent. When the public sector unions reacted to this suspension of collective bargaining rights by walking out illegally, the government responded with Bill 111, which provided:

> ...fines, imprisonment, and decertification of bargaining agents if the strike did not end immediately. The Bill exempted Quebec from the Canadian Charter of Rights and suspended sections of the Quebec Charter of Human Rights. Absence from work by covered employees was considered *prima facie* evidence of guilt. Fines and firing could take place via a simple government order. Normal legal protection such as individual trials and the right to present evidence in one's defense were also removed.
>
> (Panitch & Swartz, 1985, p. 47)

Following its 1983 re-election, the Social Credit government of British Columbia outdid Ottawa and Quebec City. Twelve new pieces of legislation coupled a restraint program to provisions rolling back the gains made by organized labour in the 1970s. At least 25 percent of public sector jobs were to be eliminated over 18 months. The current contract with government employees was legislated out of existence. A "permanent system of wage controls" for government employees, virtually suspending public sector collective bargaining rights, was created. New restrictions were placed on private sector union picketing and decisions to strike (Panitch & Swartz, 1985, pp. 47-51). There were major cuts in social spending, rent controls were terminated and the provincial Human Rights Commission was dismantled. A province-wide coalition of affected groups, "Operation Solidarity", was able to extract a few concessions – the government retracted legislation granting it the right to dismiss civil servants without cause – but if its point was blunted, its overall thrust was not deflected (Palmer, 1987; Morton, 1984, pp. 318-19; Sypowich, 1986).

In Saskatchewan, Premier Grant Devine's Conservatives, elected in April 1982, were also engaged in rolling back NDP labour legislation. Bill 104, passed in June 1983, contained many provisions designed to weaken labour's bargaining power vis-à-vis capital: it broadened the definition of workers who could be considered management, thus denying the right to union representation; it permitted non-union members of a bargaining unit to vote in strike votes; a "free speech" provision extended management's rights to "communicate" with workers during organizing drives and contract negotiations, creating more scope for the intimidation that the earlier rules had been intended to limit. Fines for contraventions of the Act were increased and made applicable to the union as a legal entity, as well as to individual members. In December 1983 Bill 24, An Act to Repeal the Construction Industry Labour Relations Act, was passed (Panitch & Swartz, 1985, pp. 52-53).

Premier Lougheed's Conservatives also reduced labour rights in Alberta. Bill 110, passed in November 1983, also applied to the construction industry. Extensive protests by the Alberta Federation of Labour kept it on the shelf, but the Labour Relations Board proceeded to reinterpret the province's Labour Code in ways that achieved the intended effect of Bill 110, and extended it to all sectors. Twenty-five hour lockouts, permitting employers to hire new employees before unions went on strike, were held to be legal, as was the practice of creating a non-union, "spin-off" corporation in order to escape an otherwise binding collective agreement. Bill 44, passed in June 1983, outlawed strikes by all nurses and hospital workers, and restricted the already limited strike rights of other public employees. All disputed collective agreements were to be submitted to arbitration, and the Minister, rather than the parties directly involved, would determine the issues to be resolved by the arbitrator. These provisions, among others, prompted the International Labour Office to condemn Bill 44. Premier Lougheed declared that he would override the Charter of Rights to ensure that Alberta Union of Public Employee members never got the right to strike (Panitch & Swartz, pp. 52-54; Nikiforuk, 1987).

Only in Manitoba, where the NDP was restored to power under the leadership of Howard Pawley in 1981, did organized labour register major gains in this period. A new labour relations act was introduced in 1982, followed by Bill 22 which streamlined certification processes, and increased the government's role in conciliation and mediation in ways favourable to labour. On a smaller scale, Ontario passed legislation in 1983 placing some limits on the use of professional strike-breakers (Panitch & Swartz, 1985, pp. 56-57).

In summary, in the decade between 1974 and 1984 the federal government pursued a "third way", interventionist but not pro-labour, between dualism and corporatism. Provincial governments, on the other hand, moved toward the poles described by Goldthorpe. The governments of British Columbia and Alberta led the way toward dualism. Quebec moved toward pro-labour corporatism until 1983, while the Blakeney government of Saskatchewan played that role for English Canada until its defeat in 1982.

Region: Province-Building and the Battle over Resource Rents

If attempts to address stagflation by suspending free collective bargaining exacerbated class differences, efforts by both orders of government to promote economic diversification and development heightened regional tensions. But because regions had provincial representatives, such conflicts of interest were manifested in, and sometimes exaggerated by, federal-provincial conflict in a way that had no parallel in the case of class conflicts. We have already traced the regional disintegration of the party system and its legacy of alienation. Now, over-burdened by the intense conflicts over energy, intergovernmental mechanisms proved incapable of functioning as instruments of joint economic policy formation. None of the institutions of federalism appeared capable of bridging the differences.

The result was an era of unprecedented "competitive state-building" and mutual frustration, as new policies developed by one government, intentionally or not, frustrated the purposes of new policies developed by others. Throughout the period, the battle over resource rents simmered in the background, poisoning the atmosphere and culminating, after the second OPEC oil price increase in 1979, in the titanic battle over the NEP.

We first sketch the matrix of industrial and regional policies developed by each order of government, including a brief discussion of the controversy surrounding the Crow's Nest Pass Rate, which well illustrates the political difficulties facing any regional/industrial policy in Canada. We then turn to a more detailed examination of the energy policies which increasingly dominated attention as the decade wore on.

The Policy Background

Provincial Industrial Policies   Several factors combined to increase the scope and ambition of provincial industrial policies in the 1970s. Increased revenues, especially in the west, enabled provinces to become "more autonomous and effective actors" by expanding the range of their policy tools, particularly public enterprises (Chandler & Chandler, 1979, p. 43). The new classes which the resource boom and state growth created became the base of the new political coalitions that insisted on the realization of that potential. Their immediate goal – to diversify and stabilize their economic base – implicitly rejected the doctrine of comparative advantage based on regional specialization and the market forces which could be expected to reinforce it.

The goal of much provincial government policy was to counteract federal policies viewed as discriminatory, ineffective or contrary to provincial economic interests. Fundamentally, provincial governments saw the province as the principal economic unit in terms of which the costs and benefits of both federal and provincial economic policy ought to be assessed. As Premier Bennett told the 1978 First Ministers' Conference on the economy: "In listening to my fellow First Ministers here, I must say that what has come out clearly to me, is...that we are not a single national economy; we are a country with distinct regions, with distinct economies unique to themselves, that need the attention and cooperation of the governments in meeting their own specific aspirations and needs" (in Brown & Eastman, 1981).

The people of each province had probably always tended to evaluate economic policy from such a perspective, but in the past their provincial governments had either lacked the resources to advance such a vision, or been run by elites ideologically opposed to large-scale state intervention. Now, except for the poorer Atlantic provinces, neither of these conditions applied. The result was that, as one survey concluded, "Many of the creative and innovative aspects of industrial policy today in Canada are to be found not at the national level, but rather within the jurisdictions of provincial governments" (Jenkin, 1983, p. 44).

While sharing a decentralizing orientation, provincial policies varied in accordance with the ideologies of government leaders, the relation of the governing parties to local interests, and the financial resources available to the provincial government.

The goal of the Western provinces was to use the revenues made available by the energy boom to strengthen and diversify their economies, to redress the historic grievances of the region, and shift the balance of economic and political power in the nation. Alberta Premier Peter Lougheed expressed these aims in a 1974 speech: "...this province's economy is too *vulnerable*, it is too dependent on the sale of depleting resources, particularly oil and gas for its continued prosperity". Alberta must plan for the "inevitable day" when the oil and gas ran out: "We can't rely on the federal bureaucrat or the establishment in Toronto to do it for us. For our objective means a fundamental change in the economy of Canada, a shift in decision-making westward, and essentially to Alberta" (in Pratt & Richards, 1979, p. 215). Albertans must, in short, reduce the degree to which their future "quality of life" depends upon "governments, institutions or corporations directed from outside the province... . We must strengthen competitive free enterprise by Albertans which to us means giving priority to our locally owned business..." (in Jenkin, 1983, pp. 52-53). In pursuit of these goals, Alberta "now employs an arsenal of policy levers comparable to that of a sovereign state", with "enormous potental for intergovernmental conflict" (Tupper, 1981, p. 94).

The Lougheed government created the Alberta Heritage Savings and Trust Fund, into which it funnelled about 30 percent of oil and gas revenues, in order to create a large pool of capital for savings and investment. By 1981 the fund held $8.6 billion in assets. The province also established a joint public-private Alberta Energy Corporation and played a major role in establishment of Nova, an Alberta corporation which grew out of the earlier Alberta Gas Trunk Line Ltd. In 1976, it bought Pacific Western Airlines, a company especially important to Alberta's role as a gateway to the North. Further processing of Alberta resources was to be pursued by the newly-created Alberta Oil Sands Technology and Research Authority and by the Alberta Research Council. Through these and other devices, funds were chanelled into development of petrochemicals, tourism, forestry, high technology and medical research. The province also used the corporate tax system and other measures to stimulate the growth of small businesses and to encourage the head offices of companies with interests in the province to relocate in Alberta.

Saskatchewan's industrial strategy was based upon greater use of public ownership. The NDP government took control of a large part of the potash industry in the 1970s, and established Crown corporations to play an important entrepreneurial role in other resource development, including oil and uranium mining. It promoted industrial development through the Saskatchewan Economic Development Corporation and a variety of other measures, including support for research and expansion of the West's largest steel maker, Interprovincial Steel. In 1983, it too established a Heritage Fund.

Traditionally, British Columbia's industrial policy had focussed on resource development – mining and forestry – supported by major rail and highway projects and the aggressive development of the province's hydro resources. W. A. C. Bennett, Social Credit Premier from 1952 to 1972, had been an agressive province-builder throughout his time in office. Some of his efforts, notably development of the Columbia River and the 1961 Columbia River Treaty with the U.S., brought him into prolonged controversy with Ottawa. And, like other Premiers who proclaimed the virtues of free enterprise, he used the power of the state to nationalize a private ferry company to create the B.C. Ferry system in 1958 and to nationalize the province's largest electric company to form B.C. Hydro in 1961. He also led efforts to create the Bank of British Columbia in 1966. In the 1970s, however, British Columbia also began to pursue a policy of diversification into manufacturing and high tech industries.

Manitoba governments were also active in promoting forestry and power developments in the northern part of the province through Manitoba Hydro and in developing a wide variety of programs of aid to manufacturing.

Newfoundland was the Atlantic province that most enthusiastically adopted the Western model of development. The intent was to gain control over natural resources and then encourage backward and forward linkages, following the failure of major "transplants" such as the Come-by-Chance oil refinery and the Stephenville Linerboard mill. Foremost among these concerns were offshore oil and gas. There was also increasing interest in the development of manufacturing equipment for the fishing industry. The government argued that in order to ensure the development of the province's resources benefitted Newfoundlanders, creating maximum employment for the province which had long endured the highest levels of unemployment in the country and doing minimum damage to the unique qualities of its community, the province must control off-shore oil and gas development and gain greater control over the fishery.

Nova Scotia's industrial policies initially focussed on the long- standing problems of the Cape Breton coal and steel industry and on developing manufacturing, especially in the Halifax-Dartmouth area. But, like Newfoundland, offshore resources – fish and oil – became increasingly important. There were also attempts to promote high technology manufacturing. New Brunswick and Prince Edward Island took a similar view of the aims of industrial policy and developed a parallel mix of incentives, subsidies, grants and government procurement policies. But none of these governments was as activist in orientation as Newfoundland: it had the largest number of provincial Crown corporations in the country (42) while the three maritime provinces had the fewest (Vining and Botterell, 1983).

The concerns of the central Canadian provinces were naturally very different from those on the periphery. Their aim was to preserve and expand their manufacturing economies in the more competitive environment that now prevailed, both nationally and internationally. Between 1970 and 1977, Ontario's share of GNP dropped from 41.9 percent to 39.9 percent; its growth rate was among the lowest in the country. Quebec, too, experienced major structural shifts, and a declining share of national GNP.

Partly because many of its supporters were averse to economic "planning" and "strategies", and partly because it sought to maintain the existing regional distribution of economic activities, Ontario's Tory government eschewed the rhetoric of "industrial strategy". Still, Ontario created an Employment Development Fund which, among other things, provided the financial aid that encouraged the Ford Motor Company to build an engine plant in the province, and promoted capital investment in pulp and paper. In 1980 the province brought all its industrial development activities under the umbrella of the cabinet Board of Industrial Leadership and Development (BILD). Low cost nuclear power was expected to encourage energy intensive industries to locate in the province, minimize dependence on expensive imported oil, and encourage the development of electrical rail and urban transit technology. Ontario also established several technology development centres. All the same, Ontarions, more than other Canadians, looked to federal economic policies.

Quebec's industrial policies after 1960 have already been discussed. In this period, the James Bay Development Corporation and agreements with Newfoundland for the production and export of Labrador hydro power, expanded its original hydro-electric strategy. Quebec also became more interested in promoting high tech industries. Pressure was placed on Ottawa and its Crown corporation, Atomic Energy of Canada Ltd. to locate experimental nuclear reactors in the province, although hopes of establishing a major nuclear industry in Quebec dimmed as the costs of nuclear power sky-rocketted in the late 1970s. Attention shifted to other hi-tech industries in the 1982 policy review entitled *Le virage technologique*. More than any other province, Quebec was also concerned with the control of investment in the province, creating a network of publicly-owned financial institutions – the Société Générale de Financement, an investment and holding corporation; the Société de Developpement Industriel, providing development loans and grants; and the Caisse de Depôt et de Placement, mobilizing assets of the Quebec pension plan for development purposes – and expanding their roles in these years. By 1982, the Caisse had assets of $14.5 billion and holdings in 183 companies. With these policies, successive Quebec governments moved deliberately to create a modern Quebec business class.

Federal Regional and Sectoral Policies   Federal industrial policy in the early 1970s remained confused and fragmented. Initiatives were divided among a number of departments and ministries, with only limited coordination among them (French, 1980). Existing programs, represented "a patchwork of industry-by-industry and some across-the-board incentives and programs, produced without much consultation with business and labour" (Doern & Phidd, 1983, p. 275). Nor were these initiatives coordinated with regional policy. The wide-ranging review of DREE, conducted between 1971 and 1973, concluded that its activities were not clearly focussed or well-integrated with provincial programs, and they had contributed to federal-provincial tensions. DREE was subsequently decentralized, with staff working more closely with individual provinces. The instrument of this new approach was the General Development Agreement (GDA), which identified general objectives and specified subsidiary agreements on particular projects. GDAs were managed by committees of provincial and local DREE officials. Funding was shared but the provinces actually operated the programs. By 1974 GDAs had been signed with all provinces (Lithwick, 1986, pp. 129-33).

As the decade advanced, there were several efforts to reform the federal industrial policy process. In 1977 Deputy Ministers in departments with policies bearing on industrial policy were brought together as "DM 10" to plan for the post-controls period. In 1978 the Board of Economic Development Ministers (BEDM) – later to become the Cabinet Committee on Economic Development and still later the Cabinet Committee on Economic and Regional Development – was created to try to coordinate development spending. The committee was served by a new central agency, the Ministry of State for Economic Development, which took control over the economic development expenditure envelope.

Ottawa's strategy paper, *Economic Development for Canada* (Ottawa, 1981), defined the national industrial strategy that the November 1981 budget sought to implement (Lithwick, 1986, pp. 133-34). It argued that the dramatic increase in the price of oil and gas over the previous eight years represented a "fundamental and essentially permanent shift...that strengthens Canada's traditional advantage in the production of basic commodities, [and] related manufactured goods on the one hand, and increases the comparative disadvantage of many standard manufactured products on the other". As a result, the best foundation for a national industrial strategy lay in "the development of Canada's rich bounty of natural resources" (Doern and Phidd, 1983, p. 437). The strategy had an important political rationale as well – it was believed that this focus would reduce inter-provincial conflicts over the location of manufacturing.

Soon, however, the slump in international oil and gas prices undermined the assumption that a permanent shift in the terms of trade had taken place. By 1984 Liberal leaders had lost faith in their capacity to predict the future and to reconcile regional economic differences. Sympathy for market "solutions" increased correspondingly, reflected in the final report (1985) of the federal Royal Commission chaired by Donald Macdonald, the former Finance Minister who had ushered in the new era of government intervention only a decade before.

Trudeau also became disillusioned with the collaborative, decentralized approach to regional policy embodied in the GDA strategy. It was perceived to give Ottawa too little credit for its regional development activities. Moreover, it reduced Ottawa's capacity to impose its priorities on development within provinces (Aucoin & Bakvis, 1984). As Prime Minister Trudeau put it in 1982: "The federal government has responsibilities in regional economic development and we plan to meet these responsibilities, and be held accountable for them, by dealing more directly with the problems and opportunities of Canadians" (in Doern, 1982b).

Economic and Regional Development Agreements (ERDAs) provided a new framework within which each government would design and operate its own programs. This implied a change in the definition of "regional policy". In the past it usually referred to policies aimed at slow growth areas, but it now meant the regional dimensions of all national policies. These changes were reflected in departmental reorganizations. DREE and ITC were combined as the Department of Regional Industrial Expansion (DRIE), in an effort to end the traditional split between DREE (aimed at the poorer regions) and ITC (aimed at serving the manufacturing interests concentrated in central Canada). A large number of DREE and ITC programs in regional and industrial development were combined under a new omnibus Industrial and Regional Development Program. Many regionally-focussed activities were allocated to other departments and all were expected to make the regional dimension a major part of their activity. The Ministry of State for Economic Development was expanded to become the Ministry of State for Economic and Regional Development (MSERD). The new program also called for better coordination of the activities of all federal Departments in the provinces, and for efforts to establish closer links between Ottawa and local economic interests through the appointment of senior federal officials, known as Federal Economic Development Coordinators, in each province.

These changes were greeted with hostility by some provincial governments, which saw them as yet another element of the attempts to reassert federal power. Interests in Atlantic Canada were afraid that the shift in focus would mean less attention to their needs. Nor did everyone in Ottawa approve. A 1982 Senate Committee report sharply attacked the changes, arguing that the GDA system had accomplished the difficult task of coordinating federal and provincial policies "magnificently" (1982, p. 82). Who now, the Committee asked "will champion the cause of the least developed regions?" (1982, p. 11). With the disbanding of MSERD in 1984, the organization of Ottawa's industrial policy, to say nothing of its substantive objectives, was again thrown into question.

The Crow's Nest Pass Rate   The re-negotiation of the Crow's Nest Pass Rate sheds light on how regional/sectoral policy changes worked after 1982. It illustrates both the difficulty faced by the federal government in devising regionally acceptable industrial policies and the changing economic bases of western regionalism.

The Crow rate, which fixed the price for transporting western grain to the ports in 1897, had long been viewed by western farmers as a *quid pro quo* for the land grants and other benefits initially given to the railways, and as partial compensation for the higher prices they had to pay for tariff-protected manufactured goods from central Canada. Unchanged since its creation, the Crow Rate had been enshrined in law in 1925, permanently fixing the price of transporting western grain. By the 1970s the economic costs of the Crow Rate were becoming intolerable. Railway revenues for grain transport were a small and declining proportion of the actual costs. Already facing severe economic problems, the railways had little incentive or revenue to undertake modernization of the western grain transportation system. Yet, such transportation problems were costing Canadian wheat farmers dearly as promised shipments to international buyers failed time and again to be delivered on time. Moreover, because only grain benefitted from the subsidized rate, economists argued that the system led to massive distortions in the allocation of resources – encouraging excess grain production on marginal land at high prices, discouraging diversification into crops not subsidized by the rate, and discriminating against such industries as feedlots and meat-packing.

In 1982, the federal government appointed the Task Force on Western Grain Transportation (The Gilson Commission). No-one seriously proposed abolishing the subsidies altogether. The issues were, rather, the products which would be subsidized, the levels of those subsidies, and the methods by which they would be paid. Would they, for example, go to the railways, allowing them to recover their actual costs and providing them with the means to upgrade a transportation system in which they and the grain elevators would continue to enjoy quasi-monopoly status? Or would they be paid directly to the wheat farmers, allowing them to make their own decisions as to how to transport their produce?

The Western Grain Transportation Act, based on the recommendations of the Gilson Commission, created a fund to be paid directly to the railways, leaving the rates paid by producers well below actual costs. Future cost increases would be shared by the producers and the federal government. The range of products to which the preferential rates applied was increased. Railways were required to invest in improvement of the transportation system, with provisions for withholding of the federal subsidy if they did not. There was a "safety net" to ensure transportation prices did not exceed a specified fraction of the price of grain. A representative Senior Grain Transportation Committee was established (although it did not include provincial government members) and there were provisions for a comprehensive review of the operation of the new policy.

The debate that ensued had many characteristics of traditional federal-provincial and east-west battles, with the family farm and the traditional prairie community ranged against an unholy alliance of the railways and the central government. But now the regional basis of these conflicts of interest was much less clear-cut. Western interests were divided: grain growers against the producers and processors of agricultural products not covered by the special rate; the Saskatchewan government championing the freedom of individual farmers to choose their preferred mode of transport against the Manitoba and Saskatchewan wheat pools which feared the erosion of the railway-linked elevator system, backed by Quebec livestock producers who feared heightened competition from the west. Western provincial governments took widely varying positions on the issue. The Saskatchewan legislature voted unanimously to oppose the federal plan; the British Columbia legislature warmly endorsed it.

The legislation went ahead. In spite of all the sound and fury many of the distortions of the old system remained. The railways benefitted over other modes of transportation; grain producers, wheat pools and the Quebec livestock industry benefitted while the western livestock and processing industry gained nothing. Nevertheless, the symbolic mould had been broken. The issue illustrated Ottawa's willingness in this period to exercise its constitutional authority on contentious issues central to the character of the economic union. It reflected the New Federalism in that there was little consultation with the provinces and a strong desire to forge direct links with the interests involved. It showed how much political energy was required to alter, even in limited ways, long-standing elements of the regional economic accomodations which underpin modern Canadian federalism. In 1984 western farmers paid an extra 2.5 cents per bushel to have their grain transported, the first increase since the inception of the Crow Rate. Yet even now, most of the original features of the Crow Rate remain intact.

Conclusions   Not all of the industrial policies developed by the federal and provincial governments were in conflict with one another. In many cases, particular policies were beneficial to province and nation. But the more diversified provinces sought to make their economies, the wider the range of industries for which they were in effective competition with each other. Many commentators were disturbed by the increased economic activism of the provinces. Politically, they argued that province-building put the welfare of the provincial part above that of the national whole, eroding the primary federal responsibility for economic management and erecting internal barriers to the free movement of citizens that would undermine a common sense of citizenship.

Economically, they argued that much provincial intervention was a wasteful, inefficient and ultimately futile effort to hold back the tide of market forces. So, for example, business economist Ed Neufeld claimed that "Inadequate coordination of industrial policies" was among the leading causes of declining productivity (1984, p. 17). Decentralization, he argued, encouraged both greater intervention and less focussed policy. Federalism, therefore, posed much greater difficulties for industrial than for macroeconomic policies. Industrial policies "will test the economic viability of the federation in a way that was not true in the earlier postwar decades when macroeconomic policies predominated" (1984, p. 29).

Those arguing for a more interventionist industrial strategy decried fragmented powers and difficulties of coordination. Those arguing for a more market-oriented strategy decried the effect of internal impediments to the internal market which threatened to dissipate the benefits of the Canadian economic union (Maxwell & Pestieau, 1980).

These concerns fused in the debate over the economic union during the constitutional negotiations. They were also manifest in federal legislation to ensure greater control over provincial purchases of airlines and, in Bill S-31, which was designed to stop provincially-owned crown corporations acquiring more than 10 percent of federally-regulated transportation and communication companies (see Tupper, 1983). The Bill had been prompted by the possibility that Quebec's Caisse de depôts might gain control over Canadian Pacific, and the fear that such control could be used to favour Quebec interests in company decisions. The Bill generated a lively debate in Quebec. Even members of the federal Liberal caucus saw it as an attack on the new Quebec business class whose growth had been fostered by agencies such as the Caisse. The Bill eventually died, but continuing concern over related matters was a major motive for appointment of the Royal Commission on the Economic Union and Development Prospects for Canada (the Macdonald Commission) in 1982.

These concerns proved exaggerated. While it was possible to draw up long lists of barriers, research conducted for the Commission indicated that their aggregate economic effects were quite small and certainly could not be considered a major cause of declining Canadian competitiveness and associated economic difficulties (Macdonald Commission, *Report*, Vol.3, 1985, p. 120). Michael Atkinson found that interprovincial competition for investment has been relatively restrained, that federal and provincial policies were as often complementary as conflicting, and that the continuing capacity of the federal government to manage the economy has "never been in doubt" (1984).

The novelty and extent of province-building initiatives was also found to be exaggerated. "Provincial governments have aimed to attract manufacturing and to stimulate diversification since the time of the National Policy" and while the use of Crown corporations increased dramatically, provincial spending on economic development, as a proportion of total spending, actually declined from 32 percent in 1951 to 14 percent in 1976 (Young, *et al*, 1984, p. 799, p. 797). Even in this heyday of province-building, federal spending on economic development-related projects dwarfed provincial efforts in sector after sector. Of $7 billion in state aid to industry in 1980, four-fifths was federal. Moreover, the federal government came to play a major role in province-building through its regional development policies. Many of the identified "distortions" to efficiency in the economic union were found to be the result of federal policies. The major distortion was in industrial assistance programs, mainly operated through Industry, Trade and Commerce and going to central Canada, rather than in regional development programs (Savoie, 1986, pp. 122-23).

Nor were federal regional and industrial development expenditures large by international standards. An important comparative study listed 20 different regional policy instruments. Canada and the United States employed far fewer than unitary states such as Britain or Norway, or than other federations, such as Germany and Australia. Unitary Italy, with disparities similar to Canada's, utilized a far greater array of instruments and was considerably more successful in reducing interregional differences in per capita income. Only France and the United States devoted a smaller proportion of government spending to direct regional assistance. Indeed, the study suggested that rather than leading to a greater commitment to regional redistribution, federalism might inhibit it, because the central government has fewer tools to undertake the task and provincial governments can be used as much to protect privilege as to bargain for greater redistribution. Because such a large proportion of regional development expenditures in a federation take the form of transfers, they may at once be more controversial, and less expansive (OECD, 1979).

Energy Policy

The difficulties of industrial policy in a federal system are two-fold. First, it must benefit all regions and strengthen linkages among them and, second, it must find an appropriate division of labour among governments in carrying them out. Nowhere were these challenges more difficult than in the energy sector between 1973 and 1983. In 1973, the OPEC capped a series of small increases with a quadrupling of prices. In 1979, following the Iranian revolution, there was a further doubling of prices. In Canada, the effect was to "internalize in the form of sharp federal-provincial conflict, the struggle raging internationally between oil importing and exporting countries" (Nelles, quoted in Doern & Toner, 1985, p. 37).

Energy divided Canada regionally as did no other issue. The territorial distribution of energy resources combined with the allocation of ownership, taxing and trade powers to maximize division. "It unveiled with shocking clarity the intergovernmental conflict of interests in Canadian energy politics" (Doern & Toner, 1985, p. 169). This had not been the case before the 1970s. Both federal and provincial governments had agreed on the need to encourage natural resource development and promote exports. With the Borden Line along the Ottawa River, a large part of the Canadian market had been reserved for western oil, which then cost more than imported oil. But now regional conflicts of interest were substantially reduced.

The consuming provinces, led by Ontario, wished to restrain price increases as much as possible to benefit both domestic and industrial users, and to ensure that the revenue gains would be shared widely across the country. Ontario argued that world oil prices bore no particular relation to the costs of production, either in Saudi Arabia or Canada, but rather were merely a reflection of the new market power of the OPEC cartel. Adopting such prices could not, therefore, be justified on efficiency grounds. Lower Canadian oil price increases would dampen inflation and provide a comparative advantage for Canadian industry.

The producing provinces wished to capitalize on their ownership of the resource by retaining full control over its management, by moving as fast as possible to world oil prices, and by capturing the lion's share of increased public revenues. Alberta and the other oil producing provinces argued that, whatever their origins, high energy prices seemed likely to prevail henceforth. Any short-term competitive gains resulting from subsidized oil prices would be more than offset in the long run as Canada's competitors became more efficient energy users. If Canada were totally self-sufficient, now or in the forseeable future, the picture might be different. But since it was not, and since maintaining prices below world energy prices would discourage new investment in exploration, Canada would have to adapt. It was better to do it now, while competitors faced the same difficulties, than later when competitors had solved their problems and Canada had not.

The federal government had a far more complex set of conflicting demands to resolve. In response to consumer interests it wanted to limit price increases, but it also wanted a single Canadian price. The greater the discrepancy between domestic and world prices, the greater would be the drain on the federal treasury in the form of subsidies for the imported oil on which the east coast still depended. On the other hand, if the discrepancy were reduced to zero, Ottawa's commitments under the existing equalization system would mushroom. Either way, Ottawa needed a greater share of windfall resource revenues. The federal government had to reconcile several other partly contradictory goals: reducing energy consumption, promoting Canadian ownership in the industry, ensuring security of future supplies, and developing new reserves in the so-called "Canada lands" in the north and off-shore. While necessarily responsive to majority interests, the federal government also saw itself as "the arbiter of provincial interests...the only government able to strike a compromise between producer and consumer interests" (Doern & Toner, 1985, p. 175).

The redistributive stakes were enormous. A 1979 Ontario government paper estimated that a $7 per barrel increase in the price of oil would add $3 billion to the coffers of the producing provinces, while adding 3.2 percent to the Ontario inflation rate and reducing its GPP by 1.5 percent (Simeon, 1980, p. 183). The revenue bonanza, Ontario argued, was creating massive inequalities in the revenues of provincial governments. By 1980, for example, Alberta's revenues from its own sources were 232 percent of the provincial average. The Ontario paper argued that "the eventual size of fiscal imbalances created by revenue flows of these orders of magnitude is staggering and represents a significant challenge to the flexibility of the central financial arrangements of Confederation". It concluded that "petrodollars, not constitutional lawyers are rewriting our constitutional system".

The Alberta government responded with a study estimating that between 1974 and 1981 the oil producing region had subsidized the other regions of the country to the tune of about $40 billion. The Economic Council of Canada, with a less immediate stake in the outcome of these statistical battles, estimated that in 1980 alone Canada's less-than-world prices represented between $12 billion and $15 billion in revenues lost to the Alberta government.

Questions of regional redistribution were so large and important that it was impossible not to believe that, in the final analysis, Ottawa's policy decision would be determined primarily by a choice between the conflicting interests of the two competing sectors and regions. Ottawa's preference for below-world prices was interpreted as a victory for the non-producing regions, not only in consequence but also in intent. "Now once again, Canada was calling on the west to...help salvage the viability of the nation. Many in the west felt that too much had been asked in the past and too much was being asked again" (Conway, 1983, p. 201).

The First OPEC Price Increase In the wake of the 1973 price hike, the federal government acted quickly. It immediately froze the price of domestically produced oil and introduced a subsidy scheme to guarantee the same lower prices to Canadian consumers east of the Ottawa River. Ottawa also announced plans to extend the pipeline carrying western oil east to Montreal. The moves were a precursor of the kind of unilateralist thrust and riposte which was to characterize energy politics throughout the decade (Doern & Toner, 1985, p. 172). Meanwhile, provinces also moved to strengthen their hands in price setting: Alberta established a Petroleum Marketing Commission in December 1973.

Both orders of government also moved to increase their share of energy revenues. Ottawa's response to increased provincial levies was to impose an export tax on oil and gas going to the United States, in order to collect the difference between the domestic and international price. The 1974 federal budget announced that henceforth provincial royalty payments could not be deducted from corporate income tax obligations, angering both the provinces and the industry which rightly felt itself caught in the intergovernmental squeeze. Faced with a "capital strike" – cancelled projects and a highly-publicized exodus of drill-rigs to the United States – governments were forced to reduce royalties and provide new incentives. Protection from this type of response, in turn, became an additional rationale for the creation of PetroCanada. Ottawa also moved to limit its escalating obligations under the equalization program which, under the existing formula, would have made Ontario (hitherto the richest province) eligible to receive federal transfers by 1977. From 1974 Ottawa would only equalize one-third of the additional revenues. In 1977 the formula was changed to take account of only half of non-renewable resource revenues and to ensure that no more than one-third of equalization payments would be derived from resource revenues. In 1978 the rule was changed again to render ineligible any province with a per capita income above the national average.

These federal moves were seen by the producing provinces as unwarranted infringements of their ownership rights. As the conflict intensified, both orders of government sought to increase their legal and political capacity to act in the energy field. In 1975 Ottawa passed the Petroleum Administration Act, giving it the power to ration supplies in an emergency, and authorizing unilateral federal action in the event of failure to reach agreement on prices with producing provinces. Provinces were concerned that this legislation might give Ottawa powers beyond the taxing and control of interprovincial and international trade, to intervene in pricing and other regulatory matters, "right down to the well-head". PetroCanada also gave the federal government leverage in negotiations with the provinces.

Alberta and Saskatchewan created new Crown corporations to participate directly in oil and gas development, and Alberta introduced a provincial marketing commission to strengthen its control. Saskatchewan introduced legislation to socialize a large part of the potash industry, to bring all freehold oil and gas rights under Crown ownership, and to ensure that the province received the windfall from the post-1973 oil price increases. Both measures were challenged in the courts, where the federal government joined private plaintiffs against Saskatchewan in defence of its powers over trade and commerce. In the potash case, the Supreme Court held the Saskatchewan legislation to be an infringement on the federal trade and commerce power. In the CIGOL case it held that the province was imposing an indirect tax and setting prices outside the province. These decisions led provincial governments to redouble their efforts to use public ownership to secure their positions and to seek protection of their power to manage resources in the constitutional arena. As Premier Blakeney put it: federal policies "led us to demand constitutional change" (in Conway, 1983, p. 212; also Blakeney, Leitch, Lougheed, Macdonald, Timbrell & Trudeau, in Meekison, 1977).

The oil and gas issues raised fundamental questions of principle and constitutional law. As the holders of the constitutional right to control the devlopment and direct taxation of their natural resources, were the producing provinces entitled to the full benefits of these revenues? Or could Ottawa legitimately claim that, while the constitution assigned these roles to the provinces, all resources were in some final sense the patrimony of the national community? "Is Canada a single community or only a loose confederation or coalition?" asked A. M. Moore, an economist, at one conference. His answer, from which clear prescriptions flowed, was: "I like to think of Canada as a single nation, a single community" (in Simeon, 1980, p. 184). As usual, the constitution itself afforded no definitive resolution to such questions. It permitted both orders of government to lay claim to oil-related revenues – Ottawa through its unlimited power to tax, and the producing provinces through royalties on production. Provincial powers flowing from ownership had to be reconciled with federal powers over international and interprovincial trade and commerce.

Despite the high constitutional, political, economic and personal stakes, the federal and provincial governments were able to achieve some form of compromise on the pricing and revenue- sharing issues in the period before the second OPEC price increase of 1979. Between 1973 and 1978, Canadian oil prices rose to 80 percent of international levels by a series of staged increases. Over the same time period the federal share of oil revenues increased from $182 million to $876 million, or from 5.2 percent to 9.5 percent of the total. The provincial share rose from $681 million to $4.3 billion, or from 27 percent to 46 percent. Both increases had been at the expense of the producing companies, whose share of total income dropped from 65 percent to 44 percent (EMR, 79; Federal Year in Review, 1979, p. 89, Table 3). Moreover, the two orders of government were able to cooperate in some developmental areas, one of the most important being their shared financing of the Syncrude oil sands plant after several private participants pulled out of the project.

The Second OPEC Price Increase   By 1979, the time of the second dramatic oil price rise, there was a new government in Ottawa. Prime Minister Clark's minority government, elected in May 1979 with 35.9 percent of the vote and 136 seats, had strong representation from the West. But the Tories were very weak in Quebec, with only 13.5 percent of the vote and two seats. Although their support in Ontario was substantial, it was also soft. The Liberals, with 40.1 percent of the vote, won 114 seats; the NDP, with 17.9 percent, won twenty six.

The Clark government was committed both to improving Ottawa's relationships with provincial governments and to a more market-oriented approach to economic questions. Partisan differences would no longer count for much, since most provincial governments, including those of the central protagonists, Ontario and Alberta, were also Conservative. If any federal government was to find compromise, it should have been this one. For these reasons, the brief tenure of the Clark government is of particular interest. When the oil pricing dilemmas arose for a second time in six years, the reaction of both orders of government affords an excellent opportunity to assess the degree to which changes in the orientation of the federal government – as distinct from the unchanged logic of regional conflicts of economic interest – affected levels of federal-provincial conflict.

The 1979 price hike was only half as large, and less of a surprise, than that of 1973. But predictions that the change in Ottawa would smooth the negotiations proved naïve. Sharp disagreement between Ontario and Alberta remained, showing that the conflicts of the previous six years were largely independent of any particular government. Where such intense regional conflicts of regional economic interest existed, federal-provincial tension would follow, even with the best will on the part of the political and bureaucratic elites. The attempt of the Conservatives to walk a tight-rope between the demands of their Alberta and Ontario party "brethren" failed, with disastrous political consequences (Doern & Toner, 1985, p. 187).

At the summer Premiers' Conference of that year Ontario released *Oil Pricing and Security*, a paper which argued strenuously against further price increases and called instead for the creation of a "National Energy and Employment Adjustment Program". Afraid of a "sell-out" and frustrated that Ontario was not at the bargaining table, Premier William Davis campaigned publicly against the energy deal he felt was being cooked up by his Tory colleagues in Ottawa. Clark's proposed price increase, he argued, was "an excessive and imprudent response to the claims of the producing provinces and the petroleum industry" and involved an "unrelenting commitment to an artificial, erratic and soaring world price – a price set by interests and circumstances foreign to Canada and *our* economic realities" (in Doern & Toner, 1985, p. 192). Ontario proposed an alternative program, to be funded by new federal revenues and a large share of the receipts of the producing provinces.

Alberta rejected the proposal as an "attempt to change the basic concept and arrangements of Confederation which left the ownership of natural resources to the provinces". Its position remained unchanged: the resources belonged to the province; they were depleting; the difference between world and domestic prices was simply a subsidy to the rest of the country. Saskatchewan supported Alberta. Premier Blakeney, speaking at Queen's University in 1980, argued that if Ontario's Tories had been willing, over the years, to develop a resource regime that captured a larger share of rents for Ontario's citizens, as opposed to foreign multinationals, it could have had its own heritage fund too. Instead, their free enterprise ideology now left them in a position in which they were obliged to try to siphon off the resource rents rightly belonging to more prudent, responsible western governments and their people.

In a long series of negotiations the Clark government tried to square the circle. It was willing to concede sharply higher prices in return for Alberta's participation in an Energy Bank and Stabilization Fund, the purpose of which was, in part, to recycle petro-dollars. Alberta rejected the idea. It is not clear whether Ottawa and Alberta negotiators ever reached a tentative agreement. But with a budget to produce, the Conservatives had to act. The December budget called for rapid price increases, a greater federal share of the resulting revenues and an 18-cent-a-gallon gasoline tax increase to finance conservation and raise revenues.

This was a fatal move for Clark's Conservative government. Despite their strong support base in the west and the influence of the Saskatchewan NDP government in their counsels, the budget was defeated with the aid of the federal NDP. Ontario's Premier Davis was conspicuous in his lack of support for the national leader of his party. Jeffrey Simpson argues that:

> [Clark] was naïve on entering the negotiations: nothing in Opposition had prepared him for the intractability of the provincial governments. He believed that by showing goodwill and by making early concessions he would consummate a speedy energy agreement that would fulfill his election promise to end the warring between Ottawa and the provinces.... He discovered that the Premiers cared at least as much about their own provinces as about the national interest and cared much more about their own political necks than about helping Joe Clark ... .
>
> (1980, p. 9, p. 204)

In the February 1980 election the Liberals were returned to power on promises to keep prices and taxes below the levels proposed in the Conservative budget. If Clark's brief government demonstrated the limited scope for reducing federal-provincial conflict by good will and conciliatory methods, the restored Trudeau government showed that conflict could still be intensified by taking a more adversarial stance.

Most westerners, particularly those in Alberta, were outraged by the election outcome. Once again there was a profound sense of having been cheated. They felt that the election had simply pitted the more populous east against them and that, having once won a seat at the table of power in Ottawa, it had now been snatched away. Two western separatist parties were formed, the Western Canada Concept and the West Fed, both of which found considerable support at public meetings throughout Alberta. The Liberal party "which to many Albertans embodied Ontario's and Quebec's dominance of the West had returned to office, partly by telling the rest of the country that Alberta was becoming too powerful and greedy". One of the prominent converts to the western separatist cause, Carl Nickle, declared that once again an election had been determined before the polls were closed in the west. Alberta was left with three alternatives, he argued: "to lie down, take it and be stomped on; continue seeking compromise as Peter Lougheed seeks; or opt for a separate Western Canadian nation". One proclaimed separatist was elected in a provincial by-election in Alberta, and polls showed considerable support for western separatism (Harrington, in Pratt & Stevenson, 1986, p. 23, p. 29).

As Nickle's characterization of the Lougheed position suggests, the Alberta government did not follow the wave of popular anger in the province by escalating its demands. Well aware of the strong popular mandate that the Trudeau government possessed, even without significant western support, Lougheed knew that his bargaining position was weaker than it had been in 1978 or 1979, and he therefore sought compromise. When negotiations with Ottawa resumed, Alberta proposed that prices be allowed to rise to 75 percent of world levels. In return, Alberta would refrain from further increases in royalties. In addition, Lougheed's government would be willing to undertake large investments in energy-related and transportation projects in other parts of Canada. Lougheed also sought, as he would throughout the constitutional talks after the Quebec referendum, cast-iron guarantees of provincial control of resources against any conceivable national majority.

But the new Trudeau government was in no mood to accept such terms. Ottawa wished to detach Canadian prices from any link to international prices, wanted a larger proportion of revenue for its own purposes, and balked at what it took to be Alberta's implicit assumption that the Government of Canada, "for want of financial wherewithal", should delegate "its responsibilities for national undertakings to a provincial government" (Institute of Intergovernmental Relations, Year in Review, 1980, p. 65). Ottawa's reply was the National Energy Program, a comprehensive strategy designed to achieve these objectives while responding to growing economic nationalist sentiments in central Ontario, directed against the oil multinationals.

Under the authority of the Petroleum Administration Act, Ottawa unilaterally established a new pricing regime. By means of new taxes on oil and gas production and exports, the program provided for an increase in the federal share of oil revenues from an estimated 12 percent in 1979 to 27.5 percent by 1982, dropping the provincial share from 49 percent to 41 percent. To promote exploration and self-sufficiency, a new Petroleum Incentives Program was established. By providing much larger subsidies for exploration in Canada Lands in the North and offshore, the program created strong incentives to move new exploration activities into the northern territories over which Ottawa had jurisdiction. By varying the size of federal grants in accordance with levels of Canadian ownership, incentives to increase the level of Canadian ownership in the petroleum industry were also created. By providing the federal government with the right to purchase up to 25 percent of all new discoveries, public ownership could supplement the private Canadianization process. A special tax to be used for the creation of a Canadian ownership account had the same object.

Ottawa justified the NEP by arguing that the price changes resulting from OPEC benefitted some parts of Canada at the expense of others. The Government of Canada had a legitimate claim to a greater share of the revenues, it was argued, "to support its energy initiatives and its broad economic management responsibilities: to cushion individual Canadians from adverse economic effects, to facilitate industrial adjustment and to see that fair play is done". The existing division of revenues was argued to be "extraordinarily unfavourable to the national government". In other countries faced by energy shocks, at least the national government could employ increased revenues to cushion the blow. But "in Canada, one provincial government – not all, and not the national government – enjoys most of the windfall.... . These policies are no longer compatible with the national interest." Provinces were receiving more than 75 percent of all public revenues from oil and gas, 80 percent of which went to Alberta, allowing it the luxuries of high expenditures, low taxes, budget surpluses and Canada's highest per capita income. "The Government of Canada believes the present system is inappropriate and unfair." Oil and gas were not being singled out unfairly for special treatment: they are so fundamental to all economic activity that they are indeed unique.

Whatever the merits of its basic objectives – Canadianization, self-sufficiency, off-shore development, a "made in Canda" oil price – the NEP was an act of *force majeure*. It was one of the principal expressions, along with the federal government's declared intent to patriate the constitution, with or without provincial consent, of the new federalism.

Provincial governments responded in kind. Earlier conflicts had often found Ontario playing the statesman role of mediator between the provinces and the federal government, and asserting the national interest. But now Ontario, faced with high oil prices, constrained finances, and worry about the future prospects of its manufacturing industry, was more self-consciously and explicitly acting as spokesman for regional and provincial interests. In this sense, Ontario became a province more like the others. Unlike the western provinces, however, Ontario's regionalist stand pushed it into a close alliance with Ottawa, an alliance which extended into other spheres, notably the constitution. In the energy context, Premier Davis defended Prime Minister Trudeau's definition of the "national interest". Current policies were damaging the "fabric of Confederation":

> When massive and unprecedented interregional shifts of tax dollars threaten to distort the economy and enfeeble (its) capacity...to meet national responsibilities, then provincial royalties are of legitimate national concern.... The stark prospect before us all is that our differences over the pricing of crude oil really have less to do with energy policy than they have to do with conflicting aspirations and convictions about the management and future of our country...energy policy must be defined in a national, not merely provincial context.
>
> (Doern & Toner, 1985, pp. 276-80)

Province-building, Premier Davis argued, should not replace nation-building; the federal government is not merely the arbiter but the guardian of the nation as a whole. The costs of higher prices for ordinary Canadians were being imposed "not by any foreign power but by a Canadian provincial government". Davis acknowledged that Ontario's heartland status was a source of envy, frustration and alienation in other parts of the country, but responded that "the record of our sharing of our wealth is clear" (Doern & Toner, 1985, pp. 276-80).

The producing provinces attacked the NEP on almost every count. It was, said Premier Lougheed, "an outright attempt to take over the resources of this province". This was fundamentally unfair because western resources were being treated quite differently from the minerals or hydro-electricity of other provinces. Central Canada had long turned a deaf ear to western complaints about higher than world prices for manufactured goods from the centre, or western taxes devoted to bailing out Chrysler or Massey-Ferguson plants in Quebec and Ontario. Albertans had already foregone over $17 billion – $8,500 for every Albertan – and they would not submit to further draining of their resources by a unilateral process:

> The attitude of Western Canada towards Confederation today is dissatisfaction and frustration.... Any unilateral action by the federal government – particularly one that's been rejected by Western Canada – will be resisted by our citizens in the most determined ways. It would be a tragic miscalculation by Ottawa if it misjudged the resolve of Albertans in this matter.
>
> (Doern & Toner, 1985, p. 266)

The NEP was also economically foolish, Lougheed argued. It would cost Canadian jobs, undermine the goals of security and self-sufficiency, hurt smaller firms, and divert resources and capital to the U.S. Beyond all of this, the way in which the NEP had been devised and was now being implemented was contrary to the postwar vision of Canadian federalism. An "inner elite" in Ottawa was imposing a "centralist, statist view of Canada", Lougheed argued, because "Ottawa could not stand any province becoming even moderately independent.... We are faced with nothing more or less than bare-faced aggression by a federal government...committed to reducing us, and taking us back to the territorial status of 1904" he declared (in Pratt & Stevenson, 1981, p. 165). The NEP was an "Ottawa program" rather than a national one. "If the country proceeds as intended by the Prime Minister, we will have a very different kind of Canada...a much different federal state – if a federal state at all." Provinces other than Quebec or Ontario would be in a "second class position" (in Doern & Toner, 1985, pp. 268-69).

Alberta launched a constitutional case, withheld approval for construction of heavy oil and tar sands projects, and announced a phased series of cutbacks in oil production, escalating to 180,000 barrels per day. Saskatchewan and British Columbia echoed Alberta's criticisms. The NEP, said Premier Blakeney, was a case of "reverse Robin Hood", a policy for one region and against another. It was no accident that regional views dominated Ottawa – but it was a "national tragedy" (in Doern & Toner,

1985, p. 282). Both provinces attacked the new taxation regime as unconstitutional. Ottawa responded with a small additional retail tax, dubbed the "Lougheed" or the "Lalonde" levy, depending upon which side one supported.

There had never been such federal-provincial conflict over resources, and pressure from various quarters mounted to call a halt to the war. The oil industry attacked the program in the financial press and followed up with another capital strike, reducing exploration expenditures, moving drilling rigs south and shelving oil sands development plans. The president of the Canadian Chamber of Commerce declared that he was "rapidly running out of patience with the political pugilists who persist in putting the nation's affairs on hold while they pursue their personal vendettas". In their 1981 Conference, the other Premiers also called for a settlement. Both orders of government seemed to sense they were a long way out on a limb, and the time had come to find a compromise.

In the spring of 1981 negotiations on oil pricing and revenue sharing resumed. By September 1981 marathon bilateral discussions achieved agreement between Ottawa and Edmonton on the basic issues. The controversial natural gas and gas liquids tax, seen by the provinces as an export levy, was reduced to zero and the petroleum and gas revenue tax was also amended. Alberta gained control of administration of Petroleum Incentive grants in the province, although federal rules still applied. Prices were to rise faster than earlier planned. Both Prime Minister Trudeau and Premier Loughheed claimed that the agreement was a reasonable compromise. Agreements were soon signed with the other producing provinces. Each was tailored to specific needs – the B.C. agreement focussed on natural gas exports; the Saskatchewan one on heavy oil. Both agreed to resume payment of taxes they had previously withheld. All three agreements left unresolved constitutional issues to one side. For example, the letter of understanding between Saskatchewan and Ottawa noted that:

> The government of Saskatchewan takes the position that the Crown in right of Saskatchewan...[is] not liable to pay taxes under the NGGLT and COSC and the Government of Canada takes the position that it has the right to levy such taxes on the Crown in Right of Saskatchewan.... . [They] have agreed however to set aside those differences of position without prejudice to them.
> (Year in Review, 1981, p. 131)

Thus, in 1981 as in 1867, agreements essential to the common welfare were achieved by putting aside fundamental differences for another day.

Another energy issue remained: off-shore oil and gas. Again, this was not new. In the 1960s British Columbia and Ottawa had gone to court over ownership of off-shore resources. The federal position had been upheld, although jurisdiction over the Strait of Georgia remained in question. As the prospects for major discoveries off the east coast grew in the 1970s, the issue arose again, especially in Nova Scotia and Newfoundland. Like the western provinces, they saw off-shore resources as the key to future prosperity and the spring-board for economic diversification. They argued these resources should be treated as provincial in a manner analogous to on-shore deposits. The matter was handled somewhat differently in the two provinces, partly because they articulated somewhat different claims.

Newfoundland had entered Confederation in 1949 after a history as a self-governing Dominion. It asserted that it had never alienated its previous rights to the continental shelf; the question simply had not arisen in 1949. Moreover, Premier Peckford argued, recognition of provincial ownership was more than a matter of revenues, it was an affirmation of Newfoundland identity and the means by which the province could preserve its traditional culture while reaping the benefits of modernization. In 1979 Prime Minister Clark had agreed to transfer ownership, but no formal agreement was signed and the new Trudeau government withdrew Clark's offer. Instead, Ottawa proposed administrative arrangements which would permit a provincial role in management, along with a split in revenues parallel to that in other provinces, at least until such time as Newfoundland and Nova Scotia were no longer have-not provinces (Doern & Toner, 1985, p. 161). Newfoundland rejected this offer.

Nova Scotia Premier John Buchanan said his province did not consider the NEP valid but, challenged by the Prime Minister to test the matter in court, Buchanan argued for a "political solution". Eventually, in March 1982 the "Canada-Nova Scotia Agreement on Off-Shore Oil and Gas Management and Revenue Sharing" was signed. The question of ownership was set aside. Nova Scotia would be represented on an "Offshore Oil and Gas Board" and would receive all "province-type revenues" until its fiscal capacity reached the national average. A $200 million fund for infrastructure development was created, along with provisions for the province to acquire part ownership in the Crown share of off-shore developments. Finally, if any province were later to sign a "better" deal, it would automatically extend to Nova Scotia.

Meanwhile, Newfoundland held out for jurisdiction. Acordingly, Ottawa referred the matter to the Courts. In 1984 the Supreme Court of Canada confirmed federal jurisdiction. By that time much of the urgency of the dispute had disappeared, owing to the dramatic fall in oil prices which slowed the pace of offshore exploration and development. The deadlock would not be broken until the September 1984 election brought Mulroney's Conservatives to power in Ottawa.

These agreements ended a decade of seemingly intractable conflict and represented a reasonable compromise among the competing interests. But it had taken a long time to reach this point and the costs along the way had been high. Ironically, no sooner was agreement achieved than the price of oil and other primary commodities, which had given rise to the conflict in the first place, collapsed. Once again, Canadian domestic politics was profoundly shaped by developments outside the country. The expected benefits of massive new exploration and development did not materialize. Instead, falling world energy and other commodity prices ended the western boom. Unemployment in Alberta soared to 11 percent in 1983, four times the 1981 level. Property values fell, and recently formed western banks fell into serious difficulties and had to be bailed out by Ottawa. The influx of new residents into the province slowed and then reversed. Far from the permanent shift in the Canadian economic balance that Ottawa's 1981 economic plans had assumed, the boom had proved temporary, as Westerners had feared all along it would.

While fears of the possibility of western (or Newfoundland) separatism were probably exaggerated, the conflicts over energy seriously strained the fabric of Canadian federalism. They raised questions about the basic premises of the Canadian political economy and reflected the break-down of a post-war accomodation. But why were these economic issues not understood primarily in class terms as wage and price controls were? Why did they not further contribute to the exacerbation of class differences in this period?

If Canada had possessed no oil, then the principal consequence of OPEC would have been a much more intense economic crisis and, with it, an intensification of class conflict. As it was, the post-war system of industrial relations was twice suspended, even though Canada was a net beneficiary of the OPEC oil price increases. Similarly, if Canada's oil and gas had been equally distributed across the country, there would have been no regional conflict, although workers and owners in the private sector would certainly have struggled with the two orders of government over the division of the windfall. In the absence of a regional dimension, that struggle, even at the federal-provincial level, might very well have been fought out in the language of class. But as it was, energy policy was seen by almost all the players, including the NDP, as a fundamental challenge to the balance of power – economic and political – between east and west.

No simple pattern of alliances between governments and the energy industry emerged either. The producing provinces had close links with the energy industry located within the province, but the federal government developed a parallel relationship with the energy industry operating on Canada lands, especially those elements that benefitted from the NEP. Moreover, there was substantial overlap between these two sets. The allegiance of other industries was less contingent on region or ownership than on which order of government most strongly favoured lower prices to subsidize them in international competition. Workers in each region were divided between those who supported the economic interest of their region, as identified by provincial governments, and those who supported their industry's (short-run) interest in subsidies.

State-centered analyses of this conflict, focussing on the federal character of the Canadian state, help to explain the form it took and the language in which it was expressed, as we shall see in the next Section. But to understand why the conflict occurred at all, we must begin with economic structures and population distributions. And to explain why it was a battle between regions rather than class factions, we must further understand the character and continuing importance of the strong identification with provincial communities characteristic of most Canadians.

The generalized debates of the period had profound consequences for the image of the country. Which community, national or provincial, was to have primacy? Which level of government was more responsive and legitimate? Was regional diversity something to be celebrated and further institutionalized, or was it a threat to be transcended and overcome by a reassertion of national will? How much should a federal system depart from simple majoritarianism? Canadians had debated such questions throughout their history, but between 1974 and 1984 they took on a form and intensity which was unparalleled. The debate did not take place in a vacuum; nor was it simply the product of power- seeking of rival elites. It took its energy from the real questions of power and influence which economic and social changes forced on the system.

Language: The PQ and the Referendum

The accession of the Parti Québécois to power on November 15, 1976 is best understood as the culmination of the trends examined in the previous chapter. Its goal was to achieve independence for Quebec while maintaining some form of economic association with the rest of Canada. The PQ promised to act gradually, to establish itself as the effective government of the province before holding a referendum on sovereignty-association. This gradual approach became known as *étapisme*. Meanwhile, the PQ would use the full powers of the Quebec government to pursue "francization" within Quebec.

The election should not be interpreted simply as a vote for sovereignty-association. Some of the PQ's activists and members may have understood it that way, but for others it was a vote for constitutional change, with the PQ as the toughest bargainers available. For still others, the issues were not so much national or linguistic as economic, the choice between the Liberals and the PQ understood primarily in class terms (See, 1987, pp. 149- 50), or simply as the desire to replace a tired and discredited government.

Nevertheless, the election of the PQ crystallized the fears for the future of the country held by many Canadians. A spate of books appeared with titles like *Must Canada Fail?* (Simeon, 1977) and *Canada and the Burden of Unity* (Bercuson, 1977). The author of the leading textbook on Canadian federalism noted that he had almost given up writing because he had not expected the federation to last long enough for his book to appear (Smiley, 1976).

As if to belie the pessimism, a host of public and private groups sponsored conferences and other activities designed to spur the search for common ground in a "third option" between the status quo and independence. Moreover, many Canadians identified with what they understood as Quebec's aspirations, and argued not only that other threats to Canadian unity were as important as that of language, but also that other provinces shared similar grievances and aspirations. Quebec's discussions of the costs and benefits of Confederation were duplicated across the country. Thus the response was not necessarily a rush to rally around Ottawa as the defender of Confederation against separatism.

In the years that followed, the struggle for the allegiance of Quebecers was fought on many fronts. The new Quebec government sought to lay the groundwork for the referendum and to pursue its domestic agenda, including social and economic reform. Its first major thrust was on language policy, designed to establish Quebec, once and for all, as a predominantly French-speaking society. The policy was enshrined in its first major piece of legislation, Bill 101, the "Charter of the French Language".

The PQ government conducted a series of major studies of the effects of Confederation on Quebec arguing, not only to Quebecers but also to those outside Quebec, that Confederation as it existed was a strait jacket for both groups, resulting in endless conflict. Both would be better off, the PQ argued, if they could get a divorce and then rearrange their relationships on a more equitable, amicable basis. A set of "economic accounts" purporting to show that Quebec received less in benefits from the federal government than it paid in taxes, was released. Federal analysts responded with contrary assesssments (Leslie and Simeon, 1977). The PQ government tried to convince Quebecers that the economic costs of separation would be small, a task made more difficult by the economic troubles of the day. Reports of investment and head offices leaving Quebec filled the newspapers.

In the autumn of 1979 the Quebec government published its White Paper, *Quebec-Canada: A New Deal*, proposing "a new partnership between equals: sovereignty-association". The paper documented the historic struggle for survival in Quebec and the permanent minority status of French Canadians. Quebec's recent experience of federalism, it argued, had been characterized by constant federal invasion of provincial powers – in culture, social policy, labour, resources and municipal affairs. Within the federal system, Quebec was treated as a province like the others; its special role as a distinct society unrecognized. Demographic trends were making Quebec ever weaker in the Confederation as a whole. Renewal in the existing system was impossible; special status an "illusion". There must be a new beginning, starting with Quebec sovereignty and a treaty of association. It would provide for a common market and a common monetary system, administered by a "Community Council" assisted by a commission of experts, a court of justice and a monetary authority. Thus, the PQ proposed to replace a ten-unit federal system with a two-unit confederal system, based on equality.

For the federal government, the PQ election signalled the climactic battle against Quebec nationalism that Pierre Trudeau and his colleagues had come to Ottawa to fight. Federal leaders countered the PQ claim on every point: they produced their own figures to show how much Quebec had gained from its participation in Confederation; they argued that Quebecers did exercise broad and effective power in Ottawa, and that a much brighter future lay in making French Canadians at home from sea to sea. They argued that sovereignty-association would not be acceptable to the rest of Canada and that the costs of achieving independence would be unacceptable. Rather than fighting for that, Quebecers should be seeking a "new federalism". The full resources of the federal government and the Liberal party were deployed to win support in Quebec. Quebecers were constantly reminded of the benefits Confederation provided. A Canadian Unity Information Office, designed to collect information on public attitudes and to generate favourable publicity, was established. In 1977 the federal government appointed the Pepin-Robarts Task Force on Canadian Unity, which held public hearings across the country. The following year it made public its constitutional reform agenda. Then, in 1979, the Pepin-Robarts Task Force issued its Final Report.

Provincial government reactions to these federal initiatives were mixed. All governments declared their opposition to negotiating sovereignty-association, but they left it to Ottawa to fight the battle. The provinces also saw in the new Quebec government an ally in their struggle for a more decentralized federation. Provincial governments, along with non-governmental study groups, including the Quebec Liberal Party and the Canadian Bar Association, developed a variety of constitutional proposals loosely labelled the "Third Option". The choice should not be the status quo or independence, they argued, but constitutional reform. Proposed reforms generally included recognition of de facto special status for Quebec, building linguistic dualism into central institutions, greater participation by provinces or regions in national policy-making, and some moves towards a less centralized federation.

The publication of the PQ's White Paper was followed by unveiling of the referendum question on December 20, 1979. The question stated the goal, sovereignty with association, promised that following negotiations no actual changes would be made without another referendum, and asked for the "mandate to negotiate the proposed agreement between Quebec and Canada". The *étapiste* strategy was thus retained. This caution reflected the state of Quebec public opinion. The proportion of the population committed to outright independence had remained stubbornly stable at about 20 percent since the 1960s. However, the *status quo* received no greater support. The majority of Quebecers were somewhere in between, their support wavering between reform and some form of sovereignty-association. Many, perhaps, were uncertain what the difference actually was between the two alternatives.

This ambivalence extended deep into the PQ and, indeed, was embodied in the complex character of its leader, René Levesque. There was a group in the party who were for independence *tout court*, and for whom association was little more than a means of sweetening the pill for the reluctant. But another, probably larger, group viewed the Canadian connection as an important part of their identity; they sought recognition of equality, "égal-à-égal", and saw sovereignty-association as the best way of asserting that principle.

Sovereignty-association might be a political and economic impossibility. Would there not, for example, be inexorable pressures for coordinated policies across virtually the whole range of economic and social issues? If so, how could a two-unit system resolve differences, especially given their differences in size and wealth, which would require the majority to defer to the minority on matters of crucial importance? But at the same time the concept retained a powerful emotional and symbolic attraction, capturing at once the desire for independence and the desire to maintain a link with Canada. Both the fleur-de-lys and the maple leaf appeared on the cover of the document "D'égal-à-égal". Before and after the referendum – indeed, ever since the formation of the PQ – Levesque had battled against the outright separatists inside and outside his party, rejecting the label when it was applied to him (Fraser, 1984).

There were also sharp differences between the conceptions of renewed federalism promoted by federal and provincial Liberals. But, despite the subtleties of the dual allegiances of most Quebecers and the numerous variations in how they sought to reconcile them, the referendum debate boiled down to a choice between independence and federalism. The question was debated in the Quebec National Assembly in March 1980, foreshadowing the campaign itself. Under the Quebec referendum law, both YES and NO sides were grouped under umbrella committees, one headed by Premier Levesque, the other by Liberal Leader Claude Ryan.

The speeches and the rhetoric of the campaign demonstrated how deeply divided Quebecers were among themselves. Competing symbols and values of nation and community contended with the most immediate material interests. While each side accused the other of underhanded tactics, what is most noteworthy in retrospect is the tolerance and openness within which such a profound debate was carried out (see Institute of Intergovernmental Relations, *The Question, 1977*).

Federal leaders, especially the Prime Minister and Justice Minister Jean Chrétien, participated actively, personifying an alternative vision of Quebec and Canada to that advocated by the PQ. In the see-saw battle, the tide seemed to turn when the "NO" campaigners switched from emphasis on the practical and economic disadvantages of separation to an explicit celebration of pan-Canadian values. Several provincial Premiers and a few citizen groups from outside Quebec added their appeal for a NO vote. But what is most remarkable is the extent to which the referendum campaign was a family affair, with English Canadians little more than fascinated on-lookers. Little public thought was given to the response in the event that the YES side won.

On May 20, 1980 the NO side won: 59.5 percent to 40.5 percent, just enough to allow the claim that a majority of all linguistic groups in Quebec had voted against the mandate. It was a terrible blow to the PQ, dividing it internally and greatly weakening its bargaining power with the other provinces and, above all, Ottawa. The referendum result, added to the 68.2 percent of the Quebec vote that the federal Liberals had received four months before in the 1980 federal election, gave Trudeau what Fraser calls "a double mandate: an authority with respect to Quebec that no federal prime minister had ever had before". Fraser goes on to argue that,

> ...the referendum transformed the Parti Québécois from a national movement into a provincial political party. It transformed René Levesque from a national leader into a provincial premier. As a national leader, he had been a figure of moderation, and a symbol of pride. As a provincial premier, he was to prove to be rigid, bitter, and weak. As a national leader, he had brought a coalition of dissent together and forged a progressive nationalist party, winning power in a surprisingly short time, and introducing a range of reforms. As a provincial premier, he failed to do what every preceding premier had managed to do since the Second World War: he failed to keep Quebec's political powers intact. The state which he...[left to Robert Bourassa was] weaker than the state which he inherited from Robert Bourassa. For René Levesque, that was...the most humiliating result of the referendum defeat.

> (1984, p. 240)

In the immediate aftermath of defeat the federal government had the initiative on the constitution. As René Levesque observed, "The ball is now in the federal court.". The PQ set itself the limited goals of resisting unilateral patriation of the constitution by Ottawa, and competent governance in Quebec. In April 1981 the PQ won re-election with 80 seats and 49 percent of the vote to the Liberals' 42 seats and 46 percent of the vote. The potentially divisive issue of sovereignty- association was pushed to one side – no-one was yet prepared to deal with it and, in any case, all energies were concentrated on the fight against Trudeau (Fraser, 1985, pp. 257-78).

Then came the second blow. On November 5, 1981, following an all- night private session from which Quebec was excluded, the federal government and the other nine provinces arrived at a constitutional deal. We discuss the deal, and the process by which it was reached, more fully in the next section. Here we are interested in its impact on Quebec society and politics. Levesque, outraged and bitter, refused to sign. Claude Morin, the Minister for Intergovernmental Relations who had negotiated with the other provinces, resigned within two weeks. The Quebec government withdrew from most intergovernmental meetings and processes. On April 17, 1982 the Constitution Act, 1982 became law. The government of Quebec responded with legislation subjecting all Quebec laws to the "notwithstanding" provisions of the Charter of Rights (Fraser, 1985, pp. 279-301).

Meanwhile, the constitutional defeat set in motion the struggle within the PQ that had hitherto been avoided. On one side were those who had always seen independence as a bargaining chip to be used to renew federalism; on the other were those who saw sovereignty-association as a step toward full independence. The political synthesis held together by the magic words "sovereignty-association" began to unravel. In the heat of the reaction to the November constitutional deal, the indépendentistes gained the upper hand. At the December 4, 1981 PQ Convention, the delegates voted down virtually all references to economic "association" in the party's constitution. The next provincial election would be fought on the issue of independence without association, to be declared unilaterally after another victory at the polls. Levesque was appalled, viewing it as the transformation of the PQ into the RIN. Two days later, in his closing speech to the Convention, he threatened to resign. On December 13, the party executive announced that there would be an internal party referendum on the question. On February 9, 1982, the results of the "René-rendum" were announced: 95 percent of the party members who mailed in their ballots supported Levesque's creed – sovereignty with continued economic association, to be negotiated only following a popular referendum, and to protect the rights of linguistic minorities as set out in Bill 101. However, only 48.8 percent of the 292,888 members to whom ballots were mailed had returned them (Fraser, 1985, pp. 302-14).

Still one more blow awaited the hapless PQ government: the recession. Quebec accounted for an incredible 44 percent of all jobs lost in Canada in this period: 219,000 jobs by August 1982, cancelling out all the gains since

December, 1977 (Fraser, 1985, p. 322). The PQ response, as we have seen, was a dramatic move to the right, unilaterally rolling back public sector wages with Bills 70 and 105. When the unions responded with a common front and illegal strikes, it looked like a re-run of Bourassa's 1972 confrontation with the Common Front, the event that threw the unions and the PQ together in the first place. But in February 1983 it was Levesque's party that brought forth Bill 111, described by L. Ian MacDonald as "the moral equivalent of the War Measures Act" (in Fraser, 1985, p. 334). The ties that bound the trade unions to the PQ were severed and the party was deprived of one of its most important bases of financial and organizational support. The battle reinforced a trend first noticed in the 1981 election: support for the PQ increasingly came from the more conservative small town rather than the urban constituencies (Fraser, 1985, pp. 322-36).

Recession and battles with labour took their toll, not only on party morale but also on voter support. By February 1983 PQ support had fallen below 20 percent (Fraser, p. 336). Meanwhile, all the other key political leaders were changing. Joe Clark was replaced as leader of the Progressive Conservative Party by Brian Mulroney in June 1983 – the first time in Canadian history that the Conservatives would be led by a Quebecer. Robert Bourassa was restored as leader of the provincial Liberals in October of the same year. Then, in February 1984 Trudeau announced that he would soon resign. His successor, John Turner, was chosen in June. In July 1984, leading by 11 points in the polls, Turner called a federal election. On August 6, Mulroney gave his Sept-Isles speech on the new era of federal-provincial cooperation that he would work for if elected. Three days later, Levesque declared his support for the principles outlined by Mulroney. The PQ was now counting on a Conservative victory to give them some progress on the constitution before they had to go to the polls themselves (Fraser, 1985, pp. 338-46).

Federal State

By 1980, intensifying conflict along all three of the traditional cleavage lines had created an unprecedented crisis of the postwar Canadian state. Other countries experienced similar traumas as "governing parties" lost power and historic compromises were breached. In Canada, because of the territorial character of two of those cleavages, and the way in which these identities were interwoven with class, this event took the form of a crisis of federalism. A system that depended on high levels of intergovernmental trust and cooperation began to seem unworkable as conflicts between governments came to be more numerous and about fundamental issues.

The territorial distribution of natural and human resources, the strength of citizen allegiances to both provincial and national communities, and regional economic structures were all conditions that could not be quickly or easily changed. Much attention therefore focussed on national political institutions, both federal and parliamentary. Their apparent inability to mediate regional and linguistic conflicts engendered a profound sense of "institutional failure". Out of this sense of failure came the drive for constitutional reform. We first examine the constitution.

Constitutional Reform

When the PQ took office in 1976 the constitutional issue was transformed. The very future of the country was now at stake. Constitutional change took on a new urgency. While the PQ laid the groundwork for the referendum, the challenge for federalists was to design a set of constitutional proposals which would prove more attractive than the PQ option. But now other provinces, especially in the West, formulated their objectives in constitutional terms: the constitution must be the vehicle to guarantee provincial control over resources, to constrain federal power, and to gain a greater regional voice in the formation of national policy. The debate now took place on two fronts, rather than one, as it had in the 1960s.

At the start, then, the constitutional crisis was the culmination of a long series of provincial challenges to federal power, and the main question was how far concessions to provincial demands would go. But, ironically, the period ended with a reassertion of federal power that left the provinces on the defensive. The traditional federalism agenda – patriation, amending formulae and divisions of powers – remained front and centre. But by the time of the 1981 agreement, many issues focussed on citizen concerns were inserted into the debate: the scope and substance of individual rights in a Parliamentary democracy; the rights of native people, women, and the handicapped; the relation between individual, minority, and majority rights, and so on.

These debates soon involved every institution and organized interest in Canadian society: leaders of federal and provincial governments were predominant throughout, but Parliament, political parties, the courts and citizen groups all became involved. Constitution-making, noted Alan Cairns, led to questioning of the efficacy of executive federalism and "precipitated a striking tendency for governments to explore their environment for greater resources, either to strengthen their bargaining power within executive federalism, or to by-pass it altogether.... The closed world of traditional federal-provincial bargaining was severely shaken" (1985, p. 112).

In many ways the debate was highly divisive. Canadians were forced to choose between competing visions of the country. The norms of constitutional civility were stretched to (some would say past) the breaking point.

The result, enshrined in the Constitution Act, was not a radical transformation. There was no reordering of the federal-provincial relationship. Patriation had been achieved; henceforth Canada would amend its constitution without any British participation. A general commitment to equalization was entrenched, as was a tidying up of jurisdiction over energy. Most important there was a Charter of Human Rights and Freedoms which opened up new directions in the relations between citizen and government. In retrospect, perhaps what was most vital was the debate itself and the process of self-examination it required. We were in important ways a different country at the end of it. Who in 1975 would have anticipated a First Ministers Conference in which native leaders in full regalia would engage the Prime Minister and the Premiers in dialogue about native rights before the television cameras? Who would have anticipated three party leaders in a bilingual debate on women's issues in the middle of an election campaign? Both, it could be argued, were made possible by the difficult, dramatic debates between 1976 and 1981. We begin our discussion of this constitutional process by exploring the issues and chief alternatives which had emerged as the negotiations got underway.

The Issues

Patriation   Patriating the constitution was viewed by the federal government (and many others) as both a requirement of full national sovereignty and an important signal to Quebecers that Canada was no longer tied to British apron strings. In March 1976 the federal government suggested that agreement to patriation by the provinces would be desirable, but that so long as the division of powers was not affected, it was not essential. This raised the issue of whether the constitution could be patriated without simultaneous agreement on an amending formula. Several provinces thought so, but most wished to ensure that if this were done, they should be fully protected in any future changes. Other provinces saw patriation and amendment as inextricably linked: it should be the culmination of the process of constitutional reform, not the start.

Preamble   Should the constitution include a statement of fundamental principles, to serve as inspiration for Canadians and a guide to interpretation by the courts? This question highlighted all the conflicts of values that have driven Canadian politics from its inception. Would there be an attempt to define the essence of Canadian federalism? Would it enshrine or inter the compact theory? Would linguistic dualism be articulated as a property of Canada, from sea to sea, or as a partnership of two societies with the special role for Quebec, perhaps even the right of self-determination, explicitly defined? Would it emphasize the sovereignty of the people as Canadians, or as members of provincial communities? Would it recognize the rights of native Canadians? What (if anything) would it say about God and the Queen? Here was a symbolic minefield. In the end it proved easier to skirt such questions, as in 1867, by avoiding a new preamble.

Amendment Formula   A crucial question that could not be begged was the amendment formula. The starting point was the Victoria Charter: the federal parliament plus the legislatures of any province which had ever had more than 25 percent of the population (Ontario and Quebec), along with any two Atlantic provinces and at least two western provinces, which together must constitute more than half the region's population. The federal government continued to support this position. But its October 1980 Resolution introduced a fundamental new principle: amendment should no longer be the exclusive preserve of governments; popular sovereignty implied that ultimately citizens should decide. Ottawa proposed a referendum device, to be used at federal discretion, in the case of intergovernmental disagreement. The Pepin-Robarts Task Force also endorsed the idea of popular ratification of amendments, calling for majorities in each of four regions. Ottawa's only potential ally here was Quebec, itself committed to a referendum on sovereignty- association. All other provinces rejected the idea, arguing that referenda would undermine legislative sovereignty and, as demonstrated by the conscription referendum, make it easier to mobilize irreconcilable divisions.

There were three challenges to the assumptions of the Victoria Charter formula, the first two articulated most strongly by Alberta. The first argued for provincial equality: whatever their variations in size, provinces were constitutionally and juridically equal. No formula should privilege the two largest provinces as the Victoria one did. Implicit here was not only a challenge to Ontario's weight in the federation, but also to the bi-national view of Quebec. Alberta's proposal, put forward in February 1979, called for assent by Ottawa together with two-thirds of the provinces, constituting 50 percent of the population (a qualification which still retained a veto power by the combined provinces of Ontario and Quebec).

The second challenge was the assertion that some provincial rights – their existing powers and privileges, and their ownership of natural resources – were inalienable. This view underpinned the argument that no amendment affecting such matters should take effect in a province which rejected it. Provinces could, in effect, "opt out" of any transfer of power to Ottawa. Later, another protection was added: if a province wished to opt out, it should not bear a financial penalty. "Fiscal compensation" should be extended to any non-participating province. The opt-out with compensation idea, pioneered in the shared cost programs of the 1960s, was thus extended into the realm of constitutional amendments. The two Alberta proposals became the "Vancouver consensus" enshrined in the Constitution Act, 1982.

The third challenge came from British Columbia, which claimed the status of a "fifth region". Its proposal called for a ratification process based on that concept. Other amendment issues were less important. Late in the process, for example, Saskatchewan argued for a formula which would limit the capacity of the Senate to block future changes. All proposals argued that any amendment affecting only a few governments should be ratified by those concerned; all would permit federal and provincial governments to amend their own constitutions when such changes did not alter the character of the federal system. Perhaps better than any other item on the table, the amendment formula highlighted the combination of high principle and power calculus that informed the positions of all governments in this process.

Language and Human Rights   Inclusion of language rights was critical to Trudeau's vision of a bilingual Canada from sea to sea. It was, therefore, the *sine qua non* of any agreement for the federal government. The Victoria Charter of 1971 had declared English and French to be official languages of Canada. Both could be used in Parliament and any of the provincial legislatures, except the three westernmost provinces. Statutes in both languages would be authoritative in Ottawa, but only in four provinces – Quebec, Ontario, New Brunswick and Newfoundland. Minority language rights would apply in the courts of the federal government, and in those of Quebec, New Brunswick and Newfoundland. There was no mention of minority language educational rights.

As before, the question now was whether language rights would be made binding on all provinces and how much variation there could be among them. There was also a renewed emphasis on the provision of services in minority languages, especially in education, stimulated by the passage of the PQ's Bill 101 in 1976. Quebec remained strongly opposed to any entrenchment of language rights that might limit the scope or effectiveness of laws aimed at controlling the province's linguistic makeup. Instead, Premier Lévesque proposed "reciprocal agreements" with other provinces, broadening access of English Canadians from outside Quebec to its English-language schools in return for improving access to French-language education elsewhere. The Pepin-Robarts Report was sympathetic to this approach, suggesting that extension of educational and other services should be left to the provinces and entrenched only when all were agreed. Except for New Brunswick the provinces agreed. Ontario, for example, committed itself to major extension of French-language services, but strongly resisted any legal or constitutional definition of itself as officially bilingual. Entrenchment was a fundamental goal for the federal government, but it realized the limits of action. Its proposal, in Bill C-60 the Constitutional Amendment Bill (1978), would extend language rights, but they would apply initially only to the federal government; provinces were free to "opt-in" later if they wished.

The Victoria Charter had been confined to familar legal and political freedoms. Now rights ranging from equality and freedom from discrimination, to geographic mobility, to women and minorities, were on the table. The federal government, seeking to mobilize support for its project by responding to the resurgence of political values, supported the expansion of the Charter. Most provinces did not. Extensions beyond basic civil rights were expected to cut into provincial powers, to override local cultural priorities in the name of nation-wide rights, and to undermine the principle of legislative sovereignty. Few were prepared to swim against the public tide by fighting against *de jure* recognition of rights – a notable exception being property rights. The real battles hinged on whether, to what degree, and under what conditions the Charter should permit either order of government to override individual rights through such devices as a qualifying preamble (rights "subject only to...") or through explicit permission, as in a notwithstanding clause.

Division of Powers   If civil and language rights had always been the primary federal objective, the division of powers had always been the chief provincial one. New issues arose here too. The most important were the desires of the resource-owning provinces to reinforce and clarify their constitutional control over the natural resources found within their borders, and their access to the revenues flowing from their development. This meant undoing the results of the Supreme Court of Canada's unfavourable decisions in the CIGOL and potash cases.

All provincial governments agreed on the importance of narrowing the broad discretionary powers assigned to the federal government under the BNA Act. Some of these powers were already virtual dead-letters. Disallowance was last used against Alberta in 1943. Reservation by the Lieutenant-Governor had been used only 11 times since 1900, four times since 1920 (Mallory, 1961, p. 133). There now seemed to be a consensus on abolishing them, although Ottawa was not unaware of their value as a bargaining chip. The federal declaratory power, which had been used nine times since 1950, was more contentious. It had in the past been an important instrument of flexibility, and had not been abused. But in the often bitter atmosphere of the present, some provinces feared it could be used to override their powers over resources. The Victoria Charter had proposed the abolition of disallowance and reservation, but made no mention of the declaratory power. The federal government's position was that it should be obligated to consult with affected provinces before using the power; the

Premiers (at their 1978 Conference) argued that it should be used only with the explicit consent of the provinces involved. Some non-governmental groups saw a role for a revised Senate in such cases.

The spending power was an even more important tool of federal flexibility, making it possible to carry out national imperatives in areas of provincial jurisdiction. There was some question as to whether this power should be subject to some form of provincial consent. On this, there was no provincial consensus. Poorer provinces depended heavily on federal spending, and were afraid that limitations would hurt them. Some wished only to require federal consultation before new programs were introduced; others would submit new federal proposals to a more formal ratification process. Opting-out with compensation was viewed by most provinces as an acceptable compromise. But as the federal government became more fearful of *de facto* special status for Quebec, it became more reluctant to follow that path. Eventually, federal leaders argued, opting-out would lead to a "chequerboard Canada", where citizens received different services in different parts of the country and had differing ties to their national government.

Many other questions about the division of powers were raised, most focussing on emergent or rapidly changing fields, such as communications. Provinces wished to affirm their exclusive jurisdiction over the development and conservation of natural resources, and to have at least some input into matters of extra-provincial trade and indirect taxation. The debate focussed primarily on which order of government's legislation ought to be paramount in cases of conflict, and whether federal powers should be limited to cases where there was an overriding "compelling national interest". For the coastal provinces, the dominant concern was to win jurisdiction over some or all aspects of off-shore resources.

At the 1978-79 First Ministers Conferences, Ottawa put two new items on the negotiating table. The first was distribution of the authority to manage economic affairs. The new focus on "micro-economic", rather than Keynesian, policy instruments brought with it the recognition that many of these instruments lay in provincial jurisdiction. In an increasingly competitive international environment in which more coherent government intervention seemed crucial to effective adjustment, Ottawa argued that existing processes of domestic policy formation were inadequate. The second issue was the integrity of the economic union. Here the call was for less government intervention by the provinces, rather than more. Ottawa argued that a growing number of provincial policies were impediments to the movement of individuals, capital, goods and services.

The federal government, in its "Pink Paper" entitled *Securing the Economic Union in the Canadian Constitution* (Chrétien, 1980), argued that "deficiencies and uncertainties" in the constitutional framework, the product of judicial interpretation limiting the scope of section 121 (which prohibits tariffs between provinces) and the scope of the federal trade and commerce power, had led to numerous internal barriers to trade. Ottawa had several proposals to rectify this situation. The Charter of Rights should entrench the right to live and work anywhere in the country. Section 121 should be expanded to prohibit all governments from laws and practices which "directly or indirectly, unduly impede" the free movement of goods services, people and capital. Provision would be made, however, to permit the federal government to depart from this prohibition in the interests of public health, morals, equalization, regional development or international obligations. These exemptions would constrain provinces, but not Ottawa. The federal trade and commerce power would be expanded to include regulation of the movement of services and capital, competition and product standards.

Ontario, while no innocent in the matter of erecting internal barriers, strongly endorsed the federal stand. Other provinces endorsed the concept of the economic union, but strenuously objected to the implied intent to limit provincial powers. To accept the federal position would be to alter drastically the balance of powers among governments. Moreover, provinces argued, the federal assertion of its capacity to act solely in the "national" interest was suspect. They interpreted much Canadian history as evidence for the reverse, that Ottawa acted largely in the interests of a dominant central Canada. Provinces were loath to give up the powers which they saw as a defence against such federal bias. Provincial governments were also reluctant to concede as much authority to the courts as the federal position implied. Finally, provinces argued that many provincially-induced barriers, such as Newfoundland's desire to give preference to Newfoundlanders in the off-shore oil industry, were justified by concerns for community preservation and sharing Canadian wealth. Thus, provinces leaned towards a Saskatchewan compromise proposal in which only the general commitment to the economic union would be constitutionally entrenched, with the details to be worked out through intergovernmental mechanisms (Whyte, Romanow & Leeson, 1985, pp. 72-73).

National Institutions   Virtually every national institution was implicated in the growing federal-provincial tensions of this decade. As early as 1968, Alan Cairns had indicted the simple majority, one member per district electoral system (1968). It exaggerated regional polarization, because interprovincial discrepancies in the distribution of seats were so much larger than the discrepancy in the vote. For example, the 20 percent of Albertans who routinely voted Liberal in federal elections often received no representation in Parliament; the same was true of Conservative supporters in Quebec. Moreover, third parties concentrated in one region, such as the Créditistes and Socreds, received far more federal seats than their share of the national vote would warrant. Conversely, when parties that were weak in a particular region – the Conservatives or NDP in Quebec – made a special effort to gain support there, the electoral system punished them for the effort. Thus, the system rewarded those parties that concentrated their political eggs in one regional basket, creating strong incentives to develop political platforms geared to regional grievances (Irvine, 1979).

The growth of government also reduced the capacity of parties to represent effectively regional interests in Ottawa by reducing the importance of regional chieftains. Cabinet ministers functioned more as policy managers, a trend reinforced by the new system of cabinet committees and the emphasis on rational policy debate. Industrial assistance, regional development, and job creation funds put patronage resources in the hands of key regional figures such as Lloyd Axworthy in Winnipeg and Alan MacEachen in Cape Breton. But their access to this patronage depended upon appointment to the cabinet, a Prime Ministerial prerogative. Their capacity to influence this decision declined as the success of the Prime Minister came to depend more on establishing a direct rapport with individual voters through television. Liberal party reforms in these years attempted to marry policy-oriented grass roots activists with a leader-centered campaign employing sophisticated polling and advertising. Regional leaders had little importance in such a pattern. Patronage continued to flow from the top down, but "the bottom" had much less to offer in return. As a result, its bargaining power vis-à-vis "the top" declined (Smith, 1981; Newman, 1968).

These developments underpinned the trend toward a "confederal" party system in Canada. In contrast to the "federal" systems of Australia or Germany which are characterized by strong personal and financial ties between the local, provincial and national levels of the major parties, Canadian provincial party leaders played little role as brokers at national party conventions, and national leaders were equally absent at the provincial level. Democratizing reforms, such as public financing of elections, also reduced the financial links between national and provincial parties. In any case, after 1976 when Bourassa's Liberals were defeated in Quebec, the Liberals had not a single provincial government with which to interact through party links.

These weaknesses carried over into the institutions of national government: Parliament, caucus and cabinet, the Senate and the Supreme Court. The formal logic of parliamentary government is majority rule and ministerial responsibility. This yields a centralized decision-making process within the governing party. Regions weakly represented within it naturally felt frozen out of power at the centre. This was exacerbated by the high level of party discipline in Parliament, which left little room for individual members to play the role of regional or provincial spokespersons. To the extent that such a role was played, it was inside the caucus and cabinet, away from public view, and so did little to alter the image of a governing party rooted in one part of the country.

The Senate did not alleviate this problem, as it does in many other countries: its regional representation role was vitiated by the federal government's exclusive power of appointment. As for the Supreme Court, despite its historically even-handed record, it is legally a creature of the federal government, a status that became more problematic as an increasing number of federal-provincial disputes were referred to the Court. Thus, national institutions failed to temper national majority rule with explicit recognition that smaller provinces should be given more weight at the centre than their population alone would warrant. As Engelmann put it, the existing institutional norms amounted to "majority rule with a vengeance" (in Pratt & Stevenson, 1981).

In this context, federalism was defined almost entirely in terms of the division of powers. This resulted in two formally autonomous systems of parliamentary government linked only by intergovernmental diplomacy. But if central institutions seemed incapable of bridging regional and other differences, the intergovernmental mechanisms developed in the previous period seemed no better. Intergovernmental relations had become, at once, more important and more intractable. Moreover, its principal forum, the Federal-Provincial Conference, was an irresponsible body. It had no legislative authority, no binding rules and no formal lines of accountability, except that of each government to its electorate. This, some argued, gave provincial governments strong incentives to articulate their interests in exclusively provincial terms and then defend those interests without compromise.

Thus the key mechanisms of representation and accommodation in liberal democratic systems – elections, parties, bicameral legislatures and the courts – were, in the Canadian case, designed in ways that limited their capacity to manage inevitable regional conflicts. Roger Gibbins (1982) argued that this failure drove dissenting regions to support strong provincial governments. Contrary to the current wisdom, he argued, Canada was not more regionally diverse than the United States. The difference between the two countries lay in their institutions. With weak party discipline, the US Congress was highly sensitive to local interests and, with equal representation in the Senate, the smaller states and regions had a stronger voice than their Canadian counterparts. Hence, regional deals were struck in the American Congress, especially on the location of military spending. By contrast, if such deals were struck at all in Canada, it was through negotiation and, in this period, confrontation, between central and provincial governments.

By the late 1960s, the rising costs of these growing confrontations inspired increasing attention to "intrastate federalism", as an alternative to the "interstate" or division of powers approach. Myriad proposals for reforms – to the electoral system, the House of Commons, the Senate, the bureaucracy and the Supreme Court – flowed from the pens of academics and other constitutional experts, in addition to both orders of governments (see Smiley & Watts, 1985; Cairns, 1979a). It soon became clear that there were two distinct approaches to intrastate reform. One sought to increase the central government's capacity to represent all regions as an alternative to devolution; the other sought to strengthen the provinces by representing their governments directly within national institutions.

Centralist approaches accepted Gibbins' analysis that the existing system under-represented some regions and that as a result citizens in those regions felt excluded from power in Ottawa. Institutional failure thus made credible provincial government claims to be the sole effective representative of the interests of their province, giving force to demands for a role in the national decision-making process on issues affecting them. Federal policy weakness, then, was not due to lack of constitutional power or of financial resources, but to lack of popular support and legitimacy. As W. P. Irvine put it:

> A large measure of the current alienation from the federal government comes from the fact that its formal power exceeds its real social power. Governments act on behalf of the whole country, but they do not have support of a majority of voters, nor do they have caucus representation from large segments of society.
>
> (1979, p. 77)

On this analysis, reforms to national institutions could reduce conflict by providing alternative avenues for the expression and accommodation of regional interests without weakening the central government. Indeed, they would provide it with a means to outflank provincial governments by rendering more plausible the claim to represent the regions as much as did the provincial governments in their areas of jurisdiction. All centralist versions of the intrastate model sought to represent citizens of regions independently of their provincial governments.

Provincialist versions of intrastate federal reform were not concerned to reverse what centralists perceived to be the waning legitimacy of the central government. Their proposals aimed at representing regions at the centre through their provincial governments. Intrastate federalism would, in effect, institutionalize the federal-provincial collaboration in national policy-making that was necessary as long as the legitimacy of provincial governments remained too strong to permit large-scale centralization.

The provincialist versions of intrastate reform appeared first. Most of them focussed on Senate reform. The most elaborate proposal of this kind was advanced by British Columbia in 1978. It called for a Senate based on five regions (one being British Columbia), comprised of provincial delegates who would vote as a bloc at the direction of the provincial government. The delegation would be headed by a provincial cabinet minister. The Senate would ratify federal appointments to the Supreme Court and some other bodies, control use of the federal spending power, and have a suspensive veto in other matters.

Several of the non-governmental contributors to the debate also advocated this type of Senate reform, including the Canadian Bar Association, the Canada West Foundation, the Ontario Advisory Committee on Confederation, the Conservative Party, the Quebec Liberal Party and, most importantly, the Pepin-Robarts Task Force. Each proposal varied in detail, but all were roughly modelled on the West German Bundesrat, building a provincial voice directly into national decision-making, providing a referee for federal actions affecting the provinces, and ratifying federal appointments in a revised Senate. Most contained at least a suspensive veto for matters clearly within federal jurisdiction, along with a provision for some form of double linguistic majority for matters relating to culture and language.

These proposals met with many objections. Eugene Forsey and others contended that a House of the Provinces would become a "House of Obstruction", blocking federal initiatives and blurring what distinctions remained between section 91 and 92 powers. Moreover, they charged, it was a misguided attempt to locate primarily executive functions, properly delegated to intergovernmental mechanisms, within a legislative body. Later provincial proposals sought to meet these objections by advocating a distinct Federal-Provincial Council, a more institutionalized FMC with powers limited to matters of direct intergovernmental concern, instead of a reformed Senate. The provincial "Best Efforts" draft of August 1980 suggested a Council of the Provinces, with equal representation for each. Its jurisdiction would be limited to legislation involving the declaratory power, the spending power, laws made under the "Peace, Order and Good Government " clause, laws to be administered by provinces, and appointments to major boards and agencies.

Centralist versions of Senate reform came a bit later. The federal government's initial suggestion, contained in Bill C-60, was very cautious: senators would continue to be appointed, but now by both orders of government. Later federal proposals, however, sought to marry growing popular pressures for a more democratic system to the concern to enhance federal power, as they had with the Charter and the idea of referenda on constitutional amendments, by advocating the direct election of senators. Proposals coming from private groups and individuals – including the Canada West Foundation, Roger Gibbins, and Gordon Robertson, from a

Joint Parliamentary Committee in 1984, and from the Macdonald Commission in 1985, also favoured an elected Senate.

But there were difficulties with these proposals. The more authority given the Senate, and the more its membership approximated equality for each province, the more it would complicate the principle of representation by population and of cabinet responsibility to the House of Commons. The more the Senate's powers were weakened to avoid this danger, the less effective it would be in regional terms. The relationship between membership in the Senate and the party system would also be complicated: some proposals wished to ensure members would be truly "regional" by denying them the ability to be cabinet ministers, join party caucuses or wear party labels; others thought the Senate should be partisan, its members making up for regional imbalances in the Commons party membership.

As the debate progressed, it also became clear that intrastate reforms would be no cure-all for the ills of Canadian federalism. Even if the goal of regional representation were met, the need for a high degree of intergovernmental cooperation and coordination would remain, since provinces would retain all their current powers. Thus, the proposal could not be a substitute for improved intergovernmental relations, unless improved regional representation at the centre was considered a prelude to dramatic centralization. Finally, all such proposals were perhaps fatally hobbled by the fact that all of the institutional players most likely to be threatened by them – provincial governments, the existing Senate and members of the House of Commons – had a veto over such changes.

Another important group of centralizing intrastate proposals sought to reform the electoral system to reduce the disparity between party electoral support and party seats at the national level. Once again, these suggestions came from private groups. None went so far as to advocate true proportional representation. Most, such as that of the Pepin-Robarts Task Force, suggested a "topping up" mechanism: in addition to voting for their individual MP, voters would cast a vote for a party list, from which additional MPs would be selected to bring each party's caucus in each region more in line with its share of the popular vote.

The final national institution to be discussed was the Supreme Court. The basic issue was whether the court should continue to be a creature of federal legislation, with all its members appointed by the central government, even though it was the last court of appeal on issues of jurisdictional dispute. Those sympathetic to the provinces proposed entrenching provisions regarding the Supreme Court – for a provincial role in appointments, for a certain number of Justices trained in the Quebec civil law, and for a particular distribution of judges across regions – in the constitution. Such proposals were frequently coupled with suggestions for an enlarged court. Finally, there were those who argued that, given the centrality of constitutional issues, a separate constitutional court should be created. Alberta, for example, called for a representative constitutional court, with randomly selected panels chosen from a pool of provincial Superior Court Judges. Quebec called for a constitutional bench, with equal numbers of Quebec and non-Quebec judges. The federal government was prepared to entrench the court and to agree to consult with the provinces on appointments. Several provinces were content with this, but others argued for ratification of judicial appointments by a reformed Senate or, in the case of Ontario, for federal appointment from a list drawn up by a National Judicial Council made up of the 11 Attorneys-General.

The Process

The dynamic of intergovernmental bargaining and alliances reflected the larger goals of each government. At this level, matters of principle were inextricably bound up with self-interest. Myriad issues were drawn into the net of constitutional discussions. Substance was frequently impossible to separate from procedure: how Canada got a new constitution might say as much about its federalism as the words written in it.

It would be necessary to resort to the Parliament of the United Kingdom to amend the BNA Act. The domestic requirements before such a request could be properly made and assented to by Britain became a central issue. Hence the battle spilled over into the UK Parliament as provinces appealed to it as the final defence against "federal majoritarianism" while Ottawa asserted that Britain was constitutionally required to honour a federal request, without looking behind it. Past failures to agree on a domestic amendment formula thus haunted the discussions and increased the acrimony. It eventually fell to the Supreme Court of Canada to define the workable formula.

The process of constitutional reform was shaped, above all, by the evolution of events in Quebec. Following the failure of the Victoria Charter in 1971, there had been little stomach for further discussions. But when the election of the PQ appeared imminent, talks and proposals multiplied. Still, provincial governments retained the initiative and they had limited incentives to agree. This dynamic was fundamentally altered when the federalists won the 1980 referendum on sovereignty-association with promises of a renewed federalism. From that point the ball was in the federal court, as René Levesque had put it, and Ottawa seized the initiative.

Before the Referendum   The first formal proposal for "renewal of the federation" was the federal government's White Paper, *A Time for Action*, and its constitutional amendment Bill, C-60, published in June 1978. It proposed a two-stage process which distinguished between those areas in which Parliament had full authority to act alone, and which were therefore not subject to provincial veto, and those where federal-provincial agreement was required.

In Phase One, to be completed by July 1, 1979, Ottawa would enact a Charter of individual and language rights, applying initially to the federal government, but with provision for provinces to "opt-in", a clarification of the role of the Governor-General and, most controversially, the replacement of the Senate with a new House of the Federation. Federal and provincial legislatures would each appoint half its 118 members, based on proportional representation from political parties. This body would have a veto both on federal bills affecting the provinces and on bills of "special linguistic significance", for which a double majority of French- and English-speaking members would be required. As an inducement to provinces to opt-in to the Charter, Bill C-60 also proposed to abolish the reservation and disallowance powers, to enlarge and entrench the Supreme Court, to provide for an annual FMC, and to include a new preamble. Phase Two, to be completed by 1981, would deal with the division of powers, the amending formula and, a new item on the agenda, native rights.

Provincial reaction to Bill C-60 was hostile. They argued that the distinction between areas where Ottawa could act and those which required agreement was artifical and unrealistic and ignored the provincial priority on the division of powers. The reformed Senate was criticized on the ground that it would affect the rights and privileges of the provinces and alter the federal balance, so that Ottawa did not, under section 91.1, have the authority to proceed unilaterally. The federal government responded by referrring the matter to the Supreme Court. Others criticized the House of the Federation on substantive grounds. The NDP argued it would perpetuate the undemocratic character inherent in any appointed Senate. Dupré and Weiler (1979) argued it would make for a more cumbersome and complex Senate without achieving any clear purpose. All comments were heard by a Special Joint Committee of the Senate and House of Commons.

Meanwhile, the Supreme Court returned its decision on the constitutional question. The majority significantly limited the authority of the federal government to amend the constitution under the 1949 amendment. The power to alter the Constitution of Canada, "subject only to specifically enumerated exceptions", said the Court, referred to the juridical entity of the government of Canada, not to the country as a whole. Moreover, it argued that the powers and mode of representation in the Senate were essential elements of the federal bargain, a protection for the "various sectional interests in Canada in relation to the enactment of federal legislation". Reform of the Senate was thus a reform to the federal system itself, and not within federal authority alone.

The Premiers called for a constitutional conference to discuss both Bill C-60 and their new division of powers proposals. In their communique of August 1978 they called for increased authority in immigration, resources, culture, communications and fisheries; and for constraints on federal authority with respect to the spending, declaratory, emergency, and treaty powers. There should be an annual First Ministers Conference (FMC), and a provincial role in judicial nominations and the creation of new provinces. They objected especially to the procedures of Bill C-60, with its two phases, deadlines and threat of unilateral action. An alliance between the Premiers and the federal Conservatives was emerging: at a meeting in Kingston the previous April, Joe Clark and a number of Premiers had come to a loose agreement on the directions for constitutional change.

The federal government accepted the proposal to meet. The FMC held in the fall of 1978 established a Continuing Committee of Ministers on the Constitution to see whether there could be agreement on "Best Efforts" drafts for specific changes, the results to be examined at the winter 1979 FMC. The federal government's attention, as Bill C-60 suggested, was on Quebec; it wanted progress on language rights, patriation and the amendment formula. Ottawa also foreshadowed its later focus on the economic union, with its own list of jurisdictional issues related to "powers over the economy".

Provincial positions varied considerably, according to their particular role in Confederation, but their agendas were very different from Ottawa's. Newfoundland called for jurisdiction over fisheries and off-shore resources, and all Atlantic provinces wanted entrenchment of the principles of equalization and a strong central government capable of redistribution. The Western provinces emphasized the distribution of powers, especially in resources. Alberta advocated an amendment formula which would provide cast-iron protection against amendments that would weaken control over resources. Its proposals were published in a document titled *Harmony in Diversity* (1978). British Columbia wanted any formula to reflect its claimed status as a "fifth region", and advocated its model for reform of the centre, also elaborated in a series of pamphlets. Ontario had few jurisdictional concerns: its focus was on protecting the common market and improving the machinery of collaborative federalism. Quebec's chief concern was to lay the groundwork for the coming referendum.

There was unanimous agreement on only a few minor matters, although considerable progress was made on others. But with the federal election in the offing, and the Quebec referendum still to come, there was little sense of urgency to reach an immediate ageement. The absence of such agreement, coupled with the Supreme Court's ruling, condemned Bill C-60 to die on the order paper. Further activity would be delayed until after the Quebec referendum.

In the meantime non-governmental groups were publishing their proposals for reform. Most important was the report of the Pepin-Robarts Task Force, published in December 1978. Its recommendations, in *A Future Together* echoed the first report of the Royal Commission on Bilingualism and Biculturalism more than a decade before, arguing that Canada was going through a "crisis of existence". Its vision of the federation was much closer to that of the provinces and Quebec federalists than to the federal Liberals. The two fundamental characteristics of the country, a source of strength as well as division, were identified as "regionalism" and "dualism", tempered with a third goal of "sharing". Institutional changes must embrace and promote these characteristics, not deny them. The Task Force took a provincialist approach to language rights: constitutional entrenchment at the provincial level should await agreement. It recommended replacement of the Senate with a 60-member Council of the Federation appointed by, and acting as delegates of, the provincial governments. It proposed to improve regional representation in the House of Commons by selecting an additional 60 MPs by proportional representation, so as to assure at least some representation from each region in all parties.

The Task Force did not devote much attention to the division of powers. Ottawa would have primary responsibility for the national economy, including the common market and regional redistribution; the provinces would also have broad economic powers and primary responsibility for their "social and cultural well-being". It accepted the possibility of *de facto* "special status" and the right of self-determination for Quebec by arguing that a democratic vote to secede must be respected. Thus, the Task Force took a very different view from that prevailing in the federal government. It saw resolution of the crisis as lying not in a reassertion of federal power but rather in embracing the linguistic and territorial diversity of Canada, by strengthening provinces and creating a more regionally sensitive federal government. It reflected the widespread view of the time "that only a looser federation could contain the pressures afoot in the nation" (Whyte, 1985, p. 9).

These assumptions were shared by most reform proposals of the period. The *Beige Paper* of the Quebec Liberal Party, for example, urged a strengthening of provincial powers (while retaining key federal powers over the national economy), and the entrenchment of the provincial right to opt-out of federal programs. It recommended abolishing the federal powers of declaration, reservation and disallowance, and subjecting other federal powers to provincial consent. It too called for a provincially-appointed body, acting as a dualist body on linguistic matters, to replace the Senate. The Supreme Court would also sit as a "dualist" bench on constitutional issues.

To critics such as Cairns (1979c), and Dupré and Weiler (1979), this formula – constraints on Ottawa, stronger provinces and collaborative policy-making – would further institutionalize linguistic and regional divisions, give too little weight to pan-Canadian values, and fragment national political authority. They gave much greater weight to reforms at the centre enhancing the federal capacity to represent all regions and to define a national purpose which transcended region.

The federal political parties diverged on these questions. In the 1979 election campaign, Conservative leader Joe Clark spoke of Canada as a "community of communities". While not spelling out a detailed constitutional program, Clark signalled his desire to work with the provinces, promising jurisdiction over off-shore resources to the provinces, along with some control over fisheries and withdrawal of Ottawa from lotteries. Generally, he promised a more consensual, cooperative federalism. Prime Minister Trudeau caricatured Mr. Clark as a "head-waiter" who would "give away the store" to the provinces, resulting in a Canada that was little more than a collection of "shopping centres" strung out across the continent.

The 1978-79 discussions ended with the 1979 federal election and the formation of the Conservative minority government. Preoccupied with learning how to govern, and uncertain how to participate in the Quebec Referendum campaign, the Clark government took no new constitutional initiatives.

After the Referendum   The sudden restoration of the Trudeau Liberals in the February 1980 election, followed by the victory of the "NO" side in the PQ referendum, transformed the debate. The PQ was in disarray: its only remaining strategy was to ally itself with other provinces, an awkward position for a party intent on showing that it was a province fundamentally different from the others, and that Ottawa was the natural government for all of English Canada. By contrast, the federal government was in a far more powerful position. Its claim to speak for Quebec was immeasurably strengthened and it had defeated provincialism on its home ground. Armed with this result and its new electoral majority, Trudeau was ready and willing to do battle against decentralizing forces on all fronts. Between 1975 and 1980 the provincialist agenda had dominated the discussion; now the federal government took the offensive.

Within 24 hours of the Quebec Referendum result, the federal Minister of Justice, Jean Chrétien, was on his way to the provincial capitals to consult about a new round of constitutional talks. Shortly thereafter, the Premiers came to Ottawa and it was agreed to open discussions on 12 issues, combining the primary concerns of both sides: patriation, amendment, a Charter of Rights, a statement of principles, the Senate and the Supreme Court, and the division of powers.

A Continuing Committee of Ministers, co-chaired by Justice Minister Jean Chrétien and Saskatchewan Attorney-General Roy Romanow, met through the summer to prepare for a summit meeting in September. The intensive discussions of this cross-country travelling road-show were complex and difficult. The continuing conflict over energy intruded to heighten tensions. The Quebec government played an active role in the talks. One of the most remarkable developments over the summer was the forging of a close alliance between Quebec and most of the other provinces, united by not only a common provincialist view of Canada, but also a suspicion of federal intentions. The provinces were particularly unhappy about the Prime Minister's insistence that if there were no agreement at the September FMC, then Parliament "would have to look to its duty to the Canadian people" and act unilaterally.

Ottawa was now less prepared to concede than before. It pressed hard on its own agenda and withdrew its support for earlier "Best Efforts" drafts. There seemed to be wide public support for its general position. A survey published on August 6, 1980 by the *Toronto Star* showed that large majorities in every province wanted a "made in Canada constitution". Furthermore, large majorities everywhere, including Quebec, wanted constitutional guarantees of human rights and supported minority language rights, to apply "where numbers warrant". The principle of equalization also received strong support everywhere. Once issues were cast outside specific regional grievances, and outside the question of legitimate procedure, Canadians appeared united. About the same time the federal government published its paper titled *Securing the Canadian Economic Union in Confederation* (which provincial governments viewed as a new challenge to their traditional economic powers) and launched an expensive advertising campaign –"Make it work. Make it right. Make it ours." – to promote its view of constitutional change.

Meanwhile, the Continuing Committee, also known as the "Uke and Toque Show", made progress on a number of issues. Optimists felt that a broad compromise, incorporating federal goals with respect to the Charter of Rights and some provincial objectives on the division of powers, was possible at the September FMC. Instead, the five days of meetings ended in failure as the deep differences that remained among the First Ministers were broadcast before the whole country. There are many possible explanations for the failure: the need for unanimity, which allowed each government to hold out for its own pet proposals; the mutual suspicion and distrust among the leaders; the fact that the existing constitution, however battered, was often preferable to accepting the alternatives proposed by others; the restriction of the participants to governments whose own interests were at stake; the leaking of a federal strategy document (the Kirby memorandum); the desire of some participants to sabotage agreement. The list could go on.

But the basic reason for failure lay in conflicting provincialist and centralist visions of Canada, fuelled by substantial policy differences. Prime Minister Trudeau and his supporters wrapped themselves in the mantle of Macdonald: "the greatest enemy is the enemy within"; Parliament is the "only group, the only assembly which can express the national will and the national interest". It followed that, "When there is a conflict between the national will and the provincial will, the national will must prevail. Otherwise we are not a nation." (in Zukowsky, 1981b). To Trudeau, provincialism, like the Quebec nationalism which he had fought for so long, threatened to destroy the country. For the provinces, the "enemy" was the tyranny of the federal government. Their historical reference was the compact theory. Provincial governments are legitimate representatives of provincial communities, which are as important as the national community. The country must be a partnership between "Section 91 and Section 92" of Canada. Both views were argued with passion and conviction in Ottawa's cavernous National Conference Centre.

At the conclusion of the conference, the Prime Minister promised to meet his caucus and cabinet. "In due course we will announce our proposed plan of action to the Canadian people and to Parliament" (in Zukowsky, 1981b, p. 56). A few days later, on October 2, Trudeau announced a "Proposed Resolution for Address to her Majesty the Queen Respecting the Constitution of Canada". Canadians, he argued, had failed to agree on a domestic amending formula after 54 years of trying; Canadian nationhood was therefore incomplete. The unanimity rule was a strait-jacket; the deadlock had to be broken: "We took the ideal of unanimity and made it a tyrant". Each Premier had used his threat of veto to "seek the particular good of a province or region...so we achieved the good of none; least of all did we achieve the good of all". He described the provincial position as a "radically new concept of Canada" – a concept of ten provinces rather than a single country. The federal Parliament had the legal authority to ask for an amendment without seeking provincial consent. It could achieve through petition to the United Kingdom what s. 91(1) prevented it from doing within Canada, and could thus by-pass the constraints of executive federalism. "Our duty", said Mr. Trudeau, "is clear: it is to complete the foundations of our independence so our freedoms.... Freedom from the paralysis of the past, with our constitution home, with our rights and freedoms guaranteed, the process of renewal can truly proceed." Parliament, drawn from all over Canada, had the right and duty to speak for all Canadians. Distinguishing between "powers for the people" and "powers for governments", he argued that the Resolution would not shift power from the provinces to Ottawa, but from both to citizens. "Freedom is not a federal-provincial question." No longer would he trade "fish for rights" in intergovernmental waters. Canadians, Trudeau argued, had given their pledge to Quebec; now it must be redeemed. "We are summoned to a great act of national will."

The Resolution would patriate the constitution, using Britain "one more time" to end the need for future requests. It would entrench an amending formula which would require consent of Ottawa, Quebec, Ontario, and two provinces – with a majority of the population in each region – from the east and from the west, and provide for a federally-sponsored referendum procedure. It would entrench a Charter of Rights and Freedoms, including both political and language rights, that would be binding on both levels. Finally, it would entrench a commitment to equalization. There were no concessions to the provincialist view of Canada and there was nothing to persuade the Premiers to accept. The federal government would appeal over the provinces to the people. This use of *force majeure* moved the debate from the intergovernmental to the Parliamentary arena, widened the range of participants, and shifted the focus of attention from questions about federalism to questions about citizen rights.

Eight provincial governments and the federal Conservatives opposed the federal initiative. "It is", said Premier Allan Blakeney of Saskatchewan, "inconsistent with our historical traditions, and with our present conception of Canada as a federal state" (Zukowsky, 1981b, p. 62). Conservative leader Joe Clark argued that:

> Because a constitution is so basic to a country, it must be the product of the broadest possible consensus. It cannot be arbitrarily imposed...by only one individual or government. Nor can it be achieved through threat, ultimatum or artificial deadline... . Mr. Trudeau tonight offers Canadians the prospect of divisive referenda, prolonged constitutional challenge in the courts, and federal-provincial turmoil. That is a betrayal of those Quebecers who voted NO in the Quebec referendum, and all other Canadians who seek genuine renewal of our confederation.
>
> (Zukowsky, 1981b, p. 62)

New Democratic Party leader Ed Broadbent supported the Resolution from the start, a stance which, as we have noted, divided his party along regional and federal-provincial lines. Such intra-party strains were much less of a problem for the Liberals: there were no Liberal provincial governments to contend with and almost no Liberal MPs from the West. The Tories were united with most of their provincial brethren on procedural grounds, but the two provincial governments that supported the federal action were also Conservative.

Premier Davis of Ontario said that the Resolution accorded closely with Ontario's constitutional goals. Not to act now would be a "victory for those who say this nation is unworkable". Despite many reservations Premier Hatfield of New Brunswick, whose position on language rights was close to that of Mr. Trudeau, added his support. The federal government was anxious to win more provincial allies and Saskatchewan Premier Alan Blakeney was equally concerned to avoid polarization, but efforts to bridge the gap between them ultimately failed. Thus was born the "Gang of Eight" provinces opposing the coalition of the federal Liberals and NDP with the Conservative governments of Ontario and New Brunswick.

The Parliamentary debate on the motion to refer the Resolution to a Special Joint Committee was ended only by invoking closure over impassioned protests. The Committee's televised hearings represented the first significant opportunity for concerned citizen groups to put forward their views. Its original deadline was extended to accommodate the 97 witnesses and the 409 individual and group briefs that were eventually submitted. The overwhelming majority of the representations focussed on various aspects of the Charter of Rights; very few on such federalist questions as the division of powers or the amending formula. Most briefs to the Joint Committee opposed the Resolution, not on the ground that unilateral action was illegitimate, or that it weakened the provinces, but rather because it was believed that the proposed Charter had too many "loopholes" and did not extend far enough. The pressure was overwhelmingly in the direction of increasing its scope and force. Many groups criticized the broad exceptions set out in section 1. Women's groups sought stronger equality provisions. The handicapped and many others wanted wider guarantees of non-discrimination. Native peoples wanted the Charter to recognize historic rights (see Zukowsky, 1981b, p. 74).

These representations led to a number of changes, some proposed by the Government and others by the Opposition parties. It was an experience of Parliament in action which Canadians had seldom witnessed and it gave the constitution a popular focus that it had not hitherto possessed. It also demonstrated how "shifts from one arena to another changed the agenda and the actors" (Cairns, 1985, p. 122). More generally, it underlined the fact that the community identities to which the Constitution must respond were no longer simply those of nation, province and language. The constitution must now speak to, and reflect, non- territorial conceptions of citizenship and community.

The debate continued in the House of Commons. While recognizing the wide popular support for much of its substance, the Conservatives continued to oppose the Resolution as a whole. Joe Clark argued that:

> The tragic irony is that at a time when there was that sense of Canadians wanting to build together and when regions which had felt inferior began to feel equal, instead of using that emotion...to build common Canadian purposes, this government brought in a measure which drives Canadians apart. Our constitu-

tion could be a source of Canadian pride and unity. Our Constitution has been made a source of Canadian shame and division.

(in Zukowsky, 1981b, p. 88)

Conservative opposition in Parliament critically undermined the legitimacy of the federal project, since it denied it the support of all but a handful of elected western representatives. Had a unanimous Parliament faced the provinces, the outcome might have been very different.

As the debate dragged on, the provinces rallied to fight the federal action. Parliamentary delay was essential to mobilizing public opposition and to mounting a court challenge. The Gang of Eight coordinated their strategies and launched reference cases in the Quebec, Manitoba and Newfoundland appeal courts. The Manitoba reference, for example, asked for an opinion as to whether the Resolution affected federal-provincial relationships or the rights, powers or privileges of the provinces; whether there was a consitutional convention requiring provincial consent to requests for such amendments; and whether Ottawa was "constitutionally required" to secure it. On February 3, 1981 the Manitoba Court of Appeal ruled 3-2 in Ottawa's favour; on March 31 the Supreme Court of Newfoundland ruled 3-0 in favour of the provinces. With the legality of the Resolution now in question, the federal government could no longer avoid getting a definitive ruling from the Supreme Court of Canada. An agreement with the Opposition led to final passage of the amended Resolution, but with no further action to be taken until the Supreme Court reference had been decided.

The legal debate also involved the question of whether the British Parliament had an obligation to pass a federal Resolution, or whether, under the Statute of Westminster, it had a residual trusteeship role to protect the federal principle. A committee of the British House of Commons, the Kershaw Committee (House of Commons [UK], 1981), argued that a trusteeship duty remained. But federal officials claimed they had a commitment from Prime Minister Thatcher to pass the Resolution without question. British MPs and Ministers were enthusiastically lobbied by representatives of both sides of the issue, including Canadian native groups. Doubts about early passage grew.

Provincial politicians countered the federal Resolution with a patriation plan of their own. In April 1981 the eight Premiers signed a document calling for immediate patriation and enactment of an amending formula, to be followed by three years of negotiations on other issues. The proposed amendment formula was adapted from one first put forward by Alberta: normal amendments could be made by Ottawa plus two-thirds of the provinces representing 50 percent of the population. Thus there would be formal equality of all provinces and no automatic veto for Quebec and Ontario. Some areas were reserved for unanimous agreement. Any province would be permitted to opt-out of an amendment affecting provincial powers and to receive appropriate fiscal compensation. There was no mention of a Charter of Rights, or of referenda. Just as Ottawa's package made no concessions to the provinces, the April accord made none to the nationalist federal agenda. Despite the televised solemnity of the interprovincial accord, it received little public support. Indeed, it appeared to demonstrate how little the provinces could agree on and how little attention they paid to the popular enthusiasm for the Charter.

There matters stood while the Supreme Court deliberated. Its decision, the first to be televised in Canadian history, was handed down on September 28, 1981. In a complex ruling, dubbed by Peter Russell as "bold statecraft" but "questionable jurisprudence" (1982), the court drove the governments back to the bargaining table. The crucial majority concluded that it would be legal for the Parliament to act without provincial consent, but that this would still be unconstitutional since it would breach an established convention of substantial provincial consent. Both sides had won; both had lost. Ottawa was told it had the narrow legal authority, but not the legitimacy, to proceed. It could do so now only at extraordinary political risk. Provinces had been warned that if they continued to delay action, Ottawa might move. The only way out was to return to the intergovernmental table. But now there was a critical difference: the convention, said the Court, did not mean unanimity; it required only "substantial consent". Two provinces was clearly not "substantial consent", but one province could no longer stop the process. The groundwork for a settlement without Quebec had been laid.

The federal government initially claimed victory. Ontario's ministers called for Ottawa to proceed on its own. But Joe Clark seemed closer to the mark: "For the government of Canada to try to proceed with its resolution would be destructive of national unity and absolutely wrong for the country" (Press Release, 30 Sept.). The Quebec National Assembly, with only nine Liberals dissenting, passed a resolution calling for immediate negotiations with "full respect for the principles and conventions which must apply to any modification of the Canadian federal system."

On September 29, the Prime Minister offered to talk to the provinces as long as there was no more delay and no further powers were given to the provinces. Bill Bennett, the Premiers' spokesman, began discussions with his colleagues. All ten Premiers met in Montreal on October 19 and 20, and the eight dissenters remained a further day. After much jockeying, it was agreed to hold a Constitutional Conference on November 2, continuing, as the Prime Minister said, "for as many hours or days are necessary until either we have reached a consensus...or it has become clear that such a consensus is not possible" (Zukowsky, 1981b, p. 20). The fixed coalitions were now dissolving: behind the scenes, Ontario, Saskatchewan, B.C. and other governments were probing for the basis of an agreement.

On November 2, the First Ministers met under extraordinary public pressure to resolve the issue. In a remarkable series of public and private encounters they forged a deal. It included patriation; the provinces' April amending formula, without the provision for opting-out with fiscal compensation (Quebec's minimum condition for accepting a formula which removed its veto power); the Charter of Rights, but with significant new limitations; and provisions on equalization and resources. It also called for future constitutional conferences, including a specific commitment to consider Native rights. Under the revisions to the Charter, the entrenched mobility right was qualified to allow any province with an employment rate below the national average to discriminate in favour of its disadvantaged residents. A "notwithstanding" clause would allow any government to suspend sections relating to fundamental freedoms, and legal and equality rights, by incorporating a provision in relevant legislation explicitly excluding it from purview of the Charter. Many details needed to be worked out, but the essential compromise had been made.

Two important modifications soon followed. With the notwithstanding clause, the agreement qualified the sexual equality provisions of earlier versions. It also dropped a carefully negotiated statement of Native rights in favour of a further conference. For both groups, the episode suggested that they had been pawns in an intergovernmental chess game. But, under the circumstances, they proved to be pawns with some political muscle. A massive, country-wide lobbying effort by women's groups forced a rapid agreement to include section 28, a clause which would be exempt from the notwithstanding clause, guaranteeing rights equally to male and female persons. A similar lobby by native rights groups resulted in a new section 35, recognizing "existing" aboriginal and treaty rights.

On November 18, 1981 the Minister of Justice introduced the Resolution that Parliament would send to Britain, the last time such a petition would be made: "We, Your Majesty's loyal subjects, the House of Commons of Canada in Parliament assembled, respectfully approach Your Majesty, requesting that you may graciously be pleased to cause to be laid before the Parliament of the United Kingdom a measure... ". The Resolution would cause Britain to enact the Constitution Act, 1982. Henceforth, "no Act of the Parliament of the United Kingdom...shall extend to Canada as part of its law." It was passed by the Canadian House of Commons on December 2, 1981, as Members spontaneously broke into "O Canada". On December 8, after Senate passage, Governor-General Edward Schreyer was presented with leather-bound copies of the Resolution by the Speakers of the House and Senate, and set off to London.

In the Parliamentary debate the Conservatives called for the restoration of full opting out, with compensation. They also proposed a modification of Charter language rights: these would not apply to Quebec if the province accepted a "Canada clause" in its own legislation, allowing any resident of Quebec to attend English schools if his/her parents had been educated in English anywhere in Canada. The Tories also pressed for restoration of the commitment to sexual equality. The NDP supported these suggestions, but argued that opting-out with compensation should apply only to Quebec. The federal government restored a measure of fiscal compensation, making it available to any province opting out of amendments affecting provincial educational or cultural powers. But the Prime Minister warned that whatever the imperfections of the intergovermental Accord, the government was bound by it and further amendments would not be accepted – a position which was to be restated a few years later with the Meech Lake Accord.

Most provincial governments could feel they had won their essential point: blocking unilateralism and gaining their preferred amendment formula. So could the federal government: it had achieved a "made in Canada" constitution and a strong Charter of Rights. Neither side won everything it wanted and there was much left unresolved on both sides (Banting & Simeon, 1983).

For the Quebec government, however, the outcome was an unmitigated defeat. The provincial alliance forged after the referendum had now been shattered. Quebec had lost the veto, and it had lost the comprehensive compensation alternative. It faced a Charter of Rights with language provisions that would soon be used to undercut important aspects of Quebec's legislative efforts to promote "francization". Quebec, argued Premier Levesque, had been the victim of "blackmail" and "nocturnal machinations". The Quebec National Assembly unanimously passed a resolution denouncing the settlement, and affirming its "traditional" right of veto. The PQ government announced that it would not participate in intergovernmental meetings, and launched a legal case asserting Quebec's constitutional right to veto any constitutional amendment bearing on its powers. It passed legislation declaring that all future Quebec legislation would be subject to the "notwithstanding" clause.

The settlement probably left Quebec constitutionally weaker than it had been at the outset. Previously, few had questioned that Quebec had a veto over constitutional changes. Virtually every proposed amendment formula had included the concept, and it had been honoured in practice: when Quebec rejected the Fulton-Favreau amendment formula in 1965, or the Victoria Charter in 1971, few had suggested that they should proceed anyway. Yet this was exactly what happened in 1981-82. Now the vision of successive Quebec governments had been rejected by both the federal government and the other nine provincial governments: the federal view of Quebec in Canada had prevailed over the view of Quebec as a distinct society and of the provincial government as its principal political expression; and the provincialist view of co-equal provinces had prevailed over the view of a binational Canada and special powers for Quebec.

How could the process of constitutional reform, initiated twenty years before primarily in response to Quebec, have ended in such an unequivocal blow to that province? From the beginning it was clear that Quebec had different priorities from other governments; it was seeking more fundamental constitutional reforms, with greater urgency. While they could all agree when the issue was a federal initiative, such as Bill C-60 or the patriation resolution, in the end the gulf became evident for all to see. It turned out that the greatest bargaining power for Quebec had been the *threat* to elect a separatist party: its bargaining power was probably less after November 15, 1976 than before. There was no obligation to negotiate directly with Quebec. Certainly Quebec's bargaining power was even less after the referendum. Despite the widespread bitterness over the 1982 settlement reflected in opinion polls and the National Assembly vote, the PQ had neither the will nor the ability to rally the people in Quebec against it, for the reasons already discussed. This, above all, was why the rest of Canada could afford to override Quebec's opposition, as it had in the Reconstruction years.

The Constitution Act was proclaimed on April 17, 1982 in a glittering ceremony on Parliament Hill. The full meaning and implication of the Act will not be known for many years. It did not end the tensions between region and nation, Quebec and Canada, which brought about the constitutional crisis. Like the British North America Act, the new constitutional document embodied the tension between Canada as a single nation in which universal citizenship is guaranteed through the national government, and Canada as a diverse federal state, built up from provincial identities, with sovereignty divided between two orders of government.

The provincialist image is found most clearly in the amending formula: change in the future will require the consent not only of the national government, but also of the governments representing the provincial communities. Those communities can protect themselves against the will of the national majority through the opting-out provisions and, if necessary, through the use of the notwithstanding clause. The document also underlines the provincial control of resources in a revised section 94.A, which has been such a strong base of provincial power.

The Charter is arguably the strongest bearer of the nationalist image of Canada. At its core is a conception of individual rights, possessed by all Canadians, independent of place. To the extent that these rights cannot be divorced from community, it is by virtue of membership in the national community, and through the guidance of a national institution – the Supreme Court – that rights are to be defined and protected. In a charter-based society, argues John Whyte, relations between citizen and state become "systematized, centralized, uniform, constant, unilateral and direct", whereas in a federal system they are "diverse, filtered, diluted, subject to mediation and complicated" (1984, p. 28).

This is not to say that collective rights are ignored in the Charter. Finding a balance between the individual and collective rights within it will be a central task for the courts. Nor are the traditional collectivities, provincial and linguistic, ignored. But they are now less fundamental, sharing equal constitutional status with collective rights defined without any reference to territory – the rights of natives, women and the handicapped. It is these considerations which led Romanow, Whyte and Leeson to see the outcome as ultimately a victory for the centralizing liberalism which Pierre Trudeau represented. Canada, they argue, is

> ...catching up to Macdonald: Less and less do Canadians see the country's virtue to be its capacity to accommodate and nurture its many local political communities. More and more, Canada is seen to be a single political unit which, in its own right, has the responsibility and, now, the will to represent the interests of all... . [T]he idea of the liberal state clashed with western regionalism and Quebec nationalism [and the liberal state won].
>
> (1985, p. 3)

Alan Cairns, a far more sympathetic critic of the federal government, agrees: "The Charter is a federal government instrument to limit the balkanisation of Canada as a moral community...and to limit the on-going provincialization of Canadian society" (1985, p. 129).

This conclusion seems premature. Trudeau cannot yet be assigned the role of vindicator of modernization theory. It is clear that the Charter now constitutes a "third pillar" of the Canadian constitutional order, along with parliamentarism and federalism. The judicial process will become a more "visible and contentious" part of the Canadian political system as it grapples with competing values and interests (Smiley, 1981, p. 51). The language of rights, which strengthens citizens against governments while simultaneously binding them to them, is also a "Canadian language, not a provincial language" and its likely thrust is progressively to Canadianize the "psyche of the citzenry" (Smiley, 1987, p. 130). But the image of the nation that it strengthens may not be a more centralized one. To lump together these two points is a serious mistake, as the drafters of the BNA Act understood.

The Charter may promote a convergence on basic political values concerning the rights of individuals and groups, but such a convergence has been going on since the Second World War in any case, and is already far advanced (Johnston, 1985). Yet, neither normative nor socio-demographic convergence implies any particular answer to the boundary question. And so far, in Canada, it has not cut against strong allegiances to subnational political communities.

Moreover, while an expansive definition of individual and group rights will undoubtedly deprive governments of some powers in some cases, in others – affirmative action is an obvious one – it will impose new responsibilities requiring new actions. We cannot safely predict whether most of the new restrictions of government rights and extensions of government duties will fall upon the federal or the provincial order. But under at least one scenario, where the federal government incurs the most restrictions and provincial governments are assigned most of the new duties, one could sensibly speak of the Charter's decentralizing impact. Under others, the effect might be roughly neutral.

If it left many issues unresolved, the constitutional outcome also opened up new vistas. Within a year, British Columbia had initiated the new amendment procedure with a resolution calling for entrenchment of property rights. The first "Section 35" conference on Native rights had been held in Ottawa. And the Charter was being invoked in a host of legal cases, large and small.

Intergovernmental Relations:
Cooperative vs. Competitive Federalism

Intergovernmental relations in this period underwent a dramatic shift with the election of the Liberal government in Ottawa in 1980. Previously, both orders of government endorsed a cooperative model of federal-provincial relations, although rising levels of conflict led them to seek as much disentanglement as policy interdependence would permit. But after 1980 Ottawa became the advocate of "competitive" federalism or, more accurately, "unilateral" federalism. The "New Federalism" rejected cooperative federalism. As the Prime Minister put it in 1980:

We have tried governing through consensus; we have tried governing by being generous to the provinces.... I thought we could build a strong Canada through co-operation. I have been disillusioned...). The old type of federalism where we give money to the province, where they kick us in the teeth because they didn't get enough...is finished.

(Various occasions, in YIR, 1982, p. 6)

Provincial leaders rejected the competitive model. Instead they sought the further institutionalization of collaboration. Provinces were privileged spokespersons for provincial interests and therefore should represent these interests in national policy-making. The federal government, as Albert Breton put it, increasingly felt that "Cooperative federalism, because it proscribes unilateral action, is...a disguised ploy to shackle the federal government" (1985, p. 493). Just as vehemently, the provinces saw the new federalism as an ideology legitimating a power grab by the federal government.

The 1970s: Cooperation and Disentanglement

Before 1980, however, the governments continued with increasing difficulty to work under the rules of cooperation, by promoting disentanglement in fiscal arrangements, and higher levels of cooperation in the spheres of consitutional reform and industrial policy formation and implementation.

Extending Intergovernmental Mechanisms   Throughout the 1970s the volume and intensity of federal-provincial interaction continued to grow: in 1973, 82 ministerial and official bodies met 151 times; by 1977, 158 bodies met 335 times. The subject matter was changing, too. Meetings on economic matters were much more frequent than those on social policy (Veilleux, 1979). But the characteristic device of what Stefan Dupre has called the era of "summit federalism" was the First Ministers' Conference (FMC), and the central issue was the constitution. Of the 29 FMCs since 1960, 17 focussed entirely on the constitution (Meekison, at OEC, 1985).

This combination of issues and processes, Dupré argues, was the worst imaginable from the point of view of achieving compromise. In contrast to the line officials who did the negotiating in the days of "administrative" federalism, the officials who prepared for and orchestrated the FMCs – from intergovernmental affairs agencies and ministries of justice – tended to have a more conflictual view of the process, and were interested in pursuing global political goals rather than substantive policy goals. Constitutional arguments contrasted sharply with fiscal debates. Constitutional issues focus on symbols, which lend themselves to all or nothing debates: either Quebec has special status or it does not. Fiscal differences, on the other hand, can easily be split. Constitutional issues also involve higher stakes. Once changed, a constitutional provision is not easily changed again, so those involved must be certain that it is a deal they can live with for a long time. The federal-provincial fiscal arrangements, on the other hand, were renegotiated every five years: if too much were given away in 1977, some could be taken back in 1982 (Dupre, 1985). Donald Smiley provides a similar assessment:

> The institutions and processes of executive federalism are disposed towards conflict rather than harmony. Federal-provincial summitry along with the related phenomenon of administrative rationalization has weakened the capacity of the

system to make piecemeal and incremental adjustments according to the norms of scientific and professional groupings. Even more crucially, the pursuit of jurisdictional autonomy takes place outside a shared acceptance of constitutional and legal norms about the respective powers of the two orders of government.

(1980, p. 116)

Not all FMCs of the 1970s focussed on the constitution. But even economic issues had become much less tractible than fiscal arrangements. The most elaborate attempt by the federal and provincial governments to collaborate on industrial policy took place in 1978, as part of the brief flirtation with tripartism that followed the termination of three years of wage and price controls. At the February FMC governments agreed on the need to restrain public spending and public sector wage settlements. The Economic Council of Canada was assigned to monitor wage and price increases and to study the costs and benefits of economic regulation. Committees of Ministers were asked to explore specific issues. Marc Lalonde declared that it was "the beginning of a more complete and puposeful intergovernmental consultation" (in Brown & Eastman, 1981, p. 41). But the second conference in November achieved little. Consensus beyond the broad orientations identified in February did not exist.

Ottawa also launched the "Enterprise 77" review of federal programs, supplemented by interviews with 5,000 firms across Canada and the subsequent organization by Industry, Trade and Commerce of 23 industry Task Forces to examine the needs of each industrial sector. The Task Force reports turned out to be little more than shopping lists, and the Tier II process that was supposed to synthesize them proved disappointing. The Blair-Carr Task Force was appointed to explore further the prospects of tripartite collaboration in a new national industrial strategy.

These proved to be the most extensive efforts yet undertaken to integrate the two axes, public/private and federal/provincial, along which any industrial strategy must be organized. Each involved different actors, different consultative forums and different policy preoccupations. The public/private axis focussed on the role of government in the economy and the shares going to the state, capital and labour; the intergovernmental axis was overwhelmingly focussed on the location of economic activity and the shares going to each order of government. Synthesis of the two proved difficult. To emphasize one axis was to diminish the other. There was also the question of the level at which consultation with the private sector should occur. While Ottawa was developing its mechanisms, so were provinces, notably Quebec with a series of "sommets économiques". In some cases, different governments had links with competing elements within the provincial business community and engaged in competitive bidding for interest group support (Thorburn, 1985).

Interprovincial mechanisms were also increasing and changing their focus. Originally they had avoided federal-provincial issues; now they were used to plan and coordinate strategies in relations with Ottawa and, despite frequent differences of interest among the provinces, to work out compromises among themselves. Chairmanship of the Premier's conference rotated annually and the chairman became the primary spokesmen for the Premiers as a group. Many federal initiatives were now regarded as illegitimate "intrusions" and the 1978 *Report of the Western Premiers' Task Force on Constitutional Trends* detailed many of them. Calls to "disentangle" federal and provincial activities, a theme pushed especially hard by Ontario and Quebec, grew louder and were strongly endorsed at the 1978 annual Premiers' Conference.

Yet at the same time, Premiers argued that national policy-making should be a collaborative affair. In their view the national interest, and the policies appropriate to implement it, could only emerge from the interaction of 11 governments. To the Prime Minister's rhetorical question at one Conference, "But who will speak for Canada?" the reply was "We all do". Hence, the Premiers called for a greater role in decisions in areas of exclusive federal jurisdiction – particularly transportation and trade – and for institutions, such as Ontario's proposed National Council of the Economy, in which to do so.

Throughout much of the 1970s federal leaders also tended to adopt this collaborative view. The 1978 Conferences on the economy, said Federal-Provincial Relations Minister Marc Lalonde, were "the beginning of a process of more complete and purposeful intergovernmental consultation" which would result in "elaboration of a national industrial strategy". Prime Minister Trudeau echoed the point (Brown, 1978-79, p. 19). Improved collaboration was also a major theme of the 1979 Conservative government. but such a process was never institutionalized and, in 1980, the federal government would change its tune.

Fiscal Arrangements: Disentanglement   The 1977 fiscal arrangements, covering the period until 1982, were developed in close federal-provincial collaboration. The result was a considerable further devolution of fiscal power and program autonomy to the provinces. It was to be the highwater mark of fiscal decentralization.

Tax Collection Agreements After the termination of the tax rental agreements in 1957 the federal government had continued to act as the tax collection agent for personal income taxes in all provinces but Quebec, and for corporate income taxes in all provinces except Quebec and Ontario. But the collection system had been modified to permit greater provincial discretion. Initially, provinces had been allowed to vary their tax rates; then they were permitted to introduce a variety of tax credits which had the effect of modifying the tax base.

By the 1970s there was increasing disquiet about the effects of these developments. The report of the Parliamentary Task Force on Federal-Provincial Fiscal Arrangements (the Breau Task Force) (1981) expressed concern that increasing divergence of tax rates from province to province could undermine nation-wide common standards and encourage inefficient allocations. It was also feared that tax revenues might be reduced by increasing provincial competition for investment. The rapid erosion of inheritance taxes, shortly after responsibility for them had been transferred to the provinces, was a sobering precedent (Sheppard, 1985, p. 193). Fears that decentralization might weaken Ottawa's fiscal policy instruments were underlined in 1977 when the federal government sought to persuade the provinces to reduce their sales taxes in order to produce short-term stimulus to consumer purchasing. The episode led to a bitter confrontation with Quebec, which eventually pursued its own program, biased to provide special assistance for Quebec-based industries.

Provincial concerns were a mirror image of the federal worries. Federal tax changes, either in tax rates or in the base on which the rates were calculated, had serious effects on provincial revenues. This was especially true for the personal income tax, because it was calculated as a percentage of the federal tax payable rather than directly on the federal base. The more aggressively the federal government used the tax system for economic policy purposes, the greater the implications for the provinces.

Shared Cost Agreements: The Creation of EPF As the negotiations for the 1977 arrangements approached, federal and provincial interests converged. Ottawa was concerned about the open-ended and uncontrolled nature of its commitment to share the rapidly-escalating costs of health care and post-secondary education, and sought a way to restrain them. Under the existing 50 percent sharing arrangements, federal spending was determined by provincial decisions. "Caps" on various transfers had been put in place in 1972, 1974 and 1975 but the larger problem remained. The federal government was also anxious to bring back more symmetry between the status of Quebec and other provinces and to end the anomaly of opting-out. As early as 1966 Ottawa sought to replace some of the shared-cost programs with looser arrangements. In the 1975 budget the federal government signalled its desire to terminate the hospital insurance program. Provincial governments wanted greater access to unrestricted funds, disentanglement of federal and provincial responsibilities, and fewer federal intrusions into areas of provincial jurisdiction. Ottawa and some of the poorer provinces were both concerned that, under shared-cost arrangements, larger amounts of federal funds flowed to the richer provinces that could match Ottawa's "fifty cent dollars".

The federal-provincial negotiations were preceded by intense provincial discussions seeking to bridge the interests of the poorer and the wealthier provinces. The result was the Federal-Provincial Fiscal Arrangements and Established Programs Financing Act, passed in 1977. Its central component was the separation of federal contributions for health and post-secondary education from any link to actual program costs: henceforth they would escalate with the Gross National Product. Federal funding would take the form of a transfer of additional equalized tax points, together with cash grants. While future federal calculations of the value of these transfers would continue to allocate them proportionally among the programs, the transfers were now seen as general revenues – not tied to a specific function – by the provinces. To provincial treasurers they no longer had a policy label attached to them.

While the financing of the programs was altered, the provisions of the Hospital Insurance and Medicare Acts were unchanged. Ottawa did request a consultative role in post-secondary education, but the overall result was a significant step back from substantive federal involvement. As the term "Established Programs Financing" implied, the mechanism for maintaining national standards was to be the will of the provincial governments and the expectations of their citizens, rather than federal controls.

The new system met the desire for fiscal restraint felt by both levels of government. Ottawa expected it to mean lower rates of increase in transfers – a hope that was soon to be dashed. Rising inflation meant that nominal GNP was rising far faster than actual health and education spending, escalating federal transfers at a higher rate than before. The provinces, however, now had strong incentives to restrain costs without losing federal dollars, and they did so with a vengeance. As a result, the federal contributions accounted for a larger and larger proportion of provincial spending, leading to charges that provinces were "underfunding" and "diverting" the transfers to alternate uses.

The 1977 arrangements represented a large step in the direction of disentanglement. It could also be argued that they represented an end of the commitment to an expanding welfare state on the part of both orders of government: the emphasis now was on holding the line. Still, in many ways the 1977 EPF agreement remained a half-way measure – reducing federal involvement but maintaining intact the federal conditions embodied in the original legislation.

Equalization: Oil Revenues and Disequilibrium The rapid rise in oil prices undermined the 1967 equalization formula, which had included natural resources among its 22 revenue sources. The enormous increase in Alberta's revenues dramatically raised the average level of provincial revenues, automatically increasing the entitlements of all provinces. The formula obliged Ottawa to meet these entitlements out of federal revenues.

In effect, Ottawa would have to tax all Canadians to compensate citizens in the poorer provinces for Alberta's windfall. Courchene (1976) estimated that for every additional dollar Alberta gained, federal equalization obligations would increase by 90 cents. If Canada went to world oil prices, and the revenues were fully equalized, the equalization payments would increase by $4 billion, necessitating a 25 percent incease in federal income taxes. Federal obligations under the program were entirely independent of federal decisions, depending solely on the revenues collected by the provinces. Between 1972 and 1977 payments rose 19 percent each year, much faster than either GNP or federal revenues.

The situation was untenable; "full" equalization had to be abandoned. Restraining price increases helped hold the payments down, but more action was necessary. Successive measures sought to cap spending and reduce the proportion of oil and gas revenues which would be equalized. In the 1977 arrangements it was agreed that only 50 percent of resource revenues would be included in the formula; later legislation excluded from equalization entitlements any province with a per capita income above the national average. This provision was directed against Ontario, which had become eligible for equalization payments under the formula, although embarrassed Ontario officials had indicated Ontario would not claim these funds.

These events raised important questions about the underlying principles of equalization. Throughout the postwar period revenue disparities among provinces had steadily narrowed; now they took a sharp upward jump. Was it consistent with fairness and common citizenship that the province of Alberta could be able simultaneously to finance generous public services, have the lowest tax levels in the country, and still salt away a good proportion of its revenues in its Heritage Savings and Trust Fund? Would such a situation result in "fiscally induced migration" as people moved to Alberta to capture a share of the increased rents? Was the goal of the program full equality in access to revenues or, less grandly, was it simply to ensure the ability of provinces to provide "reasonably comparable" levels of services without "unduly high levels of taxation" as Mitchell Sharp had formulated it? Should the equalization program become more interprovincial – with the richer provinces directly contributing into a pool from which the poorer would draw? Before 1980, no government had worked out clear answers to these questions.

After 1980: The New Federalism

Pierre Trudeau returned to Ottawa in 1980 determined to conduct federal-provincial relations on a fundamentally different set of premises from those which had operated over the last twenty years. Ottawa's New

Federalism, as we have seen, was rooted in the conviction that provincialism and decentralization had gone too far. Indeed, unless they were reversed, Trudeau argued, there was no logical stopping place, short of dismemberment of the country, or at least turning it into a loose and powerless confederation. Provincialism was now seen through the same lens as Quebec separatism, and it needed a similar reply – that cooperative federalism was both inefficient and lacking in democratic legitimacy.

The New Federalism argued that cooperative federalism was too cumbersome: it slowed down decision-making and reduced it to the lowest common denominator. It also reduced federal legitimacy. If everything had to be done jointly, and if Ottawa's relations with citizens were to be mediated through provincial governments, citizens' material and symbolic ties to the central government would be weakened. Finally, it undermined responsible government. If Ottawa were required to be responsible for its actions to provinces and if it transferred funds without condition to them, how could it be accountable to its own legislature and electorate for the way in which their money was used? How could provinces be responsible to their legislatures when so many of the dollars they spent had come from Ottawa? The new federal approach therefore eschewed formal collaboration; each government would instead look to its own responsibilities and act where it could. In this more open and competitive way, dynamism and innovation would be increased and citizens would have more control than if negotiations were conducted in secret behind closed doors. Between 1980 and 1984 the New Federalism set the tone of federal-provincial relations.

Intergovernmental Mechanisms: "Competitive Legitimation"   A s governments pursued their divergent visions of the federation they sought to mobilize support for their positions among organized interests and citizens. This struggle, which Garth Stevenson calls "competitive legitimation", took many forms. Some were bizarre: federal and provincial leaders vying with Native leaders for the support of the British Parliament; or federal and Quebec governments "bidding" for the approbation of foreign academics with research and travel grants. During this period the federal government became the largest advertiser in Canada. Grain trains became moving billboards as brightly painted cars, advertising the contributions of Ottawa, Alberta and Saskatchewan, rolled across the country. Patronage in the form of highly visible discretionary grants was now dignified by its attachment to the noble cause of national unity, rather than crass electoral politics. The Charter of Rights was attractive not only on philosophical grounds but also because of its potential for mobilizing a constituency behind the federal position on the constitution. There were many more examples.

Competitive legitimation meant that intergovernmental relations were conducted much more publicly. Conferences became a forum for projecting alternative viewpoints to citizens, rather than a meeting for negotiating between governments. Symbols, rather than the often obscure substance of government program coordination and legal responsibility, came to dominate the discussion. Media attention to the process greatly increased, with gavel-to gavel coverage and post-mortems on "The Journal". Even closed Ministerial meetings attracted more coverage; what happened inside was immediately communicated to the country through leaks or, very often, formal press conferences. These developments cast into question the sense of intergovernmental relations as a cartel of elites, conducting their affairs in private at the expense of the people. Seldom, in fact, had executive federalism been so open.

But increased openness also created more opportunities for grand-standing – talking to one's own constituency via the television cameras, rather than to the other First Ministers gathered in the room – and in an atmosphere of competitive legitimation these opportunties were frequently seized. As a result, FMCs became less and less useful as a means of dealing with serious intergovernmental problems. FMCs on the constitution have already been discussed. Those on the economy were one of the casualties of the New Federalism. Large-scale conferences, Ottawa argued, elevated Premiers to the status of national statesmen, giving them an opportunity to score easy points by attacking federal policies, and blurring any clarity in the responsibilities of the two orders of government. Moreover, summit federalism was asymmetrical: provinces demanded full consultation from Ottawa but jealously resented federal attempts to tell them what to do.

Only the pressures of the recession induced Ottawa to relent to provincial pressures for another FMC on the Economy. But the February 1982 FMC was a disaster. There was little background preparation and tensions over other issues – especially soaring interest rates – were running high. A new federal approach to fiscal arrangements – in keeping with the assumptions of the New Federalism – angered the provinces. At the end, Premiers called for a continuation of regular meetings on the economy. But the federal response was "never again". The conferences, Ottawa argued, undermined the federal role as manager of the economy and gave the provinces a platform from which to attack federal efforts, without creating any incentives for the provinces to contribute constructively to them (see YIR, 1982, p. 6).

As FMCs became less effective means of resolving federal-provincial differences, one response was increasing recourse to the courts. Of 158 cases related to the constitution to come before the Supreme Court between 1950 and 1982, 80 took place after 1975. In some cases governments joined sides with private parties; in others governments referred contentious matters for an opinion. Frequently federal lawyers were lined up against an array of lawyers from most of the provinces. By 1984 Peter Russell, a leading student of the Court, could claim that "I doubt if the judiciary of any other federation is more active than Canada's in umpiring the federal system". In doing so, he argued, the Supreme Court showed "uncanny balance" and even-handedness, with the effect of forcing the governments back to the bargaining table (1984). Not everyone agreed with Russell; many of the provinces felt that the Supreme Court of Canada was too sympathetic to the federal government which appointed all of its memebers. As a result, the more frequent recourse to the courts became, the more urgent the demand for reform of the appointment process to ensure that the Supreme Court acted as a neutral umpire in these constitutional disputes.

Fiscal Arrangements: Re-centralization   *Tax Collection Agreements: Unilateralism* Ottawa's unilateralism after 1980 produced an opposite provincial reaction in the sphere of tax collection. After federal tax changes announced in the 1981 federal budget (most of which were later rescinded), Ontario gave serious consideration to withdrawing from the Tax Collection Agreements and establishing its own collection system, paralleling Quebec's (Courchene, 1986, pp. 89-91). In the end Ontario chose not to follow this course, explaining that it did not wish to fragment the Canadian economic union any further, or to lose the benefits to taxpayers of administrative simplicity. However, Alberta withdrew from the federal corporate tax collection system in order to develop one that it argued would be more appropriate to the needs of Alberta industry. British Columbia, fearing Alberta competition, also announced its intention to withdraw, but did not do so (Courchene, 1986, pp. 84-88).

Shared Cost Arrangements: Return to Conditionality The harmony of interest and strategy that led to the 1977 EPF agreements did not inform the discussion of the 1982 arrangements. Several factors combined to make the latter much more difficult. Most important was the New Federalism and Ottawa's overriding interest in regaining its authority and initiative vis-à-vis the provinces. Also important, however, was the urgent need to gain greater control over its own expenditures at a time when the provinces were also facing difficult financial pressures. Further, there was the need to respond to the intense political pressures from health-related interests, universities and others concerned about erosion of standards and budgets in these fields. Finally, there was the continuing need to adapt the federal-provincial fiscal arrangements to the ongoing volatility of economic circumstances, and to sustained pressures on the equalization system engendered by resource revenues. Each of these would have created difficulties on its own; taken together, and mixed with the high levels of mistrust surrounding the constitution and other issues, they made agreement impossible to reach for the first time in the post-war period.

The question for the 1982 round of the fiscal arrangements was whether to extend the logic of the 1977 EPF by eliminating all federal conditions attached to the shared cost programs covered under that agreement, or to return to a greater federal policy role through clearly articulated and enforceable conditions. The federal government sought the latter. It wanted to control its deficit and eliminate what it called a fiscal imbalance by reducing the total level of transfers. It wanted to reinforce its control over the economy by linking fiscal arrangements and tax collections to a code of conduct on the economic union. Most important, it wanted to reassert a role in education and health policy. Provinces, argued federal ministers, had "diverted" federal transfers to other uses and were "underfunding" in these areas.

Responding to growing public concern over the perceived erosion of health and education standards, the federal government wanted to reintroduce the link between transfers and program conditions. To this end it proposed that transfers for health and education continue, but that new legislation should clarify and implement national standards in health, and should depend on "satisfactory progress" towards defining a role for Ottawa in post-secondary education. The revenue guarantee would finally be ended. Provinces bitterly opposed both the reduction of funds and the reimposition of federal conditions. This time the negotiations did not result in a compromise agreement. Instead, after a few modifications, the federal legislation was enacted in 1982 without provincial approval.

To enlist support for its position, the federal government sponsored a parliamentary Task Force on Federal-Provincial Fiscal Arrangements (the Breau Task Force) (1981). It was the first time there had ever been extensive Parliamentary scrutiny of federal-provincial fiscal arrangements before they were negotiated. Like the parliamentary committee on the constitution, the Task Force was not concerned with the niceties of federal-provincial relations, or with concepts of federalism and the constitution. For them the focal points were the substance of social policy and the need to enhance accountability. As with the constitutional committee, the Task Force provided a golden opportunity to many groups to voice their concerns about the future of social policy. While they provided little support for the federal intention to cut costs, they provided much political support for increased conditionality, roundly criticizing provinces for their cost-cutting measures and calling for federal intervention (Simeon, 1982).

In 1983 the federal government reasserted the separate allocations to health and education and "capped" its contribution to the education component according to the "six and five" guidelines. This reduced transfers, made them less predictable and reintroduced directly targetted funds.

Ontario claimed that the "cap" cost the province $94 million in 1983-84. By this time, the quality of medical care had become a major public issue, as citizens responded to provincial efforts to reduce costs by imposing user-fees and permitting the growth of extra billing. In December 1983 the federal government introduced a new Canada Health Act. It redefined the conditions of provincial eligibility for federal funds so as to exclude explicitly these practices. It also provided for direct sanctions, in the form of dollar-for-dollar reductions in federal transfers, against provinces that violated these conditions. The legislation also called for more detailed accounting by the provinces and for "appropriate recognition" of federal financial support for the programs.

Again, the negotiations ended in stalemate. Ottawa, the provinces argued, was putting them in an impossible position: increasing program demand with one hand and cutting or limiting transfers on the other. In the name of abstract concepts such as accountability and national standards, other critics argued, the federal government was undermining some of the basic virtues of federalism, especially its encouragement of experiment and innovation. In the current climate of restraint, that meant the ability to experiment with more "efficient" delivery mechanisms (Courchene, 1984). The Bill was passed, and sanctions began to be introduced in 1984. Polls suggested that in this battle Ottawa had public support on its side. All federal opposition parties supported the legislation. Unlike energy and the constitution, health care was not an issue that divided the country regionally: this time the provinces were on their own. No changes were made in post-secondary education, but a number of alternatives to increase the federal role were actively explored within the government.

The discussions raised basic issues about the future of Canadian federalism. First, how in an era of stagnant or declining revenues would governments share the taxation pie? Second, how could traditional norms of accountability of governments to citizens and legislatures be reconciled with unconditional grants, if they required a clear assignment of responsibility to one government? Third, were there to be "national standards" in basic social programs? Similarly, were post-secondary institutions to be seen as essential elements in planning for national manpower and research needs? Finally, how (if at all) was the public to have input into the crucial discussions that were being made between governments concerning social policy? No consensus had emerged on these questions by the end of this period.

Equalization Events, the second oil price hike and proposals to locate equalization in the Charter, forced citizens and governments to address more systematically the issues that had been left hanging at the end of the 1970s. While the debates on principles went on, two practical problems had to be dealt with immediately. First, how to treat resource revenues so as to remain faithful to the traditional principles of equalization without generating excessive payments. Second, how to devise a rational formula which would not have the effect of designating Ontario as an eligible recipient for federal equalization transfers.

The federal solution, spelled out in the 1981 Budget Paper, *Fiscal Arrangements in the Eighties*, maintained the representative tax system. But rather than equalizing to the "national average", the standard became a single province, Ontario. This meant that, by definition, Ontario could never become a recipient. Moreover, since Ontario had so few resource revenues, they could be included in the formula without generating significant payments. Since Ontario's other revenue sources were relatively buoyant, equalization payments overall would continue to rise. But the new arrangement specified that they could not rise at a rate greater than growth in GNP.

The provinces roundly attacked the proposal in a *Provincial Report on the Revised Equalization Program Proposal*. Basing equalization on one province, however large, would introduce greater volatility in payments than would the national average standard. It would virtually eliminate resources as a basis for equalization; indeed, provinces with natural resource-based economies were penalized, since any new income they derived from this source would cut into their equalization entitlements. Tensions were increased because the new formula would also have differential effects on various provinces, and because new population figures demonstrated that in the immediately preceding years there had been "over-equalization" of $217 million, which the provinces would have to return.

At the February 1982 federal-provincial conference, Ottawa proposed as an alternative changing the Ontario standard into one based on five provinces – Ontario, Quebec, British Columbia, Saskatchewan and Manitoba. This was more balanced, since it excluded the "extremes" of Alberta and the Atlantic provinces. The federal government also proposed to broaden further the formula's tax base, and to introduce a guaranteed floor to cushion provinces against any drastic alteration in their equalization entitlements resulting from changed economic conditions. A transitional adjustment was also to cushion any province, such as Manitoba, which stood to lose by the modified arrangements (Courchene, 1984, Ch. 11).

Thus, the federal government was prepared to concede more to the poorer provinces on equalization than it was on EPF. Nevertheless, the changes in equalization implied a reduced capacity to maintain the principle of comparable services at comparable levels of taxation. In the 1950s and 1960s there had been considerable convergence in per capita provincial revenues and very similar rates of taxation. In the 1970s large variations in provincial tax rates reappeared, and differences in per capita revenues grew.

Conclusions

The battle over the constitution and Trudeau's New Federalism left federal-provincial relations in disarray. Each order of government had a quite different sense of how the federation should operate. Unilateral action and recourse to the courts often displaced negotiation and compromise. Federal-provincial relations became an arena for expressing deep divisions over a wide range of tightly interwoven issues. Intergovernmental machinery, it was often argued, failed to coordinate policies, failed to accommodate regional and national interests, and failed to meet the standards of democratic accountability and participation. In spite of these failures, complete paralysis was not the result. There were agreements on the great issues, like energy. Although strained, cooperation continued on many specific programs sheltered from the high-noon atmosphere of First Ministers Conferences.

In the wake of these extraordinary levels of federal-provincial conflict, it is worth asking a number of related questions. To what degree, and in what ways, did federal institutions contribute to the deep conflicts of this period? In those cases in which federalism did not cause these conflicts, could reforms to federalism be expected to reduce them? Was the enormous energy poured into the criticism of existing institutions, and the imagining of alternatives, warranted by the potential returns?

There can be no definitive answers to such questions, only provisional ones. Federalism did not cause the regionalization of the party system that reduced the legitimacy of the central government in the Atlantic and Western provinces. Nor would better regional representation at the centre have been sufficient to reduce regional tensions to manageable levels, as the short-lived Clark government discovered. But, given the existence of such regional conflicts of economic interest, provincial governments were endowed with powerful resources with which to defend and promote them – resources that they would not have had in a unitary state system. The same logic applies with respect to francophones in Quebec. Federalism thus gave more effective voice to national minorities that would otherwise have been quieter if not silent. How one evaluates this depends upon one's attitudes to pluralist democracy.

Federalism also changed the terms in which these interests, and conflicts between them, were understood and articulated. It transformed questions of substance – what energy policy? – into questions about the efficacy and legitimacy of federalism itself. In order to justify the means by which they sought to achieve their substantive goals – to their constituencies, to other citizens and to the courts – governments developed sharply divergent views of the federal system. The energy debate, for example, was not only about prices, but about the authority to set prices; not only about revenues, but about the right to revenues. Thus, the interests of provincial communities were transmuted into a political discourse focussing on the rights of provincial governments.

But, more deeply, were federal and provincial governments responsible for creating and promoting ideologies which led to conflict in the first place as Cairns, among others, has argued? Public opinion data gives us some purchase on this question, and enables us to trace the evolution of citizen attitudes to the institutions of federalism, their sense of identification with national and provincial communities, and the relation between the two.

The polls throughout this period told a contradictory story. They revealed much hostility to the federal government and, generally, to the "fairness" of the federal system. The federal government was seen to be remote, unresponsive and biased in favour of some regions over others. Provincial governments were felt to be closer to the people, more responsive and effective. Many citizens felt that their provincial government should be "tougher" in dealings with Ottawa; a plurality said they would support the province in a federal-provincial fight. More Canadians wanted further decentralization than wanted further centralization. While there was increasing hostility to all governments, the federal government appeared to be the lightning rod (Johnston, 1986).

But this evidence of regional hostility to Ottawa coexisted with many elements of commonality. Citizens across all regions seemed to share similar conceptions of the good society, and of the role of government in promoting it. In matters of social, economic and cultural policy, there was evidence of convergence across both regional and linguistic lines. There was evidence of strong nation-wide support for uniform standards of public health care and for equalization and sharing within the federation. Most citizens looked to the federal goverment to oversee such programs. Most important, all the evidence suggests that citizens strongly identified with both the national community and their provincial community, even in Quebec. Both were viewed positively. They were not seen to be incompatible or inherently in conflict. Rather, they were complementary and mutually reinforcing (Johnston, 1986).

This meant that the increasingly polarized visions of community (national versus provincial) and federalism (cooperative versus competitive) pursued by governments in the 1970s and early 1980s, the subtle arguments about constitutional interpretation, and the expensive symbols and propaganda found little sympathy among the majority of Canadian citizens. The political elites did not profoundly re-shape citizen identities – the product of a long, historical process operating primarily at the level of day-to-day experience – as they had hoped they would. Instead, they remained constrained by their citizens' beliefs and democratic institutions, as they always had been. It was possible to push beyond these constraints for brief periods, especially immediately after elections, but as the inter-governmental battles intensified a growing number of Canadians became convinced that their governments were missing the point. Their purpose was to arrive at a fair solution to the nation's economic and social problems – fair in both regional and individual terms – and not to glorify "la patrie", whether at the level of province or country, for its own sake. Most Canadians were more upset with both orders of government for failing to negotiate and cooperate than they were with one level of government for acting unfairly. By 1982 there was widespread public and governmental agreement that a more effective relationship must be worked out.

When Pierre Trudeau stepped down as Prime Minister in 1984, a remark-able era in Canadian federalism came to an end. Between 1980 and 1984 he had sought not only to stop, but to reverse, the direction in which the federal system had been evolving for a quarter century. He had invoked a liberal, individualist image of the nation to counter the more communitarian image that underpinned the growing provincialism and Quebec nationalism, and had institutionalized that image in a Charter of Rights. He had repudiated cooperative federalism and tested the limits of federal power in field after field.

The most enduring legacy of these efforts, and the most important, will almost certainly be the Charter of Rights. It will transform constitutional discourse, as Mallory has argued: no longer will battles over basic civil and political rights have to be fought out and decided in the language of jurisdiction; no longer will fundamental issues of individual and collective rights hinge on a finding of *intra vires* or *ultra vires* (1985, p. 54). In the longer run, it may also transform the language of individual and collective identity. The Charter seems likely to enhance the status of individuals vis-à-vis communities, but it also grants constitutional recognition to new bases of collective identity, such as gender (see Taylor, 1985; Cairns & Williams, 1985a). Whatever the changing balance among these identities in the future, the basis for thinking and acting on them is forever changed. Beyond discourse, the Charter gives hitherto politically disadvantaged groups, par-ticularly those that are not territorially concentrated, a potentially powerful new institutional avenue for political mobilization.

The lasting significance of the New Federalism is much more problematic. Prime Minister Trudeau succeeded in pushing through the Canada Health Act, and its basic principles seem likely to endure. But the National Energy Policy, implemented over the vociferous objections of provincial governments, had already been dismantled. In other areas – strengthening federal economic powers, defining new rules to govern the economic union, and asserting a greater federal voice in post-secondary education – there was little success even at the outset. Taken as a whole, the efforts to increase the relative power of the federal government, and particularly its capacity unilaterally to control and manage the economy, were only successful at the margin. In part this was due to the constitutional assignment of powers and determined provincial government resistance. But wage and price controls in 1975, and the NEP in 1981, showed that Ottawa had wide latitude to act in the economic field, and the limits of the Trade and Commerce power have yet to be fully explored.

The larger reasons for Ottawa's limited capacity to manage the economy lie outside federal-provincial dynamics. International factors have significantly constrained federal powers. Canada's integration with the United States and the world financial system has sharply limited Ottawa's capacity to operate independent and effective fiscal and monetary policies. International trade agreements have effectively removed tariffs and many types of subsidy and incentive which, in this context, become "non-tariff barriers", as instruments of federal economic policy. Most of the instruments that remain are shared with, or primarily occupied by, provincial governments.

At the same time, there have been domestic barriers to effective federal economic management. Divergent regional economic interests have always made it difficult to form a consensus on a national economic strategy. Now, with the declining regional economic integration that is the legacy of the International Policy, that task has become more difficult than ever. Even if such a policy could be formulated, it would be difficult to execute it effectively without the cooperation of organized labour and capital. Yet neither the Liberals nor the Conservatives was able to forge even the limited kind of tripartism that has been constructed by NDP and PQ provincial governments.

Nevertheless, it may well be that, whatever the hostilities it engendered and however imperfectly it was realized, Trudeau's New Federalism was cathartic. Perhaps nothing other than a "damn the torpedoes" approach would have broken the log-jam on patriation and the amending formula, or won a Charter of Rights. Perhaps, too, the climactic confrontation with Quebec nationalism forced citizens to clarify the alternatives and define a realistic balance between their allegiances to national and provincial communities. In the tradition of Macdonald, Trudeau pushed hard on the outer limits of federal power, providing his successors with a benchmark that will doubtless inform their deliberations about desirable levels of centralization and modes of interaction between governments for a long time to come.

On the other hand, the crude political reality of the New Federalism often amounted to little more than the mobilization of a central Canadian majority to by-pass provincial governments and the majorities that they represented. By 1984 the costs of this strategy were evident. Most Canadians believed that intergovernmental mistrust and hostility reduced the nation's capacity to deal effectively with its economic problems, and these were the problems that people now worried about more than anything else. The desire for less tension and conflict, for a more consensual style that would be more sensitive to regionalism and provincialism, was widespread. Perhaps the most compelling of Brian Mulroney's promises in the 1984 election campaign, therefore, was his pledge of "National Reconciliation".

Chapter 11

The Renewal of Collaborative Federalism, 1984-87

On September 4, 1984 Brian Mulroney led the Progressive Conservatives to victory, with 50 percent of the vote and 211 of the 282 seats in the Commons. The national dimensions of the sweep were remarkable. The Tories won at least 70 percent of the seats in every region. Their long drought in Quebec was ended. Forging a coalition of disaffected Liberals and Péquistes and emphasizing his own Québécois identity Mulroney won more than three-quarters of the province's seats. No party had won a victory like this since the last great Tory sweep of 1958.

"National Reconciliation" lay at the core of the Tory's campaign message. They promised to "bring Quebec back in" to a constitutional consensus and reduce the tension and hostility between Ottawa and the provinces. The Prime Minister pledged a return to cooperative federalism, reforging the linguistic, regional and intergovernmental accommodations which had been shattered by the combination of international forces and Trudeau's New Federalism. He set out the central elements of reconciliation during a campaign speech in Sept Iles. (6 August, 1984).

There is room in Canada for all identities to be affirmed, for all aspirations to be respected.... Our first task is to breathe a new spirit into federalism. The serious deterioration of federal-provincial relations is not exclusively the result of constitutional deficiencies. Centralistic and negative attitudes are much more to blame.... Let us replace the bias of confrontation with the bias of agreement.

He promised to work with the "duly elected" government of Quebec to "convince the Quebec National Assembly to give its consent to the new Canadian constitution". He committed his government to ending regionally discriminatory policies – including dismantling the hated National Energy Program – and promised to mount a renewed attack on regional disparities.

At the level of the federal state, Mulroney committed his government to end federal intrusions into provincial jurisdiction and to respect provincial priorities:

> We will ensure that we do not duplicate provincial programs or launch programs that are incompatible with provincial programs. ...we will put an end to federal attempts to smother the expansion of legitimate instruments for collective development, such as the Caisse de depôt du Québec.... A Progressive Conservative government will be guided by the principle of respect for provincial authority.
>
> (Extracts from address, Sept Iles, 6 August, 1984)

Intergovernmental collaboration in policy development was to be rejuvenated:

> To end parallel or incompatible planning once and for all between the two orders of government, we will set up a federal-provincial advisory and coordinating body which will operate at the highest level, namely with 11 leaders themselves working together in an appropriate institutional framework advising as to the options envisaged and the directions to take.
>
> (Extracts from address, Sept Iles, 6 August, 1984)

Such cooperation, the new Prime Minister argued, was essential to achieving economic recovery It was difficult to imagine a clearer rejection of the Trudeau model, or a more explicit statement of politics as elite accommodation.

The new government was equally committed to reducing the role of the state in Canadian economic life. It was pledged to fiscal restraint and an attack on the federal deficit through spending cuts and trimming the public service, to a limited degree of privatization and to deregulation. This thrust had become common currency throughout the western democracies and, indeed, was foreshadowed in the last years of the Trudeau government and the brief interregnum of John Turner. But at the same time Mulroney the vote-seeking politician was careful in his campaign to stress that essential elements of the Canadian welfare state remained a "sacred trust".

These thrusts were enshrined in the two major initiatives of the Mulroney government. In May 1987 he and the 10 provincial Premiers signed the Meech Lake Accord. It proposed to entrench in the constitution the principle of Quebec as a distinct society, to modify the amending formula adopted in 1982, to provide a provincial role in nomination of Senators and Supreme Court Justices, to define and limit the federal spending power and to give constitutional status to First Ministers Conferences. By the fall of 1988, following the procedures adopted in 1982, it had been ratified by the federal House of Commons and the legislatures of eight provinces. Two provinces, New Brunswick and Manitoba, had yet to give their consent, and its eventual adoption was uncertain.

In 1985 Mulroney undertook to negotiate a comprehensive trade agreement with the United States and in 1987 signed the Canada-U.S. Free Trade Agreement.

It is premature to attempt a full analysis of the four years of the first term of the Progressive Conservative government. We remain caught up in constantly-changing events, lacking the distance to discern clear patterns and lasting effects, to separate the significant from the ephemeral.

With these caveats (and the realization that we are writing history not current events, much less prognostications) we depart somewhat in this chapter from the pattern followed until now. We use the opportunity to recapitulate the model that has animated our study, and within that framework seek to identify some of the continuing dilemmas of Canadian federalism which these two initiatives illustrate. We do not ask what lasting impact the Mulroney approach will have, but rather how its initiatives and the debates they have inspired relate to the continuing themes of federal state and federal society within a changing global context.

Federal Society

The Economic Context

From the begining we have examined the dynamics of state and society in terms of the wider political economy. In the immediate postwar period, we saw how the new International policy and Keynesian economic management ushered in a sustained period of economic growth in which both the manufactured products of Central Canada and the resources of other regions were in demand. Hence growth was reasonably evenly shared and regional economic conflicts were muted. Moreover, the new International policy, aimed at monetary stability and tariff reduction, was essentially a federal responsibility. Provinces may have been the beneficiaries, but there was little reason for them to become enmeshed in international economic relations.

In the 1970s we saw how a changed international situation, with its dramatic shift in the terms of trade, began to strain the Canadian fabric much more seriously, driving a massive wedge between Canada's regions and providing the essential fuel for the deep conflicts of the period. Moreover, these altered conditions led to much more activist industrial policies, at both levels, ushering in the period of rival "province" and "nation-building" strategies. These events also made the provinces much more aware of the consequences of global developments for their own economic well-being, and in this period we saw a considerable increase in provincial activities abroad. Moreover, the attention of global agencies such as the GATT were shifting to the impact of non-tariff barriers. Hence, their decisions were increasingly likely to reach beyond Ottawa to engage provincial industrial policies. And, given the Canadian treaty power, it appeared that provincial acquiescence if not active participation was necessary if Canada were effectively to pursue its goals in international forums. In the Tokyo Round of the GATT careful attention was paid to consultation with the provinces.

By the 1980s the increasingly interdependent global environment had virtually obliterated the boundary between domestic and international policy and politics. Simultaneously it dissolved the notion that federalism ended at the Canadian border.

Between 1982 and 1988 the Canadian economy recovered strongly from the sharp recession of 1981-82, pulled along primarily by an earlier and stronger recovery in the United States. Real GDP grew by an average of 4.2 percent between 1982 and 1987, leading all the other major industrial countries (ECC, 1986, p. 9; OECD, 1988). The annual rate of inflation was cut to about four percent and interest rates, though still high in real terms, edged downwards. Unemployment remained stubborn, finally dropping below eight percent in 1988. The number of new jobs created increased dramatically, but unemployment, especially among youth, remained unacceptably high.

Regional specialization has always meant that cycles of growth and recession have had different impacts and timing in the various parts of the country. But despite the lags, the movements had usually been in the same direction: recovery in manufacturing would spill over to increased demand from resource producers; recovery in resource producing areas would stimulate demand for manufactured goods from central Canada. The most striking aspect of the post-1982 recovery was its remarkable concentration in Southern Ontario and, to a lesser extent, western Quebec, and in the major service industries.

Southern Ontario and especially the booming Toronto region outpaced the rest of the country. Growth in the other eight provinces was much slower to materialize. In 1987, British Columbia still suffered double-digit unemployment, while the rate in Alberta was twice its pre-recession level (*Financial Post*, Dec. 28, 1987).

Lying behind these regional differences was a massive shift in the terms of trade, reversing the experience of the 1970s. Now led by oil and wheat, mainstays of the prairie economy, resource prices were in collapse. Observed the Economic Council of Canada, "Today, far from being a locomotive of growth, the resource sector is acting as a brake" (ECC: 1986, p. 43). In the eight months prior to July 1986, the well-head price of Alberta crude fell 61 percent, to $14.54 from its peak of $37.24 (Leslie, 1987, p. 6). This collapse rippled through all parts of the western economy, affecting oil and gas producers, the exploration and service firms which depended on them, real estate and retailing, and the financial institutions which had financed the boom. Two predominantly regional banks collapsed and many other institutions were in serious difficulty. For Newfoundland and Nova Scotia the price changes meant that the golden promise of off-shore oil and gas would be indefinitely delayed.

Mineral production, faced with a combination of diminished demand and in many cases with much cheaper production elsewhere, also fell, with especially severe economic impacts in British Columbia, Saskatchewan (where potash crumbled) and parts of Ontario and Quebec. In 1982-83, timber prices fell dramatically, hitting B.C. especially hard (Carmichael, 1986, p. 10), although a considerable recovery had occurred in this sector by 1987. A world glut of wheat, combined with a costly subsidy war between the European Community and the United States, ravaged the prairie wheat economy. Wheat prices dropped 20 percent to 30 percent between 1985 and 1986 (Leslie, 1987, p. 7); the value of grain exports in 1986 was 29 percent below 1982 (Little, *Report on Business* Magazine, August, 1987, p. 13).

The Economic Council of Canada drew the obvious implication of these events: "The slide in energy and other commodity prices is threatening to exacerbate the regional stresses within this country" (1986, p. 66). There were also important implications for federalism. The price drops cut deeply into provincial government revenues, while at the same time increasing demands on their welfare and income support systems. Provinces were running large deficits. In 1979 the provinces had a combined surplus of $1.7 billion (fuel for Ottawa's contention that the modern form of fiscal imbalance was in the provinces' favour). By 1982 the combined provincial deficit was $5.6 billion, declining to $2.5 billion in 1984. This changed fiscal climate lead all governments (with the important exception of Ontario) to practice the politics of restraint.

The second major effect was to bring about a return to a more traditional model of the Canadian political economy, restoring Ontario to its dominant position. Migration flows to the West were halted, then reversed, and the province regained its position as the leader in per capita incomes. This in turn helped change the pattern of regional and intergovernmental alliances. In the 1970s, Ontario's firm links with Ottawa on the constitution and energy were rooted in the realization that only though the use of federal power could Ontario establish a claim to western resources. Now the basis for that alliance had faded and Ontario was faring well by itself. More important, interest in the West had been in resisting such claims; it needed autonomy from Ottawa. With its own resource base now weakened, it was more important for the West to establish a claim for assistance from Ottawa. The focus shifted from independence from the centre to the need for influence over it. It is thus not surprising that support for an elected Senate which would institutionalize such influence grew rapidly and that the Alberta government, hostile to intrastate federalism as a threat to provincial freedom of action in the 1970s, now joined the movement for a "Triple E" (Elected, Equal, Effective) Senate. Once again the Canadian federal system was being driven by external events.

These events also undermined the faith in activist "province-building" policies, although the lure of the mega-project, – whether James Bay electricity, Alberta and Saskatchewan heavy oil and tar sands, or Newfoundland's Hibernia – remained undiminished despite the now unfavourable economic conditions. While they acknowledged that the Free Trade Agreement would inhibit the scope of provincial policy, the western provinces were now more concerned with the security of access to American markets they hoped it would bring.

This period also saw renewed concerns about the international trading environment. These now came to be focussed almost entirely on the relationship with the United States. Several elements converged. First, there was no let-up in the huge Canadian dependence on American markets. Second, that market looked increasingly threatened by a resurgence of protectionist sentiment in the United States, as it confronted massive trade deficits and the relative decline of a number of major industries. American trade actions against Canadian exports developed in numerous sectors, each of which was crucial to particular regions.

Shakes and shingles, softwood lumber, steel and fish were all on the list (ECC, 1986, p. 19). Americans were also becoming increasingly hostile to a number of Canadian domestic policies, ranging from timber royalties to unemployment insurance to regional development grants, all of which were held to constitute "unfair" subsidies to Canadian producers.

These developments called into question many aspects of Canadian policies to alleviate regional disparities. Equally important, they now implicated a large number of provincial activities. In the softwood lumber case, for example, it was provincial forest management practices which American interests contested. In 1988, it was provincial liquor pricing policies which attracted the ire of the GATT. An effective Canadian response to the external threat, therefore, required coordination among the Canadian governments, each of which brought somewhat differing interests to the table.

In the softwood lumber case, an arrangement was eventually reached. With provincial consent, Ottawa imposed an export tax on lumber. It was to remain in place until the provinces adjusted their own policies to the satisfaction of the Americans and, in the meantime, the proceeds were to be returned to the provinces.

The implications, however, were clear. Actions in the external environment were reaching to the provincial level and international third parties were now a new presence at the federal-provincial bargaining table. Better ways would have to be found to coordinate Canada's voice in these international arenas.

Region

There were strong grounds for anticipating a decline in the importance of regional tensions. On one hand, the decline of energy prices radically reduced the intensity of conflict between Ontario and the West. On the other, the capacity and will of the new federal government to manage the tensions seemed much enhanced by the national dimensions of its majority.

The new government moved quickly to restore harmony. The first step was to go a very long way to meeting Newfoundland's claim for jurisdiction over offshore oil and gas. It was enshrined in the Atlantic Accord of 1985. Only a year before, the Supreme Court had upheld federal jurisdiction. Now a new model of shared responsibility would be adopted, giving effect to an informal agreement between Brian Mulroney and Premier Peckford made before the election. Management of the off-shore resources would be the responsibility of a Canada-Newfoundland Offshore Petroleum Board, made up equally of federal and provincial nominees, with a neutral chairman. The means and pace of development would be decided by the Board, with federal paramountcy until such time as national self-sufficiency had been achieved; after that Newfoundland would be paramount. Ottawa would retain responsibility for taxes and Canadianization policy. Pricing would also be shared, with Ottawa again retaining the final word. Revenues, including all "provincial type" royalties and taxes, were to be treated as if they were on land. When – or if – revenues started to flow, Newfoundland would not lose equalization benefits; they would be phased out very gradually. Other benefits for the province included local preference rules for labour and supplies, concentration of research and development activities in the province, and creation of a $300 million development fund, three quarters of which would come from Ottawa. Similar provisions were extended to Nova Scotia. There could be no clearer indication of Mulroney's vision of renewed federalism; henceforth, offshore oil development would be developed according to provincial priorities.

The second specific grievance laid to rest was the hated NEP. (For a good narrative and analysis, see Hawkes and Pollard, 1987.) Lower prices meant that prices and revenues were now less contentious. The new government's market-based ideology, together with the desire for warmer relations with the private sector and foreign economic interests, meshed well with provincial and energy industry concerns.

The Western Accord was signed in March 1985. Henceforth, with a provision to allow intervention if prices escalated rapidly or supply was threatened, prices would be set by the market. Taxation of the industry would shift from taxes on gross revenues to taxes on profit. A host of taxes associated with the NEP, including the Petroleum and Gas Revenue Tax (PGRT), and the Petroleum Compensation Charge (PCC), were to be eliminated or quickly phased out. (Details in Hawkes and Pollard, 1987, p. 156.) The "PIP grants" would also be phased out, replaced by tax based-incentives, and the bias in favour of exploration on Canada lands would be eliminated.

The Western Accord was followed in November by an agreement among Ottawa, Alberta, Saskatchewan and B.C. deregulating natural gas prices. A related new Frontier Energy Policy was also aimed at stimulating private investment and ending the favourable treatment of PetroCanada and other Canadian-owned firms. The dismantling of the NEP responded to three sets of pressures – from the provinces, industry and the United States. With respect to federalism it marked, in the Prime Minister's words, "More than any other initiative of the federal government, the advent of reconciliation among Canadians and our progress toward renewed federalism". (Remarks at FMC on the Economy, Halifax, November, 1985).

But the agreements did not depend solely on the changed political climate; they depended equally on the international oil market. Rapidly rising prices forced government intervention in the 1970s, collapsing prices could have a similar effect. As the Western recession grew in response to the drop in 1985-86, with only a slight recovery later, voices were raised in the West for measures to save jobs and stimulate exploration and production. Saskatchewan Premier Grant Devine advocated a new minimum or "floor price" for oil, as did the Senate Energy Committee. Industry sources also called for a survival plan, including a proposal for Ottawa to enter long-term contracts at above-market prices to support development for the future. The changed environment was underlined by none other than the premier of Alberta, Don Getty: "If it is proven to me that the floor price or some kind of stabilization is necessary, I couldn't care less what's been said in the past" (In Hawkes and Pollard, p. 162). At the 1986 Premiers' Conference Alberta's call for a national rescue plan for the industry, including subsidies and price stabilization, was endorsed.

But Ottawa, having met one set of demands, was not in a position easily to reverse its direction, although it did hasten the elimination of the PGRT. The inability or reluctance to do more helped fuel a growing sentiment in Alberta that electing a Tory government did not automatically generate the hoped for economic benefits. But now the criticism was that Ottawa was not doing enough to help the West, not that it was robbing the region's resources.

A similar pattern developed with respect to western grain farmers, even harder hit by world over-supply and by the effects of subsidies in other countries. Pressure grew on Ottawa to help rescue them as well. Early in 1986, on the eve of a Saskatchewan election, it committed $1 billion to support farm incomes through a variety of measures. In 1987 it was predicted that more than half of farmers' incomes were to come from government. Yet farm bankruptcies, partly as a result of the hang-over of high debt from over-expansion in the 1970s, continued to climb.

The federal government saw its initiative for free trade with the United States, unveiled in the fall of 1985, as another way of alleviating regional tensions. Westerners and Maritimers had traditionally been the strongest advocates of free trade and their Premiers provided the strongest support for the Tory proposal. The federal government adopted the same reasoning as the Macdonald Commission (*Report*, Vol. I, Chap. 6). To put the final nails in the coffin of the National Policy would end the historic grievances rooted in the idea that resource producers were forced to sell their products in volatile world markets, or to artificially shielded domestic markets, while they were simultaneously required to pay higher prices to tariff-protected central Canadian manufacturers. Now, it was argued, this unfairness would be ended and each region would buy and sell where the price was best. Central power would no longer be used to distort the terms of trade among regions and Ottawa's ability to discriminate would be reduced.

The free trade debate again pitted Ontario against the West and the East. But this time Ottawa was lined up with the latter and the Quebec government, which had played a minor role in the energy battles of the 1970s, was also part of the free trade coalition. Even in Ontario, the business community, which historically had tended to support protection and the National Policy, was now committed to free trade with the U.S. Its fortunes were now at least as dependent on foreign, especially American, markets as on the domestic market. Indeed, as the debate unfolded, it focussed as much or more on class and other divisions as it did on region.

The free trade debate returned to other continuing themes. What was the link between unity within Canada and the country's relationship with the United States? Did the strengthening of north-south ties – and the final end to the National Policy with its dream of building an east-west economy – imply a weakening of the economic and, perhaps, other linkages among Canadians? Would it reduce the commitment to regional sharing? Would the rules of free trade mean that the federal role as nation-builder would be reduced? Would the capacity of the federal government to act as the balance-wheel, to redistribute resources from richer to poorer regions, and to promote regional development be eroded?

These were questions for the future. In the first years of its mandate, as it sought on the one hand to respond to the changing character of regional problems and on the other to consolidate its political support, especially in Quebec, the federal government, like its predecessors, engaged in the highly visible use of discretionary spending, whether in industrial grants or defence procurement. These also fostered interregional tensions. None did so more than the decision to locate service facilities for the F-18 fighter plane with Canadair in Montreal, rather than with the competing (and technically superior) bid from Bristol Aerospace, based in Winnipeg. The decision provoked a storm of protest in Manitoba, with echoes elsewhere. Once again it appeared to westerners that Ottawa was responsive to the electoral weight of central Canada.

Again, like its predecessors, the Mulroney government continued to tinker with regional development policy as traditionally defined. In the 1984 campaign the Conservatives had argued that the combining of DREE with Industry, Trade and Commerce into the Department of Regional Industrial Expansion, and the elimination of the Ministry of State for Economic and Regional Development by the short-lived Turner government, "left Canada's least developed regions without their traditional voice" and reduced "the importance attached by the federal government to the task of combatting regional disparity" (quoted in Savoie, 1986, p. 90). A Conservative government would give renewed attention to regional disparities, increasing the policy instruments available to deal with them and working much more closely with the provinces.

Once in office, the new government did not initially make any changes. Economic and Regional Development Agreements which had been negotiated with seven provinces remained in place and new ones were signed with Ontario, British Columbia and Quebec. They reflected the commitment to less emphasis on federal direct delivery and more on supporting the provinces (Savoie, 1985). Those "striking symbols of waste and mismanagement", the heavy water plants in Cape Breton, were finally closed and an "enriched" program of tax incentives announced for Cape Breton (Graham, 1986, p. 353).

The Mulroney government saw regional development as another area in which to demonstrate the virtues of the new federalism. After extensive discussions through the winter, the 11 governments endorsed a joint declaration which restated regional development as a central goal of federalism – to be an element in all fields of policy, from fiscal to trade and transportation – and which asserted the intergovernmental character of responsibility for regional development.

Many of the older dilemmas about regional policy remained: was it directed specifically at the poorest regions, or to be oriented to all regions; was it to be part of overall industrial policy, or a separate function; was it aimed at national efficiency and adjustment (including the promotion of mobility), or was it to concentrate on "place prosperity"? What were the appropriate federal and provincial roles, and to what extent should federal actions be shaped by provincial priorities? Did the new economic imperatives mean that we must pay less attention to regional, and interpersonal, redistribution? Was regional redistribution perpetuating, rather than curing, regional dependency, as the Forget Comission on Unemployment Insurance, appointed by the federal government, and the House Commission, established by Newfoundland, suggested? Was the logic of the new government's economic policy – with market incentives and free trade – fundamentally at odds with the political logic of responding to regional economic development needs? Such questions had fed the constant tinkering with regional development institutions since the 1960s. The process continued under the Tories as new, locally-based agencies were created in the Atlantic and Western regions (the Atlantic Opportunities Agency and the Western Diversification Fund), and DRIE underwent yet another transformation, to join with the Ministry of Science and Technology to become the Ministry of Industry, Science and Technology in 1988.

All these questions, along with fiscal restraint, meant that there was some question about the continued capacity for the federal government to act as the "shock absorber" for the federal system (Leslie, 1987). The coincidence of economic factors and the genuine federal commitment to national reconciliation had indeed attenuated regional conflict. It had by no means eliminated it.

Language: The End of Quebec Nationalism?

The Parti Québécois and the nationalism it represented never recovered from the defeats of the 1980 Referendum, the 1982 Constitution Act and the failure of their efforts to block it in the courts. Even before its defeat in 1985 by the Liberals under Robert Bourassa, morale, membership and, most important, internal party consensus on its fundamental rationale, Quebec sovereignty, had eroded. The party was wracked with internal dissension even as it continued to be the party of government in difficult economic circumstances. The contradiction between the character of the PQ as a social movement and as a conventional party which must trim its sails to maximize votes became more serious.

An increasingly exhausted Premier Levesque battled to bring the party back to a more moderate, étapiste position, forcing an internal party referendum in which his position won 95 percent of the votes cast. But the price was that many members and several leading ministers, including Jacques Parizeau and Camille Laurin, left the party. In September 1985, following a year of turmoil in his party over whether or not to pursue the grail of independence, René Levesque stepped down as leader. An era in which Canadian politics had been fascinated by the struggle between Levesque and Pierre Trudeau, each acting out on the national stage the two great traditions of thought about federalism in Quebec, was over. Graham Fraser wrote a fitting political epitaph:

> They burst into politics and government in the 1960s: Mr. Levesque, Mr. Trudeau and all those who joined and followed them. Now 25 years later, a year after Mr. Trudeau, Mr. Levesque is leaving. Paradoxically, it is in part thanks to his success that the next generation lacks the same passion and fascination. Chips have dropped off shoulders. Quebec now has the luxury of turning away from politics. The talented and ambitious are no longer fuelled by rage and humiliation. Not only have the battles over language and pride been largely won, Pierre-Marc Johnson's classmates now have opportunities that Mr. Levesque's classmates never had. What sometimes looks like the failure of a dream is perhaps the price of success.
> (Graham Fraser, *The Globe and Mail*, 27 October, 1985)

Levesque's successor as leader of the PQ, Pierre-Marc Johnson, son of the former Union nationale Premier, took the position that sovereignty was to be a long term goal, an insurance policy for the future; for the moment the party would concentrate on a "national affirmation" not greatly different from that of Mr. Bourassa. But he, too, made little headway and finally resigned in 1987 to be replaced by PQ Finance Minister Jacques Parizeau, who renewed the commitment to independence. Now, however, there seemed to be little general support for the dream.

Thus, the wave of nationalism which had dominated Quebec politics for a generation seemed to be spent and was not likely to be revived for a considerable time. What accounts for this turn of events? There are two broad but contradictory answers.

First, the decline of Quebec nationalism could be seen as the consequence of failure. Enormous energy had been spent in the run-up to the referendum and, again, in the battle against patriation in 1980-81. The outcome of those negotiations had been disastrous. English Canada had rejected not only the ideals of the PQ but also the essentials of a reformed federalism which had been advocated by every Quebec government in the modern era. There was no recognition of Quebec as a distinct society, or of its government as the primary political instrument of a people. There was neither a general devolution of power to the provinces nor a specific recognition of "special status". The new amending formula did not mention the long-standing Quebec claim to a veto. The language rights provisions promised to undermine the Quebec government's capacity to shape the province's own linguistic environment and were soon followed by a number of successful court challenges to Bill 101. Most telling, perhaps, was that the new constitution had been achieved over the direct objections of the Quebec government; it now seemed that Quebec could be excluded with impunity. Despite fruitless rear-guard actions – a continued court challenge, a withdrawal of Quebec from participation in many intergovernmental forums, and passage of legislation subjecting all Quebec laws to the "notwithstanding" provisions of the Charter of Rights – there was no wave of hostile public opposition to the constitutional dénouement. The reaction, rather, appeared to be one of resignation and exhaustion. It would be a long time before the advocates of independence could summon the energy to fight again.

If failure it was, there were many explanations at hand. The loss of PQ support could be interpreted less as a rejection of independence than a simpler reaction of the electorate against a party grown tired in power. A party which, saddled with the task of governing in an extraordinarily difficult period, was unable to maintain the committed coalition essential to achieve its primary goal. Economic pressures forced the government into budget restraint measures which directly attacked some of the chief elements of its nationalist coalition, notably the public and para-public sectors and the trade unions.

The economic insecurities of the time were hostile to the kind of political adventure embodied in the PQ project. Despite the "battle of the balance sheets" the party was unable to convince enough Quebecers that Confederation hobbled Quebec's economic growth, or that independence could be achieved without economic cost. The PQ had been born in a period of rapid economic growth. It was a product not only of traditional Quebec grievances but also of affluence, and the optimism that permitted. Its appeal declined as economic uncertainty increased.

Moreover, it was also a product of the period when, in all western societies, there was tremendous confidence in the capacity of governments to mould and shape society, to be the instrument of popular will, the benign instrument of change. By the mid-1970s this optimism had vanished in many countries, but not in Quebec. The euphoria after November 15, 1976 was fuelled by the faith that anything was possible. Such confidence in the role of the state was essential to the new nationalism. It was no longer rooted in a set of distinctive religious or cultural values, nor in the idea of a simple partnership of French- and English-speaking Canadians. Rather, it was defined in terms of the *political* category of *les québécois*. It not only required a strong Quebec state, but also depended on faith in that state for its own legitimacy. When Quebecers lost confidence in the capacity of the state, the credibility of a state-based nationalism declined as well, and it now had no other powerful body of ideas on which to fall back. In addition, the PQ was born in a period when independence and self-determination were dominating ideas; it died as an independence movement when global interdependence had become the dominating idea. Now, the emphasis had shifted from opportunity to constraint.

Ultimately Quebecers were convinced that they could not negotiate successfully the divorce and remarriage which sovereignty-association implied. English Canadians could not accept the blow to their own national identity. Nor could they accept a two-unit confederacy, with its implication that crucial economic decisions would be made in an equal partnership of two countries differing so greatly in population and wealth.

But a quite different interpretation might also be offered. The decline of Quebec nationalism was also a consequence of success. The grievances which fuelled the search for a "new deal" between Canada and Quebec had been met to a surprising degree.

In the 1960s, the Royal Commission on Bilingualism and Biculturalism starkly demonstrated the differences in incomes between French- and English-speaking employees. Within Quebec, francophones were at the bottom of the economic heap. The economic elite in Quebec, and especially Montreal, was overwhelmingly English-speaking. Management positions were dominated by the minority and French-speaking Canadians who wanted to progress had to "hang up their language with their hat" every morning. By the mid-1980s, linguistic disparities in average incomes had disappeared (Vaillancourt, 1985). Francophones had entered the management ranks of anglophone firms, which in turn used French much more often in their internal operations. More important, francophone-owned firms, often with strong initial assistance from Quebec government agencies, had emerged to play a vital role in the economic life of the province and of Canada as a whole. What the state had helped make possible now rendered the state less necessary.

Similarly, in the 1960s much of the public face of Montreal had been anglophone and a high proportion of immigrants had been assimilating into the anglophone milieu. Successive Quebec language laws had changed that too. The sense of linguistic insecurity among francophones had substantially declined, although it had by no means disappeared.

Other grievances had been at least partly redressed as well. As a result of the Official Languages Act, the work of the Commissioner of Official Languages, and other measures, the federal government was now much better equipped to serve its French-speaking citizens. The proportion of francophones at the upper levels of the civil service had increased. The Liberals had made good on their promise to increase "French power" in Ottawa. Throughout the 1970s many of the most powerful Ministers, Marc Lalonde, Jean Chrétien and others, were Quebecers. The PQ argument that Ottawa was no more than the national government of English Canadians and that Quebec interests would always be sacrificed in a majoritarian Parliament now had less credibility.

Furthermore, it was difficult to sustain the argument that federalism had been a strait-jacket for Quebec in the 1960s and 1970s. None of Quebec's initiatives in social and economic policy had been blocked by the constitution. "Nation-building" whether in language policy or creation of new state enterprises had proceeded within the framework of Confederation. And while it was true that the constitution still did not recognize Quebec's distinctive character, a number of political changes consistent with that position had been made. Regular First Ministers' meetings, the annual Premiers' Conference, and a federal-provincial secretariat – all of which had been on the agenda for change enunciated by Premier Lesage in the 1960s – were now established features of the intergovernmental scene. Opting-out, Established Programs Financing, provincial variations in federal programs such as youth allowances, and a provincial role in immigration procedures all addressed concerns raised by Quebec. If they had by no means met the more expansive goals of nationalists, these changes had indeed altered the face of Canadian federalism.

Finally, it would be wrong to suggest that the choice for Quebecers was simply between head and heart, profitable federalism against equality and independence. Quebecers, it turned out, had positive attachments to both the provincial and the national community.

From this perspective, the outcome of the referendum and the constitutional battles represents not defeat, but affirmation. René Levesque and Pierre Trudeau, for all their passionate struggle, were complementary forces. Arising from the same postwar intellectual ferment in Quebec, each had helped make the success of the other possible, and each had helped shape contemporary Canadian federalism. The drive went out of the independence movement because so many of its fundamental premises had been achieved within Confederation.

Each of these interpretations was persuasive for different groups and individuals – the "moderates" accepted the success story and those still committed to full independence held to some version of the story of failure – but the common denominator was reduced interest in further efforts to promote the program of the PQ.

The future evolution of Quebec nationalism remains unclear, but we are not writing its epitaph. Some form of ethnic community-based politics has characterized Quebec political life from the beginning, changing in light of changes within Quebec society and in its economic and political relations with the rest of the country. It is virtually inconceivable that Canadian politics and the evolution of Canadian federalism will not continue to be shaped by the relationships between French- and English-language groups, and between Quebec and the other governments in Canada. Quebec's low birth-rate, the continuing assimilation of many immigrants into anglophone Quebec, and Quebec's declining proportion of both the Canadian and North American population will ensure that fears for linguistic survival, and the need for government to ensure it, will never be far below the surface, even of an affluent, outward-looking Quebec.

Tom Courchene (1986) has suggested that the energies and ambitions of Quebecers are being channelled increasingly into the private sector and toward more personal sources of achievement. The newest phase of Quebec nationalism, he argues, might be called "market nationalism", reflecting the political and cultural ascendency of a newly self-confident and successful francophone business class. The model for the new Quebecer to emulate was "no longer the arch-bishop or even the deputy-minister", but the "entrepreneur" (Leslie, 1987, p. 84). Brian Mulroney and the new wave of Quebec MPs he brought to Ottawa had strong links with this class; so did the Bourassa Liberals. While policies such as the highly successful Quebec stock savings plan (an innovation of PQ finance minister Jacques Parizeau), huge export-oriented hydro-electric projects, and institutions such as the Caisse would remain in place, the Bourassa government was the first since Lesage not to see a powerful Quebec state as the chief instrument of Quebec's economic advance. A series of reports and studies prepared for the new government committed the province to a market orientation, including deregulation, cutbacks to the welfare state and reduced public spending. In fact, the process of adopting an "incentive-oriented, entrepreneurial or people's capitalism", Courchene points out, had begun in the last years of the PQ government. It represented an "integrated strategy...for the control of economic institutions by Québécois, and from a location within Quebec, namely Montreal" (quoted in Leslie, 1987, p. 85).

Public pump-priming, however, was not excluded. There were strong pressures on the Mulroney government to support these ambitions. The province wanted – and got – assistance to maintain the petro-chemical industry in Montreal, a massive loan to General Motors to keep open its plant in Ste. Thérèse and, most controversially, a massive contract to service new jet fighters to Canadair in Montreal, after an expert panel had recommended it go to Winnipeg-based Bristol Aerospace.

Quebec's new openness, and its orientation to global and American opportunities, was reflected in the powerful support Premier Bourassa lent to the free trade initiative, which allied him with the federal Tories and against the national Liberals. The deep fears about independence and cultural autonomy which the agreement tapped in English Canada seemed to have little expression in Quebec. Jacques Parizeau, elected leader of the PQ in 1987, was equally committed to free trade at least partly because reducing Quebec's reliance on the pan-Canadian market would, in the long run, minimize the economic costs of Quebec independence.

Despite these new orientations, Quebec's exclusion from the Constitutional Accord of 1981-82 continued to rankle. It was widely believed that the legitimacy of the Constitution Act, 1982, would be forever suspect if means were not found to bring Quebec in voluntarily. The implications of the Charter for the goal of making Quebec a predominantly francophone society remained controversial. Outside Quebec, preoccupation with Quebec had virtually vanished after the events of 1981-82. But "bringing Quebec back in" or "completing the circle" as the aboriginals had phrased their goal, was a central objective for the new federal government. Confederation was incomplete without that. Any further constitutional change could be frustrated by Quebec's refusal to participate. The longer-run fear was that in any renewal of nationalist pressure, the "imposition" of the new constitution on Quebec would be a potent rallying cry.

Thus, both Mulroney and Bourassa had strong reasons for renewing the constitutional dialogue, and there was much common ground between them. Yet both were sensitive to the dangers of reviving passions so recently cooled and to the risk of raising hopes only to fail again. The federal side had to reckon with the now firmly-established view that all provinces must receive equal treatment, and with the complacency about Quebec which meant few would be willing to pay a high price for its support. The Quebec side had to recognize the continuing danger of being outflanked by the nationalists and a repeat of the humiliating turn-around Bourassa had to make in 1971. Thus, initial discussions were private and low key, first on a bilateral basis and then in private meetings with other provinces.

The Quebec Liberals' 1985 election platform, *Mastering Our Future*, argued that "nothing less than Quebec's dignity is at stake" and committed the government to "negotiate a constitutional agreement which will restore to Quebec its proper place in the Canadian federation" (in Leslie, 1987, p. 77).

In May 1986 Quebec's Minister of Intergovernmental Affairs, Gil Remillard, set out "Quebec's conditions for participating in a new constitutional accord" at a conference of officials and academics. Quebec was ready to negotiate with its "federal partners... . But we want to negotiate with partners who first indicate to us concretely their desire to rectify the injustice that the Constitution Act of 1982 represents for Quebec" (Leslie, 1986, pp. 97-105). He then set out Quebec's five conditions: recognition of Quebec as a distinct society; constitutionally extended powers in immigration; limitation of the federal spending power; the right to veto constitutional amendments; and a role in appointing judges of the Supreme Court of Canada (Leslie, 1986, p. 99).

Mulroney responded quickly. He appointed Senator Lowell Murray, who had voted against the 1982 settlement because it excluded Quebec, as Minister of State for Federal-Provincial relations with responsibility for the Accord. He worked closely with the new Secretary to the Cabinet for Federal-Provincial relations, Norman Spector, to lay the groundwork with the other provinces. To reopen the issue, and to fail, would be worse than leaving it alone. At the 1987 Premiers' Conference, Bourassa's colleagues agreed to place Quebec's concerns at the top of the constitutional agenda. Meanwhile the federal New Democrats, anxious to cement their growing strength in Quebec, had developed a position broadly similar to the evolving agreement. So had the federal Liberals, although not without much internal dissension as the "new guard" of Quebec Liberals, led by John Turner's Quebec Lieutenant, Raymond Garneau, contended with those still faithful to the Trudeau model. Thus the stage was set for the First Ministers to gather at Meech Lake in April 1987.

Outside Quebec, the most bitter language dispute of the decade occurred in Manitoba. In 1979, the repudiation of its constitutional obligations dating from 1890 finally came home to roost when the Supreme Court ruled the 1890 Act *ultra vires* of the provincial legislature. This meant that all Manitoba's laws were to be passed in both French and English. In order to avoid having to reenact all the legislation passed since 1890, the Manitoba NDP government tried to find a political solution, trading improved French-language services for the need to translate a century's worth of statutes. The attempt failed in the face of massive hostility mobilized by the provincial Tories. In 1984, Robert Bilodeau challenged the validity of a traffic ticket. The appeal in his case was combined with a federal reference seeking a comprehensive ruling on the status of all Manitoba's laws. In 1985, the Supreme Court duly held that the laws were all unconstitutional, and gave the province several years to translate them all (Hogg, 1985, pp. 812-813; Pollard, 1986, pp. 207-216). Manitoba's denial of French language rights had been repeated in Saskatchewan and Alberta when they became provinces. Language rights in the Northwest Territories Act had been like those in Manitoba, and in 1988 the Supreme Court held that these rights had not been extinguished when the new provincial regimes were created. However, since they had been enshrined in legislation rather than in the constitution, they were subject to legislative action. Thus it was open to the provinces to enact new provisions. Saskatchewan did so, removing the language commitment and agreeing to translate only a few statutes. Western francophones argued that this was a repudiation of an historic, if unenforced, commitment and that it constituted a violation at least in spirit of the Meech Lake injunction for all governments to "preserve" minority language rights. Saskatchewan Premier Grant Devine replied that his limited concessions were an advance over the practice of the previous decades. Similar debates occurred over the use of French in Alberta.

New Brunswick, the model of provincial bilingualism, was also the scene of bitter linguistic controversy. 1984 saw the report of the Task Force appointed to review progress under the province's official bilingualism policy. The Bastarache Report demonstrated continued underrepresentation of francophones in the public service and called for affirmative action to redress the balance. Public meetings held across the province to explain the findings and seek reaction were the scene of ugly confrontations, focussed on anglophone fears of the loss of employment oppprtunities, especially in light of civil service cut-backs (Pollard, 1986, pp. 196-99).

In Quebec, anglophone groups were among the most ardent opponents of the Meech Lake Accord, believing it would legitimate further attacks on their language rights in the name of preserving and promoting Quebec's distinct society. In Ontario the new Liberal government edged closer to making the province officially bilingual, but refused to take the final plunge. All these developments reinforced the sense that only in Quebec did francophone Canadians constitute a secure community; and this in turn legitimated the claim to distinct status.

Meech Lake

The Constitutional Accord, 1987, was finally signed by all eleven First Ministers in the early morning of June 2, 1988 following a marathon session that had begun the previous day. The debate it sparked replayed all the themes which had driven constitutional discussion since the 1960s (*Canadian Public Policy*, 1988; Rogerson and Swinton, 1988; Schwartz, 1988; *Queen's Quarterly*, 1988). The answer the Accord gave to the question of how to define the relations between French and English Canadians was a marked shift from the position so long espoused by Prime Minister Trudeau and enshrined in the Constitution Act, 1982. It constitutionalized the Quebec-centered model.

The Accord began with a new interpretive clause defining Canadian dualism simultaneously as the presence throughout Canada of French- and English-speaking Canadians – one group centered in Quebec, but also present elsewhere, the other centered outside Quebec, but also present in the province. It defined Quebec as a distinct society within Confederation. It required that the constitution be interpreted in a manner consistent with these fundamental facts. It also charged all governments to "preserve" national dualism. Quebec, and not the federal government, is further given responsibility for "promoting" its distinct identity. However, any transfer of jurisdiction associated with this role is explicitly excluded. The only transfer of responsibility in the Accord is a constitutionalizing, and extension, of earlier agreements between Quebec and Ottawa concerning immigration.

The Quebec veto over constitutional changes was restored, partly by extending the range of matters for which unanimity would be required in the future, and partly by extending the right of fiscal compensation for a province which does not participate in a transfer of powers to Ottawa. Both principles had been inserted in the constitution in 1982. Quebec's concerns about the structure of the Supreme Court were met by constitutionalizing the requirement that three of the judges must come from Quebec and by requiring that the federal government select judges from provincial nominations. Quebec's historic desire to restrict the federal spending power, a matter of almost constant debate since World War II, was partially met through a provision stating that provinces may opt-out, with compensation, of new national shared-cost programs in areas of provincial jurisdiction. But there was the important proviso that to qualify for compensation the province must establish its own programs "compatible with the national objectives". Thus, on the one hand Quebec made an important concession, accepting the constitutional legitimacy of the federal spending power; on the other it constitutionalized the right to opt out under certain circumstances. Quebec's long-standing interest in institutionalizing federal-provincial relations was met through provisions establishing a requirement of annual First Ministers Conferences on the economy and on constitutional matters.

Quebec's essential conditions, set out a year earlier, had been achieved. "Today", said the Prime Minister at the formal signing ceremony, "we welcome Quebec back to the Canadian constitutional family... . And tomorrow we get on with the business of building a new Canada... ." Replied Premier Robert Bourassa, "It is with much pride and a certain emotion that we accept, and that we express our profound satisfaction and joy to reintegrate with the Canadian constitution."

While Quebec nationalists felt the Accord did not go far enough, and especially criticized the spending power provision for explicitly recognizing the idea that Ottawa could act in areas of exclusive provincial jurisdiction, the Accord was quickly ratified in Quebec. In the House of Commons, the Accord was endorsed by both the Liberal and the NDP leaders. Both parties saw flaws in the Accord, but argued that the achievement of securing Quebec's voluntary consent outweighed any weaknesses.

The Liberals, however, were deeply split. The thrust of the Accord, if not its still unknown practical consequences, was a repudiation of Pierre Trudeau's vision of Quebec in Canada. It appeared to give only grudging recognition to linguistic minorities and national bilingualism, while accepting the fundamental Quebec nationalist premise of the province as a distinct society, with the Quebec government having a special, if limited, role in promoting it. Mr. Trudeau denounced the Accord as a craven sell-out to provincialism and as a giant first step down the slippery slope towards independence.

All provincial Premiers signed the Accord and pledged themselves to ratify it. It was carefully designed to ensure that the principle of provincial equality, entrenched in the 1982 amending formula, was maintained. Thus, the unanimity and opting-out rules were extended to all provinces, as was the right to nominate Senators and judges. Moreover, provisions such as those on the spending power and entrenching FMCs responded to a provincialist as well as a Quebec agenda. Several other provincial concerns, notably Senate reform, were inscribed on the agenda for the annual FMCs on the constitution.

Nevertheless, there were serious provincial misgivings, and these crystallized as time passed and provincial elections began to change the leaders at the table. The Liberals, under Premier Frank McKenna, swept the Hatfield Conservatives out of office in New Brunswick. The new government, especially concerned that the rights of New Brunswick francophones might be undermined, announced it would not ratify the agreement without important changes. In Manitoba the New Democrats were defeated and a minority Conservative government came to power with a revitalized provincial Liberal party holding the balance of power. Its Leader, Sharon Carstairs, denounced the Accord, and pledged to ensure it would not be passed. By the summer of 1988, however, eight provinces had ratified the Accord. Once again, the unanimity rule which had bedevilled previous rounds of constitution-making, and which was now a central part of the amending formula, made it clear that change could be achieved only with a very high degree of consensus.

The debate on the Accord recapitulated all the debates on language and federalism we have described throughout this work. It gave constitutional entrenchment to many of the practices of federalism which grew up through this period. For example, "opting-out" had been practised by Duplessis, but at considerable cost to his province; it was legislated in the opting-out legislation of the 1960s; it was constitutionalized for the first time in the 1982 amending formula; and now it was extended. Successive Quebec governments had put forward the notion of Quebec as a distinct society; now it was constitutionally legitimated. The spending power had always been exercised with great sensitivity to provincial concerns; now that, too, was written down in the constitutional document. Quebec representation on the Supreme Court was part of the federal Supreme Court Act; now it was part of the constitution. First Ministers Conferences, as we have seen, have long been an important policy-making forum, nowhere mentioned in the constitution; now they were. So in one sense the Accord could be seen as little more than formalizing existing law and practice. For its defenders, it represents the successful resolution of long-standing issues, reforging both symbolically and constitutionally the fundamental linguistic accommodation. Hence it lays the groundwork for the creative adaptation of federalism to the new problems that the country faces, unburdened by the weight of past, unresolved conflicts.

But in another sense it can be seen as repudiating the more recent thrust of constitutional change. 1982 had rejected the Quebec-centered model and had enacted the Charter of Rights. The Charter placed national dualism above the Quebec-centered model and generally emphasized individual rights over collective ones. Both concepts were hostile to the concept of distinct society. Opponents of the Accord feared that if courts were required to interpret the constitution, especially section 1, in light of Quebec's role in promoting its distinct society, then individual rights in the Charter might be undermined. For example, the Quebec anglophone community, among the bitterest critics of Meech Lake, argued that Quebec could be allowed a freer hand to promote the security of the French language in Quebec at the expense of anglophone linguistic rights. From this perspective, then, Meech Lake does not so much transcend the past as tie us even more firmly to it.

In the 1980s, then, the intensity of conflict between Quebec and Ottawa declined dramatically from earlier periods. The causes lie primarily in the internal shifts of opinion, notably the demise of state-based nationalism, in Quebec. But they also lie in the change in the federal stance towards Quebec, from one which rejected the basic premises of Quebec's legal distinctiveness to one which accepted them. By 1988 the legitimacy of the federal system in Quebec seemed less in question than at any time since the onset of the Quiet Revolution.

Class, Gender and Native Peoples

Meech Lake was a response to the classic and continuing dilemmas of the federal society and the operation of federal institutions. It was aimed at ending the constitutional isolation of Quebec while also meeting some traditional concerns of the other provinces, especially the desire to remove the capacity of national majorities, or the central government, to infringe on their fundamental powers and interests. It affirmed dualism and the distinct society and made adjustments to the operation of federal institutions – the Supreme Court and Senate, the spending power and executive federalism. All these were matters which had been on the constitutional agenda since the 1960s. The constitutional controversy it engendered was the familiar one of centralization versus decentralization, a province- or a nation-centered federalism.

But as we saw in the previous chapter, the constitutional agenda was now much broader. It was no longer only about federalism. The Charter of Rights and Freedoms had introduced a broad new pillar to the Canadian constitutional framework. It had given much greater prominence both to the concept of individual rights and to the constitutional recognition of identities and interests other than those of region and province – women, aboriginal Canadians, Canadians of multi-cultural origin, and others.

The Meech Lake debate demonstrated that the politicization of these groups, and the symbolic importance of their inscription in the Canadian constitutional order, had fundamentally changed the character of constitutional politics. By far the most telling criticism of the Accord derived from just these groups.

Throughout this study we have sought to explore the implications of federalism for non-territorial interests. We have criticized those who saw in the emergence of modern industrial society the obsolescence of federalism, and shown that those who predicted the "displacement" of federal divisions by the "modern" and "creative" politics of class were proven wrong. But we have also noted that both federal society and federal institutions did inhibit the mobilization of new divisions and did place hurdles, though not insurmountable ones, to the response of governments to their concerns. Thus, federalism both slowed the adoption of welfare state policies in Canada and greatly affected the form they took, the language in which they were debated, and the level of government by which they were delivered. In turn, we have seen how the mobilization of new groups, and the policy thrusts they articulated, also helped shape the character of the modern federal state.

The tensions between the territorial and non-territorial dimensions of Canadian politics were central to the Meech Lake debate. The revolt of women's groups against their exclusion from the late-night agreement in November 1981, and their successful mobilization to restore the equal rights clause, had been a catalytic event in the politicization of gender in Canada. It left women's groups sensitive to the implications of constitutional politics and highly suspicious of the process of executive federalism. Not surprisingly, therefore, they emerged as the most articulate critics of Meech Lake. Their chief concern was that the entrenchment of the distinct society clause as a new interpretive principle might be used to undermine the hard-won guarantees of the Charter. Could the desire of some future Quebec government to promote its population growth, for example, infringe on women's equality? From this perspective what was needed was a strengthening of the Charter, by removing the notwithstanding clause, for example, not its weakening. For some commentators, such as Peter Hogg and William Lederman, such fears were unwarranted, but in the nature of things there could be no certainty until the clause was tested in the courts.

Especially in the postwar period, "progressive" movements in Canada have often looked first to the federal government for redress, largely on the grounds that it has had the resources and at least the potential capacity to ensure national standards. Hence, women's groups were concerned that the limitation on the federal spending power in S. 106A might weaken the federal capacity to introduce new social programs or to ensure nation-wide standards. For some these fears were justified, as a proposed new federal strategy for promoting day care was to be operated jointly with the provinces.

Women's groups also mounted a strong attack on the process by which Meech Lake was achieved. They, and many other critics, argued that it was a classic example of federal and provincial governments meeting behind closed doors to exclude alternative interests and arrange matters in their own interest. For this reason, women's groups were also hostile to the future role for executive federalism implied by the provisions for annual FMCs. Similarly, they were suspicious that provincial nomination of judges would sensitize the court to regional perspectives to the possible exclusion of other concerns and other bases of representation.

The failure of the Meech Lake Accord to extend recognition to communities which did not fall within the traditional concerns of the federal system was particularly poignant in the case of Canada's aboriginal peoples. The Meech Lake agreement came only a few weeks after the failure of the final Conference instructed by the 1982 Accord to find a formula for entrenchment of aborginal rights in the constitution. Native groups had been represented in these conferences, but no compromise could be found between the aboriginal claim for a substantial measure of self-government and the concerns of several provinces that the implications for their programs, revenues and jurisdiction were so great that the parameters of self-government must be fully negotiated before they could be entrenched. Understandably bitter aboriginal leaders contended that the white governments could settle their own affairs but lacked the commitment to do the same for them.

Canada's multicultural groups had also found some recognition in the 1982 settlement. They, too, criticized Meech Lake because it seemed to enshrine the dualism of French and English Canada as the fundamental sociological fact of the Canadian community, relegating the multi-cultural dimension to a lesser role. While the practical consequences would probably be minor, and while the Mulroney government passed a Multiculturalism Act celebrating Canadians' ethnic diversity, the criticism underlined how much the constitutional agenda had expanded and how important its symbolic aspects had become.

These perspectives on Meech Lake suggested, just as Porter, Horowitz and others had in an earlier period, that there is a fundamental disjunction between the society constitutionalized in the federal state, which represents and privileges territorial interests and identities, and an emerging society in which territory may be far less salient. While many critics sought a reconciliation between the distinct society notion and the individual rights of the Charter, and while others denied there was any real danger of a contradiction, there could be no denying the profound logical tension between the two concepts.

As we have shown, such tensions are not new. They are to be found in all Canadian constitutional documents, from the Constitution Act, 1867, to the Constitution Act, 1982. Successive constitutional documents have expanded the competing concepts and shuffled the cards among them differently. But they have always left it to the political process, including (now more than ever) the courts, to define the relationships and the accommodations over time. We have added new concepts of community, identity and citizenship, but we have not displaced older ones. Instead, we have woven them together in a complex web. And while emerging movements have often challenged federalism, it is also true that federalism at its heart legitimates the concept of a Canada based on diverse communities, at once autonomous and part of the whole – a model which in recent years has helped legitimate such newer concerns as multi-culturalism and aboriginal self-government.

If the new movements challenged the institutions and practices of federalism, so in the Mulroney period federalism continued to interact with the politics of class-based economic divisions. As Keith Banting observes, "basic structural changes in the economies of western nations and ideological shifts have transformed the politics of the welfare state". (1987, p. 21). The dominant pattern in this period has been "the dreary process of restraint and retrenchment, for the most part incremental, but occasionally more dramatic" (p. 11).

As a result, these were also difficult times for organized labour. Its primary task was to preserve as many of the gains of the previous generation as possible. In this, Canadian labour leaders appeared to be much more successful than their counterparts in the United States and the United Kingdom, where union density fell dramatically and the political power of trade unions was sharply curbed.

The new federal government was not bent on a Thatcherite revolution for Canada, despite its market orientation. The government quickly backed down in the face of popular mobilization after it announced early in its term that it would limit the rate of increase in Old Age Security. It established a Royal Commission on Unemployment Insurance, the Forget Commission, which recommended, among other things, the elimination of extended regional benefits in order to minimize its redistributive effects and cast it more as a true insurance system. But the government did not adopt this recommendation. While some highly visible and contentious spending cuts were made, the government relied at least as much on increased taxation in its only-partially-successful battle against the budget deficit.

The government's market orientation was most dramatically displayed in the free trade initiative. Trade unions feared that a completely open border would in the long run greatly increase the power of mobile capital over static labour and would set in motion pressures for harmonization with American policies which would be likely to erode some of Canada's more progressive social and taxation policies. Thus trade unions were among the leaders of the coalition of groups which mobilized to attack the agreement.

It was at the provincial level, and especially in the western provinces hard hit by the recession and the subsequent slow recovery, that restraint cut most deeply. As before, class conflict was most evident at the provincial level and some of the provincial governments manifested the most thorough-going neo-conservative positions. Thus, in British Columbia, Alberta and Saskatchewan, further legislation limiting trade union power was introduced in this period (See Panitch and Schwartz, 1985, p. 1988). Similar battles were fought in Quebec and Newfoundland. Several provinces introduced draconian cuts in services and in public service employment. As Banting points out "virtually all provinces curtailed other aspects of their social assistance programs: eligibility rules were made more restrictive...payments for special needs were reduced and in some cases eliminated; and more aggressive monitoring and enforcement procedures were put in place" (1987, p. 189). But the patterns were by no means uniform. The new Liberal minority government in Ontario, flush with buoyant revenues and bound by an agreement with the NDP, was particularly active in many areas of social legislation, including path-breaking pay equity legislation.

The complexities of federalism have in the past been understood as a mild brake on development of the welfare state. In the 1980s most "innovation" in social policy was aimed at restraining its growth, redirecting it towards the promotion of increased efficiency, targetting its spending more effectively and experimenting with alternative delivery systems. Banting suggests that this altered climate allows us to test two distinct meanings of the proposition that federalism is a "conservative" force. It could limit "progressive" expansion or, alternatively, it could restrain change in either direction. His tentative conclusion is that the evidence of the 1980s suggests that federalism "constrains both rapid expansion and contraction in the scope of state activity". It complicates the task of radical movements whether of the left or the right, and the process of federal-provincial negotiation "diversifies the range of interests and ideologies that are brought to bear" (p. 206).

Banting also argues that in a period of retrenchment the federal government is likely to be more constrained than the provinces. The federal government has a more diverse constituency and must balance a greater range of interests. Therefore, it is less likely than more homogeneous provinces to be captured by a single interest. A greater proportion of federal spending is found in statutory transfers to individuals and provinces, which are politically difficult to change. Ottawa's role as regional balance wheel means that equalization and regional development spending is difficult to cut. Ottawa's control over fiscal and monetary policy places it under less harsh budgetary constraints than the provinces. And when the federal government does consider cuts in programs such as Unemployment Insurance, the effect is to push additional costs on to provinces and to damage constituencies that have the ear of provincial governments. Therefore, provinces (of whatever ideological stripe) are likely to join the chorus opposing them. On the other hand, cuts at the provincial level do not create the same incentives for Ottawa. Indeed they reduce its obligations under the Canada Assistance Plan. Accordingly, the provinces, if they are so inclined, are freer than the federal government to move in a conservative direction and the federal government has little incentive to try to stop them. The interaction between federalism and the agendas suggested by labour and by class divisions therefore remain complex. In this period, neither labour nor the NDP mobilized to attack trends in federalism, such as the Meech Lake Accord.

Federal State

Throughout the postwar period the scope of intergovernmental relations and their role in the policy-making process has become increasingly important. The fundamental reason lies in the extraordinary interdependence of federal and provincial governments, coupled with the salience of regional divisions and the political weight of both orders of government, which has precluded massive transfers of responsibility from one to the other. But the growth of intergovernmental relations, and its distinctive Canadian form of executive federalism has, as we have seen, generated a number of dilemmas. On one hand have been questions of efficacy and effectiveness: how has federalism affected the ability of Canadian governments to respond to the policy challenges facing the country? On the other hand, there have been questions of democratic accountability. Is the intergovernmental process consistent with the norms and values of responsible parliamentary government?

In the previous chapter we saw that the 1980-84 Trudeau government responded with at least a partial no to each of these questions. It sought to reassert federal power and check what it saw as a drift to provincialism which was undermining Canada's policy effectiveness. Further, it sought to establish a more direct accountability between the federal government and Canadian citizens. It adopted a more competitive style of intergovernmental relations, seeking to deemphasize cooperative federalism.

In its turn, the Mulroney government promised to restore harmonious intergovernmental relations by reinstating collaborative federalism at the heart of the governing process. It moved quickly to bring provinces "inside the circumference of federal-policy-making" and to honour the promise of the Sept Isles Speech. The provinces, the government stated at the November 1985 First Ministers Conference, were to be involved in national policy-making as "trusted partners in the business of managing the federation, partners equally dedicated to its unity and prosperity" (quoted in Milne, 1986, p. 221). Said the Prime Minister: "I believe in a federalist state you should govern, to the extent humanly possible, in harmony with the provinces" (quoted in Graham, p. 391). There was a veritable explosion of intergovernmental meetings at all levels. There had been an annual average of five First Ministers' Conferences between 1980 and 1984; in the first year of the Mulroney mandate, there were 13. There were 353 Ministerial meetings, compared to an annual average of 82 in the previous four years, and 72 Deputy Ministers meetings, compared with an average of 45 in the previous period. Many more of the meetings were now held outside Ottawa, more of them concentrated on the provinces' agenda, and more were chaired by provincial ministers or officials.

This commitment to cooperative federalism was manifested in a wide variety of policy areas. In fiscal federalism, for example, the government's desire to reduce spending clashed directly with its desire not to antagonize the provinces. They were insulated from the first round of budget cuts, but in the Tories' first budget in May 1985, the Finance Minister announced Ottawa's intention to limit the rate of growth of fiscal transfers "in order to effect savings amounting to about $2 billion in 1990-91" with the "place and manner of achieving these savings" to be the subject of future discussions. Despite provincial protests, Ottawa persisted. The rate of increase in EPF payments would no longer be tied to inflation, but rather to the rate of growth in GNP, less two percent.

Tax reform was also high on the government's agenda. The government sought to simplify the income tax system, reducing marginal rates while closing loopholes, and to move towards a comprehensive national sales tax. The close integration of federal and provincial tax systems, one of the achievements of the federal system, meant that it was "inconceivable that comprehensive reform could proceed in Canada without intensive consultation with and, indeed, the substantial agreement of, the provinces" (Stewart, 1987, p. 122). It was necessary to ensure that the provinces would not occupy any new tax room opened by the federal reform. More important, given the presence and variations in existing provincial sales taxes, any new integrated National Sales Tax would, whatever its advantages in economic efficiency and ease of compliance for tax-payers, await federal-provincial agreement.

Similarly, post-secondary education remained on the national agenda. In the spring of 1985 A. W. Johnson, a former senior federal official who had been commissioned by the previous government, issued a report which supported those who argued that provinces were "diverting" post-secondary education transfers to other purposes. The actual federal share of the operating costs of the institutions, he calculated, ranged from 60 percent to 107 percent. In five provinces the value of the transfer exceeded the provinces' own spending. There was a widespread feeling that Ottawa and the provinces had failed "to establish any coherent and coordinated federal-provincial national priorities for higher education" (Watts, 1986, p. 171).

But the continuing dilemmas about national purpose versus provincial variation were posed most sharply in the debates on Meech Lake and free trade.

Free trade posed the question of how federalism could be adapted to the exigencies of a world in which global and North American interdependence pressed ever more sharply on domestic policy-making institutions. So long as international trade policy emphasized tariffs, monetary policy and the like, then federal dominance in the area was assured. But increasingly, institutions such as the GATT were turning their attention to subsidies, procurement policies and other non-tariff barriers. Many of these, inevitably, would be programs and activities undertaken by provincial governments. Similarly, from the start it was clear that American negotiators in the free trade discussions were anxious to include provincial practices in any agreement and to ensure that it would be binding on the provinces. Already actual or threatened American trade actions against Canadian soft-wood lumber, cedar shakes and shingles, fish and other products – all based on alleged "unfair" subsidies or trade practices – were aimed at either provincial policies or federal policies directed to stimulating regional development.

These developments meant that the "constitutional gap" identified by the Macdonald Commission was becoming less and less tenable (*Report*. Vol. III, pp. 151-56). The Constitution Act assigned to Ottawa the power to speak for Canada abroad and to negotiate international agreements. But, as we noted earlier, when it came to treaty implementation the federal-provincial division of powers was to prevail. The underlying question, therefore, was whether federalism, with its divided authority in such matters, would hobble Canadian efforts to develop a coherent, unified bargaining position and to adapt its economic and social policies to the new exigencies. Would federalism have important consequences for Canada's ability to project its interests abroad and, in the long run, would the changed international environment itself alter the internal dynamics of Canadian federalism?

The first question for the free trade discussions was what role should the provinces play at each stage. Most provinces warmly endorsed the free trade initiative, and at the November 1985 FMC, they agreed on the principle of "full provincial participation" in the trade talks, without defining the phrase. To Premier Peterson of Ontario and some others it meant that the negotiations would be from first to last a joint responsibility and should be directed ultimately by the First Ministers, to whom the Chief Trade Negotiator, Simon Reisman, should report. To the federal government, it meant that the the provinces should be informed and consulted.

By the summer of 1986, a procedure was in place (Brown, 1989). The First Ministers met every 90 days throughout the process to review progress. A Continuing Committee of officials monitored the discussions even more closely. The final agreement appeared to have been written to infringe as little as possible on provincial jurisdiction, but it did include a clause in which Ottawa committed itself to use all available powers to ensure provincial compliance where they were affected.

But there remained many uncertainties of the sort that we have explored throughout this volume. Federalism had "worked" in these negotiations, but would it work in the future? Many voices had argued that federalism was "obsolete" given the new challenges governments faced in the Depression era. Now it could be argued that the new global environment equally required major adaptation of the federal system. Would the costs of diversity inhibit Canada's ability to respond? And if so, was the appropriate response to centralize the power to implement international agreements, as in the U.S. and Australia, or was it once again to search for a new collective mechanism for intergovernmental agreement on such matters?

And what of the effects on federalism? Some critics of the trade agreement, such as the government of Ontario, (which, along with Prince Edward Island remained opposed to some aspects of the arrangement) saw in it another "new face of centralism". They pointed out that while the agreement placed few limits on existing provincial activities, it indirectly affected many more. It opened the possibility that the courts might now expand the scope of the federal trade and commerce power, catching in its net many provincial activities which had before gone unchallenged.

Others saw the long-run effect of a free trade agreement as decentralizing. In the short run, the most direct constraints would operate on the federal government. Historically the tariff had always been the primary instrument of federal industrial policy; now it would no longer be in the armoury. Other instruments of industrial policy, such as the ability to favour domestic industries in investment or to use energy policy as a means of economic development, would be sharply constrained. Generally, the logic of Canada-

U.S. free trade could be seen as undermining one of the central rationales for the very existence of a federal government since 1867 – the creation of an east-west economy and the stimulation of economic linkages among Canadians. Some also saw a threat to another central rationale for Ottawa within the Canadian political economy – its ability to act as a balance wheel, redistributing resources and development across Canadian regions.

From this perspective, each Canadian region would be on its own in the global and North American environment, trading wherever the opportunities were greatest, with no preference for strengthening economic linkages with other Canadians. With the federal rationale undermined and its instruments constrained, it was possible that, while they would also be constrained, provinces would play a greater relative role in economic development.

Finally, as the Ontario government pointed out, the closer intermeshing of the Canadian and American economies and the linking of their economic policies could mean that there would henceforth be another presence at the federal-provincial bargaining table. The Agreement itself would constrain the kinds of federal-provincial arrangements which might emerge and American negotiators might put pressure on the federal government to monitor and control provincial activities more closely.

It is impossible to predict such consequences with any certainty. But from the longer perspective of this study, it should be realized that the trade agreement is simply the latest step in the evolution of the new international policy which Canada adopted after World War II. Many of the external pressures and constraints which the agreement underlines are the product of this larger historical development and would exist in one or another form with or without it. In this sense, the agreement underlines a larger lesson about the blurring of the distinctions between international forces and domestic policy with important consequences for the operation of the federal state.

The Meech Lake Accord was less a response to a changing international environment than it was an attempt to resolve continuing dilemmas within the domestic framework of federalism. It too raised questions about centralization and decentralization, national versus provincial purposes, and the management of the interdependence characteristic of modern federalism. The Accord made no major change in the division of powers, except to broaden and to constitutionalize the provinces' role in immigration, already an area of joint constitutional authority. But in other respects it further institutionalizes and entrenches the provincialist shift which, with the exception of the 1980-84 period, has characterized the evolution of Canadian federalism since the 1950s. It does so in a number of ways.

At the level of constitutional amendment, it extends the logic of the 1982 Constitution Act by making it even more difficult for a national majority to impose its conception of national purpose on a dissenting province. It does so by expanding the number of areas in which unanimous agreement is necessary to make an amendment and by increasing the availability of fiscal compensation for a province which does not participate in an amendment altering the division of powers. The amending process thus continues to demand a very high level of intergovernmental consent. It is designed to protect provinces against the power of national majorities.

Second, the Accord partially provincializes two of the central institutions of federalism. Supreme Court Justices and Senators (at least until further Senate reform is agreed upon) will be appointed from lists of provincial nominees. This underlines a model of federalism which sees these institutions as the guarantors of the federal bargain rather than as institutions of the national government. These provisions are also a first formal recognition of the intra-state model in which federalism is to be manifested not only in relations between levels of government but also in the operations of the central government itself. As we discussed earlier, such models can be designed either to represent governments, and thus to reinforce provincial governments as representative of regions, or to represent citizens directly and thus, at least potentially, to undercut provinces. Meech Lake reflects the former variant.

The tension between national purpose and provincial variation is most clearly reflected in the new section 106A which concerns the federal spending power. By providing an explicit constitutional base for the federal spending power, it reinforces the idea that the federal government can act in areas of provincial jurisdiction in the pursuit of national purposes. But by providing that provinces adopting programs "compatible with the national objectives" may opt-out with fiscal compensation, it also constitutionalizes the idea that provinces may carry out these national purposes and that they may do so in varying ways. There are many ambiguities in this formulation, but at heart it restates the way the spending power has been used in practice throughout the modern period. As we have seen, opting-out has a long history. Shared-cost programs have always involved provincial delivery of services with relatively few, loose conditions; and have always provided for considerable provincial variation within them. They have never been used to ensure detailed intervention by the federal government. The balance between national purposes and provincial variation has always been a matter of negotiation. Again, this provision extends and constitutionalizes a past evolution, rather than reversing it.

All these provisions also reinforce the necessity of extensive collaborative federalism. Governments must jointly decide on amendments, use of the federal spending power, and appointment of judges and Senators. In recognition of this, the Accord (also for the first time) places the machinery of intergovernmental relations in the constitution, calling for annual First

Ministers' Conferences on the Economy and on the Constitution. The change is formal and symbolic. Such Conferences emerged as a central part of Canada's governing machinery throughout our period, a product of the inevitable interdependence among governments and of the political strength behind each of them. No new roles or responsibilities are assigned to them.

The debate on the Accord echoes and sharpens debates about the federal state we have traced throughout this volume. Those who argue for the primacy of the national community and of the national government as its advocate believe that the Accord entrenches provincial powers which make such a vision more difficult to achieve. Those who argue that contemporary policy challenges require more centralized authority see in Meech Lake a tilt the other way. Those who seek common, national standards see a legitimation of provincial differences. Those who believe that the political system needs to be reoriented to minimize the salience of territory, giving greater weight and attention to other needs and interests, see a set-back to such aspirations.

On the other hand, those who believe that nation-building must be constructed on a foundation of representing and incorporating regional and linguistic differences, and who see the equal legitimacy of federal and provincial governments and communities, find their conception embraced in the Accord. Those who seek to protect provincial interests against national majorities and a national government necessarily dependent on the votes of the more populous regions are reassured. Those who regard the essence of federalism as the ability of government to vary policy responses in light of the differing preferences of their constituencies see encouragement in Meech Lake.

If Meech Lake triggered renewed debate on such questions, it also triggered one on the relationship between federalism and the quality of democracy in Canada. It has highlighted the growing tensions among the conceptions of democracy embedded in each of the three major "pillars" of Canadian government. We have already discussed the tensions between the "distinct society" clause, with its conception of the rights of a provincial linguistic community, and the idea of individual rights in the Charter. As early as the 1950s voices were being raised about the potential tensions between federalism and Parliamentary government. The logic of parliamentary government is one of majority rule; federalism entrenches rule by multiple majorities and, as we have seen, constrains the ability of national majorities to impose their will on provincial majorities. The abiding issue is which kinds of majorities are appropriate for which kinds of purposes.

But the primary democratic critique of contemporary federalism lies in the relationship between executive federalism and democratic accountability. The Breau Task Force on fiscal federalism (Canada, 1981) and others had queried how effectively the federal government could be held accountable if a significant proportion of the funds it raised were transferred to provinces with limited conditions. And how could provincial governments be held accountable to their electorates when they were spending funds they had not raised? The more governments were enmeshed with each other and the more central to decision-making intergovernmental agreements became, the more the accountability of governments to their own legislatures was eroded. The more intergovernmental conferences were to take on the roles of a legislature, the greater the concerns about their own lack of accountability.

These concerns crystallized in the Meech Lake debate. It was to be enacted according to the procedures adopted in 1982, and in important ways these were more consistent with parliamentary norms than previous processes. Prior to 1982 most amendments were agreed to by executives alone, although requests to Britain required a Resolution by Parliament. Now, every legislature would have an opportunity to assess proposed changes. Nevertheless, the carefully balanced intergovernmental compromise was presented as a fait accompli. Any amendment to it in any legislature would be likely to unravel it, forcing a return to the intergovernmental bargaining table with no certainty of renewed agreement. Hence, the governments said that only undefined "egregious" errors in the text would be cause for reopening discussion. Thus legislatures were faced with the simple alternatives of voting the agreement up or down. To many critics this rendered the legislative debate and committee hearings a sham.

Some criticism went further, suggesting that even the wide support for the Accord by both governments and opposition parties in most legislatures did not meet the desirable test of democratic legitimacy for constitutional enactments. For them the test must be popular ratification through referendum, as proposed but rejected in 1980-81, an indication of just how much recent events had shifted the constitution from a bargain among governments to a bargain between citizens and government.

The most thorough-going critique of executive federalism has been suggested by Albert Breton (1985). For Breton, the virtue of federalism lies principally in the opportunity it provides for governments to compete for popular support. In so doing they increase the likelihood of responsiveness to citizen preferences. This virtue is undercut by a federalism which emphasizes collaboration and agreement among governments. The danger is that these governments will constitute a closed "elite cartel" who will arrange matters to their own benefit, collectively agreeing to exclude broader concerns and to ensure their own continuing power and status. Moreover, in emphasizing agreement, they will sacrifice the benefits of policy variation. Breton therefore advocates a more competitive model of federalism in which governments openly compete for public support and act unilaterally within their assigned powers. Coordination will occur as each adjusts to the actions of others. Intergovernmental relations should be relegated to the tidying up of administrative arrangements once the basic policy decisions have been made through an open political process.

The logic of policy-making through the collective agreement of independent executives has been criticized in other settings as well. Fritz Scharpf analyzes the "joint decision trap" which characterizes decision-making in the European Community and in the wide sphere of "joint tasks" in the German federation. In both cases, decisions effectively require unanimity. Instead of the creativity and flexibility offered by multiple levels of government, Scharpf suggests, the result of shared decision-making is often "either inefficient, or inflexible, or unnecessary and, in any case, quite undemocratic" (Scharpf, 1988, p. 247). The bureaucratic self-interests of governments are likely to predominate. Policy is difficult to change because non-agreement assures the continuation of the status quo, and at least one government is likely to prefer that to any alternatives on the table. Unanimity in joint decision-making can work only if the participants share common interests or a common sense of the costs of failure to agree.

These are indeed serious dilemmas. They may help explain how difficult it has been for the Mulroney government to translate the spirit of "reconciliation" into major new intergovernmental policy initiatives, despite the best of intentions. Certainly, the "joint decision trap" bedevils constitutional negotiations in which unanimity is required for a number of critical kinds of change. Explicit mutual agreement is required in few other areas of policy-making, but the intermeshing of joint programs and fiscal arrangements does require a high degree of cooperation. A central challenge for federal-provincial relations, therefore, is to find the means whereby the cooperation, coordination and consultation rendered imperative by the shared occupancy of the policy space can be reconciled with the virtues of competition, variety and governmental autonomy in charting policy and responding to citizen preferences. If the Trudeau era underlined the dangers of confrontation, the Mulroney experiment reveals the dangers of cooperation and conflict-avoidance.

Throughout our history we have seen examples of both competition and collaboration. In the immediate postwar period the model was collaborative, but under federal leadership and within a broad consensus on the role and purpose of the state. Between 1960 and the early 1980s, the primary model was one of unrestrained competition in many forums. The literature in this era concentrated on the costs of this competition and suggested that in their competitive struggle for power, governmental elites were exaggerating and accentuating the underlying differences, constituting the "other crisis" in Canadian federalism (Cairns, 1976). At the outset of the Mulroney era many argued that there was a need to find bases for greater harmony and cooperation in order to get away from the destructive conflict which had marked intergovernmental relations in the preceding period.

Meech Lake is an example of just such intergovernmental collaboration. Those who oppose it see it as a prime example of elite conspiracy against a larger public interest. Those who defend it argue that, given the underlying dissension, it is only through elite accommodation that the delicate compromises necessary for resolving such complex issues can be found. They argue it reflects a nation-building state-craft attainable in no other way, resolving a constitutional failure which could not be tenable in the long run. Thus for some, Meech Lake epitomized the vices of collaborative federalism; for others, its virtues. But in the longer run, the mechanisms set up by the Meech Lake Accord would not themselves predetermine whether the practice of federalism would be cooperative or competitive. The mechanisms of the Accord do indeed force governments to collaborate. But as they discuss Supreme Court appointments or new shared cost programs in the FMCs, they may do it openly or behind closed doors, cooperatively or competitively. The Accord itself says nothing about how the mechanisms will be used. They could equally be an arena for harmony or conflict, for increasing public awareness or for deeper secrecy.

Conclusion

Thus the Mulroney approach to federalism, epitomized in the Meech Lake Accord, does not predetermine the future course of federalism any more than previous federal governments have done. By 1988, federal-provincial conflict was greatly muted in comparison with the preceding periods. Much of the credit must go to the government's commitment to national reconciliation and, especially, its commitment to reconciliation with Quebec. But equally, this increased harmony is a product of the kinds of larger forces which, throughout our study, have driven the evolution of Canadian federalism. The primary dilemma lies in the fact that federalism and intergovernmental relations are now conducted in an environment made more complex and multi-dimensional by changes both within Canadian society and in the global environment.

In the preface to the second edition of *Canada in Question*, D.V. Smiley confessed that he almost failed to complete it, so disheartened was he by the fear that the federation could not survive the "compound crisis" of French-English relations, regional tensions and relations with the United States. In the preface to his 1987 sequel, *The Federal Condition in Canada*, Smiley reverses his view. Federalism was now to be understood as a highly resilient and stable system of government for Canada. "In retrospect, it appears that I and most other observers...very much over-estimated the strength of Quebec nationalism and provincialist influences else-where...and very much underestimated the capacity of the system to respond effectively to such divisive pressures" (1987, p. xi).

Our analysis suggests that there is much truth to this statement. Even at the height of the battles over Quebec sovereignty, energy and the like, surveys showed that most Canadians attached great importance both to the national and their provincial communities. Only a small percentage of Quebecers ever supported separation *tout court*; even tinier minorities supported western separatism. And the federal system, however messily, did indeed provide a framework for accommodation. Even before the end of the Trudeau era the drive had gone out of the current phase of Quebec nationalism. Agreements on energy and other matters had been worked out. It may indeed have been the case that the academics' fascination with crisis and conflict and the politicians' interest in exacerbating differences overemphasized the depth of conflict and the strains on the system. But it would be equally wrong to see these conflicts as artifacts of the expansionist drives of politicians. These conflicts were linked to fundamental differences in political economy and in basic values and identities; they were a product at once of a changing society and changing roles of government; they placed enormous strains on the Canadian political fabric and, for a time, did indeed have the potential to end the Canadian political experiment. Thus, the question is not so much whether we have exaggerated the depth of conflict in the past, but rather whether we have captured the forces, domestic and international, societal, institutional and personal, which account for changes over time.

Chapter 12

Conclusions

Our model does not provide a crystal ball which allows us to predict the future. It has identified some of the primary variables which, according to their direction and magnitude, have shaped Canadian federalism in the past and which may be expected to determine its evolution in the coming years. The pivotal point of our analysis has been the way in which the changing economic and social roles of the state have cast and re-cast the essential character of Canadian federalism, defining the purposes and the dilemmas of intergovernmental relations. Our thesis in this regard could be stated as: federal form follows state function. But changes in the degree of centralization of the federation can take place even in the absence of fundamental changes in the role of the state, as with the birth of classical federalism in 1896, and in the decentralizing trend of modern federalism since the Reconstruction decade. We sketched the dynamics of the societal accommodations and political alliances that give rise to these changes in the substance and division of state functions. Finally, we grounded these dynamics in the evolution of international and domestic political economic structures.

In the 1940s and 1950s we saw that issues of federalism – debates about the structures of federalism framed in terms of rival conceptions of Canadian identity and nationality – were muted. Federalism was by no means unimportant but the driving forces, to which federalism was required to adapt, came from other sources. In Chapter 7 we examined some of the reasons for this, from a benign international climate which minimized regional economic conflicts of interest to a political preoccupation with the building of the Keynesian welfare state which did not threaten enduring provincial identities and loyalties outside Quebec. Many observers saw in these developments the obsolescence, if not the disappearance, of federalism.

In the 1960s and 1970s we saw how both domestic and international forces combined to increase the salience of regional differences of interest, to energize regional loyalties and to exacerbate intergovernmental tension.

More recently still, we have noted several straws in the wind, difficult to assess because they are so new, which suggest a return to a federal dynamic more similar to that of the 1940s and 1950s than to that of the 1960s and 1970s. The international climate is at once less regionally divisive and more threatening to the country as a whole, suggesting that economically rooted regional tensions may decline in political prominence. Issues of social justice and national economic renewal, which are more likely to divide Canadians along class, gender and ethnic lines than along linguistic and regional lines, increasingly preoccupy the Canadian electorate. The emergence and growing strength of entirely new bases of political organization, rooted in new definitions of collective identity such as the critique of traditional gender roles developed by contemporary feminists, injects a very different agenda into Canadian politics. Moreover, the existence of the Charter – a document largely hostile to regional identities and particularities, and as available to non-territorially organized interests as to territorially organized ones – provides such movements with an important new political instrument for the realization of their goals outside traditional federalist institutions.

But if these indicators all point towards a politics less dominated by issues framed in terms of provincial identities and interests, we do not wish to suggest that what we are observing is a simple pendulum swing back to the *status quo ante* of the 1940s and 1950s. Much less do we wish to argue yet another version of the displacement thesis we criticized earlier. The regional and linguistic identities so sharpened in the experiences of the last two decades were not new; nor are they likely to disappear. They preceded the most recent round of province-building initiatives and they will remain as it subsides. Moreover, provincial governments now command a much greater share of fiscal and bureaucratic resources than they did in the postwar era. We are not likely to see an acquiescence to federal tutelage as in the late 1940s. Even then, it is worth recalling, provincial governments had the institutional capacity and political support to ensure that there would only be a limited shift of constitutional power to Ottawa. The amendment formula adopted in 1982, as modified in 1987, enhances the capacity of provincial governments to block such changes in the future. Fiscal restraint limits the capacity of any future federal government to undertake the kind of centralizing push attempted by Trudeau after 1980, even if it shared his political vision and will.

Thus, to argue that territorial divisions are likely to be muted and intergovernmental tensions less global and ideological is neither to predict a rapid expansion of central government authority nor to suggest that the "spirit of Meech Lake" augurs a generation of intergovernmental harmony. Indeed, it is always possible to envision conditions which would falsify even our cautious predictions of increased harmony. International developments could well greatly exacerbate regional disparities and conflicts of economic interest, as they did in the seventies, while diminishing the capacity of the federal government to respond to them fairly and effectively. Domestic developments could also exacerbate tensions. Relative demographic or economic decline in Quebec, for example, could well stimulate a resurgence of Quebec nationalism, particularly if it were accompanied by a reduction of the federal government's commitment to bilingualism.

All this is to say that Canada is and will remain incorrigibly federal at both societal and constitutional levels. Our history makes it clear that this virtually rules out some paths of development. First, at the level of collective identity, no vision of Canadian politics predicated upon the assumption that either the national or the provincial dimensions of Canadian identities can or will or ought to dominate the other is ever likely to prevail. The failure of Prime Minister Trudeau's "new federalism" attests to the first half of this proposition; the defeat of Premier Levesque's sovereignty-association option to the second. The Canadian political nationality must be based on the acceptance of the reality and legitimacy of citizen loyalties to both types of political community because the great majority of Canadian citizens strongly identify with both communities and view this "internal duality" as stable and beneficial rather than contradictory and undesirable.

Second, and closely related, no vision of Canadian politics which asserts that territorially organized identities and communities will or ought to be entirely displaced by non-territorial ones , such as class or gender , will succeed. Territorially organized communities are core constituents of collective identity in capitalist nation states for at least two reasons. First, because the regional economic specialization which develops "naturally" in a market or quasi-market system creates close linkages between territorially defined communities and the economic interests of their inhabitants vis-à-vis those of other regions. Second, because such communities correspond to, and are nurtured by, the way in which political power is organized, that is, by states, whether federal or unitary, which claim sovereign jurisdiction over territorially defined communities.

This is not to suggest that other, non-territorially organized identities cannot or will not emerge. But they will always coexist, synthetically or syncretically, with great scope for variation from one province to the next, with territorially organized identities. This, in turn, means that attempts to attach these new identities and interests exclusively to one order of government, rather than recognizing that they must be expressed and pursued through both orders of government, are doomed to fail. This is a lesson which the NDP, with its experience of provincial government and its endorsement of the Meech Lake Accord now appears to have learned.

At the level of the state, there are parallel lessons. No global, centralizing model of federalism can succeed. Sir John A. Macdonald did not; neither did Pierre Trudeau, despite the exercise of enormous political will. On the other hand, no radical decentralizing project will succeed either. What is remarkable about the combined result of Meech Lake and the 1982 constitutional changes is that there is virtually no shifting of power among levels of government, despite the important changes in other respects. Centralizers will always be able to veto decentralizers, and vice versa. This is not simply a product of the amending formula. Governments in the future, as in the past, will often be unable to use even the powers that they do undeniably possess because they run against the grain of popular opinion and organized interests. Several lessons follow from this.

First, "province" and "nation-building" should not be seen as antithetical. Economic and social development in every province, not just the poorer ones, is absolutely dependent upon the exercise of federal power. But, on the other hand, without an extension of federal authority beyond the limits which are conceivable in the absence of a political or economic catastrophe, national economic and social development will continue to require the exercise of provincial jurisdiction.

Second, if one is committed to nation-building in the sense of extending the federal government's capacity for leadership, there are alternative means of trying to achieve this goal. One historical thread runs from Macdonald to Trudeau asserting, in effect, that national leadership is only possible in the space created by the absence of provincial power. But a second line, running from Laurier to Pearson, is equally nation-building in its commitment to making the nation wealthier and more just, yet recognizes the national dimensions of provincial activity and is willing to work with and through provincial governments. It may not be a coincidence that the 1963-68 Pearson regime was not only among the most activist in social and economic policy in Canadian history, but also the one that made most concessions to active provinces, particularly Quebec.

Clearly there will be tension between the aims and methods of the two orders of government in many cases. The issue, which parallels the debate in France between Jacobin centralizers and those such as de Tocqueville who defended the existence of intermediary institutions, is whether these tensions are, by and large, healthy. We return to this issue, and the various meanings which might be given to the term "healthy" below.

Third, as long as the majority of Canadians remain committed to an extensive state role in social and economic policy, it follows that there is no escaping the interdependence of federal and provincial governments. Our history describes the extension of this overlapping and shared responsibility in one policy field after another. The growth of government took place at both levels; neither monopolized the new agenda. Indeed, with the free trade negotiations, and the general extension of international trade agreements to non-tariff barriers, we have recently seen a major extension of interdependence to the international arena. For some, the implication is clear: federal domestic economic powers should be correspondingly extended. But this, too, appears impossible, not only because of the limited federal power to implement treaties but also because a national consensus in support of such an extension does not exist.

If the centralizing alternative is blocked, our history also indicates it is unlikely that we may return to a sharp delineation of "watertight" compartments – the pre-war, classical model of federalism – in a redefined division of powers. All the movement has been the other way. While there will continue to be shifts between which order of government is the leader and innovator in a particular policy field, and more or less successful efforts to "tidy up" overlaps by administrative means will also continue, shared and divided responsibility is a permanent condition in Canada. Accordingly, it seems inevitable that Canada will be governed as a partnership between both orders of government as we deal now with the recurring questions of the past and as we confront new questions in the future.

As Albert Breton (1985) reminds us, this does not and ought not to imply that all decisions are made jointly, or that action by either order of government cannot take place without first gaining the consent of the other. Jurisdictional overlap also entails competition in meeting citizen needs, and a public process of seeking to define issues and alternatives which increases the representativeness of the political system as a whole. The language of province and nation-building implies an image of provincial and central states engaged in the kind of zero-sum opposition that we associate with conflicts between nation-states. Our analysis argues, instead, that both federal and provincial governments must be seen as elements in a single Canadian state with overlapping, if distinct, constituencies and perspectives.

It might be thought inappropriate to end our history with a normative question – how well have Canadians been served by the federal system and how might the workings of that system be improved? – since our prime focus has been on describing and explaining the evolution of that system. But if our empirical arguments are correct and Canada will remain federal, both societally and constitutionally, then it is important to bring the historical experience examined here to bear on our political fate as Canadians and the ways in which that fate may be rendered as happy as possible. The important dilemmas that confront contemporary Canadian federalism may be organized around five major political values that stand in some form of tension with the institutions and practices of federalism: community, equity, liberty, democracy and efficacy.

The conception of community represented and expressed through our federal institutions remains problematic. We have seen how the commentary about Meech Lake revolved around the relative primacy of national and provincial communities, and alternative means of institutionalizing French-English relations. The Accord strikes a balance between the polar visions that emerged in the 1970s: a bilingual citizenry from sea to sea, and two unilingual nations. The optimistic view of this is that language could be set aside as a major source of conflict, opening the way to new political agendas and new coalitions cutting across the language barrier. The more pessimistic view is that demographic changes both inside and outside Quebec, along with new political values undermining the legitimacy of collective goals may soon erode the linguistic gains of the past quarter-century. If the struggles over bilingualism and special status come to seem remote, passé and perhaps even irrelevant to an increasing number of English Canadians animated by this new agenda, the way will be opened to the marginalization of French Canadians outside Quebec and, in the longer run perhaps, inside Quebec as well. Such developments could increase the importance of ethnic divisions once again, so that federal institutions would be asked to respond to imperatives pointing in very different directions.

Setting aside this potential source of a revival of a politics dominated by ethnic divisions, what are the new axes of Canadian politics likely to be, and what implications do they have for federalism? We can see two types of axes that may well become more salient in the near future: first, collectivist challenges to federalist preoccupations and procedures, predicated upon non-territorially-based identities such as class and gender; and second, libertarian or individualist challenges to the value and rights of territorial communities and the governments that defend their interests.

The new collectivist bases of identity and political mobilization give rise to challenges to the justice of existing economic and political institutions. These challenges often issue in demands for the extension of the roles of the state, whether to reverse the degradation of the environment, distribute the costs and benefits of dramatic economic adjustment more equitably, or socialize costs of child care hitherto borne by individual families. But at the same time these non-territorially based actors are often highly critical of the intergovernmental processes that rapidly growing governments have found necessary (if not sufficient) to the effective execution of their new policies on the ground that these processes are undemocratic. We consider the relation between federalism and democracy below. Here we merely note that there is a deep tension between the demands of these groups for new processes of decision-making and their concern to expand the roles of the state.

The traditional response of the "progressive" movements to this dilemma was to advocate a dramatic centralization of the federation. We have already suggested why we view this as an unrealistic "solution", but this empirical critique does not address the view that says centralization may well be politically impossible in the foreseeable future, but so much the worse for social justice. To this position it may be replied that progressive innovations have been pioneered at the provincial level at least as often as at the federal level in Canadian history. More deeply, the "strength" of the state , if by this is meant its capacity to act in the interests of the less economically powerful against the more powerful , is not a function of its centralization, but of its legitimacy. And legitimacy is a function of the degree of correspondence or "fit" between the processes by which policies are formed and the substance of those policies, or between popular conceptions of procedural and substantive justice. The kind of federalism which now exists appears to exhibit such a correspondence. Hence, if the Canadian state lacks the legitimacy to carry out the reform agendas now or in the future, it will not be because modern federalism has weakened the state. Moreover, one reason Ottawa has often disappointed the progressives is precisely because it has necessarily had to be concerned with national unity and with balancing often conflicting regional interests. We saw how this blunted the federal reform drive in the depression and postwar years. International constraints will press harder and harder on the policy instruments – trade, tariff and fiscal policy – which the federal government does control. Coherent policies of either the right or the left are more likely to emerge at the provincial level.

Libertarian challenges, rooted in the new third pillar of the constitution – the Charter of Rights – go to the rights of individuals against communities, whether territorial or non-territorial in character. The Charter recognizes rights other than individual rights, but it has become a basis for such challenges to language legislation and to various aspects of aboriginal self-government. It may also be used to restrict the rights of federal and provincial governments to make policy in areas encroaching on private property rights, including free collective bargaining, transforming long-standing relations between governments and populations, as well as limiting parliamentary sovereignty.

Furthermore, such challenges will raise fundamental political and philosophical questions about the appropriate way of conceiving the relation between individual autonomy and the requirements of the communities within which those individual autonomies are constituted. Canadian political and legal culture is steeped in the language of how to reconcile or balance the conflicting needs of different communities, but the battles that are shaping up in the future will pose difficult new challenges.

The debates surrounding Meech Lake also underline continuing dilemmas concerning the relationship between federalism and democratic values. Critics of the Accord challenge not only its substance but also the process of intergovernmental elite accommodation by which it was achieved. The legitimation of federalism as intergovernmental collaboration accentuates long-standing tensions between the norms of federalism and those of Parliamentary government. So long as governments operated in "watertight" compartments this tension did not exist; both orders of government were directly accountable to their respective legislatures. But the overlapping of federal and provincial responsibilities blurs the neat lines of formal accountability. The negotiation of intergovernmental arrangements which can be subject to legislative scrutiny and debate but cannot be easily modified further strengthens executives against legislatures. It will be important in the future to seek more ways to ensure that citizens and groups gain access to intergovernmental processes in advance of the negotiation of Accords, and to improve the capacity of legislatures to scrutinize effectively the conduct of governments in the intergovernmental arena.

Senate reform will raise similar dilemmas within the federal Parliament. In a truly revitalized Senate could the government remain accountable only to the Commons? Moreover, all serious proposals for Senate reform are predicated on the assumption that Parliament must move away from the principle of simple majority rule to one in which smaller regions are weighted more heavily, and provinces, not individual citizens, are weighted equally. Indeed, such "reforms at the centre" may pose more problems for democratic norms than the intergovernmental process. Certainly they cannot be regarded as a resolution of the tensions between democratic and federalist values.

The obvious tension between federalism and the emergence of executive federalism does not tell the whole story about the relationship between democracy and political institutions. Executive federalism is just one manifestation of the larger tension between participant democracy and executive power in the modern administrative state. And federalism is much more than the intergovernmental relations we have stressed. It is also a system of multiple, responsive governments, dealing with the issues that arise in differentiated political communities. Such a model allows for a better fit between citizen preferences and public policies than a centralized model could.

Finally, the issue of the capacity of federal institutions to respond effectively to future policy challenges will remain. One perspective, already noted as the traditional position of the Canadian left, is that federalism limits Canada's ability to adapt and respond to international pressures. Such pressures seem to carry the implication that it is vital to ensure all domestic actors are able to develop a common position, to speak with one voice, and to bend domestic forces to a common task. The diversity of interests in a federal society and the fragmentation of authority entailed by a federal constitution, are held on this view to make such national cohesiveness in the face of external threat extremely difficult. Moreover, both dimensions of federalism may make it more difficult to achieve the collaboration among labour, government and business which many see as an equally essential prerequisite of international competitiveness.

But we would argue that just as "new-corporatism" as practiced in a number of European countries can make it easier to accommodate and respond effectively to international challenges in highly class divided societies, so also with our federal institutions in a society that is territorially divided. Nor should federalism necessarily be incompatible with neo-corporatist institutions, although they will undoubtedly require that we develop a uniquely Canadian, more decentralized version. This is not beyond our capacities. We have pioneered a form of federalism that is at once decentralized and effective at reconciling the kinds of conflicts with which federalism was designed to deal. Federalism is more than a necessity for Canada; it is a form of territorially dispersed authority possessing virtues which have been well summarized by Martin Landau:

> It promotes geographical equity, increases popular capacity to inspire responsibility and accountability, enables easier access to decision-points, reduces conflict, and is more democratic. It is also more effective and efficient. It improves the delivery of services, solves the problem of switch-board overload, allows for careful consideration of local needs, encourages invention and innovation, provides more accurate descriptions of problems – it even eases national planning problems through the provision of a more reliable information base.
> ("On the Concept of Decentralization", 1981, p. 10).

As Landau observes, these are claims rather than hard facts, but we believe that our survey of modern Canadian federalism provides considerable support for their validity. Without sacrificing the vitality and responsiveness of federalism, we have adapted the Canadian state to shifting political concerns and conceptions of the appropriate role of the state. The idea that federalism has been a strait-jacket on public policy cannot be easily sustained. Decentralization can enhance flexibility in an era of increased complexity, accelerating change and growing uncertainty.

In this sense, the evolution of our federal system over the last forty years has probably provided Canadians with a comparative advantage over nations characterized by more centralized, hierarchical political institutions. It is surely obvious by now that the interpenetration of political and economic institutions is so complex and profound in capitalist industrial democracies that such comparative political advantages carry with them important comparative economic advantages as well.

We are confident that Canada's federal institutions equip us well to meet current and future economic challenges.

Bibliography

Abel, Albert S. 1980. *Towards a Constitutional Charter for Canada*. Toronto: University of Toronto Press.

Abella, Irving. 1973. *Nationalism, Communism and Canadian Labour, 1935-1956*. Toronto: University of Toronto Press.

———. 1975. *The Canadian Labour Movement 1902-1960*. Ottawa: Canadian Historical Association.

Adams, Ian, et. al. 1971. *The Real Poverty Report*. Edmonton: Hurtig Publishers Ltd.

Adamson, Agar. 1971. "The Fulton-Favreau Formula: A Study of its Development, 1960-67". *Journal of Canadian Studies*. 3: pp. 45-55.

Advisory Commission on Intergovernmental Relations. 1971. *In Search of Balance: Canada's Intergovernmental Experience*. Washington: U. S. Government Printing Office.

Aitken, Hugh G. J., ed. 1959. *The State and Economic Growth*. New York: Social Science Research Council.

———. 1964. "Government and Business in Canada: An Interpretation". *Business History Review*. 38: pp. 4-21.

———. 1981. "Defensive Expansionism: The State and Economic Growth in Canada". In *Approaches to Canadian Economic History* edited by W. T. Easterbrook and M. H. Watkins. Toronto: Macmillan of Canada.

Alberta. 1984. *Harmony in Diversity: Proposals for an Industrial and Science Strategy for Alberta*. Edmonton: Queen's Printer.

Allen, Robert C. and Gideon Rosenbluth, eds. 1986 *Restraining the Economy: Social Credit Economic Policies for B.C. in the Eighties*. Vancouver: New Star Books.

Anderson, B. 1983. *Imagined Communities*. London: Verso.

Anderson, F. J and N. C. Bonsor. 1986. "Regional Economic Alienation: Atlantic Canada and the West". In *Disparities and Interregional Adjustment* edited by Kenneth Norrie. Volume 64 of the Research Studies prepared for the Royal Commission on the Economic Union and Development Prospects for Canada, pp. 185-221. Toronto: University of Toronto Press.

Anisman, Philip. 1986. "The Regulation of the Securities Market and the Harmonization of Provincial Laws". In *Perspectives on the Harmonization of Law in Canada* edited by R. Cuming. Volume 55 of the Research Studies prepared for the Royal Commission on the Economic Union and Development Prospects for Canada, pp. 77-168. Toronto: University of Toronto Press.

Arès, Richard. 1966. "La Confédération: pacte ou loi?" *Relations* 26: pp. 328-340.

Archibald, Bruce. 1971. "Atlantic Regional Underdevelopment and Socialism". In *Essays on the Left: Essays in Honour of T. C. Douglas* edited by Laurier Lapierre, pp. 103-120. Toronto: McClelland and Stewart.

Armstrong, Christopher. 1981. *The Politics of Federalism*. Toronto: University of Toronto Press.

Armstrong, C. and H. V. Nelles. 1975. "Private Property in Peril: Ontario Businessmen and the Federal System 1898-1911". In *Enterprise and National Development: Essays in Canadian Business and Economic History* edited by Glenn Porter and Robert Cuff, pp. 20-38. Toronto: Hakkert.

Arnopoulos, Sheila M. and Dominique Clift. 1980. *The English Fact in Quebec*. Montreal & Kingston: McGill-Queen's University Press.

Arsenault, Michael. 1988. "Quebec: The Party's Over". *Saturday Night*. (February) pp. 19-20.

Atkinson, Michael M. 1984. "On the Prospects for Industrial Policy in Canada". *Canadian Public Administration* 27: pp. 454-67.

Aucoin, Peter, ed. 1985a. *Regional Responsiveness and the National Administrative State*. Volume 37 of the Research Studies prepared for the Royal Commission on the Economic Union and Development Prospects for Canada. Toronto: University of Toronto Press.

——, ed. 1985b. *Party Government and Regional Representation in Canada*. Volume 36 of the Research Studies prepared for the Royal Commission on the Economic Union and Development Prospects for Canada. Toronto: University of Toronto Press.

——. ed. 1985c. *Institutional Reforms for Representative Government*. Volume 38 of the Research Studies prepared for the Royal Commission on the Economic Union and Development Prospects for Canada. Toronto: University of Toronto Press.

——. ed. 1981. *The Politics and Management of Restraint in Government*. Montreal: Institute for Research in Public Policy.

Aucoin, Peter and Herman Bakvis. 1984. "Organizational Differentiation and Integration: The Case of Regional Economic development Policy in Canada". *Canadian Public Administration* 27: pp. 348-71.

Axline, Andrew, et al. 1974. *Continental Community? Independence and Integration in North America*. Toronto: McClelland and Stewart.

Badgley, Robin. F. and Samuel Wolfe. 1967. *Doctors' Strike: Medical Care and Conflict in Saskatchewan*. Toronto: Macmillan of Canada.

Bakvis, Herman. 1981. *Federalism and the Organization of Canadian Political Life: Canada in Comparative Perspective*. Kingston: Institute of Intergovernmental Relations.

——and William Chandler, eds. 1987. *Federalism and the Role of The State*. Toronto: University of Toronto Press.

Bankes, Nigel D., Constance Hunt and J. Owen Saunders. 1986. "Energy and Natural Resources: The Canadian Constitutional Framework". In *Fiscal Federalism* edited by M. Krasnick, Volume 65 of the Research Studies prepared for the Royal Commission on the Economic Union and Developmet Prospects for Canada, pp. 53-138. Toronto: University of Toronto Press.

Banting, Keith. 1987. *The Welfare State and Canadian Federalism*. 2nd edition. Montreal and Kingston: McGill-Queen's University Press.

——, ed. 1986a. *State and Society: Canada in Comparative Perspective*. Volume 31 of the Research Studies prepared for the Royal Commission on the Economic Union and Development Prospects for Canada. Toronto: University of Toronto Press.

——, ed. 1986b. *The State and Economic Interests*. Volume 32 of the Research Studies prepared for the Royal Commission on the Economic Union and Development Prospects for Canada. Toronto: University of Toronto Press.

——and Richard Simeon, eds. 1983. *And No One Cheered: Federalism, Democracy and the Constitution Act*. Toronto: Methuen.

——and Richard Simeon, eds. 1985. *Redesigning the State: The Politics of Constitutional Change in Industrial Nations*. Toronto: University of Toronto Press.

Barry, Brian. 1975. *Sociologists, Economists and Democracy*. Chicago: University of Chicago Press.

——. 1985 "Does Democracy Cause Inflation: Political Ideas of Some Economists". In *The Politics of Inflation and Stagflation* edited by Leon S. Lindberg and Charles S. Maier. Washington, D.C.: Brookings Institution.

Beaudoin, Gérald-A. 1983. *Le Partage des Pouvoirs*. Troisième ed. Ottawa: Editions de l'Université d'Ottawa.

Beck, J. M. 1968. *Pendulum of Power: Canada's Federal Elections*. Toronto: Prentice-Hall.

——, ed. 1971. *The Shaping of Canadian Federalism: Central Authority or Provincial Right?* Toronto: Copp Clark.

Beck, Stanley and and Ivan Bernier, eds. 1983. *Canada and the New Constitution: The Unfinished Agenda*. Two volumes. Montreal: Institute for Research on Public Policy.

Beckton, Clare and A. Wayne MacKay, eds. 1986. *The Courts and the Charter*. Volume 58 of the Research Studies prepared for the Royal Commission on the Economic Union and Development Prospects for Canada. Toronto: University of Toronto Press.

———. 1986. *Recurring Issues in Canadian Federalism*. Volume 57 of the Research Studies prepared for the Royal Commission on the Economic Union and Development Prospects for Canada. Toronto: University of Toronto Press.

Beer, Samuel. 1973. "The Modernization of American Federalism". *Publius*. 3: pp. 49-96.

Behiels, Michael D. 1984. *Prelude to Quebec's Quiet Revolution: Liberalism versus Neo-Nationalism, 1945-60*. Montreal and Kingston: McGill-Queen's University Press.

Bélanger, Gérard. 1986. "The Division of Powers in a Federal System: A Review of the Economic Literature". In *Division of Powers and Public Policy* edited by Richard Simeon. Volume 61 of the Research Studies prepared for the Royal Commission on the Economic Union and Development Prospects for Canada, pp. 1-28. Toronto: University of Toronto Press.

Bell, Daniel. 1970. "The Cultural Contradictions of Capitalism". *The Public Interest*. 21: pp. 16-43.

Bell, D. V. J. and L. Tepperman. 1979. *The Roots of Disunity*. Toronto: McClelland and Stewart.

Bellamy, David J. et. al. 1976. *The Provincial Political Systems: Comparative Essays*. Toronto: Methuen.

Bercuson, David, ed. 1977. *Canada and the Burden of Unity*. Toronto: Macmillan of Canada.

———, J. L. Granatstein, and W. R. Young. 1986. *Sacred Trust? Brian Mulroney and the Conservative Party in Power*. Toronto: Doubleday of Canada.

Berger, Carl. 1970. *The Sense of Power: Studies in the Ideas of Canadian Imperialism, 1867-1914*. Toronto: University of Toronto Press.

———. 1976. *The Writing of Canadian History*. Toronto: University of Toronto Press.

Bergeron, Gérard. 1966. *Du Duplessisme au Johnsonnisme*. Montréal: Editions parti pris.

———. 1978. *Ce Jour-là...le Referendum*. Montréal: Editions Quinze.

———. 1984. *Pratique de l'Etat au Québec*. Montréal: Les Editions Québec/Amerique.

Bernard, André. 1978. *What Does Quebec Want?* Toronto: James Lorimer.

Bernier, Ivan and Andrée Lajoie, eds. 1985a. *Law, Society and the Economy*. Volume 46 of the Research Studies prepared for the Royal Commission on the Economic Union and Development Prospects for Canada. Toronto: University of Toronto Press.

———, eds. 1985b. *The Supreme Court of Canada as an Instrument of Political Change*. Volume 47 of the Research Studies prepared for the Royal Commission on the Economic Union and Development Prospects for Canada. Toronto: University of Toronto Press.

Bernier, Ivan, Nicholas Roy, Charles Pentland and Daniel Soberman. 1986. "The Concept of Economic Union in International and Constitutional Law". In *Perspectives on the Canadian Economic Union* edited by Mark Krasnick. Volume 60 of the Research Studies prepared for the Royal Commission on the Economic Union and Development Prospects for Canada, pp. 35- 153. Toronto: University of Toronto Press.

Berry, Glyn. 1974. "The Oil Lobby and the Energy Crisis". *Canadian Public Administration* 12: pp. 600-635.

Birch, Anthony. 1955. *Federalism, Finance and Social Legislation in Canada, Australia and the United States*. London: Oxford University Press.

———. 1986. "Political Authority and Crisis in Comparative Perspective". In *State and Society: Canada in Comparative Perspective*, edited by Keith Banting. Volume 31 of the Research Studies prepared for the Royal Commission on the Economic Union and Development Prospects for Canada, pp. 87-130. Toronto: University of Toronto Press.

Bird, Richard. 1970. *The Growth of Government Spending in Canada*. Toronto: Canadian Tax Foundation.

————. 1978. "The Growth of the Public Service in Canada". In *Public Employment and Compensation in Canada*, edited by D. K. Foot. Montreal: Institute for Research in Public Policy.

————. 1986. *Federal Finance in Comparative Perspective*. Toronto: Canadian Tax Foundation.

Black, Conrad. 1976. *Duplessis*. Toronto: McClelland and Stewart.

Black, Edwin R. 1968. "British Columbia: The Politics of Exploitation". In *Exploiting Our Economic Potential* edited by R. Shearer, pp. 23-41. Toronto: Holt, Rinehart & Winston.

Black, Edwin R. 1975. *Divided Loyalties: Canadian Concepts of Federalism*. Montreal & Kingston: McGill-Queen's University Press.

Black, Edwin R. and Cairns, Alan C. 1966. "A Different Perspective on Canadian Federalism". *Canadian Public Administration* 9: pp. 27-44.

Blais, André, ed. 1986a. *The Political Sociology of Industrial Policy*. Volume 45 of the Research Studies prepared for the Royal Commission on the Economic Union and Development Prospects for Canada. Toronto: University of Toronto Press.

————, ed. 1986b. *Industrial Policy*. Volume 44 of the Research Studies prepared for the Royal Commission on the Economic Union and Development Prospects for Canada. Toronto: University of Toronto Press.

Blishen, Bernard, et al, eds. 1961. *Canadian Society: Sociological Perspectives*. Toronto: Macmillan of Canada.

Bliss, Michael, ed. 1966. *Canadian History in Documents, 1763-1966*. Toronto: The Ryerson Press.

————. 1980. "Rich by Nature, Poor by Policy". in *Entering the Eighties: Canada in Crisis* edited by R. Kenneth Carty and Peter W. Ward. Toronto: Oxford University Press.

————. 1982. *The Evolution of Industrial Policies in Canada: An Historical Survey*. Ottawa: The Economic Council of Canada.

Block, Fred. 1977. *The Origins of International Economic Disorder*. Berkeley: University of California Press.

Bluestone, Barry and Bennett Harrison. 1982. *The Deindustrialization of America*. New York: Basic Books.

Boadway, Robin. 1985. "Federal-Provincial Transfers in Canada: A Critical Review". In *Fiscal Federalism* edited by Mark Krasnick. Volume 65 of the Research Studies prepared for the Royal Commission on the Economic Union and Development Prospects for Canada, pp. 1-95. Toronto: University of Toronto Press.

Bonenfant, Jean-Charles. 1966. "L'Evolution du statut de l'homme politique canadien-français". *Recherches sociographiques* 7: pp. 117-125.

Borins, Sandford F. 1983. *The Language of the Skies: The Bilingual Air Traffic Control Conflict in Canada*. Montreal and Kingston: McGill-Queen's University Press.

Bothwell, Robert, Ian Drummond and John English. 1981. *Canada Since 1945: Politics, Power and Provincialism*. Toronto: University of Toronto Press.

————. 1987. *Canada 1900-1945*. Toronto: University of Toronto Press.

Bourque, Gilles and Nicole Laurin-Frenette. 1972. "Social Class and Nationalist Ideologies in Quebec". In *Capitalism and the National Question in Canada* edited by Gary Teeple, pp. 185-210. Toronto: University of Toronto Press.

Brady, Alexander. 1947. *Democracy in the Dominions: a Comparative Study in Institutions*. Toronto: University of Toronto Press.

————. 1959. "Quebec and Canadian Federalism". *Canadian Journal of Economics and Political Science* 25: pp. 250-270.

Brazeau, Jacques. 1966. "Les nouvelles classes moyennes". *Recherches Sociographiques* 7: pp. 151-164.

Breton, Albert. 1964. "The Economics of Nationalism". *Journal of Political Economy* 72: pp. 376-386.

————. 1965. "A Theory of Government Grants". *Canadian Journal of Economics and Political Science* 31: pp. 175-187.

————. 1985. "Supplementary Statement". In Royal Commission on the Economic Union and Development Prospects for Canada *Report*, Vol. III.

————and Anthony Scott. 1978. *The Economic Constitution of Federal States*. Toronto: University of Toronto Press.

————. 1980. *The Design of Federations*. Montreal: Institute for Research in Public Policy.

Breton, Albert, et. al. 1964-65. "An Appeal for Reason in Politics". *Canadian Forum* 44: pp. 29-33.

Brittain, Samuel. 1977. *The Economic Contradictions of Democracy*. London: Temple Smith.

Britton, John N. H. and James Gilmour. 1978. *The Weakest Link: Technological Perspectives on Canadian Industrial Underdevelopment*. Ottawa: Science Council of Canada.

Brodie, M. Janine and Jane Jenson. 1980. *Crisis Challenge and Change: Party and Class in Canada*. Toronto: Methuen.

Brown, Douglas. 1978. *The Federal Year in Review, 1977-8*. Kingston: Institute of Intergovernmental Relations.

————, 1979. *The Federal Year in Review, 1979*. Kingston: Institute of Intergovernmental Relations.

————. 1987-88. "The Federal-Provincial Consultation Process". In *Canada: the State of theFederation: 1987- 88* edited by Peter M. Leslie and R. L. Watts, pp. 77-96. Kingston: Institute of Intergovernmental Relations.

Brown, Douglas and Julia Eastman, with Ian Robinson. 1981. *The Limits of Consultation: The Debate among Ottawa, the Provinces and the Private Sector on an Industrial Strategy*. Ottawa: The Science Council of Canada and Kingston: Institute of Intergovernmental Relations.

Brown, M. Paul. 1983. "Responsiveness versus Accountability in Collaborative Federalism: The Canadian Experience". *Canadian Public Administration* 26: pp. 629-639.

Bryce, R. B. 1957. "Discussion". *Proceedings*, Ninth Annual Conference. Toronto: Institute of Public Administration of Canada. 162-164.

————. 1986. *Maturing in Hard Times*. Toronto: Institute of Public Administration of Canada and McGill-Queen's University Press.

Bryden, Kenneth. 1974. *Old Age Pensions and Policy-Making in Canada*. Montreal and Kingston: McGill-Queen's University Press.

Bryden, Marion. 1965. *Occupancy of Tax Fields in Canada*. Toronto: Canadian Tax Foundation.

Brym, Robert, ed. 1986. *Regionalism in Canada*. Toronto: Irwin Publishing.

Bucovetsky, M. W. 1975. "The Mining Industry and the Great Tax Reform Debate". In *Pressure Group Behaviour in Canadian Politics* edited by A. Paul Pross, pp. 87-114. Toronto: McGraw-Hill Ryerson.

Burns, R. M. 1965. "The Machinery of Federal-Provincial Relations". *Canadian Public Administration* 8: pp. 527- 534.

————. 1971. *One Country or Two?* Montreal and Kingston: McGill-Queen's University Press.

————. 1976. *Conflict and its Resolution in the Administration of Natural Resources*. Kingston: Centre for Resource Studies.

————. 1980. *The Acceptable Mean: The Tax Rental Agreements. 1941-1962*. Toronto: Canadian Tax Foundation.

Byers, R. B. and Robert Reford, eds. 1979. *Canada Challenged: The Viability of Confederation*. Toronto: Canadian Institute of International Affairs.

Cairns, Alan C. 1970. "The Living Canadian Constitution". *Queen's Quarterly* 77: pp. 1-16.

——. 1971. "The Judicial Committee and its Critics". *Canadian Journal of Political Science* 4: pp. 301-345).

——. 1977. "The Governments and Societies of Canadian Federalism". *Canadian Journal of Political Science* 10: pp. 695-725.

——. 1979a. "The Other Crisis in Canadian Federalism". *Canadian Public Administration* 22: pp. 175-195.

——. 1979b. *From Interstate to Intrastate Federalism in Canada*. Kingston: Institute of Intergovernmental Relations.

——. 1979c. "Recent Federalist Constitutional Proposals: A Review Essay". *Canadian Public Policy* 3: pp. 348-65.

——. 1985. "The Politics of Constitutional Renewal in Canada". In *Redesigning the State: The Politics of Constitutional Change in Industrial Nations* edited by Keith Banting and Richard Simeon, pp. 95-145. Toronto: University of Toronto Press.

——and Cynthia Williams. 1985a. *Constitutionalism, Citizenship and Society in Canada*. Volume 33 of the Research Studies prepared for the Royal Commission on the Economic Union and Development Prospects for Canada. Toronto: University of Toronto Press.

——. 1985b. *The Politics of Gender, Ethnicity and Language in Canada*. Volume 34 of the Research Studies prepared for the Royal Commission on the Economic Union and Development Prospects for Canada. Toronto: University of Toronto Press.

Cameron, David. 1974. *Nationalism, Self-Determination and the Quebec Question*. Toronto: Macmillan of Canada.

——. 1978. "The Growth of the State". *American Political Science Review* 72: pp. 1243-1261.

——. 1984. "Social Democracy, Corporatism, Labor Quiescence and the Representation of Economic Interests in Advanced Capitalist Society". In *Order and Conflict in Contemporary Capitalism*, edited by John Goldthorpe, pp. 143- 178. Oxford: Clarendon Press.

——. 1985. "The Growth of Government Spending: The Canadian Experience in Comparative Perspective". In *State and Society: Canada in Comparative Perspective*, edited by Keith Banting. Volume 31 of the Research Studies prepared for the Royal Commission on the Economic Union and Development Prospects for Canada, pp. 21-51. Toronto: University of Toronto Press.

Campbell, Colin. 1983. *Governments Under Stress: Political Executives and Key Bureaucrats in Washington, London and Ottawa*. Toronto: University of Toronto Press.

Campbell, Robert M. 1987. *Grand Illusions: the Politics of the Keynesian Experience in Canada*. Peterborough: Broadview Press

Canada. 1945. *White Paper on Employment and Income*. Ottawa: King's Printer.

——. 1968a. *Federalism for the Future*. Ottawa: Queen's Printer.

——. 1969a. *The Constitution and the People of Canada*. Ottawa: Queen's Printer

——. 1969b. *Federalism and International Relations*. Ottawa: Queen's Printer.

——. 1969c. *Federal-Provincial Grants and the Spending Power of Parliament*. Ottawa: Queen's Printer.

——. 1969d. *Income Security and Social Services*. Ottawa: Queen's Printer.

——. 1969e. *The Taxing Powers and the Constitution of Canada*. Ottawa: Queen's Printer.

——. 1978. *The Constitutional Amendment Bill: Text and Explanatory Notes*. Ottawa: Supply and Services.

——. 1985. *Progress Report on Federal-Provincial Relations*. Ottawa: Federal-Provincial Relations Office.

——. 1987. *A Guide to the Constitutional Accord*. Ottawa: Government of Canada. .

————. 1981. Canadian Unity Information Office. *Federalism and Decentralization: Where do we Stand?*. Ottawa: Supply and Services.

————. Various years. Commissioner of Official Languages. *Annual Report*. Ottawa: Supply and Services.

————. 1950. Constitutional Conference. *Proceedings*. Ottawa: King's Printer.

————. 1971. Constitutional Conference. *Proceedings*. Ottawa: Information Canada.

————. 1981. Consultative Task Force on Industrial and Regional Developments (Blair-Carr Task Force). *Report*. Ottawa: Supply and Services.

————. 1980. Department of Energy, Mines and Resources. *The National Energy Program*. Ottawa: Supply and Services.

————. 1982. Department of Energy Mines and Resources. *NEP Update*. Ottawa: Supply and Services.

————. 1981. Department of Finance. *Fiscal Arrangements in the Eighties: Proposals of the Government of Canada*. Ottawa: Supply and Services.

————. 1986. Department of Finance. *Securing Economic Renewal: The Budget Speech*. Ottawa: Supply and Services.

————. 1973. Ministry of Health and Welfare. *Working Paper on Social Security for Canadians*. Ottawa: Information Canada.

————. 1986. Department of Justice. *A Consolidation of the Constitution Acts, 1867 to 1982*. Ottawa: Supply and Services.

————. 1960. Dominion-Provincial Conference. *Proceedings*. Ottawa: Queen's Printer.

————. 1987. First Ministers' Conference on the Constitution. *Verbatim Transcript*. Ottawa: Canadian Intergovernmental Conference Secretariat.

————. 1980. Health Services Review. *Canada's National Provincial Helath Program for the 1980s*. Ottawa: Health and Welfare Canada.

————. 1977. Mackenzie Valley Pipeline Inquiry (The Berger Inquiry). *Report*. Ottawa: Supply and Services.

————. 1981. Parliamentary Task Force on Federal-Provincial Fiscal Arrangements. (Breau Task Force) *Fiscal Federalism in Canada*. Ottawa: Supply and Services.

————. 1986. Privy Council Office. (Federal-Provincial Conference, October, 1966). *Proceedings*. Ottawa: Queen's Printer.

————. 1971. Constitutional Conference. *Proceedings*. Ottawa: Information Canada.

————. 1957. Royal Commission on Canada's Economic Prospects. (Gordon Commission) *Report*. Ottawa: Queen's Printer.

————. 1965. Royal Commission on Bilingualism and Biculturalism. *A Preliminary Report*. Ottawa: Queen's Printer.

————. 1969. Royal Commission on Bilingualism and Biculturalism. *Report*. 3 vols. Ottawa: Queen's Printer.

————. 1940. Royal Commission on Dominion-Provincial Relations. (Rowell-Sirois Commission) *Report*. 3 vols. Ottawa: King's Printer.

————. 1985. Royal Commission on the Economic Union and Development Prospects for Canada. (Macdonald Commission) *Report*. 3 vols. Ottawa: Supply and Services.

————. 1951. Royal Commission on National Development in the Arts, Letters and Sciences. (Massey Commission) *Report*. Ottawa: King's Printer.

————. 1970. Royal Commission on the Status of Women. *Report*. Ottawa: Information Canada.

————. 1971. Royal Commission on Taxation. (Carter Commission). *Report*. Ottawa: Information Canada.

———. 1986. Royal Commission on Unemployment Insurance. (Forget Commission). *Report*. Ottawa: Supply and Services.

———. 1971. Senate Committee on Poverty. *Report*. Ottawa: Information Canada.

———. 1982. Senate Standing Committee on National Finance. *Government Policy and Regional Perspectives*. Ottawa: Supply and Services.

———. 1972. Special Joint Committee of the Senate and the House of Commons on the Constitution of Canada. *Final Report*. Ottawa: Information Canada.

———. 1987. Special Joint Committee of the Senate and House of Commons on the 1987 Constitutional Accord. *Report*. Ottawa: Queen's Printer.

———. 1972. Task Force on Foreign Investment. (The Gray Task Force). *Report*. Ottawa: Information Canada.

———. 1979. Task Force on National Unity. *Report: A Future Together: Observations and Recommendations*. Ottawa: Supply and Services.

———. 1979. *A Time to Speak: Views of the Public*. Ottawa: Supply and Services.

Canadian Annual Review of Public Affairs. Various years. Toronto: University of Toronto Press.

Canadian Bar Association. Committee on the Constitution. 1978. *Towards a New Canada*. Montreal: Canadian Bar Association.

Canadian Broadcasting Corporation. Research Services. 1980. *A Question of Country*. Toronto: Canadian Broadcasting Corporation.

Canadian Intergovernmental Conference Secretariat. 1974. *The Constitutional Review, 1968-71*. Ottawa: Information Canada.

———. 1978. *Proposals on the Constitution, 1971-78*. Ottawa: Supply and Services.

Canadian Tax Foundation. Various years. *The National Finances*. Toronto: Canadian Tax Foundation.

———. Various years. *Provincial and Municipal Finances*. Toronto: Canadian Tax Foundation.

Canadian Trade Committee. 1965. *Canadian Economic Policy Since the War*. Ottawa: Carleton University.

Careless, Anthony. 1977. *Initiative and Response: The Adaptation of Canadian Federalism to Regional Economic Expansion*. Montreal and Kingston: McGill-Queen's University Press.

Careless, J. M. S. 1965b. "Metropolitanism and Nationalism". In *Nationalism in Canada* edited by Peter Russell, pp. 271-283. Toronto: McGraw-Hill.

———and R. Craig Brown. 1967. *The Canadians 1867-1967*. Toronto: Macmillan of Canada.

Carmichael, Michael. 1986. *New Stresses on Confederation: Diverging Regional Economies*. Toronto: C. D. Howe Institute.

Carter, George F. 1971. *Canadian Condititonal Grants Since World War II*. Toronto: Canadian Tax Foundation.

Carty, R. Kenneth and Peter W. Ward, eds. 1980. *Entering the Eighties: Canada in Crisis*. Toronto: Oxford University Press.

———, eds. 1986. *National Politics and Community in Canada*. Vancouver: University of British Columbia Press.

Chandler, Marsha A. 1986. "Constitutional Change and Public Policy: the Impact of the Resource Amendment (Section 92A)". *Canadian Journal of Political Science*. 19: pp. 103-126.

———and William M. Chandler. 1979. *Public Policy and Provincial Politics*. Toronto: McGraw-Hill Ryerson.

Chaput, Marcel. 1961. *Pourquoi je suis séparatiste*. Montréal: Editions du jour.

Cheffins, R. I. and Tucker, R. N. 1976. *The Constitutional Process in Canada*. Toronto: McGraw-Hill Ryerson.

Chevalier, Michel and James Taylor. 1971. *Dynamics of Adaptation in the Federal Public Service.* A study prepared for the Royal Commission on Bilingualism and Biculturalism. Ottawa: Queen's Printer.

Chrétien, Jean. 1980. *Securing the Canadian Economic Union in the Constitution.* Ottawa: Supply and Services.

————. 1986. *Straight from the Heart.* Toronto: Seal Books.

Clark, S. D. 1962. *The Developing Canadian Community.* Toronto: University of Toronto Press.

————. 1975. "The Post Second World War Canadian Society". *Canadian Review of Sociology and Anthropology.* 12: pp. 25-32.

Clarke, Harold D., Lawrence Leduc, Jane Jenson and Jon Pammett. 1979. *Political Choice in Canada.* Toronto: McGraw-Hill Ryerson.

Clarkson, Stephen. 1982. *Canada and the Reagan Challenge.* Toronto: James Lorimer.

Clement, Wallace. 1983. *Class, Power and Property: Essays on Canadian Society.* Toronto: Methuen.

————. 1984. "Canada's Social Structure: Capital, Labour and the State, 1930-1980". In *Modern Canada, 1930s-1980s* by Michael S. Cross and Gregory Kealey, pp. 81-101. Toronto: McClelland and Stewart.

Clift, Dominique. 1982. *The Decline of Nationalism in Quebec.* Montreal and Kingston: McGill-Queen's University Press.

Coffey, William J. and Mario Polèse, eds. 1987. *Still Living Together: Recent Trends and Future Directions in Canadian Regional Development.* Montreal: Institute for Research in Public Policy.

Cohen, Lenard, Patrick Smith and Paul Warwick. 1987. *The Vision and the Game: Making the Canadian Constitution.* Calgary: Detselig Enterprises.

Coleman, William. 1984. *The Independence Movement in Quebec.* Toronto: University of Toronto Press

Conway. J. F. 1983. *The West: The History of a Region in Confederation.* Toronto: James Lorimer.

Cook, Ramsay. 1966. *Canada and the French-Canadian Question.* Toronto: Macmillan of Canada.

————. 1971. *The Maple Leaf Forever: Essays on Nationalism and Politics in Canada.* Toronto: Macmillan of Canada.

Corbett, Edward M. 1967. *Quebec Confronts Canada.* Baltimore: Johns Hopkins University Press.

Corry, J. A. 1939a. *Difficulties of Divided Jurisdiction.* A Study prepared for the Royal Commission on Dominion-Provincial Relations. Ottawa: King's Printer.

————. 1939b. *The Growth of Government Activities Since Confederation.* Ottawa: King's Printer.

————. 1958. "Constitutional Trends and Federalism". In *Evolving Canadian Federalism* edited by A. R. M. Lower et al, pp. 92-125. Durham, NC: Duke University Press.

————. 1979. "The Uses of a Constitution". In *Special Lectures, 1978 --The Constitution* by the Law Society of Upper Canada. Toronto: Law Society of Upper Canada.

————. 1981. *My Life and Work: A Happy Partnership.* Kingston: Queen's University.

Courchene, Thomas J. 1984. *Equalization Payments Past Present and Future.* Toronto: Ontario Economic Council.

————. 1986a. *Economic Management and the Division of Powers.* Volume 67 of the Research Studies prepared for the Royal Commission on the Economic Union and Development Prospects for Canada. Toronto: University of Toronto Press.

————. 1986b. "Market Nationalism". In *Policy Options* 7: (October) pp. 7-12.

————. 1987. *Social Policy in the 1990s: Agenda for Reform*. Toronto: C. D. Howe Institute.

————, et al, eds. 1985. *Ottawa and the Provinces: the Distribution of Money and Power*. 2 vols. Toronto: Ontario Economic Council.

Craig, Gerald M., ed. 1963. *Lord Durham's Report*. Toronto: McClelland and Stewart.

Craven, Paul and Tom Traves. 1979. "National Policy, 1872- 1933". *Journal of Canadian Studies* 14: pp. 14-38.

Creighton, Donald. 1939. "Conservatism and National Unity". In *Essays in Canadian History Presented to George Mackinnon Wrong* edited by R. Flenley, pp. 154-177. Toronto: Macmillan of Canada.

————. 1970. *Canada's First Century*. Toronto: Macmillan of Canada.

Crépeau P.-A. and C. B. Macpherson, eds. 1965. *The Future of Canadian Federalism*. Toronto: University of Toronto Press.

Cross, Michael S. and Gregory Kealey. 1984. *Modern Canada, 1930s-1980s*. Toronto: McClelland and Stewart.

Crouch, Colin. ed. 1979. *State and Economy in Contemporary Capitalism*. London: Croom Helm.

————. 1985. "Conditions for Trade Union Restraint". In *The Politics of Inflation and Stagflation*, edited by Leon Lindberg and Charles Maier, pp. 105-139. Washington, DC: Brookings Institution.

Crozier, Michael, et. al. 1975. *The Crisis of Democracy*. New York: New York University Press.

Cuming, R. ed. 1986. *Perspectives on the Harmonization of Law in Canada*. Volume 55 of the Research Studies prepared for the Royal Commission on the Economic Union and Development Prospects for Canada. Toronto: University of Toronto Press.

————. 1986b. *Harmonization of Business Law in Canada*. Volume 56 of the Research Studies prepared for the Royal Commission on the Economic Union and Development Prospects for Canada. Toronto: University of Toronto Press.

Cumming, Peter. 1986. "Equitable Fiscal Federalism: The Problems in Respect of Resource Revenue Sharing". In *Fiscal Federalism*, edited by Mark Krasnick. Volume 65 of the Research Studies prepared for the Royal Commission on the Economic Union and Development Prospects for Canada, pp. 49-95. Toronto: University of Toronto Press.

Dafoe, J. W. 1963. *Laurier: A Study in Canadian Politics*. Toronto: McClelland and Stewart.

Dahl, Robert. 1961. *Who Governs?*. New Haven, CT: Yale University Press.

————and Charles E. Lindblom. 1953. *Politics, Economics and Welfare*. New York: Harper.

————and Edward Tufte. 1973. *Size and Democracy*. Stanford: Stanford University Press.

Dalfen, Charles M. and Laurence Dunbar. 1986. "Transportation and Communications: The Constitution and the Canadian Economic Union". In *Perspectives on the Canadian Economic Union*, edited by Mark Krasnick. Volume 60 of the Research Studies prepared for the Royal Commission on the Economic Union and Development Prospects for Canada, pp. 139-202. Toronto: University of Toronto Press.

Dawson, R. M. 1933. *Constitutional Issues in Canada: 1900-1931*. London: Oxford University Press.

Desbarats, Peter. 1965. *The State of Quebec: A Journalist's View of the Quiet Revolution*. Toronto: McClelland and Stewart.

Deutsch, John. 1970. *Study on Maritime Union*. Fredericton: Maritime Union Study.

Dion, Léon. 1961. "De l'ancien au nouveau régime". *Cité libre* 12: pp. 3-15.

————. 1963. "The Origin and Character of the Nationalism of Growth". *Canadian Forum* 43: pp. 179-183.

————. 1966. "La polarité des idéologies: conservatisme et progressisme". *Recherches Sociographiques* 7: pp. 23-35.

————. 1967. *Le Bill 60 et la société Québécoise*. Montréal: Editions HMH.

————. 1980. *Le Québéc and le Canada: les voies de l'avenir*. Montréal: Les éditions Québecor.

Dodge, William, ed. 1978. *Consultation and Consensus: a New Era in Policy Formulation?*. Ottawa: The Conference Board in Canada.

————, ed. 1982b. *How Ottawa Spends*. Ottawa: School of Public Administration, Carleton University.

————and Richard Phidd. 1983. *Canadian Public Policy: Ideas, Structure, Process*. Toronto: Methuen.

————and Glen Toner. 1985. *The Politics of Energy: the Development and Implementation of the NEP*. Toronto: Methuen.

Donnelly, Murray. 1963. *The Government of Manitoba*. Toronto: University of Toronto Press.

Downs, Anthony. 1957. *An Economic Theory of Democracy*. New York: Harper.

Drache, Daniel and Duncan Cameron. 1985. *The Other Macdonald Report*. Toronto: James Lorimer.

Draper, James A. 1971. *Citizen Participation: Canada*. Toronto: New Press.

Drummond, Ian. 1972. *The Canadian Economy: Structure and Development*. Georgetown, ON: Irwin-Dorsey.

Dunn, Shelagh. 1982. *The Year in Review, 1981: Intergovernmental Relations in Canada*. Kingston: Institute of Intergovernmental Relations.

————. 1983. *The Year in Review, 1982: Intergovernmental Relations in Canada*. Kingston: Institute of Intergovernmental Relations.

Dupré, Stefan. 1964. "Contracting Out: A Funny Thing Happened on the Way to the Centennial". *Proceedings*, pp. 209-218. 18th Tax Conference. Toronto: Canadian Tax Foundation.

————. 1980. "Reflections on the Fiscal and Economic Aspects of Government by Conference". *Canadian Public Administration* 23: pp. 54-59.

————. 1985. "Reflections on the Workability of Executive Federalism". In *Intergovernmental Relations* edited by Richard Simeon. Volume 63 in the Research Studies prepared for the Royal Commission on the Economic Union and Development Prospects for Canada, pp. 1-32. Toronto: University of Toronto Press.

------ et. al. 1973. *Federalism and Policy Development: The Case of Adult Occupational Training in Ontario*. Toronto: University of Toronto Press.

————and Paul Weiler. 1979. "A Sense of Proportion and a Sense of Priorities: Reflections on the Report of the Task Force on Canadian Unity". *Canadian Bar Review* lvii: pp. 446-471.

Dwivedi, O. P. ed. 1982. *The Administrative State in Canada*. Toronto: University of Toronto Press.

Dyck, Rand. 1976. "The Canada Assistance Plan: The Ultimate in Cooperative Federalism". *Canadian Public Administration* 19: pp. 587-602.

————. 1986. *Provincial Politics in Canada*. Toronto: Prentice-Hall.

Easterbrook, W. T. and Aitken, Hugh. 1980. *Canadian Economic History*. Toronto: Gage.

————and M. H. Watkins, eds. 1967. *Approaches to Canadian Economic History*. Toronto: McClelland and Stewart.

Economic Council of Canada. Various dates. *Annual Review*. Ottawa: Supply and Services.

————. 1977. *Living Together: A Study of Regional Disparities*. Ottawa: Supply and Services.

————. 1982. *Financing Confederation Today and Tomorrow*. Ottawa: Supply and Services.

————. 1983. *The Bottom Line: Trade, Technology and Income Growth*. Ottawa: Supply and Services.

Elkins, David and Richard Simeon. 1980. *Small Worlds: Provinces and Parties in Canadian Political Life*. Toronto: Methuen.

Epstein, David F. 1984. *The Political Theory of The Federalist*. Chicago: University of Chicago Press.

Epstein, Leon D. 1964. "A Comparative Study of Canadian Parties". *American Political Science Review* 58: pp. 46-59.

Esman, Milton, ed. 1977. *Ethnic Conflict in the Western World*. Ithaca, NY: Cornell University Press.

———. 1984. "Federalism and Modernization: Canada and the United States". *Publius* 14: pp. 21-38.

Ethier, Mireille. 1986. "Regional Grievances: The Quebec Case". In *Disparities and Inter-regional Adjustment* edited by Kenneth Norrie. Volume 64 of the Research Studies prepared for the Royal Commission on the Economic Union and Development Prospects for Canada, pp. 159-184. Toronto: University of Toronto Press.

Fairley, Scott. 1986. "Constitutional Aspects of External Trade Policy". In *Case Studies in the Division of Powers* edited by Mark Krasnick. Volume 62 of the Research Studies prepared for the Royal Commission on the Economic Union and Development Prospects for Canada, pp. 1-51. Toronto: University of Toronto Press.

Falardeau, Jean-Charles. 1961. "Le Canada-français politique vue de l'interieur". *Recherches sociographiques* 2: pp. 295-340.

———. 1966. "Des élites Traditionaelles aux élites nouvelles". *Recherches sociographiques* 7: pp. 131-151.

Faribault, Marcel. 1962. *Le Canada-français d'Aujourd'hui*. Montréal: Trust General du Canada.

———and Robert M. Fowler. 1965. *Ten to One: the Confederation Wager*. Toronto: Mc-Clelland and Stewart.

Favreau, Guy. 1965. "National Leadership in Canadian Federalism". In *Concepts of Federalism* edited by Gordon Hawkins, pp. 46-51. Toronto: Canadian Institute of Public Affairs.

Feldman, Elliott and Neil Nevitte. 1979. *The Future of North America: Canada, the United States and Quebec Nationalism*. Cambridge: Harvard University Press.

Firestone, O. J. ed. 1974, *Regional Economic Development*. Ottawa: University of Ottawa Press.

Flenley, R. ed. 1939. *Essays in Canadian History Presented to George Mackinnon Wrong*. Toronto: Macmillan of Canada.

Fletcher, Frederick J and Donald C. Wallace. 1986. "Federal-Provincial Relations and the Making of Public Policy in Canada". In *Division of Powers and Public Policy* edited by Richard Simeon. Volume 61 of the Research Studies prepared for the Royal Commission on the Economic Union and Development Prospects for Canada, pp. 125-206. Toronto: University of Toronto Press.

Foot, D. K. ed. 1978. *Public Employment and Compensation in Canada*. Montreal: Institute for Research in Public Policy.

Forbes, H. D., ed. 1985. *Canadian Political Thought*. Toronto: Oxford University Press.

Forget, Claude E. 1986. "The Harmonization of Social Policy". In *Fiscal Federalism*, edited by Mark Krasnick. Volume 65 in the Research Studies prepared for the Royal Commission on the Economic Union and Development Prospects for Canada, pp. 97-128. Toronto: University of Toronto Press.

Forsey, Eugene. 1962. "Canada: Two Nations or One?". *Canadian Journal of Economics and Political Science* 28: pp. 485-501.

———. 1964-65. "The British North America Act and Bilculturalism". *Queen's Quarterly* 71: pp. 141-149.

Foster, Peter. 1983. *The Sorcerer's Apprentices: Canada's Super-Bureaucrats and the Energy Mess*. Toronto: Totem Books.

Fournier, Pierre. 1976. *The Quebec Establishment*. Montreal: Black Rose.

Fowke, V. C. 1952. "The National Policy Old and New". In *Canadian Journal of Economics and Political Science* 18: pp. 271-286.

————. 1957. *The National Policy and the Wheat Economy*. Toronto: University of Toronto Press.

Francis, R. Douglas and Donald B. Smith. eds. 1982. *Readings in Canadian History, Post Confederation*. Toronto: Holt, Rinehart and Winston of Canada.

Franks, C. E. S. 1987. *The Parliament of Canada*. Toronto: University of Toronto Press.

Fraser, Blair. 1967. *The Search for Identity: Canada: Postwar and Present, 1945-1967*. Garden City, NJ: Doubleday.

Fraser, Graham. 1972. *Fighting Back: Urban Renewal in Trefann Court*. Toronto: Hakkert.

————. 1984. *PQ: René Levesque and the Parti Quebecois in Power*. Toronto: Macmillan of Canada.

French, Richard. 1980. *How Ottawa Decides: Planning and Industrial Policy-making, 1965-1980*. Toronto: James Lorimer.

Friesen, Gerald. 1984. *The Canadian Prairies: A History*. Toronto: University of Toronto Press.

Friesen, J. and H. K. Ralston, eds. 1980. *Historical Essays on British Columbia*. Toronto: Gage.

Gagnon, Alain, ed. 1984. *Quebec State and Society*. Toronto: Methuen.

Gallant, Edgar. 1965. "The Machinery of Federal-Provincial Relations". In *Canadian Public Administration* 8: pp. 515-526.

Garigue, Philippe. 1963. *L'Option politique du Canada français*. Montréal: Editions du Levrier.

Gaventa, John. 1980. *Power and Powerlessness: Quiescence and Rebellion in an Appalachian Valley*. Urbana, IL: University of Illinois Press.

Gellner, Ernst. 1983. *Nations and Nationalism*. Ithaca: Cornell University Press.

Gerin-Lajoie, Paul. 1950. *Constitutional Amendment in Canada*. Toronto: University of Toronto Press.

————. 1957. "Looking to a New Era in Federal-Provincial Relations". In *Canadian Tax Journal* 5: pp. 62-68.

Gibbins, Roger. 1980. *Prairie Politics and Society: Regionalism in Decline*. Toronto: Butterworths.

————. 1982. *Regionalism: Territorial Politics in Canada and the United States*. Toronto: Butterworths.

Gillespie, W. I. 1979. "Postwar Canadian Fiscal Policy Revisited, 1945-75". *Canadian Tax Journal* 27: pp. 265- 276.

Gilligan, Carol. 1982. *In a Different Voice*. Cambridge: Harvard University Press.

Glenday, Daniel, Hubert Guindon and Allan Turowetz, eds. 1978. *Modernization and the Canadian State*. Toronto: Macmillan of Canada.

Goldthorpe, John. 1982. "Problems of Political Economy after the End of the Postwar Period". Nuffield College: Mimeographed.

————, ed. 1984. *Order and Conflict in Contemporary Capitalism*. Oxford: Clarendon Press.

Gollner, Andrew B. and Daniel Salee. 1988. *Canada Under Mulroney: an End of Term Report*. Montreal: Vehicule Press.

Gough, Ian. 1982. *The Political Economy of the Welfare State*. London: Macmillan.

Gourevitch, Peter. 1986. *Politics in Hard Times: Comparative Responses to International Economic Crises*. Ithaca, NY: Cornell University Press.

Grant, George. 1965. *Lament for a Nation*. Toronto: McClelland and Stewart.

Guest, Dennis. 1980. *The Emergence of Social Security in Canada*. Vancouver: University of British Columbia Press.

Graham, Ron. 1986. *One-eyed Kings: Promise and Illusion in Canadian Politics*. Toronto: Collins.

Granatstein, J. L. 1975. *Canada's War*. Toronto: University of Toronto Press.

———. 1982. *The Ottawa Men: The Civil Service Mandarins 1935-1957*. Toronto: Oxford University Press.

Great Britain. 1942. Interdepartmental Committee on Social Insurance and Allied Services. *Report*. (The Beveridge Report.) London: Her Majesty's Stationery Office.

Groulx, L'Abbé. 1985. "Tomorrow's Tasks". In *Canadian Political Thought* edited by H. D. Forbes, pp. 255-270. Toronto: Oxford University Press.

Guindon, Hubert. 1964-5. "Social Unrest, Social Class, and Quebec's Bureaucratic Revolution". *Queen's Quarterly* 71: pp. 150-162.

Gwynn, Richard. 1968. *Smallwood: The Unlikely Revolutionary*. Toronto: McClelland and Stewart.

Habermas, Jurgen. 1975. *Legitimation Crisis*. Boston: Beacon Press.

Hamelin , J. and F. Harvey. 1976. *Les travailleurs québécois 1941-1971*. Québec: Cahiers de l'Institut Superieur de Sciences Humaines: Université Laval.

Haggart, Ron, and Aubrey E. Golden. 1971. *Rumours of War*. Toronto: New Press.

Hall, Peter. 1986. *Governing the Economy*. Oxford: Oxford Uuniversity Press.

Hamilton, Richard and Maurice Pinard. 1982. "The Quebec Independence Movement". In *National Separatism* edited by Colin H. Williams, pp. 203-234. Vancouver: University of British Columbia Press.

Hampson, Fen. 1986. *Forming Economic Policy: the Case of Energy in Canada and Mexico*. New York: St. Martin's Press.

Hardin, Herschel. 1974. *A Nation Unaware: The Canadian Economic Culture*. Vancouver: J. J. Douglas.

Hawkins, Gordon, ed. 1965. *Concepts of Federalism*. Toronto: Canadian Institute of Public Affairs.

Heilbroner, Robert L. 1975. *The Economic Problem*. 4th ed. Englewood Cliffs, NJ: Prentice-Hall.

Heintzman, Ralph. 1983. "The Political Culture of Quebec, 1840-1960". *Canadian Journal of Political Science* 16: 3-59.

L'Heureux, Jacques. 1985. "Municipalities and the Division of Powers". In *Intergovernmental Relations*, edited by Richard Simeon. Volume 63 of the Research Studies prepared for the Royal Commission on the Economic Union and Development Prospects for Canada, pp. 179-214. Toronto: University of Toronto Press.

Hirsch, F. and J. Goldthorpe, eds. 1978. *The Political Economy of Inflation*. London: Martin Robertson.

Hirschman, Albert. 1970. *Exit, Voice and Loyalty*. Cambridge: Harvard University Press.

———. 1987. *Shifting Involvements*. Princeton, NJ: Princeton University Press.

Hockin, Tom, ed. 1971. *Apex of Power: The Prime Minister and Political Leadership in Canada*. Toronto: Prentice-Hall of Canada.

Hodgetts, J. E. 1966. "Regional Interests and Policy in a Federal Structure". *Canadian Journal of Economics and Political Science* 32: pp. 3-14.

———. 1973. *The Canadian Public Service: A Physiology of Government 1867-1970*. Toronto: University of Toronto Press.

———and O. P. Dwivedi. 1969. "The Growth of Government in Canada". *Canadian Public Administration* 12: pp. 224- 238.

————and O. P. Dwivedi. 1974. *Provincial Governments as Employers*. Montreal and Kingston: McGill-Queen's University Press.

Hogg, Peter. 1985. *Constitutional Law in Canada*. 2nd ed. Toronto: The Carswell Company Limited.

Hood, W. C. 1964. "Economic Policy in Our Federal State". *Canadian Tax Journal* 12: pp. 389-397.

Horowitz, Gad. 1966. "Conservatism, Liberalism and Socialism in Canada: An Interpretation". *Canadian Journal of Economics and Political Science* 32: pp. 143-171.

————. 1968a. "Toward the Democratic Class Struggle". In *Agenda 1970: Proposals for a Creative Politics* edited by Trevor Lloyd and Jack McLeod, pp. 241-255. Toronto: University of Toronto Press.

————. 1968b. *Canadian Labour in Politics*. Toronto: Uuniversity of Toronto Press.

Howard, John and William Stanbury. 1984. "Measuring Leviathan". In *Understanding Leviathan* edited by George Lermer, pp. 87-110. Vancouver: Fraser Institute.

Hueglin, Thomas O. 1984. *Federalism and Fragmentation*. Kingston: Institute of Intergovernmental Relations.

Hum, Derek. 1983. *Federalism and the Poor: A Review of the Canada Assistance Program*. Toronto: Ontario Economic Council.

Hurley, James Ross. 1966-67. "Federalism, Coordinate Status and the Canadian Situation". *Queen's Quarterly* 73: pp. 157-166.

Inglehart, Ronald. 1977. *The Silent Revolution: Changing Values and Political Styles among Western Publics*. Princeton, NJ: Princeton University Press.

Innis, Harold A. 1956. *Essays in Canadian Economic History*. Toronto: University of Toronto Press.

Innis, Hugh R. 1873. *Bilingualism and Biculturalism: An Abridged Version of the Royal Commission Report*. Toronto: McClelland and Stewart.

Institute of Intergovernmental Relations. 1969. *Report: Intergovernmental Liaison on Fiscal and Economic Matters*. Ottawa: Queen's Printer.

————and Economic Council of Canada. 1979. *Proceedings: Workshop on the Political Economy of Confederation*. Ottawa: Supply and Services.

————. 1980. *The Question: The Debate on the Referendum Question, Quebec National Assembly, March 4 to 20, 1980*. Kingston: Institute of Intergovernmental Relations.

Irvine, William P. 1979. *Does Canada Need a New Electoral System?*. Kingston: Institute of Intergovernmental Relations.

Irving, John A. 1959. *The Social Credit Movement in Alberta*. Toronto: University of Toronto Press.

Jamieson, Stuart. 1968. *Times of Trouble: Labour Unrest and Industrial Conflict in Canada, 1900-1966*. Ottawa: Privy Council Office.

Jenkin, Michael. 1983. *The Challenge of Diversity: Industrial Policy in the Canadian Federation*. Background Study No. 50, Science Council of Canada. Ottawa: Supply and Services.

Johnson, A. W. 1968. "The Dynamics of Federalism". In *Canadian Journal of Political Science* 1: pp. 18-39.

————. 1975. "Canada's Social Security Review". In *Canadian Public Policy* 1: pp. 456-472.

————. 1985. *Giving Greater Point and Purpose to The Federal Financing of Post-Secondary Education and Research in Canada*. Ottawa: Secretary of State.

Johnson, Daniel. 1965. *Egalité ou indépendance*. Montréal: Les éditions Renaissance.

Johnson, Harry G. 1963. *The Canadian Quandry*. Toronto: McGraw-Hill.

Johnson, Leo. 1972. "The Development of Class in Canada in the Twentieth Century". In *Capitalism and the National Question in Canada* edited by Gary Teeple, pp. 142-183. Toronto: University of Toronto Press.

Johnston, Richard. 1980. "Federal and Provincial Voting: Contemporary Patterns and Historical Evolution". In *Small Worlds: Provinces and Parties in Candian Political Life* edited by David Elkins and Richard Simeon, pp. 131-178. Toronto: Methuen.

———. 1986. *Public Opinion and Public Policy in Canada.* Volume 35 of the Research Studies prepared for the Royal Commission on the Economic Union and Development Prospects for Canada. Toronto: University of Toronto Press.

Jones, Richard. 1972. *Community in Crisis: French-Canadian Nationalism in Perspective.* Toronto: McClelland and Stewart.

Joy, Richard. 1972. *Languages in Conflict.* Toronto: McClelland and Stewart.

Katzenstein, P. 1976. "International Relations and Domestic Structures: Foreign Economic Policies of Advanced Industrial States". In *International Organization* 30: pp. 1021- 1034.

———. 1985. *Small States in World Markets.* Ithaca, NY: Cornell University Press.

Katznelson, Ira and Aristide Zolberg. 1986. *Working Class Formation.* Princeton, NJ: Princeton University Press.

Kent, Tom. 1962. *Social Policy in Canada: Towards a Philosophy of Social Security.* Ottawa: Policy Press.

Keohane, Robert. 1984. "The World Political Economy and the Crisis of Embedded Liberalism". In *Order and Conflict in Contemporary Capitalism* edited by John Goldthorpe. Oxford: Clarendon Press.

———and Joseph Nye. 1977. *Power and Interdependence.* Boston: Little, Brown.

Keyfitz, Nathan. 1963-64. "Canadians and Canadiens". In *Queen's Quarterly* 70: pp. 163-182.

Keynes, J. M. *The General Theory of Employment, Interest and Money.* London: Macmillan.

King, Anthony. 1975. "Overload: Problems of Governing in the 1970s". In *Political Studies* 23: pp. 284-296.

Kitchen, Harry M. and M. L. McMillan. 1986. "Local Government and Canadian Federalism". In *Intergovernmental Relations* edited by Richard Simeon. Volume 63 of the Research Studies prepared for the Royal Commission on the Economic Union and Development Prospects for Canada, pp. 215-261. Toronto: University of Toronto Press.

Kong, Shiu L. and Riten Ray, eds. 1978. *Unity Within Diversity.* Toronto: University of Toronto Press.

Kornberg, A. and H. D. Clarke, eds. 1983. *Political Support in Canada: The Crisis Years.* Durham, NC: Duke University Press.

Korpi, Walter and Michael Shalev. 1979. "Strikes, Industrial Relations and Class Conflict in Capitalist Society". In *British Journal of Sociology* 30: pp. 164-187.

Krasner, Stephen. 1976. "State Power and the Structure of International Trade". *World Politics* 28: pp. 317-347.

Krasnick, Mark, ed. 1986a. *Perspectives on the Canadian Economic Union.* Volume 60 in the Research Studies prepared for the Royal Commission on the Economic Union and Development Prospects for Canada. Toronto: University of Toronto Press.

———, ed. 1986b. *Case Studies in the Division of Powers.* Volume 62 of the Research Studies prepared for the Royal Commission on the Economic Union and Development Prospects for Canada. Toronto: University of Toronto Press.

———, ed. 1985c. *Fiscal Federalism.* Volume 65 of the Research Studies prepared for the Royal Commission on the Economic Union and Development Prospects for Canada. Toronto: University of Toronto Press.

Kresl, R. K. 1974. "The New Nationalism and Economic Rationality". In *American Journal of Canadian Studies* 4: pp. 2-19.

Kruhlak, Orest et. al. eds. 1970. *The Canadian Political Process: A Reader*. Toronto: Holt, Rinehart and Winston.

Kumar, Pradeep. 1986. "Union Growth in Canada: Retrospect and Prospect". In *Canadian Labour Relations* edited by Craig Riddell. Volume 16 of the Research Studies prepared for the Royal Commission on the Economic Union and Development Prospects for Canada, pp. 95-160. Toronto: University of Toronto Press.

Kwavnick, D. 1965. "The Roots of French-Canadian Discontent". *Canadian Journal of Economics and Political Science* 31: pp. 509-523.

————. 1972. *Organized Labour and Pressure Politics: The CLC, 1956-1968*. Montreal and Kingston: McGill-Queen's University Press.

————, ed. 1973. *The Tremblay Report*. Toronto: McClelland and Stewart.

La Forest, Gérard V. 1967. *The Allocation of Tax Fields Under the Canadian Constitution*. Toronto: Canadian Tax Foundation.

Lajoie, Andrée, Pierette Mulazzi and Michelle Gamache. 1986. "Political Ideas in Quebec and the Evolution of Canadian Constitutional Law, 1945 to 1985". In *The Supreme Court of Canada as an Instrument of Social Change* edited by Ivan Bernier and Andree Lajoie. Volume 47 of the Research Studies prepared for the Royal Commission on the Economic Union and Development Prospects for Canada, pp. 1-103. Toronto: University of Toronto Press.

Lamarsh, Judy. 1969. *Memoirs of a Bird in a Gilded Cage*. McClelland and Stewart.

Lamontagne, Maurice. 1954. *Le fédéralisme canadien*. Québec: Presses de l'Université Laval.

Landau, Martin and Eva Eagle. 1981. "On the Concept of Decentralization". Berkeley, CA: University of California, mimeographed.

Lapierre, Laurier, et. al., eds. 1971. *Essays on the Left: Essays in Honour of T. C. Douglas*. Toronto: McClelland and Stewart.

Laski, Harold. 1939. "The Obsolescence of Federalism". In *The People, Politics and the Politician* edited by A. N. Christensen and E. M. Kirkpatrick, pp. 53-76. New York: Holt, Rinehart and Winston.

Latouche, Daniel. 1974. "La vraie nature de la Révolution tranquille". In *Canadian Journal of Political Science* 7: pp. 524-536.

————. *Canada and Quebec: Past and Future*. Volume 70 in the Research Studies prepared for the Royal Commission on the Economic Union and Development Prospects for Canada. Toronto: University of Toronto Press.

Laux, Jeanne and Maureen Molot. 1988. *State Capitalism: Public Enterprise in Canada*. Ithaca, NY: Cornell University Press.

Laxer, James. 1976. *Canada's Unions*. Toronto: James Lorimer.

————. 1983. *Oil and Gas: Ottawa, the Provinces and the Petroleum Industry*. Toronto: James Lorimer.

Lederman, W. R., ed. 1964. *The Courts and the Canadian Constitution*. Toronto: McClelland and Stewart.

————. 1971. "Cooperative Federalism". In *Queen's Quarterly* 78: pp. 7-17.

————. 1981. *Continuing Canadian Constitutional Dilemmas*. Toronto: Butterworths.

Léger, Jean-Marc. 1957-58. "Aspects of French-Canadian Nationalism". In *University of Toronto Quarterly* 27: pp. 310-329.

————. 1963. "The New Face of Centralism". In *Canadian Forum* 43: pp. 155-6.

Leman, Christopher. 1980. *The Collapse of Reform: Political Institutions and the Poor in Canada and the U.S.* Cambridge, MA: Massachusets Institute of Technology.

Leslie, Peter M., ed. 1986, 1987. *Canada: the State of the Federation, 1985*. Kingston: Institute of Intergovernmental Relations.

———, ed. 1987. *Canada: the State of the Federation, 1986*. Kingston: Institute of Intergovernmental Relations.

———. 1987. *Federal State, National Economy*. Toronto: University of Toronto Press.

———. 1986. "Canada as a Bicommunal Polity". In *Recurring Issues in Canadian Federalism* edited by Clare Beckton and A. Wayne MacKay. Volume 57 in the Research Studies prepared for the Royal Commission on the Economic Union and Development Prospects for Canada, pp. 113-144. Toronto: University of Toronto Press.

———and R. L. Watts, eds. *Canada: the State of the Federation: 1987-88*. Kingston: Institute of Intergovernmental Relations.

Lermer, George, ed. 1984. *Probing Leviathan: An Investigation of Government in the Economy*. Vancouver: The Fraser Institute.

Levesque, René. 1968. *An Option for Quebec*. Toronto: McClelland and Stewart.

———. 1986. Translated by Philip Stratford. *Memoirs*. Toronto: McClelland and Stewart.

Levitt, Kari. 1970. *Silent Surrender: The Multinational Corporation in Canada*. Toronto: Macmillan of Canada.

Lindberg, Leon, Colin Crouch, and Claus Offe, eds. 1975. *Stress and Contradiction in Modern Capitalism: Public Policy and the Theory of the State*. Toronto: Lexington.

———and Charles Maier. 1985. *The Politics of Inflation and Stagflation*. Washington, DC: Brookings Institution.

Lipset, S. M. 1960. *Political Man: The Social Bases of Politics*. New York: Doubleday.

———. 1968. *Agrarian Socialism: The Cooperative Commonwealth Federation in Saskatchewan*. Revised ed. Garden City, NJ: Anchor Books.

———. 1970a. "Canada and the United States: A Comparative View". In *Poverty and Social Policy in Canada* edited by W. E. Mann, pp. 488-498. Toronto: Copp Clark.

———. 1970b. "Revolution and Counter-Revolution: The United States and Canada". In *The Canadian Political Process: A Reader* edited by Orest Kruhlak et. al., pp. 13-38. Toronto: Holt, Rinehart & Winston.

———and Stein Rokkan. 1965. *Party Systems and Voter Alignments: Cross-National Perspectives*. New York: Basic Books.

Lithwick, Harvey. 1967. *Economic Growth in Canada: A Quantitative Analysis*. Toronto: University of Toronto Press.

———. 1986. "Federal Government Economic Development Policies: An Evaluative Survey". In *Disparities and Interregional Adjustment* edited by Kenneth Norrie. Volume 64 of the Research Studies for the Royal Commission on the Economic Union and Development Prospects for Canada, pp. 109-157. Toronto: University of Toronto Press.

Livingston, William S. 1956. *Federalism and Constitutional Change*. Oxford: Oxford University Press.

Lloyd, Trevor and Jack McLeod. 1968. *Agenda 1970: Proposals for a Creative Politics*. Toronto: University of Toronto Press.

Lower, A. R. M. 1973. *Canada: An Outline History*. Toronto: McGraw-Hill Ryerson.

------ et. al. 1958. *Evolving Canadian Federalism*. Durham, NC: Duke University Press.

Lukes, Steven. 1977. "Power and Structure". In *Essays in Social Theory*. London: Macmillan.

Lumsden, Ian, ed. 1970. *Close the 49th Parallel*. Toronto: University of Toronto Press.

Lynn, James H. 1967. *Federal-Provincial Fiscal Relations*. Study prepared for the Royal Commission on Taxation. Ottawa: Queen's Printer.

Macdonald, Donald C., ed. 1975. *Government and Politics in Ontario*. Toronto: Macmillan of Canada.

MacDonald, L. Ian. 1984a. *From Bourassa to Bourassa: a Pivotal Decade in Canadian History*. Toronto: Harvest House.

———. 1984b. *Mulroney: The Making of the Prime Minister*. Toronto: McClelland and Stewart.

MacKay, A. Wayne and Richard Bauman. 1985. "The Supreme Court of Canada: Reform Implications for an Emerging National Institution". In *The Courts and the Charter* edited by Clare Beckton and A. Wayne MacKay. Volume 58 of the Research Studies prepared for the Royal Commission on the Economic Union and Development Prospects for Canada, pp. 37-131. Toronto: University of Toronto Press.

———and Clare Beckton. 1986. "Institutional and Constitutional Arrangements: An Overview". In *Recurring Issues in Canadian Federalism* edited by Clare Beckton and A. Wayne MacKay. Volume 57 of the Research Studies prepared for the Royal Commission on the Economic Union and Development Propsects for Canada, pp. 1-76. Toronto: University of Toronto Press.

Mackintosh, W. A. 1967. *The Economic Background of Dominion-Provincial Relations*. Carleton Library edition. Toronto: McClelland and Stewart.

McLarty, Robert. 1967. "Organizing for a Federal-Provincial Fiscal Policy". *Canadian Tax Journal* 15: pp. 412-420.

Magnusson, Warren, et. al. 1984. *The New Reality: The Politics of Restraint in British Columbia*. Vancouver: New Star Books.

Maier, Charles. 1975. *Recasting Bourgeois Europe*. Princeton, NJ: Princeton University Press.

Mallory, J. R. 1948. "Disallowance and the National Interest: The Alberta Social Credit Legislation of 1937". In *Canadian Journal of Economics and Political Science* 14: pp. 342-357.

———. 1961. "The Lieutenant Governor's Discretionary Powers". In *Canadian Journal of Economics and Political Science* 27: pp. 518-522.

———. 1958. "The Five Faces of Federalism". In *The Future of Canadian Federalism* edited by P.-A. Crepeau and C. B. Macpherson, pp. 3-15. Toronto: University of Toronto Press.

———. 1954, 1976. *Social Credit and the Federal Power In Canada*. Toronto: University of Toronto Press.

Macpherson, C. B. 1962. *Democracy in Alberta: Social Credit and the Party System*. 2nd ed. Toronto: University of Toronto Press.

Mann, W. E. ed. 1970a. *Poverty and Social Policy in Canada*. Toronto: Copp Clark.

———, ed. 1970b. *Social and Cultural Change in Canada*. 2 Vols. Toronto: Copp Clark Pitman.

Mansell, Robert L. and Lawrence Copithorne. 1986. "Canadian Regional Economic Disparities: A Survey". In *Disparities and Interregional Adjustment* edited by Keneth Norrie. Volume 64 of the Research Studies prepared for the Royal Commission on the Economic Union and Development Prospects for Canada, pp. 1- 51. Toronto: University of Toronto Press.

Manthorpe, Jonathan. 1974. *The Power and the Tories: Ontario Politics 1943 to the Present*. Toronto: Macmillan of Canada.

Manzer, Ronald. 1974. *Canada: A Sociopolitical Report*. Toronto: McGraw-Hill Ryerson.

———. 1985. *Public Policies and Political Development in Canada*. Toronto: University of Toronto Press.

Marr, William L. and Donald G. Paterson. 1980. *Canada: An Economic History*. Toronto: Gage.

Marsh, Leonard. 1975. *Report on Social Security for Canada 1943*. Toronto: University of Toronto Press.

Martin, Andrew. 1977. "Political Constraints on Economic Strategies in Advanced Industrial Countries". In *Comparative Political Studies* 10: pp. 323-354.

————. 1986. "The Politics of Employment and Welfare: National Policies and International Dependence". In *The State and Economic Interests* edited by Keith Banting. Volume 32 of the Research Studies prepared for the Royal Commission on the Economic Union and Development Prospects for Canada, pp. 157-241. Toronto: University of Toronto Press.

Maslove, A. and G. Swimmer. 1980. *Wage Controls in Canada 1975-78*. Montreal: Institute for Research in Public Policy.

Mathias, Philip. 1971. *Forced Growth*. Toronto: James Lewis and Samuel.

Matthews, Ralph. 1983. *The Creation of Regional Dependency*. Toronto: University of Toronto Press.

————and Campbell Davis. "The Comparative Influence of Region, Status, Class and Ethnicity on Canadian Attitudes and Values". In *Regionalism in Canada* edited by Robert Brym, pp. 89-122. Toronto: Irwin Publishing.

Maxwell, Judith and Caroline Pestieau. 1980. *Economic Realities of Contemporary Confederation*. Montreal: C. D. Howe Research Institute.

McAdam, Doug. 1982. *Political Process and the Development of Black Insurgency, 1930-1970*. Chicago: University of Chicago Press.

McAllister, James A. 1984. *The Government of Edward Schreyer: Democratic Socialism in Manitoba*. Montreal and Kingston: McGill-Queen's University Press.

McCall-Newman, Christina. 1982. *Grits: An Intimate Portrait of the Liberal Party of Canada*. Toronto: Macmillan of Canada.

McConnell, W. H. 1969. "The Genesis of the Canadian New Deal". In *Journal of Canadian Studies* 4: pp. 31-41.

McDougall, A. K. 1986. *John P. Robarts: His Life and Government*. Toronto: University of Toronto Press.

McDougall, John N. 1982. *Fuels and the National Policy*. Toronto: Butterworths.

McFetridge, D. G., ed. 1985a. *Canadian Industry in Transition*. Volume 2 of the Research Studies prepared for the Royal Commission on the Economic Union and Development Prospects for Canada. Toronto: University of Toronto Press.

————, ed. 1985b. *Canadian Industrial Policy in Action*. Volume 4 of the Research Studies prepared for the Royal Commission on the Economic Union and Development Prospects for Canada. Toronto: University of Toronto Press.

McKercher, William R., ed. 1983. *The U. S. Bill of Rights and the Canadian Charter of Rights and Freedoms*. Toronto: Ontario Economic Council.

McLarty, Robert A. 1967. "Organizing for a Federal-Provincial Fiscal Policy". In *Canadian Tax Journal* 15: pp. 412-20.

McNaught, Kenneth. 1969. *The Pelican History of Canada*. Revised edition. Toronto: Penguin of Canada.

McRae, Kenneth, ed. 1974. *Consociational Democracy: Political Accommodation in Segmented Societies*. Toronto: McClelland and Stewart.

McRoberts, Kenneth. 1985. "Unilateralism, Bilateralism and Multilateraliasm: Approaches to Canadian Federalism". In *Intergovernmental Relations* edited by Richard Simeon. Volume 63 of the Research Studies prepared for the Royal Commission on the Economic Union and Development Prospects for Canada, pp. 71-130. Toronto: University of Toronto Press.

————and Dale Posgate. 1980. *Quebec: Social Change and Political Crisis*. Toronto: McClelland and Stewart.

McWhinney, Edward. 1979. *Quebec and the Constitution, 1960-1978*. Toronto: Uuniversity of Toronto Press.

————. 1982. *Canada and the Constitution, 1979-1982*. Toronto: University of Toronto Press.

Meekison, J. Peter. 1971, 1977. *Canadian Federalism: Myth or Reality?* 2nd ed., 3rd ed. Toronto: Methuen.

Miliband, Ralph. 1969. *The State in Capitalist Society*. London: Wiedenfeld and Nicolson.

Milne, David. 1982. *The New Canadian Constitution*. Toronto: James Lorimer.

——. 1986. *Tug of War: Ottawa and the Provinces Under Trudeau and Mulroney*. Toronto: James Lorimer.

Moe, Terry. 1980. *The Organization of Interests*. Chicago: University of Chicago Press.

Monahan, Patrick J. 1986. "The Supreme Court and the Economy". In *The Supreme Court as an Instrument of Political Change* edited by Ivan Bernier and Andree Lajoie. Volume 47 of the Research Studies prepared for the Royal Commission on the Economic Union and Development Prospects for Canada, pp. 105-178. Toronto: University of Toronto Press.

——. 1987. *Politics and the Constitution: the Charter, Federalism and Supreme Court of Canada*. Toronto: Carswell.

Morin, Claude. 1972. *Le pouvoir québecois en negociation*. Montreal: Les Editions Boréal Express.

——. 1976. *Quebec versus Ottawa: The Struggle for Self- Government, 1960-72*. Toronto: University of Toronto Press.

Morley, J. Terence, et. al. 1983. *The Reins of Power: Governing British Columbia*. Vancouver: Douglas and McIntyre.

Moore, A. Milton and J. Harvey Perry. 1966. *Financing Confederation: The First Hundred Years*. Toronto: Canadian Tax Foundation.

Moore, Barrington. 1966. *Social Origins of Dictatorship and Democracy*. Boston: Beacon Press.

——. *Injustice: the Social Bases of Obedience and Revolt*. New York: Sharpe.

Morrison, J. C. 1961. *Oliver Mowat and the Development of Provincial Rights in Ontario*. Toronto: Ontario Department of Public Records and Archives.

Morton, Desmond. 1984. *Working People*. Toronto: Copp Clark Pitman.

——. 1986. *The New Democrats, 1961-86:The Politics of Change*. Toronto: Copp Clark Pitman.

Morton, W. L. 1972. *The Canadian Identity*. 2nd ed. Toronto: University of Toronto Press.

——. 1967. *Manitoba: A History*. 2nd ed. Toronto: University of Toronto Press.

Mulroney, Brian. 1984. Election Address, Sept-Isles, Quebec. 6 August. Mimeographed.

Mullan, David J. 1985. "Administrative Tribunals: Their Evolution in Canada from 1945 to 1984". In *Regulations, Crown Corporations and Administrative Tribunals* edited by Ivan Bernier and Andree Lajoie. Volume 48 of the Research Studies prepared for the Royal Commission on the Economic Union and Development Prospects for Canada, pp. 155-201. Toronto: University of Toronto Press.

Naylor, Tom. 1975. *The History of Canadian Business, 1868-1914*. Toronto: James Lorimer.

Neatby, H. Blair. 1963. *William Lyon Mackenzie King*. Volume 2 (1924-1932). Toronto: University of Toronto Press.

——. 1972. *The Politics of Chaos: Canada in the Thirties*. Toronto: Macmillan of Canada.

——. 1976. "Mackenzie King and French Canada". In *Journal of Canadian Studies* 11: pp. 3-13.

Nelles, H. V. 1974. *The Politics of Development: Forests Mines and Hydro-electric Power in Ontario, 1849-1941*. Toronto: Macmillan of Canada.

Nevitte, Neil and Allan Kornberg. 1985. *Minorities and the Canadian State*. Oakville: Mosaic Press.

Newfoundland. Royal Commission on Employment and Unemployment. 1986. *Report: Building on our Strengths*. St. John's: Queen's Printer.

Newman, Peter. 1963. *Renegade in Power*. Toronto: McClelland and Stewart.

————. 1968. *The Distemper of Our Times: Canadian Politics in Transition, 1963-8.* Toronto: McClelland and Stewart.

Norrie, Kenneth. 1976. "Some Comments on Prairie Economic Alienation". In *Canadian Public Policy* 2:211-224.

————, ed. 1986. *Disparities and Interregional Adjustment.* Volume 64 of the Research Studies prepared for the Royal Comission on the Economic Union and Development Prospects for Canada. Toronto: University of Toronto Press.

Norrie, Kenneth, Richard Simeon and Mark Krasnick. 1985. *Federalism and the Economic Union in Canada.* Volume 59 of the Research Studies prepared for the Royal Commission on the Economic Union and Development Prospects for Canada. Toronto: University of Toronto Press.

O'Connor, James. 1973. *The Fiscal Crisis of the State.* New York: St. Martin's Press.

Oliver, Michael, ed. 1961. *Social Purpose for Canada.* Toronto: University of Toronto Press.

Olson, Mancur. 1965. *The Logic of Collective Action.* Cambridge, MA: Harvard University Press.

————. *The Rise and Decline of Nations.* New Haven, CT: Yale University Press.

Ontario. Advisory Committee on Confederation. 1967, 1970. *Background Papers and Reports.* 3 Vols. Toronto: Queen's Printer.

Ostrom, Vincent. 1987. *The Political Theory of the Compound Republic.* Lincoln, NB: University of Nebraska Press.

OECD. 1977. *Towards Full Employment and Price Stability.* (The McCracken Report). Paris: OECD.

————. 1978. *From Marshall Plan to Global Interdependence.* Paris: OECD.

————. 1979. *The Role of Industrial Incentives in Regional Development.* Paris: OECD.

————. 1981. *The Welfare State in Crisis.* Paris: OECD.

Ornstein, Michael. 1986. "Regional Politics and Ideology". In *Regionalism in Canada* edited by Robert Brym, pp. 47- 88. Toronto: Irwin Publishing.

Ossenberg, Richard. 1971. *Canadian Society: Pluralism, Change and Conflict.* Toronto: Prentice-Hall.

Owram, Doug. 1982. *The Economic Development of Western Canada: An Historical Overview.* Ottawa: Economic Council of Canada.

Pal, Leslie A. 1981. "Keynesian Commitment, Keynesian Illusion: The Politics of Canadian Fiscal Policy, 1943-1963". Thesis. Queen's University.

Palmer, Bryan. 1987. *Working Class Experience: the Rise and Reconstitution of Canadian Labour, 1800-1880.* Toronto: Butterworths.

Panitch, Leo, ed. 1977. *The Canadian State: Political Economy and Political Power.* Toronto: University of Toronto Press.

————and Don Swartz. 1985. *From Consent to Coercion: The Assault on Trade Union Freedoms.* Toronto: Garamond Press.

Peacock, Donald. 1968. *Journey to Power: The Story of a Canadian Election.* Toronto: The Ryerson Press.

Pelletier, Gérard. 1971. *The October Crisis.* Toronto: McClelland and Stewart.

————. 1983. *Years of Impatience: 1950-1960.* Toronto: Methuen.

————. 1987. *Years of Choice 1960-1968.* Toronto: Methuen.

Penniman, Howard, ed. 1975. *Canada at the Polls: the General Election of 1974.* Washington, DC: The American Enterprise Institute.

Pepin, Gilles. 1985. "The Problem of Section 96 of the Constitution Act, 1867". In *The Courts and the Charter* edited by Clare Beckton and A. Wayne MacKay. Volume 58 of the Research Studies prepared for the Royal Commission on the Economic Union and Development Prospects for Canada, pp. 223-227. Toronto: University of Toronto Press.

Pépin, Jean-Luc. 1964-65. "Cooperative Federalism". In *Canadian Forum* 44: pp. 206-210.

Perlin, George. 1980. *The Tory Syndrome*. Montreal and Kingston: McGill-Queen's University Press.

Phidd, Richard and G. Bruce Doern. 1978. *The Politics and Management of Canadian Economic Policy*. Toronto: Macmillan of Canada.

Phillips, Paul. 1979. "The National Policy Revisited". In *Journal of Canadian Studies* 14: pp. 3-13, 39-49.

————and Stephen Watson. 1984. "From Mobilization to Continentalism: The Canadian Economy in the Post-Depression Period". In *Modern Canada, 1930s-1980s* by Michael S. Cross and Gregory Kealey, pp. 20-45. Toronto: McClelland and Stewart.

Pickersgill, J. W. and Donald Forster. 1961-70. *Mackenzie King Record*. Toronto: University of Toronto Press.

Pigeon, Louis-Philippe. 1951. "The Meaning of Provincial Autonomy". In *Canadian Bar Review* 29: pp. 1126-1135.

Pinard, Maurice. 1971. *The Rise of a Third Party*. Englewood Cliffs, NJ: Prentice-Hall.

Pollard, Bruce. 1984. *The Year in Review, 1983: Intergovernmental Relations in Canada*. Kingston: Institute of Intergovernmental Relations.

————. 1986. *Managing the Interface: Intergovernmental Affairs Agencies in Canada*. Kingston: Institute of Intergovernmental Relations.

————. 1987. "Minority Language Rights in Four Provinces". In *Federal State, National Economy* by Peter M. Leslie, pp. 193-222. Toronto: University of Toronto Press.

Porter, Glenn and Robert Cuff, eds. 1975. *Enterprise and National Development: Essays in Canadian Business and Economic History*. Toronto: Hakkert.

Porter, John. 1965. *The Vertical Mosaic: An Analysis of Social Class and Power in Canada*. Toronto: University of Toronto Press.

Preston, Richard, ed. 1972. *The Influences of the United States on Canadian Development*. Durham, NC: Duke University Press.

Prang, Margaret. 1986. "Networks and Associations and the Nationalizing of Sentiment in English Canada". In *National Politics and Community in Canada* edited by R. Kenneth Carty and W. Peter Ward, pp. 48-62. Vancouver: University of British Columbia Press.

Pratt, Larry. 1976. *The Tar Sands: Syncrude and the Politics of Oil*. Edmonton: Hurtig Publishers Ltd..

————. 1982. "Energy: The Roots of National Policy". In *Studies in Political Economy* 7: pp. 27-59.

————, ed. 1986. *Socialism and Democracy in Alberta*. Edmonton: NeWest Press.

————and Garth Stevenson, eds. 1981. *Western Separatism: The Myths, Realities and Dangers*. Edmonton: Hurtig Publishers Ltd..

Presthus, Robert. 1973. *Elite Accommodation in Canadian Politics*. Toronto: Macmillan of Canada.

Prince, Michael, ed. 1987. *How Ottawa Spends, 1986-7*. Toronto: Methuen.

Pritchard, J. R. S., ed. 1983. *Crown Corporations in Canada*. Toronto: Butterworths.

Pross, A. Paul, ed. 1975. *Pressure Group Behaviour in Canadian Politics*. Toronto: McGraw-Hill Ryerson.

Provencher, Jean. 1974. *René Levesque: Portrait of a Québécois*. Toronto: Gage.

Przeworski, Adam. 1980. "Social Democracy as a Historical Phenomenon". In *New Left Review* 122: pp. 27-58.

———. 1985a. "Marxism and Rational Choice". In *Politics and Society* 14: pp. 379-409.

———. 1985b. *Capitalism and Social Democracy*. Cambridge: Cambridge University Press.

Québec. 1977. *Les comptes économiques du Québec*. Québec: Conseil executif.

Québec. Conseil Executif. 1979. *Québec-Canada: A New Deal*. Québec: Editeur Officiel du Québec.

Québec. 1954. Royal Commission of Inquiry on Constitutional Problems. *Report*. (The Tremblay Report). Québec: Editeur Officiel du Québec.

Québec Liberal Party. Constititional Committee. 1980. *A New Canadian Federation*. Montréal: Québec Liberal Party.

———. Policy Commission. 1985. *Mastering our Future*. Montréal: Québec Liberal Party.

Quinn, Herbert F. 1979. *The Union Nationale: Québec Nationalism from Duplessis to Levesque*. 2nd ed. Toronto: University of Toronto Press.

Radwanski, George. 1978. *Trudeau*. Toronto: Macmillan of Canada.

Rae, K. J. 1985. *The Prosperous Years: The Economic History of Ontario, 1939-75*. Toronto: University of Toronto Press.

Rawlyk, George. 1968. "Nova Scotia Regional Protest, 1867-1967". In *Queen's Quarterly* 75: pp. 105-123.

Reich, Robert. 1983. *The Next American Frontier*. New York: Penguin.

Reid, Malcolm. 1972. *The Shouting Signpainters: Literary and Political Account of Quebec Revolutionary Nationalism*. Toronto: McClelland and Stewart.

Reuber, Grant L. 1980. *Canada's Political Economy: Current Issues*. Toronto: McGraw-Hill Ryerson.

Richards, John and Larry Pratt. 1979. *Prairie Capitalism: Power and Influence in the New West*. Toronto: McClelland and Stewart.

Riddell, Craig, ed. 1985. *Canadian Labour Relations*. Volume 16 of the Research Studies prepared for the Royal Commission on the Economic Union and Development Prospects for Canada. Toronto: University of Toronto Press.

Rioux, Marcel. 1965. "Conscience éthnique et conscience de classe au Québec". *Recherches Sociographiques* 6: pp. 23-32.

Roberts, Wayne and John Bullen. 1984. "A Heritage of Hope and Struggle: Workers, Unions, and Politics in Canada, 1930-1982". In *Modern Canada, 1930s-1980s* by Michael S. Cross and Gregory Kealey, pp. 105-143. Toronto: McClelland and Stewart.

Roberts, Leslie. 1957. *The Life and Times of Clarence Decatur Howe*. Toronto: Clarke Irwin and Company.

Robertson, Gordon. 1979. "The Role of Intergovernmental Conferences in the Decision-Making Process". In *Confrontation and Collaboration:Intergovernmental Relations in Canada Today* edited by Richard Simeon, pp. 78-88. Toronto: Institute of Public Administration of Canada.

———. 1985. "Northern Political Development Within Canadian Federalism". In *The North* edited by Michael S. Whittington. Volume 72 of the Research Studies prepared for the Royal Commission on the Economic Union and Development Prospects for Canada, pp. 123-132. Toronto: University of Toronto Press.

Robin, Martin. 1972. *The Rush for Spoils: The Company Province, 1871-1933*. Toronto: McClelland and Stewart.

———, ed. 1971. *Canadian Provincial Politics*. Toronto: Prentice-Hall.

Robinson, Ian. 1987. "The Logic of Solidarity". Unpublished manuscript. Yale University.

Rodgers-Magnet, Sanda and Joseph Eliot Magnet. "Mobility Rights: Personal Mobility and the Canadian Economic Union". In *Perspectives on the Canadian Economic Union* edited by Mark Krasnick. Volume 60 of the Research Studies prepared for the Royal Commission on the Economic Union and Development Prospects for Canada, pp. 195-270. Toronto: University of Toronto Press.

Rogers, Norman McL. 1931. "Government by the Dead". In *Canadian Forum* 12: pp. 46-49.

Rogowski, Robert. 1974. *Rational Legitimacy: a Theory of Political Support*. Princeton, NJ: Princeton University Press.

Rokkan, Stein and Derek Urwin. 1983. *Economy, Territory Identity*. London: Sage Publications.

Romanow, Roy, John Whyte and Howard Leeson. 1984. *Canada Notwithstanding: The Making of the Constitution, 1976-1982*. Toronto: Carswell/Methuen.

Rotstein, Abraham. ed. 1965. *The Prospect of Change: Proposals for Canada's Future*. Toronto: McGraw-Hill.

Rowe, Frederick W.1980. *A History of Newfoundland and Labrador*. Toronto: McGraw-Hill Ryerson.

Roy, Nicolas. 1986. *Mobility of Capital in the Canadian Economic Union*. Volume 60 of the Research Studies prepared for the Royal Commission on the Economic Union and Development Prospects for Canada. Toronto: University of Toronto Press.

Russell, Peter. 1982. *The Court and the Constitution*. Kingston: Institute of Intergovernmental Relations.

————. 1983a. "Bold Statescraft, Questionable Jurisprudence". In *And No One Cheered: Federalism, Democracy and the Constitution Act*. edited by Keith Banting and Richard Simeon, pp. 210-238. Toronto: Methuen.

————. 1983b. "The Political Purposes of the Canadian Charter of Rights and Freedoms". In *Canadian Bar Review* 61: pp. 30-54.

————. 1985a. "The First Three Years in Charterland". In *Canadian Public Administration* 28: pp. 367-396.

————. 1985b. "The Supreme Court and Federal-Provincial Relations: The Political Use of Legal Resources". In *Canadian Public Policy* 11: pp. 161-170.

————. 1987. *The Judiciary in Canada: The Third Branch of Government*. Toronto: McGraw-Hill Ryerson.

————, ed. 1965a. *Leading Constitutional Decisions*. Toronto: McClelland and Stewart.

————, ed. 1965b. *Nationalism in Canada*. Toronto: McGraw- Hill.

Rutherford, Paul. 1982. "Tomorrow's Metropolis: the Urban Reform Movement in Canada, 1880-1920". In *Readings in Canadian History, Post Confederation* edited by R. Douglas Francis and Donald B. Smith, pp. 303-320. Toronto: Holt, Rinehart and Winston of Canada.

Ryerson, Stanley B. 1972. "Quebec: Concepts of Class and Nation". In *Capitalism and the National Question in Canada* edited by Gary Teeple, pp. 220-240. Toronto: University of Toronto Press.

Sabel, Charles. 1984. *Work and Politics*. Cambridge: Cambridge University Press.

Safarian, A. E. 1970. *The Canadian Economy in the Great Depression*. Toronto: McClelland and Stewart.

————. 1980. *Ten Markets or One? Regional Barriers to Economic Activity in Canada*. Toronto: Ontario Economic Council.

Sage, Walter N. 1982. "British Columbia Becomes Canadian (1871-1901)". In *Readings in Canadian History, Post Confederation* edited by R. Douglas Francis and Donald B. Smith, pp. 10-20. Toronto: Holt, Rinehart and Winston of Canada.

Sargent, John, ed. 1985a. *Postwar Macroeconomic Developments*. Volume 20 of the Research Studies prepared for the Royal Commission on the Economic Union and Development Prospects for Canada. Toronto: University of Toronto Press.

————, ed. 1985b. *Fiscal and Monetary Policy*. Volume 21 of the Research Studies prepared for the Royal Commission on the Economic Union and Development Prospects for Canada. Toronto: University of Toronto Press.

————, ed. 1985c. *Economic Growth: Prospects and Determinants*. Volume 22 of the Research Studies prepared for the Royal Commission on the Economic Union and Development Prospects for Canada. Toronto: University of Toronto Press.

Saunders, J. Owen. ed. 1986. *Managing Natural Resources in a Federal State*. Toronto: Carswell.

Savoie, Donald. 1981. *Federal-Provincial Collaboration: The Canada-New Brunswick General Development Agreement*. Montreal and Kingston: McGill-Queen's University Press.

————. 1986. *Regional Economic Development: Canada's Search for Solutions*. Toronto: University of Toronto Press.

————, ed. 1986. *The Canadian Economy: A Regional Perspective*. Toronto: Methuen.

Scarrow, Howard A. 1960. "Federal-Provincial Voting Patterns in Canada". In *Canadian Journal of Economics and Political Science* 26: pp. 289-298.

Schattschneider, E. E. 1942. *Party Government*. New York: Holt, Rinehart and Winston.

————. 1966. *The Semi-Sovereign People*. New York: Holt, Rinehart and Winston.

Schonfield, Andrew. 1965. *Modern Capitalism: The Changing Balance of Public and Private Power*. New York: Oxford University Press.

Schull, Joseph. 1978. *Ontario Since 1867*. Toronto: McClelland and Stewart.

Schultz, H.J., M. A. Ormsby, J. R. H. Wilbur and B. J. Young. 1967. *Politics of Discontent*. Toronto: University of Toronto Press.

Schultz, Richard. 1979. *Federalism and the Regulatory Process*. Montreal: Institute for Research in Public Policy.

————. 1980. *Federalism, Bureaucracy, and Public Policy: The Politics of Highway Transport Regulation*. Montreal and Kingston: McGill-Queen's University Press.

————and Alan Alexandroff. 1985. *Economic Regulation and the Federal System*. Volume 42 of the Research Studies prepared for the Royal Commission on the Economic Union and Development Prospects for Canada. Toronto: University of Toronto Press.

Schmitter, Philippe and Gerhard Lehmbruch. 1979. *Trends Toward Corporatist Intermediation*. Beverley Hills: Sage.

Schwartz, Brian. 1987. *Fathoming Meech Lake*. Winnipeg: Legal Research Institute, University of Manitoba.

Schwartz, Mildred. 1967. *Public Opinion and Canadian Identity*. Toronto: Prentice-Hall.

————. 1971. *Politics and Territory*. Montreal and Kingston: McGill-Queen's University Press.

Scott, Anthony, ed. 1976. *Natural Resource Revenues: A Test of Canadian Federalism*. Vancouver: University of British Columbia Press.

Scott, F. R. 1947. "The Special Nature of Canadian Federalism". In *Canadian Journal of Economics and Political Science* 13: pp. 13-25.

————. 1951. "Centralization and Decentralization in Canadian Federalism". In *Canadian Bar Reviw* 29: pp. 1095-1125.

————. 1961. "Social Planning and Canadian Federalism". In *Social Purpose for Canada* edited by Michael Oliver, pp. 394-407. Toronto: University of Toronto Press.

————. 1977. *Essays on the Constitution: Aspects of Canadian Law and Politics*. Toronto: University of Toronto Press.

Scott, F. R. and Michael Oliver. 1964. *Quebec States her Case*. Toronto: Macmillan of Canada.

Scott, Stephen A. 1986. "The Canadian Constitutional Amendment Process: Mechanisms and Prospects". In *Recurring Issues in Canadian Federalism* edited by Clare Beckton and Wayne MacKay, pp. 77-112. Toronto: University of Toronto Press.

See, Katherine O'Sullivan. 1986. *First World Nationalisms: Class and Ethnic Politics in Northern Ireland and Quebec*. Chicago: University of Chicago Press.

Sheppard, Robert and Michael Valpy. 1982. *The National Deal: The Fight for a Canadian Constitution*. Toronto: Fleet Books.

Sherman, Paddy. 1966. *Bennett*. Toronto: McClelland and Stewart.

Shearer, R., ed. 1968. *Exploiting Our Economic Potential*. Montreal: Holt, Rinehart and Winston.

Sheppard, Anthony F. 1985. "Taxation Policy and the Canadian Economic Union". In *Fiscal Federalism* edited by Mark Krasnick. Volume 65 of the Research Studies prepared for the Royal Commission on the Economic Union and Development Prospects for Canada, pp. 149-210. Toronto: University of Toronto Press.

Sidelsky, Robert. 1979. "The Decline of Keynesian Politics". In *State and Economy in Contemporary Capitalism* edited by Colin Crouch, pp. 55-87. London: Croom Helm.

Siegfried, André. 1966. *The Race Question in Canada*. Carleton Library edition. Toronto: McClelland and Stewart.

Silver, A. I. 1982. *The French-Canadian Idea of Confederation, 1864-1900*. Toronto: University of Toronto Press.

Silzer, Nola and Mark Krasnick. 1986. "The Free Flow of Goods in the Canadian Economic Union". In *Perspectives on the Canadian Economic Union* edited by Mark Krasnick. Volume 60 of the Research Studies prepared for the Royal Commission on the Economic Union and Development Prospects for Canada, pp. 155-194. Toronto: University of Toronto Press.

Simeon, Richard. 1972. *Federal-Provincial Diplomacy: The Making of Recent Policy in Canada*. Toronto: University of Toronto Press.

——. 1975. "Regionalism and Canadian Political Institutions". In *Queen's Quarterly* 82: pp. 499-511.

——. 1980. *A Citizen's Guide to the Constitutional Issues*. Toronto: Gage.

——. 1982. "Fiscal Federalism in Canada: A Review Essay". In *Canadian Tax Journal* 30: pp. 41-51.

——. 1982-83. "Criteria for Choice in Federal Systems". In *Queen's Law Journal* 18: pp. 131-57.

——. 1986. "Considerations on Centralization and Decentralization". In *Canadian Public Administration* 29: pp. 445-461.

——. 1987. "Federalism and Free Trade". In *Canada: The State of the Federation, 1986* edited by Peter M. Leslie, pp. 189-214. Kingston: Institute of Intergovernmental Relations.

——, ed. 1977. *Must Canada Fail?* Montreal and Kingston: McGill-Queen's University Press.

——, ed. 1979. *Confrontation and Collaboration: Intergovernmental Relations in Canada Today*. Toronto: Institute of Public Administration of Canada.

——, ed. 1985a. *Division of Powers and Public Policy*. Volume 61 of the Research Studies prepared for the Royal Commission on the Economic Union and Development Prospects for Canada. Toronto: University of Toronto Press.

——, 1985b. *Intergovernmental Relations*. Volume 63 of the Research Studies prepared for the Royal Commission on the Economic Union and Development Propsects for Canada. Toronto: University of Toronto Press.

——and Donald Blake. 1980. "Regional Preferences". In *Small Worlds: Provinces and Parties in Canadian Political Life* by David Elkins and Richard Simeon, pp. 77-105. Toronto: Methuen.

——and Robert Miller. 1980. "Regional Variations in Public Policy". In ibid pp. 242-284.

Simpson, Jeffrey. 1980. *Discipline of Power*. Toronto: Personal Library.

Skocpol, Theda. 1979. *States and Social Revolutions: A Comparative Analysis of France, Russia and China*. Cambridge: Cambridge University Press.

Sloan, Thomas. 1965. *Quebec: The Not-So-Quiet Revolution*. Toronto: Ryerson Press.

Smiley, Donald V. 1962. "The Rowell-Sirois Report, Provincial Autonomy and Postwar Canadian Federalism". In *Canadian Journal of Economics and Political Science* 28: pp. 54-69.

———. 1963a. *Conditional Grants and Canadian Federalism*. Toronto: Canadian Tax Foundation.

———. 1963b. *The Rowell/Sirois Report/Book I*. Toronto: McClelland and Stewart.

———. 1964. "Public Administration and Canadian Federalism". In *Canadian Public Administration* 7: pp. 371-388.

———. 1965a. "Federalism, Nationalism and the Scope of Public Activity in Canada". In *Nationalism in Canada* edited by Peter Russell, pp. 95-111. Toronto: McGraw-Hill.

———. 1965b. "The Two Themes of Canadian Federalism". In *Canadian Journal of Economics and Political Science* 31: pp. 80-97.

———. 1967. *The Canadian Political Nationality*. Toronto: Methuen.

———. 1971. "The Structural Problem of Canadian Federalism". In *Canadian Public Administration* 14: pp. 326-343.

———. 1972. *Canada in Question: Federalism in the Seventies*. Toronto: McGraw-Hill Ryerson.

———. 1974. *Constitutional Adaptation and Canadian Federalism*. Document 4, Royal Commission on Bilingualism and Biculturalism. Ottawa: Queen's Printer.

———. 1975. "Canada and the Quest for a National Policy". In *Canadian Journal of Political Science* 8: pp. 40-62.

———. 1976. *Canada in Question: Federalism in the Seventies*. 2nd ed. Toronto: McGraw-Hill Ryerson.

———. 1979. "An Outsider's Observations of Federal-Provincial Relations Among Consenting Adults". In *Confrontation and Collaboration: Intergovernmental Relations in Canada Today* edited by Richard Simeon, pp. 105-113. Toronto: Institute of Public Administration of Canada.

———. 1980. *Canada in Question: Federalism in the Eighties*. 3rd ed. Toronto: McGraw-Hill Ryerson.

———. 1981. *The Canadian Charter of Rights and Freedoms, 1981*. Toronto: Ontario Economic Council.

———. 1984. "Public Sector Politics, Modernization, and Federalism: The Canadian and American Experiences". In *Publius* 14: pp. 39-59.

———. 1985. *An Elected Senate for Canada? Clues From the Australian Experience*. Kingston: Institute of Intergovernmental Relations.

———. 1987. *The Federal Condition in Canada*. Toronto: McGraw-Hill Ryerson.

———and R. L. Watts. 1985. *Intrastate Federalism in Canada*. Volume 39 of the Research Studies prepared for the Royal Commission on the Economic Union and Development Prospects for Canada. Toronto: University of Toronto Press.

Smith, A. D. 1981. *The Ethnic Revival*. Cambridge: Cambridge University Press.

Smith, David E. 1975. *Prairie Liberalism: The Liberal Party in Saskatchewan: 1905-71*. Toronto: University of Toronto Press.

———. 1981. *The Regional Decline of a National Party: Liberals on the Prairies*. Toronto: University of Toronto Press.

Snell, James G. and Frederick Vaughan. 1985. *The Supreme Court of Canada: History of the Institution*. Toronto: University of Toronto Press.

Stairs, Dennis and Gil Winham, eds. 1985. *Canada and the International Political/Economic Environment*. Volume 28 of the Research Studies prepared for the Royal Commission on the Economic Union and Development Prospects for Canada. Toronto: University of Toronto Press.

Stanbury, W. T. ed. 1982. *Government Regulation: Scope Growth, Process*. Montreal: Institute for Research in Public Policy.

Stein, Michael. 1973. *The Dynamics of Right Wing Protest: a Political of Social Credit in Quebec*. Toronto: University of Toronto Press.

Stevenson, Garth. 1974. "Continental Integration and Canadian Unity". In *Continental Community? Independence and Integration in North America* by Andrew Axline, et al, pp. 194-220. Toronto: McClelland and Stewart.

———. 1977. "Federalism and the Political Economy of the Federal State". In *The Canadian State: Political Economy and Political Power* edited by Leo Panitch, pp. 71-100. Toronto: University of Toronto Press.

———. 1979. *Unfulfilled Union*. Toronto: Macmillan of Canada.

———. 1981. "The Political Economy Tradition and Canadian Federalism". In *Studies in Political Economy* 6: pp. 113-133.

———. 1985. "The Division of Powers". In *Division of Powers and Public Policy* edited by Richard Simeon. Volume 61 of the Research Studies prepared for the Royal Commission on the Economic Union and Development Prospects for Canada, pp. 71- 124. Toronto: University of Toronto Press.

Steinfels, Peter. 1979. *The Neo-Conservatives*. New York: Simon and Schuster.

Stewart, Ian. 1987. "Tax Reform and the Federation". In *Canada: The State of the Federation* edited by Peter M. Leslie, pp. 109-128. Kingston: Institute of Intergovernmental Relations.

Studnicki-Gizbert, K. W., ed. 1974. *Issues in Canadian Transport Policy*. Toronto: Macmillan of Canada.

Stursberg, Peter. 1975. *Diefenbaker: Leadership Gained*. Toronto: University of Toronto Press.

———. 1976. *Diefenbaker: Leadership Lost*. Toronto: University of Toronto Press.

Swainson, Donald, ed. 1970. *Historical Essays on the Prairie Provinces*. Toronto: McClelland and Stewart.

———, ed. 1972. *Oliver Mowat's Ontario*. Toronto: Macmillan of Canada.

Swainson, Neil A. 1979. *Conflict Over the Columbia: The Canadian Background to an Historic Treaty*. Montreal and Kingston: McGill-Queen's University Press.

Swinton, K. E. and C. J. Rogerson. 1988. *Competing Constitutional Visions: the Meech Lake Accord*. Toronto: Carswell.

Symons, T. H. B. 1971. "Ontario's Quiet Revolution". In *One Country or Two?* by R. M. Burns, pp. 169-204. Montreal and Kingston: McGill-Queen's University Press.

Szablowski, George J. 1986. "Treaty-making Power in the Context of Canadian Politics: An Exploratory and Innovative Approach". In *Recurring Issues in Canadain Federalism* edited by Clare Beckton and A. Wayne MacKay. Volume 57 of the Research Studies prepared for the Royal Commission on the Economic Union and Development Prospects for Canada, pp. 145-85. Toronto: University of Toronto Press.

Tarrow, Sydney D. 1977. *Between Centre and Periphery*. New Haven, CT: Yale University Press.

Taylor, Charles. 1970. "Nationalism and the Intelligentsia: A Case Study". In *Social and Cultural Change in Canada*, edited by W. E. Mann, pp. 274-287. Toronto: Copp Clark.

———. 1985. "Alternative Futures: Legitimacy, Identity and Alienation in Late Twentieth Century Canada". In *Constitutionalism, Citizenship and Society in Canada* edited by Alan Cairns and Cynthia Williams. Volume 33 of the Research Studies prepared for the Royal Commission on the Economic Union and Development Prospects for Canada, pp. 183-230. Toronto: Unviersity of Toronto Press.

Taylor, Malcolm G. 1978. *Health Insurance and Canadian Public Policy*. Montreal and Kingston: McGill-Queen's University Press.

Teeple, Gary, ed. 1972. *Capitalism and the National Question in Canada*. Toronto: University of Toronto Press.

Teryakian, Edward and Ronald Rogowski. 1985. *New Nationalisms in the Developed West*. Boston: Alen and Unwin.

Thirsk, Wayne R. 1986. "Interprovincial Trade and the Welfare Effects of Marketing Boards". In *Perspectives on the Canadian Economic Union* edited by Mark Krasnick. Volume 60 of the Research Studies prepared for the Royal Commission on the Economic Union and Development Prospects for Canada, pp. 1- 33. Toronto: University of Toronto Press.

Thomson, Clive, ed. 1988. *Navigating Meech Lake*. Kingston: Institute of Intergovernmental Relations.

Thomson, Dale C. 1967. *Louis St. Laurent: Canadian*. Toronto: Macmillan of Canada.

———. 1984. *Jean Lesage and the Quiet Revolution*. Toronto: Macmillan of Canada.

———, ed. 1974. *Quebec Society and Politics: Views From the Inside*. Toronto: McClelland and Stewart.

Thorburn, H. G. 1973. "Needed: A New Look at the Two Nations Theory". In *Queen's Quarterly* 80: pp. 268-273.

———. 1984a. *Party Politics in Canada*. 5th ed. Toronto: Prentice-Hall.

———. 1984b. *Planning and the Economy: Building Federal- Provincial Consensus*. Ottawa: Canadian Institute for Economic Policy.

———. 1985. *Interest Groups in the Canadian Federal System*. Volume 69 of the Research Studies prepared for the Royal Commission on the Economic Union and Development Prospects for Canada. Toronto: University of Toronto Press.

Touraine, Alain. 1983. *Solidarity: Poland: 1980-81*. Cambridge: Cambridge University Press.

Trebilcock, Michael. 1986. *The Political Economy of Adjustment*. Volume 69 of the Research Studies prepared for the Royal Commission on the Economic Union and Development Prospects for Canada. Toronto: University of Toronto Press.

———, et al., eds. 1983. *Federalism and the Economic Union*. Toronto: Ontario Economic Council.

Tremblay, Guy. 1986. "The Supreme Court of Canada: Final Arbiter of Political Disputes". In *The Supreme Court as an Instrument of Political Change*, edited by Ivan Bernier and Andrée Lajoie. Volume 47 of the Research Studies prepared for the Royal Commission on the Economic Union and Development Prospects for Canada, pp. 179-209. Toronto: Unviersity of Toronto Press.

Trudeau, Pierre-E. 1956. *La Grève de l'amiante: une étape dans la révolution industrielle au Québec*. Montréal: Les editions Cité libre.

———. 1958. "Federalism, Nationalism and Reason". In *The Future of Canadian Federalism* edited by P.-A. Crépeau and C. B. Macpherson, pp. 16-35. Toronto: University of Toronto Press.

———. 1962. "La nouvelle trahison des clercs". In *Les éditions Cité libre* 48: pp. 3-16.

———. 1968. *Federalism and the French Canadians*. Toronto: Macmillan of Canada.

———. 1987. "Say Goodbye to the Dream of One Canada". In Toronto *Star*, 27 May.

Tupper, Allan. 1978. "Public Enterprise as Social Welfare: The Case of the Cape Breton Development Corporation". In *Canadian Public Policy* 4: pp. 530-546.

———. 1979. "The State in Business". In *Canadian Public Administration* 22: pp. 124-50.

———. 1981. "Mr. Trudeau and the West". In *Western Separatism: The Myths, Realities and Dangers* edited by Larry Pratt and Garth Stevenson, pp. 85-104. Edmonton: Hurtig Publishers Ltd..

————. 1982. *Public Money in the Private Sector*. Kingston: Institute of Intergovernmental Relations.

————. 1983. *Bill S-31 and the Federalism of State Capitalism*. Kingston: Institute of Intergovernmental Relations.

Tupper, Allan and G. Bruce Doern, eds. 1981. *Public Corporations and Public Policy in Canada*. Montreal: Institute for Research in Public Policy.

Underhill, Frank. 1937. "The Fathers of Confederation". In *Canadian Forum* 17: pp. 226-228.

————. 1943. "The Canadian Party System in Transition". In *Canadian Journal of Economics and Political Science* 9: pp. 300-313.

————. 1953-54. "Canada and the Canadian Question". In *Queen's Quarterly* 60: pp. 462-475.

————. 1961. *In Search of Canadian Liberalism*. Toronto: Macmillan of Canada.

Urquhart, M. C. and K. A. H. Buckley, eds. 1965. *Historical Statistics of Canada*. Toronto: Macmillan.

Vallières, Pierre. 1968. *White Niggers of America*. Toronto: McClelland and Stewart.

Van Loon, Richard. 1979. "Reforming Welfare in Canada". *Public Policy* 27: pp. 469-504.

Vanderkamp, John. 1986. "The Efficiency of the Interregional Adjustment Process". In *Disparities and Interregional Adjustment* edited by Kenneth Norrie. Volume 64 of the Research Studies prepared for the Royal Commission on the Economic Union and Development Prospects for Canada, pp. 53-108. Toronto: Unviersity of Toronto Press.

Veilleux, Gérard. 1979. "L'Evolution des mechanismes de liaison intergouvernementale". In *Confrontation and Collaboration:Intergovernmental Relations in Canada Today*, pp. 35-77. Toronto: Institute of Public Administration of Canada.

Verney, David. 1986. *Three Civilizations, Two Cultures, One State*. Durham, NC: Duke University Press.

Vining, Aiden R. and Robert Bottrell. 1983. "An Overview of the Origins, Growth, Size and Functions of Provincial Crown Corporations". In *Crown Corporations in Canada* edited by J. R. S. Pritchard, pp. 303-367. Toronto: Butterworths.

Wade, Mason. 1964. *The French Canadian Outlook*. Toronto: McClelland and Stewart.

————. 1955; rev. ed. 1968. *The French Canadians, 1760-1967*. 2 Vols. Toronto: Macmillan of Canada.

————, ed. 1960. *Canadian Dualism: Studies of French-English Relations*. Toronto: University of Toronto Press.

————, ed. 1969. *Regionalism in the Canadian Community, 1868-1967*. Toronto: University of Toronto Press.

Waite, P. B., ed. 1963. *The Confederation Debates in the Province of Canada, 1865*. Toronto: McClelland and Stewart.

Walker, Michael, ed. 1978. *Confederation at the Crossroads: The Search for a Federal-Provincial Balance*. Vancouver: The Fraser Institute.

Ward, Norman and Duff Spafford, eds. 1968. *Politics in Saskatchewan*. Toronto: University of Toronto Press.

Wardhaugh, Ronald. 1983. *Language and Nationhood: The Canadian Experience*. Vancouver: New Star.

Watts, R. L. 1970. *Multicultural Societies and Federalism*. Studies of the Royal Commission on Bilingualism and Biculturalism. Ottawa: Information Canada.

————. 1986. "Financing Post-Secondary Education and Research". In *Canada: the State of the Federation, 1985, 1986* edited by Peter M. Leslie, pp. 467-488. Kingston: Institute of Intergovernmental Relations.

Weil, Simone. 1978. *The Need for Roots*. London: Routledge and Kegan Paul.

Westell, Anthony. 1972. *Paradox: Trudeau as Prime Minister*. Toronto: Prentice-Hall.

Westin, Alan F. 1983. "The United States Bill of Rights and the Canadian Charter: A Socio-Political Analysis". In *The U.S. Bill of Rights and the Canadian Charter of Rights and Freedoms* edited by William R. McKercher, pp. 27-50. Toronto: Ontario Economic Council.

Westmacott, Martin and D. J. Phillips. "Transportation Policy and National Unity". In *Canada Challenged: The Viability of Confederation* edited by R. B. Byers and Robert Reford, pp. 293-315. Toronto: Canadian Institute of International Affairs.

Whalley, John and Irene Trela. 1986. *Regional Aspects of Confederation*. Volume 68 of the Research Studies prepared for the Royal Commission on the Economic Union and Development Prospects for Canada. Toronto: University of Toronto Press.

Wheare, K. C. 1964. *Federal Government*. 4th ed. New York: Oxford University Press.

Whitaker, Reginald. 1977. *The Government Party: Organizing and Financing the Liberal Party of Canada, 1930-58*. Toronto: University of Toronto Press.

———. 1980. "Reason, Passion and Interest: Pierre Trudeau's Eternal Liberal Triangle". In *Canadian Journal of Political and Social Theory* 4: pp. 5-30.

———. 1983. *Federalism and Democratic Theory*. Kingston: Institute of Intergovernmental Relations.

Whittington, Michael S., ed. 1985. *The North*. Volume 72 of the Research Studies prepared for the Royal Commission on the Economic Union and Development Prospects for Canada. Toronto: University of Toronto Press.

———and Glen Williams, eds. 1984. *Canadian Politics in the 1980s*, 2nd ed. Toronto: Methuen.

Whyte, John. 1985a. "Constitutional Aspects of Economic Development Policy". In *Division of Powers and Public Policy* edited by Richard Simeon. Volume 61 of the Research Studies prepared for the Royal Commission on the Economic Union and Development Prospects for Canada, pp. 29-70. Toronto: University of Toronto Press.

———. 1985b. "Reinventing Canada: The Meaning of Constitutional Change". Toronto: Public Law Workshop, Osgoode Hall Law School. Mimeographed.

———. 1986. "A New Look for Federal Powers over the Economy?". Toronto: University of Toronto Law School. Mimeographed.

Wilensky, Harold. 1975. *The Welfare State and Equality*. Berkeley, CA: University of California Press.

Williams, Colin H., ed. 1982. *National Separatism*. Vancouver: University of British Columbia Press.

Williams, Glen. 1983. *Not for Export:Toward a Political Economy of Canada's Arrested Industrialization*. Toronto: McClelland and Stewart.

Williamson, J. G. 1965. "Regional Inequality and the Process of National Development: A Description of Patterns". In *Economic Development and Cultural Change* 13: pp. 3-45.

Wolfe, David A. 1984a. "The Crisis in Advanced Capitalism: An Introduction". In *Studies in Political Economy* 12: pp. 32-36.

———. 1984b. "The Rise and Demise of the Keynesian Era in Canada: Economic Policy, 1930-1982". In *Modern Canada, 1930s-1980s* by Michael S. Cross and Gregory Kealey, pp. 46-78. Toronto: McClelland and Stewart.

———. 1985. "The Politics of Deficits". In *The Politics of Economic Policy* edited by G. Bruce Doern. Volume 40 of the Research Studies prepared for the Royal Commission on the Economic Union and Development Prospects for Canada, pp. 111-162. Toronto: University of Toronto Press.

Woodcock, George. 1981. *Canada Betrayed*. Vancouver: Harbour Publishing.

Woolstencroft, T. 1982. *Organizing Intergovernmental Relations*. Kingston: Institute of Intergovernmental Relations.

Young, R. A., Philippe Faucher and André Blais. 1984. "The Concept of Province-Building: A Critique". In *Canadian Journal of Political Science* 17: pp. 783-818.

Young, Walter D. 1969a. *The Anatomy of a Party: The National CCF, 1932-61*. Toronto: University of Toronto Press.

———. 1969b. *Democracy and Discontent: Progressivism, Socialism and Social Credit in the Canadian West*. Toronto: McGraw-Hill/Ryerson.

Zukowsky, Ronald. 1981a. *Intergovernmental Relations in Canada: The Year in Review, 1980*. Kingston: Institute of Intergovernmental Relations.

———. 1981b. *Struggle over the Constitution: From the Quebec Referendum to the Supreme Court*. Kingston: Institute of Intergovernmental Relations.

Zysman, John. 1977. *Political Strategies for Industrial Order: State, Market and Industry in France*. Berkeley, CA: University of California Press.

———. 1983. *Governments, Markets and Growth: Financial Systems and the Politics of Industrial Change*. Ithaca, NY: Cornell University Press.